Indian Economic Reforms

Also by Raghbendra Jha

CONTEMPORARY MACROECONOMIC THEORY AND POLICY

INDUSTRIAL EFFICIENCY: An Indian Perspective

MACROECONOMICS FOR DEVELOPING COUNTRIES

MODERN PUBLIC ECONOMIES

Indian Economic Reforms

Edited by

Raghbendra Jha
Australia South Asia Research Centre
Australian National University
Canberra
Australia

palgrave
macmillan

First published 2003 by
PALGRAVE MACMILLAN
Houndmills, Basingstoke, Hampshire RG21 6XS and
175 Fifth Avenue, New York, N. Y. 10010
Companies and representatives throughout the world

PALGRAVE MACMILLAN is the global academic imprint of the Palgrave Macmillan division of St. Martin's Press, LLC and of Palgrave Macmillan Ltd. Macmillan® is a registered trademark in the United States, United Kingdom and other countries. Palgrave is a registered trademark in the European Union and other countries.

ISBN 1–4039–0796–X

This book is printed on paper suitable for recycling and made from fully managed and sustained forest sources.

A catalogue record for this book is available from the British Library.

Library of Congress Cataloging-in-Publication Data

Indian economic reforms / edited by Raghbendra Jha.
p. cm.
Includes bibliographical references and index.
ISBN 1–4039—0796–X
1. India--Economic policy--1980- 2. India--Economic conditions--1947-
I. Jha, Raghbendra

HC435.2.I5554 2003
330.954--dc21

2003049801

10 9 8 7 6 5 4 3 2 1
12 11 10 09 08 07 06 05 04 03

Printed and bound in Great Britain by
Antony Rowe Ltd, Chippenham and Eastbourne

To the children of India — with the hope
that they design even better economic policy

CONTENTS

List of Figures

List of Tables

Notes on Contributors

Apte, Pradeep, Ferguson College, Pune, India.

Athukorala, Prema-Chandra, Professor of Economics, Division of Economics, Research School of Pacific & Asian Studies, The Australian National University, Canberra, Australia.

Banga, Rashmi, Associate Professor of Economics at Jesus and Mary College, University of Delhi, India.

Basu, Parikshit, lecturer in finance and economics at Charles Sturt University, Bathurst, Australia.

Basu, Saswati, part-time lecturer in economics at the School of Marketing and Management, Charles Sturt University, Bathurst, Australia.

Bhide, Shashanka, National Council of Applied Economic Research, New Delhi, India.

Bose, Dhritidyuti, Assistant Adviser in the Reserve Bank of India's Department of Economic Analysis and Policy, Mumbai, India.

Chakraborty, Chandana, Associate Professor of Economics, School of Business of Montclair State University, New Jersey, USA.

Chand, Satish, Fellow with the Research School of Pacific & Asian Studies and a Senior Lecturer in Economics at The Australian National University, Canberra, Australia.

Dahiya, Shri Bhagwan, Department of Economics, Maharshi Dayanand University, Rohtak, India.

Dutta, Dilip, Senior Lecturer in Economics and Director of the Centre for South Asian Studies at the University of Sydney, Australia.

Gupta, Desh, Senior Lecturer in Economics at the University of Canberra, Australia.

Gupta, Santanu, Lecturer at Gokhale Institute of Politics and Economics, Pune, India, and is currently on the Ratan Tata Fellowship to London School of Economics and Political Science, UK.

Jha, Raghbendra, Rajiv Gandhi Chair Professor of Economics and Executive Director of the Australia South Asia Research Centre, Research School of Pacific & Asian Studies, The Australian National University, Canberra, Australia.

Kalirajan, Kaliappa, Professor of Economics, GRIPS/ Foundation for the Advanced Studies on International Development, Joint Graduate Program, Tokyo, Japan.

Kumari, Anita, Researcher at the Institute of Economic Growth, Delhi, India.

McKibbin, Warwick, Professor of Economics and Convenor of the Economics Division in the Research School of Pacific & Asian Studies, The Australian National University, Canberra, Australia. He is also a non-resident Senior Fellow at the Brookings Institution in Washington D.C, and President of McKibbin Software Group.

Maitra, Pushkar, Senior Lecturer in the Department of Economics, Monash University, Melbourne, Australia.

Mallick, Soumitra Kumar, Senior Lecturer of Economics, Finance & Control at the Indian Institute of Social Welfare & Business Management, Calcutta, India.

Rath, Deba Prasad, Economic Research Department, Reserve Bank of India, and Director, Publications Division, Mumbai, India.

Roy, Kalyan K., Professor of Financial Management, at the Indian Institute of Social Welfare & Business Management, Calcutta, India.

Saggar, Mridul, Director of the Econometrics Division, Reserve Bank of India, Mumbai, India.

Sarkar, Amitava, Professor of Economics, Macro-Economics, and International Economics & Finance, Indian Institute of Social Welfare & Business Management, Calcutta, India.

Sen, Kunal, School of Development Studies, University of East Anglia, UK

Sen, Partha, Professor of Economics, Delhi School of Economics, Delhi University, India.

Shand, Ric, Visitor, Division of Economics, Research School of Pacific & Asian Studies, The Australian National University, Canberra, Australia.

Sharma, Anurag, PhD Scholar, Division of Economics, Research School of Pacific & Asian Studies, The Australian National University, Canberra, Australia.

Singh, Kanhaiya, Ministry of Foreign Trade, Government of India, New Delhi, India.

Thapa, Prem Jung, Research Fellow, Economics Program, Research School of Social Sciences, The Australian National University, Canberra, Australia. He is also affiliated with the Institute for Integrated Development Studies based in Kathmandu, Nepal.

Tutakne, Sadanand, Business Analyst, Risk, Information and Banking — India, American Express (India) Pvt. Ltd. and is pursuing a doctoral degree in economics from the University of Maryland at College Park, USA.

Wilson, Edgar, Associate Professor, Department of Economics, University of Wollongong, Australia.

PART I

INTRODUCTION

1

Indian Economic Reforms: An introduction to the volume

Raghbendra Jha

Indian economic reforms started unfolding in earnest in July 1991 but had been in the making for at least four years prior to it. The change in economic philosophy begun at that time has permeated economic policy and academic as well as business debate. Though there are important arguments about the structure, sequencing and speed of economic reforms *per se*, there is hardly any serious body of opinion challenging their need, indeed their indispensability. This victory for economic reforms is remarkable for a country such as India with a vibrant, if not bitter, history of disagreements about economic policy.

Against this background, the present volume downplays the current prevalent route of listing what reforms have taken place and trying to put together a road map for the future. Several studies have done that and a short bibliography appears at the end of this chapter. Nor is it only an 'update' on the Indian economy. Several banks and business consulting houses, not to mention government departments and international bodies such as the World Bank and the IMF do this on a regular basis. The main concern of this volume is to examine the impact of the reforms on the Indian economy in a structured manner and the overwhelming majority of the papers in this volume are analytical. They model the impact of the reforms on various sectors as well as the macro economy and, where possible, try to draw lessons for better policy design.

The first section of the book consists of seven papers on monetary and financial sector developments in the aftermath of the reforms. The chapter 'Monetary regimes in India' by Warwick McKibbin and Kanhaiya Singh argues that an important issue currently facing India is the choice of an appropriate regime for conducting monetary policy. This chapter summarizes the state of the current policy debate on selecting a monetary regime for India and presents estimates of the impact of alternative monetary regimes in the face of a variety of shocks. The impacts of shocks to aggregate demand, productivity growth and risk perceptions are considered under the three policy regimes of money targeting, inflation targeting and nominal income targeting.

In their chapter, 'On the Endogenity of the Money Multiplier in India', Raghbendra Jha and Deba Prasad Rath argue that an endogenous money multiplier framework is best suited for analyzing the money supply process in India and question the simplifying assumptions tending to justify stability and predictability of the money multiplier especially in the context of a deregulated financial system with market determined interest rates. An empirical analysis conducted using monthly data for the period April 1980 through March 2000 establishes this and traces the source of the endogeneity of multipliers to a range of macroeconomic variables. Thus monetary targeting is becoming increasingly difficult.

Amitava Sarkar, Kalyan Roy and Soumitra Mallick, in their chapter 'Financial Fragility in Indian Stock Markets: The Decade of the Nineties', use cointegration techniques to model the behaviour of Indian stock markets in the aftermath of the reforms. It attempts to model the behaviour of stock prices for 7638 companies for the period 1988 to 2001. Apart from structural modeling, the chapter examines the financial fragility of Indian stock markets and attempts to identify periods of crises in stock markets.

In his chapter, 'A Perspective on Saving, Investment and Macroeconomic Policies in India in the 1990s', Mridul Saggar examines the behaviour of savings and investment aggregates for the Indian economy. The gains in private saving were largely the result of financial deepening. Failure of fiscal reforms to keep pace with the wide-ranging reforms may have been largely responsible for limited gains in saving and investment. A sharp decline in public saving rate during the reforms period has contributed to a rise in the private saving rate, but the rise failed to fully compensate for the fall in public saving rate and resulted in lowering the overall gross domestic savings rate from the level it could have attained, if the fiscal reforms would have progressed at a desired pace.

Partha Sen, in his chapter 'Exchange Rate Policy in India', examines the Indian exchange rate experience since the start of the liberalization process. He analyzes macroeconomic data pertaining to the external sector and the relationship between foreign capital flows and the exchange rate. In the last decade, the various items in the capital account of the balance of payments have had governmental controls removed. The exchange rate can be said to be increasingly 'determined' by these flows (and, of course, the policy stance in response to the flows). Sen argues that it is premature to institute capital account convertibility in India.

In the chapter on 'Macroeconomics of Credit: An Indian Perspective' Deba Prasad Rath and Dhritidyuti Bose model the behaviour of credit in

India. The credit-output relationship is shown to be bi-directional. A time series model estimated for the reform period shows that industrial output continues to exert predominant influence on credit demand and supply. From the policy angle, credit turns out to be as weak a target variable as money in view of its long-term velocity displaying higher degree of volatility than the broad money velocity.

In their chapter 'The Fiscal Constraint on India's Economic Growth' Raghbendra Jha, Satish Chand and Anurag Sharma review the evidence on the sustainability of the fiscal deficit in India. Results of tests with and without structural breaks are reported. Contours of a policy to improve the fiscal health of the economy within the broader context of a policy of tax reform are discussed.

The second section of the book deals with the industrial sector of India. Using company level data for the engineering industry, Anita Kumari models the determinants of export performance and the impact of economic reforms thereupon, in her chapter 'Technology, Productivity and Export Growth of Engineering Industry in India'. She finds that exports increased in both the periods but export growth declined during the post-reform period. Productivity growth had a positive impact on export growth in both periods, but particularly in the post-reform period.

The chapter on 'Public and Private Investment expenditure and its linkages with FDI: A case study of India' by Sadanand Tutakne, Santanu Gupta and Pradeep Apte, develops an overlapping generations model to investigate the role of public investment on private investment and FDI for India and analyzes the role of the reforms program. The analysis is conducted for India as a whole as well as for three states: Andhra Pradesh, Gujarat and Maharashtra. At the national level, they find some evidence of public investment having a positive impact on private investment. At the state level, it is only in Andhra Pradesh that reforms have had a positive and significant impact on private investment.

Prema-Chandra Athukorala and Kunal Sen, in their chapter 'Liberalization and Business Investment in India', specify an empirical model to examine the impact of liberalization on business investment in India. The results suggest that the level of capital stock and rental cost of capital are important determinants of business investment along with changes in output and public investment. It is evident that the net impact of the reforms on corporate investment has been salutary.

Shri Bhagwan Dahiya and Desh Gupta in their chapter, 'The Current State of Corporate Governance in India', argue that India was slow in moving towards changes in corporate governance in the early part of the post-reform period, despite a higher number of scandals. But starting from 1997, with the introduction of the SEBI Takeover Code, reforms have been introduced firstly through CII's voluntary Code and then through implementations of the recommendations of the KMB committee. These have set in place a Code of Corporate Governance and have moved India's corporate goverance regime away from one dominated and monitored by insiders and towards the Anglo–Saxon model, seeking an arm's length relationship. Conflicts of interest are clearly highlighted and an attempt is made to resolve them. But problems of corporate governance remain — particularly in the area of implementation.

The next section on India's Exposure to the Global Economy consists of two chapters. Kaliappa Kalirajan in his chapter 'The Impact of a Decade of India's Trade Reforms' reviews changes in trade policy — particularly tariffs and non-tariff barriers. India has taken major steps towards trade liberalisation since 1991, partly on its own initiative and partly from its commitments to the WTO. Nevertheless the direction of trade policy has been overly cautious and influenced by domestic pressures for protection. Tariff levels are too high by ASEAN standards.

Rashmi Banga in her chapter 'Do Productivity Spillovers from Japanese and U.S. Firms Differ?' models the impacts of FDI from Japan and the U.S. on the Indian economy. US FDI in manufacturing is usually undertaken in technologically sophisticated industries with not yet standardised products that are more capital-intensive in nature, while Japanese FDI generally enters industries that are less capital-intensive, producing standardised products that are less technology-intensive. She finds that Japanese equity has a significant positive impact on the total factor productivity growth of the domestic firms but US equity has had no significant effect.

The next part deals with Sectoral and Regional issues and consists of four chapters. In their chapter 'Growth in India's State Economies before and with reforms: shares and determinants', Shashanka Bhide and Ric Shand consider the characteristics of economic growth for 14 major states of India during the period 1993 to 1999. The chapter discovers patterns in such growth and argues that the behaviour of determinants of economic growth across these states is broadly consistent with the observed pattern of growth in their state domestic products. The chapter also examines the role of various constraints — such as the fiscal deficit, quality of infrastructure — to economic growth at the state level.

Edgar Wilson's 'Testing Market Integration in Indian Agriculture' develops a simultaneous vector autoregressive model of non-stationary prices, which is estimated using Johansen's full information likelihood estimation techniques to derive efficient and consistent parameter estimates. The chapter also quantifies a short run equilibrating price elasticity, which indicates the ability of individual markets to return to equilibrium when faced with short-term commodity price shocks. The elasticities are estimated and tested for their significance using end-of-month wholesale price data for selected markets for wheat, jower, paddy rice, groundnut, rapeseed and mustard seed and the periods prior to and after agricultural marketing liberalisation compared.

In their chapter 'Indian Software Industry: Growth Patterns, Constraints and Government Initiatives' Chandana Chakraborty and Dilip Dutta provide an analytical framework for examining the size and ownership of the Indian software industry. The degree of foreign participation and concentration are examined. The size of the industry is discussed in the context of relative magnitudes of domestic and foreign markets. Export performance of this industry and national policy towards this strategic industry are also examined.

Raghbendra Jha and Prem Thapa in their chapter 'India's Infrastructure Sector' examine the spatial distribution of infrastructure services across India. They also consider several policy reforms particularly for the electricity sector.

The final part of this book examines India's Social Sector and consists of three chapters. In their chapter 'Income Generation Program and Empowerment of Women — A Case Study in India', P. Basu and S. Basu review the increasingly important role of accountability and a participatory approach in the empowerment of women under the umbrella of an economic reform agenda in India in recent years. The study has used a socio-economic case study in the district of South 24 Parganas in West Bengal, India involving a private NGO and a government organization both of whom were responsible for designing and implementing anti-poverty programs. The chapter reveals that recipients are, in general, more satisfied with the performance of the private NGO.

In his chapter 'Are the Poor more vulnerable to Income Shocks? An analysis of consumption in rural India' Pushkar Maitra examines the extent of consumption insurance against income risk by households in rural India. Motivated by the theory of risk sharing, he estimates the effects of income changes on consumption after controlling for aggregate shocks through changes in village level consumption and household size. The results show that the null hypothesis of full insurance is rejected both for the population as a whole and for the different land classes. Consumption tracks income more closely for poorer households compared to the richer households.

In the chapter entitled 'Rural Poverty in India: Structure, determinants and suggestions for policy reform' Raghbendra Jha presents estimates of poverty in India at both national and sub-national levels. Characteristics of the rural poor as well as their experiences in asset, credit and labour markets are discussed. Finally the chapter reviews the working of some key poverty reduction programs and outlines steps that would facilitate an improvement in their functioning.

Each chapter in the volume has a contribution to make in terms of the design of future reforms. It is best to let readers discover these themselves.

Economic Reforms: Some Suggested Directions

Much work needs to be done to push forward the reforms process and my comments here will be very brief. Perhaps the most important step is for the economic reforms begun at the central level to percolate to the level of individual states. The list of urgent state level reforms includes control of the fiscal deficit, reform of state electricity boards, reforming and harmonizing state taxes, breaking down barriers to internal trade and better targeting and provision of public services. On the macroeconomic side fiscal deficits of both central and state governments have to be reined in. This in itself requires considerable tax and expenditure reform and rational use of user fees for public services. The reform of public sector undertakings is well overdue. To function well, public sector undertakings must have more autonomy. Further, many of the assets (such as prime land other facilities) of these undertakings can be revenue earning but the government has been unable to give these undertakings the freedom to pursue such activities. The government's privatization programs needs to be pursued in right earnest. To stimulate growth in the industrial sector all remaining barriers to entry must be removed. The climate for FDI investment needs to be improved further. Further, much needs to be done to improve the efficiency of capital and labor markets so that resources can be accumulated more efficiently and factor markets can function more smoothly. India's infrastructure development — particularly roads, ports and electricity — is urgent if she is to grow fast. Public funds are scarce and developing a legal and industrial framework for the involvement of the private sector in such development is a matter of priority. To stimulate rural development and lower rural poverty on an emergent basis, public investment should be redirected toward the rural sector and well targeted in terms of regions — those with high poverty and rainfed areas[1] — as well as people, the landless and small farmers. Rural, non-agricultural development is crucial for poverty reduction. Infrastructural investment would be crucial for this. Thus pressures for additional public investment continue. There is a pressing need for tax/GDP ratios and public savings to pick up. There is certainly a need for private investment but the private sector would not be interested in the poorest areas of India without substantial inducement.

[1] Fan and Hazell (2000) provide evidence of the effectiveness of investment in rainfed areas.

Reform of price policy with regard to inputs is necessary to ensure that such investment is not mistargeted. User cost pricing of ground water would lead to redirection of private investment away from excessive use of pumps and overuse of groundwater resources, which lead to lowering of the water table. Deep structural and financial reforms of the state electricity boards are well overdue.

In order to facilitate human resource development policies are required to ensure that adequate provisions are made for expenditures in education and training and that these are allocated equitably. The design and implementation of education and training programs for the poor need much improvement. It is particularly important to ensure universal access to good basic education since this is beneficial from the standpoint of poverty alleviation. This very brief review of necessary reforms only seems to underline the important observation that economic reforms do not necessarily mean less government — but only a different kind of government. The public sector will continue to play a key role in India for the foreseeable future. To do this successfully it needs to improve its productivity and help in resource generation as well as enhance its regulatory performance. Government machinery needs to undergo a sea change in areas of governance and outlook toward regulation and the private sector. Such attitudinal changes are the hardest to bring about — but they remain the key to sustained economic prosperity.

Acknowledgements

Some of the chapters in this volume were first presented at a conference to mark ten years of economic reforms in India held in the Australia South Asia Research Centre of the Australian National University during November 2001. I am grateful to all the conference participants for their invaluable contributions. Other authors picked up the baton and provided some further articles to help make this volume an integrated, cohesive analytical inquiry into Indian economic reforms. My first debt of gratitude is to all these authors. Bonnie Allan and Julie Barnes made excellent arrangements for this conference. I am obliged to James Fox, Director of the Research School of Pacific and Asian Research of the ANU for providing financial assistance for holding the conference and to Warwick McKibbin, Director of the division of economics of the Research School of Pacific and Asian Research for his encouragement and support. Stephanie Hancock provided crucial secretarial support in not just organizing this volume but also producing camera-ready copies and helping in the editing. Amanda Watkins of Palgrave–Macmillan provided unflinching support and encouragement throughout the production of this volume. To all these people I express my sincere gratitude.

References

Ahluwalia, M.S., *Perspectives on India's Reforms* (New Delhi: Oxford University Press, 1999).
Desai, M., 'Democracy and Development: India 1947–2002', K.R. Narayanan Lecture (Canberra: Australia South Asia Research Centre, Australian National University, 2002).
Fan, S. and P. Hazell, 'Should Developing Countries Invest more in Less-Favoured Areas? — An Empirical Analysis of Rural India' *Economic and Political Weekly,* 35(12) (2000), 1455–64.
Joshi, V. and I. Little (eds), *India's Economic Reforms 1991–2001* (New Delhi: Oxford University Press, 2002).
Kelkar, V., *India's Economic Reforms Agenda: Micro, Meso and Macro Economic Reforms,* Fourth Annual Fellows' Lecture (Centre for the Advanced Study of India, University of Pennsylvania, 2001).
Rangarajan, C., *Economic Reforms: An Assessment,* Dr. B.R. Ambedkar Lecture (University of Mumbai, 2001).
Sachs, J., A. Varshney and N. Bajpai, *India in the Era of Economic Reforms* (New Delhi: Oxford University Press, 1999).
Srinivasan, T.N., *Eight Lectures on Indian Economic Reforms* (New Delhi: Oxford University Press, 2000).

PART II

FINANCIAL SECTOR DEVELOPMENTS

2
Issues in the Choice of a Monetary Regime for India

Warwick J. McKibbin and Kanhaiya Singh

1. Introduction

In the face of ongoing economic reform, the choice of the appropriate monetary regime for India is a fundamentally important question. Many developing countries including India are considering adopting inflation targeting as the basis for monetary policy, yet there are concerns as to whether a regime that works well in developed economies, should also work well in a developing economy. This chapter summarizes the state of the current policy debate on selecting a monetary regime for India and presents estimates from an empirical model of India,[1] of the impact of alternative monetary regimes in the face of a variety of shocks to the Indian economy. The impacts of shocks to aggregate demand, productivity growth and country risk premia are considered under the three policy regimes of money targeting, inflation targeting and nominal income targeting. It is concluded that a monetary target performs worst among the three regimes while the results of income targeting are most encouraging. Inflation targeting performs well for demand shocks but causes greater volatility in real output under both productivity shocks and risk reassessment shocks. Although nominal income targeting works well in the model, the way this could be implemented in a developing economy needs more research. It is often argued that because nominal income targeting has not been observed in practice in any countries it should not be considered. However, much the same could have been said about inflation targeting until the end of the 1980s.

There have been two broad objectives of monetary policy in India: (1) to maintain a reasonable degree of price stability and (2) to help accelerate the rate of economic growth (Rangarajan 1998, p. 60). However, the relative

---

1 Based on McKibbin and Singh (2002).

emphasis between the two objectives has been changing. The policy statement of Reserve Bank of India (RBI) by Governor Bimal Jalan, on Monetary and Credit Policy for the year 1999–2000 (RBI 1999b) brought the issue of price stability into the fore. The main basis of monetary policy in India since the mid-1980s is due to the Chakravarty Committee Report (RBI 1985), which recommended a monetary targeting approach. The intermediate target was chosen to be the supply of broad money aggregate M3[2] instead of the interest rate under the contention that the demand function for money in India has remained fairly stable with respect to 'select set of variables' (Rangarajan 1998, pp. 63–4). The Chakravarty Committee (RBI 1985) had presumed a target of 4 per cent for inflation. However, annual inflation as measured by wholesale price index (WPI) was 9 per cent during 1970s, 8 per cent during 1980s and 10 per cent during 1990–95 (Rangarajan 1998, p. 63).

The report of the Chakravarty Committee (RBI 1985), while recommending monetary targeting qualified that 'mechanical application of constant money supply growth rule has no place' due to significant structural changes required to facilitate the growth process. It is clear from Table 2.1 that the RBI does not follow an absolutely fixed growth rate of money supply. The money supply growth target in India is derived from the long-run money demand function, where income is represented by the exogenously given 'anticipated' growth rate and 'tolerable' rate of inflation. Applying these projections to a long run income elasticity of the demand for money leads to a projection of money supply growth for one year (Vasudevan 1999).

Since 1960, the Reserve Bank of India (RBI) has had a range of monetary policy instruments at its disposal including direct (quantity) and indirect (price) instruments.[3] The main direct instruments included cash reserve ratio (CRR),[4] Statutory liquidity ratio (SLR),[5] quantitative controls on reserve bank lending to the banks and the commercial sector ('refinance'),

---

2 M3 =Currency with public+Demand deposit with the banking system+Other deposits with the RBI+Time liability portion of savings deposits with the banking system+Certificates of deposits issued by banks+Term deposits (excluding FCNR (B) deposits) with contractual maturity with the banking system+Call borrowing from 'Non-Depository' financial corporations by the banking system

3 For a comprehensive detail see Joshi and Little (1994), Sen and Vaidya (1997)

4 Since 1962 the RBI is empowered to vary the CRR between 3 per cent and 15 per cent of total demand and time liability. It rose to 15 per cent in 1994–95 but since then it is brought down to below 10 per cent. CRR in excess of 3 per cent is currently remunerated at 4 per cent per annum (Reddy 1999b).

5 Over and above the CRR banks are required to maintain a minimum amount of liquid assets in cash, gold, and government securities that amounted to at least 25 per cent of their demand and time liabilities.

and quantitative credit controls. The indirect instruments had been operating through the administrative setting of various interest rates. The CRR and SLR have been quite powerful instruments in the hands of the RBI. While the CRR affects adjusted reserve money directly by immobilizing banks' cash holdings, the SLR affects reserve money indirectly by reducing the monetisation of the fiscal deficits. The government finds a 'captive' market for its securities in the form of SLR. This leads to diversion of large amount of bank resources to government; as a result it rose to 37.4 per cent in 1992.

Table 2.1: Performance of Monetary Targeting in India

Year	M3 (% growth)[5]		GDP (% growth)[1]		Inflation (%)[2]	
	Target	Actual	Target (objective)	Actual	Target (objective)	Actual
1983–84	< 16.2	18.2	-	8.3	-	7.6
1984–85	<18.2[3]	19.0	-	3.8	Curb Inflation	6.0
1985–86	<19.0[4]	16.0	~3.8	4.1	Avoid resurgence	4.8
1986–87	<17.5	18.6	> 4.1	4.8	Continue check	5.1
1987–88	<18.6	16.0	5.0	4.3	Avoid re-emergence	10.7
1988–89	<16.9	17.8	-	10.6	-	5.7
1989–90	<17.1	19.4	4-5	6.9	-	9.1
1990–91	<15.4	15.1	~5.0	5.4	-	12.1
1991–92 (April)	<14.0[5]	19.3	4.0	0.8	Max 7.0	13.6
1991–92 (Oct)	<13.0		3.0		Max 9.0	
1992–93	<11.0[6]	15.7	-	5.3	8.0	7.0
1993–94	~12.0	18.4	5.0	6.2	Further Moderation	10.8
1994–95 (April)	14.0–15.0	22.3	5.0	5.3	~ 6.8	10.4
1994–95 (Oct)	16.0 (Max)		5.5			
1995–96	15.5 (Max)	13.7	5.5	7.2	~ 8.0	5.0
1996–97	15.5–16.0	16.2	6.0	7.5	6.0	6.9
1997–98	15.0–15.5	17.6	6.5–7.0	5.1	5.0-6.0	5.3
1998–99	15.5–16.0		6.0–7.0		~5.0	

Notes: Some of the values specifically before 1990–91 are taken from the implied statements like 'less than previous year' or 'less than average of last four years' etc.

1 GDP: Gross Domestic product at factor cost at 1980–81 prices.

2 Inflation: Based on wholesale price index.

3 Growth of liquidity and primary money creation

4 Liquidity Growth.

5 M3 Target was made consistent with the containment of gross fiscal deficit to 6.5 per cent of GDP in 1991–92

6 M3 Target was made consistent with the containment of gross fiscal deficit to 5.0 per cent of GDP in 1992–93

Sources: (1) Mohanty and Mitra (1999); (2) Reserve bank of India Annual Report, various issues; (3) Circulars issued by Credit Planning Cell/Monetary Policy Department, Reserve Bank of India.

Table 2.2: Central Bank Independence, Seigniorage, and Indicators of Financial Deepening in Selected Countries, 1980–95

Country	CBI Rank 1980s (%)	Seigniorage to GDP* (%	Inflation Tax# (%	Real Interest Rate on deposits 1980–89 (%)		Broad Money to GDP (%)	Nom. GDP per Capita (US$) 1995
				Geometric Average	Standard Deviation		
New Zealand	12	0.23	7.5	2.1	4.2	47.9	16650
Canada	4	0.22	4.7	4.3	1.5	49.6	19249
U.K.	7	0.25	5.7	0.7	2.1	70.0	18986
Sweden	6	0.47	6.4	2.5	2.6	51.4	26070
Finland							
Australia	8	0.32	5.8	3.1	2.9	49.9	19257
Spain	11	1.30	7.7	0.9	2.4	76.1	14465
Israel	24	1.60	33.1	N/A	N/A	78.8	15689
India	**21**	**1.30**	**8.7**	**-0.3**	**2.7**	**45.7**	**345**
Chile	36	1.34	15.9	7.8	9.6	37	4868
Korea	28	0.51	6.8	4.0	4.6	37.5	10146
Mexico	32	3.22	29.6	-6.2	13.3	26.1	3164
Indonesia	26	0.52	8.5	5.4	6.1	29.8	1034
Philippines	18	0.95	11.1	-0.3	10.9	32.6	1072

Notes: * Annual Monetary base multiplied by the inflation tax and divided by nominal GDP, except for Israel where foreign currency deposits were excluded from the monetary base.

\# Defined as: (CPI inflation/(100+CPI inflation)), a bounded measure of the real losses on holding of money balances.

Sources: (Masson, et al. 1997), Table 4; CBI rank from (Cukierman 1992), Table 21.1.

Following economic liberalization and financial sector reforms[6] the RBI has been moving away from quantitative controls towards an interest rate channel for monetary transmission. The central bank actively uses a combination of Open Market Operations (OMO), auction of Government Securities and Private Placements to maintain medium and long-term interest rates. This is particularly important in view of the management of government borrowings, which has increased since abolition of automatic monetisation. It is considered that monetary policy in India is neither wholly subsidiary to fiscal policy nor it is heavily constrained by the balance of payments.[7] Cukierman (1992) placed India at 21st position in ranking of central bank independence (see Table 2.2). The extent of the

6 The reforms include inter-alia free floating exchange rate, decontrol of interest rate, development of securities markets, greater reliance on open market operations, auctions of government securities, phased decontrol of capital account. For a comprehensive details see Reddy (1999b; Sen and Vaidya (1997). Also see IMF (1998); Rangarajan (1995); Rangarajan (1998); Reddy (1999a); Reddy (1999c); Reddy (1999f)

7 Joshi and Little (1994).

monetisation of the fiscal deficit as percentage of gross domestic product has fallen from an average of 2.28 per cent for the period 1985 to 1990, to 0.61 per cent for 1991 to 1997. Subsequently the automatic monetisation of fiscal deficit was abolished (RBI 1998).

The RBI now heavily relies on OMO including repo operations in conjunction with the Bank Rate, however more conventional instruments such as CRR, and sectoral refinance (export) continue. The reserve requirements are considered a tax on intermediation and therefore, in the process of financial sector reform, they are systematically being reduced, while the structure of administered interest rates has been almost[8] totally dismantled since 1994. The statutory minimum for SLR has been brought down to 25 per cent since then, yet many banks hold SLR more than the statutory prescription (Reddy 1999b). The quantity control through ratios of this type impairs the profitability of banks and introduces inefficiency in resource allocation and deprives the private sector of capital in favor of government. To minimize the role of quantity variables the RBI took initiatives to activate the rate variables through development of government securities market as part of its policy reform in 1992. With the development of a voluntary government securities market the RBI can now effectively buy and sell government securities as a part of its open-market operations, depending on its assessment of liquidity requirements in the system. According to the current RBI annual report (RBI 1999) a number of measures taken to improve securitization of the money market, including permission to foreign institutional investors to invest in Treasury Bills (TB), are helping to deepen the securities market.

A market based exchange rate system has been operational since March 1993 with occasional intervention from the RBI against speculative attacks. There have been significant steps towards Capital Account Convertibility (IMF 1998). In addition to relaxing restrictions on banks' overseas borrowing and investment activities, norms for Indian investment overseas have been liberalized.

Clearly the Indian economy is passing through a stage where monetary policy needs to be re-examined. The success of monetary targeting as stated earlier depends upon (i) the reliability of relationship between the monetary-aggregate being targeted and the goal variables (output and inflation) and (ii) control by the central bank of the target monetary aggregate so that credibility of the central bank is maintained. During the pre-reform period these conditions were largely met with fully

---

8 Currently there is a prescribed rate of 4.5 per cent for saving bank accounts. Interest rate on smaller advances up to Rs. 200,000 should not exceed prime lending rate, which each bank is statutorily required to announce.

administered interest rates, liquidity ratios, exchange rate and capital flows. With reforms in place and the opening up of the economy, a complete break down of monetary targeting and its abandoning cannot be ruled out.

There is a vigorous debate on the appropriate monetary regime in India. Vasudevan (1999) observes that the fact that the actual money supply (Table 2.1) has exceeded the announced targets in most years raises doubts about the stability of the money demand function or the correctness in adapting the operating procedure of targeting bank reserves. Reddy (1999d), also recognizes that in a dynamic setting with continuous evolution in technology and financial systems, stability of the demand for money function may be undermined. In a similar vein Mohanty and Mitra (1999) observe that, with increasing market orientation of the financial structure and international capital flows, it needs to be considered whether a monetary targeting approach could ensure internal and external stability. Even if the money demand function show some kind of stability, it cannot be guaranteed that in a changing environment of external and financial sector reforms which enhance the sensitiveness of quantity variable to their market-determined price, money growth rate targeting would remain optimal. In was inevitable that inflation targeting would be considered. Kannan (1999) reviewed this possibility in the Indian context and argued for accomplishing the financial sector reforms before implementing inflation targeting.

2. The Theory of Monetary Regime Design

A monetary policy regime is concerned with the choice of instruments, operating targets and intermediate targets with the objective of meeting the ultimate goals of policy. This process results in a systematic rule (either simple or very complex) for adjusting the instrument (quantity or price) in response to new information. The goal variables are the ultimate variables of interest to policymakers and typically include inflation, output or unemployment. Intermediate targets include exchange rates, broader monetary aggregates, nominal output, and more recently inflation forecasts. Operating targets could be bank reserves or overnight inter-bank short-term rates (like call money rates). The instruments are the variables which the central bank finds in its direct control and which are easily manipulated to achieve a desired value for the operating targets and the intermediate targets. Instruments include interest rates on borrowings from the central bank (interest rate on reserve money like overnight rates, 'repo' rates or 90 days bill rates) or a reserve requirement ratio (like cash reserve ratio, CRR) or central banks' holding of government securities (treasury bills, TB). The problem facing the monetary authorities is to choose an appropriate instrument and intermediate target/targets, and a rule defining their interrelationship. This is what constitutes the regime of monetary policy. The problem that arises is which regime performs better in a given economic environment? Many answers are theoretically ambiguous and thus the ultimate answer is to be found by empirical analysis of the regimes in simpler models like that demonstrated in de Brouwer and O'Regan (1997), Cecchetti (1998), Svensson (1998) among others or global models like the McKibbin–Sachs Global (MSG2) model.[9] These models are used to generate profiles of inflation and output variability that can be compared across regimes. For a current discussion on performance of different monetary policy regimes reference see Mishkin (1999) and McCallum (1999).

Why should the central bank follow rules at all? This question has been discussed in the literature on the discretion vs. rule debate. Cecchetti (1998) gives two important arguments in support of rules. A) The now established finding that when policymaking is based on pure discretion rather than rules, dynamic inconsistency can lead to high steady state inflation is relevant (Walsh 1998, pp. 321–35). B) Policy transparency is helps establish central bank credibility. If the central bank follows a rule it appears directly accountable. Such arguments have found favor in Australia, Canada, New Zealand, Spain, United Kingdom, Sweden, and Israel.

There are several approaches followed in the literature on implementing monetary regimes. These range from simple ad hoc rules[10] to analytically derived optimal feedback rules. We now discuss the theory behind some of the popular instruments and the rules for a monetary policy regime.

2.1 The Instrument Choice Problem

Modern central banks work through a fractional reserve banking system where the two most common modes of operations are legislative controls and OMO. In several economies the central bank holds the power to specify CRR requirements within legislative specified limits, which allows it to have direct quantitative control on the monetary aggregates. In OMO the central bank buys or sells government securities to influence the operating targets. The central bank has the choice to use either quantity or price of the securities as the instrument. Since the price of the security is inversely related to the interest rate and changes in the stock of securities determines the changes in the reserve money and hence monetary aggregates, the choice is between monetary aggregate and the interest rate

---

9 See for example Bryant, et al. (1993); McKibbin (1993), Henderson and McKibbin (1993); Henderson and McKibbin (1993a); McKibbin (1997); McKibbin, et al. (1998).

10 Nominal money rule, 'Taylor rules' (Taylor 1993b), Henderson and McKibbin (1993) (or CC) rule, nominal-income targeting rules (McCallum 1989); and inflation forecast targeting (Svensson 1996a; Svensson 1998a).

as the instrument. The classic analysis of this question (Poole 1970) which has since been extended in a number of other articles and has been useful in a variety of settings even beyond monetary policy issues like fixed versus flexible exchange rate and nominal versus indexing of wages.[11].

The choice of an instrument is an endogenous decision and it would become more complicated when more than one variable is included in the objective function of the central bank. For example a policy maker may be interested in minimizing the variance of output as well as inflation with some weights assigned to them. Similarly when expectations and the supply disturbances are also included in the model and monetary policy affects both real and nominal magnitudes, various tradeoffs emerge. The choice of the instrument does not appear to be model invariant. A good survey of several supply-demand models including neutrality and non-neutrality of monetary policy is Friedman (1990). Another issue is the problem of price level indeterminacy (Sargent and Wallace (1975)). This result, due to the assumption of complete market clearing and rational expectations, lead them to conclude that the interest rate instrument was not only inferior to a money instrument but was implausible on an *a priori* basis. This lead to the notion that only money could be the instrument, until McCallum (1981) demonstrated that this indeterminacy of prices under an interest rate instrument would follow only in the case in which the central banks' policy rule placed no weight on price (case of 'pure interest rate peg' where money is entirely disregarded). As long as some weight is placed on price in the policy rule function of the central bank, determinacy would prevail. A similar outcome has been demonstrated by Henderson and McKibbin (1993a). In addition to the above purely theoretical reasons, the role of nominal anchor has been emphasized in the literature ((Barro and Gordon 1983; Kydland and Prescott 1977; Mishkin 1999)), particularly as a constraint on the discretionary policy that helps in reducing the time-inconsistency problem.[12]

2.2 Intermediate Target Problem

Traditionally, central banks appear to use some kind of intermediate target for conducting their monetary policy. The most common variable for an intermediate target has been growth of broader aggregates of money, nominal income or the nominal exchange rate. Inflation forecasts have also been adopted as targets by some central banks. The intermediate target

---

11 For example see Roper and Turnovsky (1980), Aizenmann and Frenkel (1985), Gray 1976, Fischer (1977b)

12 Walsh (1998) defines a policy as time-consistent if an action planned at time t for time t+i remains optimal to implement when time t+i actually arrives. If it was not optimal to respond as planned originally then such policy is time-inconsistent.

variables are in fact endogenous. As noted by Svensson (1996a, pp. 14–5), an ideal intermediate target 'is highly correlated with the goal, easier to control than the goal, easier to observe by both the central bank and the public than the goal, and transparent so that central bank communication with the public and public understanding and public prediction of the monetary policy are facilitated'. Observations for such variables are available on a more timely and continuous basis than the ultimate target variables like output and prices. The main idea behind using an intermediate target is the fact that these variables are more up-to-date in information content than the ultimate target variables. The selected instrument, whether an interest rate or non-borrowed reserves or base money itself and the intermediate target, together form a policy rule in a form that the intermediate target could be systematically influenced by the instrument variables. Several such variables can provide potentially useful information but selecting a variable for an intermediate targets is an empirical problem. The choice of a monetary policy regime is all about choosing intermediate target and the instrument, which give minimum variability to the ultimate target variables in a complete model of the economy.

The information contained in the intermediate target variable could be used in two ways. One way obviously is to choose the instrument setting in such a way that the expected deviation in the intermediate target variable from its target be minimized. The second way of using the information content of an intermediate target is to use the information to derive an optimal feedback rule by relating the value of the policy instrument to the observed value of the information variable. Under the optimal feedback rule, the information in the intermediate target is used to choose the value of the policy coefficient that minimizes the loss function itself. Thus the stress here is to minimize the expected deviation of the goal variable from its target instead of minimizing the expected deviation of the intermediate target variable from its target. This use of the information variable dates back to Kareken, et al. (1973). Friedman (1975, 1977) demonstrated that intermediate targeting is inefficient compared to optimal feedback rule with both an interest rate as the instrument or reserves as the instrument. Rules obtained in the case of the former did not minimize the variance in the output when compared to the later. Walsh (1998) draws similar conclusion where the objective function is to minimize expected squared deviations of the inflation rate around a target level. It is shown that the optimal feedback rule out-performs intermediate money targeting, however an intermediate target does better than a policy which does not respond to new information so long as money-demand shocks are small. The results of the intermediate-target problem are also not model invariant. In a comparison of nominal income targeting with money supply targeting, Bean (1983) used a rational expectation model and measured the desirability of policies by their effect on variance of output around a certain full information level and concluded that monetary policy based on nominal income as an intermediate target is likely to be preferable to a policy based on exogenously determined money provided elasticity of aggregate demand with respect to real balances be less than one. However. West (1986), showed that, if the objective of monetary policy is to minimize the unconditional variance of output, then nominal income targeting can be preferred to fixed money stock if and only if the elasticity of aggregate demand with respect to real balances is greater than one, a completely opposite result to Bean (1983). In the case of an inflation forecast as the intermediate target, Svensson (1996a) claims it to be an ideal intermediate target as it is by definition the current variable that is most correlated with the goal.

2.3 Representation of Regimes by Simple Rules

Calculating An Optimal Feedback Rule Requires a complex process of constrained optimization in which the policy instrument is supposed to respond to a range of information in a given time period. In practical models there could be vector of targets or goal variables, a vector of predetermined state variables, a vector of forward looking variables and a vector of innovations to the state variables. This brings about uncertainty about the true model and complicates the derivation of the optimal feedback rule. McKibbin (1997) indicates the difficulty in distinguishing between discretion and a complex rule and advocates the use of simple rules as an alternative. At the same time he cautions that such rules must be robust to different models of the economy in addition to the model in which that was developed. Some of the popular rules are summarize in table 3.

3. An Overview of the MSG2 Multi-Country Model

Full documentation of the MSG2 model and an analysis of its properties and tracking performance can be found in McKibbin and Sachs (1991). Information on the latest model can be found on the world wide web at www.sensiblepolicy.com. A summary of the key features of the model are presented in table 4 and the coverage of the model used in the current article are listed in table 5. The version used in this chapter is the 'India model' version 44M (see McKibbin 1998b). The theoretical structure of the model is outlined in McKibbin and Singh (2002).

The MSG2 multi-country model is a fully specified dynamic intertemporal general equilibrium model (DIGEM) with careful treatment of stock-flow relations such as the accumulation of investment into capital stocks and the accumulation of fiscal deficits into net asset stocks. Both the short run demand and supply sides of the major economies are incorporated. In the long run, supply is determined by neoclassical growth theory. The model incorporates a number of financial markets such as share markets and markets for short and long bonds in each of the industrial regions where prices are determined by intertemporal arbitrage relations as well as long run sustainability conditions on fiscal deficits and current account positions. In addition, the assumption of rational expectations in these financial markets as well as some forward looking behavior in real spending decisions means that the effects of anticipated policy changes are well handled. The regimes that are included in the model are explicitly modeled and since we use a structural model with rational expectations, the model is essentially immune from the Lucas (1976) Critique.

Table 2.3: Alternative Instrument Rules

Money Rule:	$i_t = \bar{i}_t + \beta(m - \bar{m}_t)$	(1)
Nominal-Income Rule:	$i_t = \bar{i}_t + \beta(p_t + y_t - \overline{p_t + y_t})$	(2)
Bryant-Hooper-Mann Rules:		(3)
Henderson-McKibbin (or CC) Rule:	$i_t = \bar{i}_t + \alpha(\pi_t + y_t - \overline{\pi_t + y_t})$	(3a)
Taylor Rule:	$i_t = \bar{r}_t + \pi_t + 0.5(\pi_t - \bar{\pi}_t) + 0.5(y_t - \bar{y}_t)$	(3b)
Inflation-only rule:	$i_t = \bar{r}_t + \pi_t + \gamma_1(\pi_t - \bar{\pi}_t)$	(4)
Change rule:	$i_t = \bar{i}_t + \pi_t + \gamma_1(\pi_t - \bar{\pi}_t) + \gamma_2(y_t - \bar{y}_t)$	(5)
Constant-real-interest rate rule:	$i_t = c + \pi_t$	(6)

Where:

i = nominal interest rate;

r = real interest rate;

π = inflation rate;

p = log of price level;

y = log of output;

m = log of money and

c = constant

a bar over a variable indicates a desired value

Sources: McKibbin 1997 #8; Brouwer, 1997 #5

Table 2.4: Main Features of the MSG2 Model

- both the demand and supply side of the major economies are explicitly modelled;
- demand equations are based on a combination of intertemporal optimizing behavior and liquidity constrained behavior;
- the supply side takes explicit account of imported intermediate goods especially the role of imported capital goods in investment in economies;
- major flows such as physical investment, fiscal deficits and current account imbalances cumulate into stocks of capital, government debt and net external debt which in turn change the composition and level of national wealth over time.
- Wealth adjustment determines stock equilibrium in the long run but also feeds back into short-run economic conditions through forward-looking share markets, bond markets and foreign exchange markets.
- Asset markets are linked globally through the high international mobility of capital.

Table 2.5: Regional Coverage of the MSG2 Model used here (version 44M)

Regions

Structural
United States
Japan
Canada
Ger many
United Kingdom
France
Italy
Rest of the Euro Zone (denoted REMS)
Mexico
Rest of the OECD (denoted ROECD)
India

Non-Structural
Oil exporting countries (denoted OPEC)
Non-oil developing Countries (denoted LDCs)
Easter European economies and the former Soviet Union (denoted EEFSU)

Sectors
one good in each country/region

It is important to note that investment and consumption behavior is modeled as a weighted average of intertemporal optimizing behavior (with rational expectations of the future path of the global economy), and backward looking behavior based on current income. Thus expected changes in policy and changes in future stocks of assets leads to an initial (although quite damped) response of households and firms. Investment is based on the cost of adjustment approach of Lucas (1967) and Treadway (1969), which yields a model with investment partially determined by Tobin's *q*, along the lines of Hayashi (1982). A full derivation of the model can be found in McKibbin and Sachs (1991).

Apart from the shocks and underlying model structure, the results also depend on the assumptions about fiscal and monetary closure, or more specifically the fiscal and monetary regimes in place in each economy. In this chapter, policy regime assumptions are changed in all countries at the same time as changing these regimes in India. In all countries, fiscal policy is assumed to be implemented such that all governments maintain a fixed share of government spending to GDP and adjust taxes to service any changes in debt. The fiscal deficit adjusts endogenously to any changes in real activity or interest rates.

4. Implementing Alternative Monetary Regimes in the MSG2 Model

We now discuss the properties of three monetary regimes in a model of India. The model used in this chapter has contributed to the literature on regime choice, both from the point of view of a single country or region (Argy, et al. 1989), as well as from a global perspective (Henderson and McKibbin 1993; McKibbin and Sachs 1991; McKibbin and Sachs 1988). Rather than focus on optimal rules, as in the above studies, we focus on the impact of three simple rules for monetary policy.

Monetary policy in this model is assumed to be implemented with a feedback rule for interest rates on some target variable (either the stock of money relative to target, the level of nominal income relative to target, or the rate of inflation relative to target). Here we take an extreme value for each feedback coefficient such that the target variables are targeted exactly in each year. An alternative approach is either to use an arbitrary coefficient to capture partial adjustment or one can calculate an 'optimal' feedback coefficient such that some objective function written in terms of ultimate target variables is optimized (McKibbin 1993). In that earlier article the 'optimal' degree of adjustment for a monetary target rule, given the historically estimate variance covariance matrix of shocks, was found to be exact targeting on money.

The three monetary regimes used in this chapter are summarized in equations (1), (2) and (4) in Table 2.3. Take equation (1) for example. This says that the short term nominal interest rate (i) equal to the baseline nominal interest rate plus a coefficient times the gap between the actual stock of money (m) and the target stock of money (m_t^{bar}). The range of alternative regimes could be explored but are not done so in the current paper. This will be the focus of future research.

5. The Consequences of Alternative Monetary Regimes for India

In this section we subject the model to 5 shocks: a persistent rise in domestic demand in India; a temporary rise in domestic demand in India; a persistent rise in domestic supply in India; a temporary rise in domestic supply in India; and a permanent increase in the perceived risk of investing in Indian assets.[13] The demand shocks are a rise in private consumption of 1 per cent of GDP and the supply shock is a rise in the level of labour productivity of 1 per cent. The results for each simulation are summarized in six figures — one figure for each variable: real GDP, Inflation (defined in terms of a consumer price index); the nominal exchange rate (defined as $US/Rupee); short term nominal interest rates; trade balance and the stock market value. Each figure contains results under the three alternative regimes of a monetary target, and inflation target and a nominal income target.

We first solve the model from 1996 to 2070 given exogenous assumptions about tax rates, productivity growth and population growth by country as well as a range of other exogenous variables under alternative monetary regimes. Each shock is then imposed on the model as a surprise in the year 2000. In the results, all variables are expressed as deviations from what otherwise would have occurred along the baseline of the model. The deviation units differ across variables: GDP, exchange rates and stock market values are expressed as per cent deviation from baseline; inflation and interest rates are all expressed as percentage point deviation from baseline; and the trade balance is expressed as per cent of baseline GDP deviation from base.

5.1 Persistent Demand Shock

The results for a persistent rise in domestic demand are shown in figures 2.1 through 2.6. Note that although the shock to the exogenous component

---

[13] We also simulated a shock to money demand but due to space limitations don't report these results in detail. As expected from the theoretical literature, the money rule performs very badly for this shock relative to the other regimes, which can almost offset the shock completely.

of consumption is permanent, the endogenous components of consumption tend to fall over time so that aggregate private consumption is not permanently higher forever (it can't be given budget constraints in the model). This shock should be considered as just more persistent than the temporary demand shock.

Figure 2.1: Real GDP Under a Permanent Domestic Demand Shock

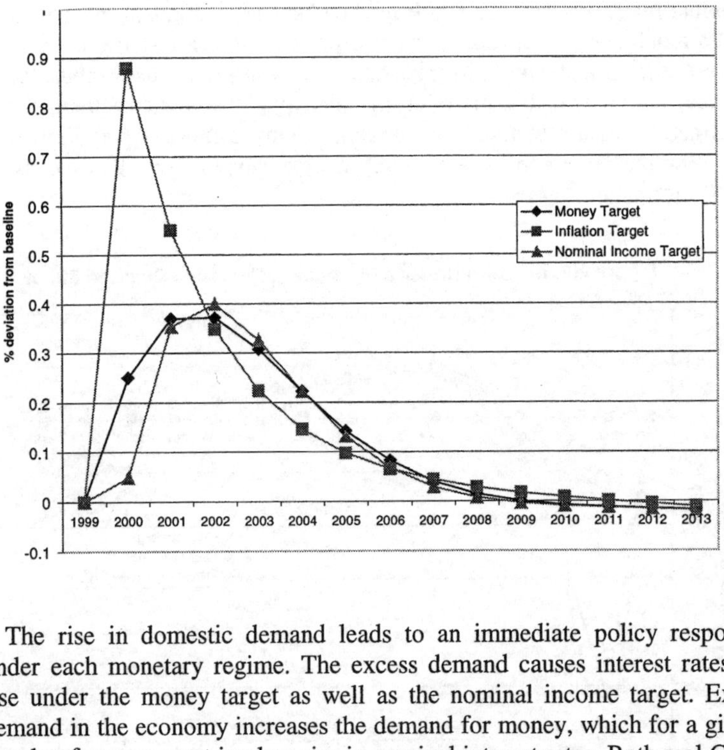

The rise in domestic demand leads to an immediate policy response under each monetary regime. The excess demand causes interest rates to rise under the money target as well as the nominal income target. Extra demand in the economy increases the demand for money, which for a given supply of money must imply a rise in nominal interest rates. Both real GDP and domestic producer prices rise and thus interest rates must rise under a nominal income target. It is interesting that interest rates fall slightly under an inflation target. This is because the inflation rate (defined in terms of the consumer price index) actually falls. The rise in domestic demand causes a capital inflow, which leads to an appreciation of the nominal exchange rate and a fall in import prices. The import price fall dominates the rising domestic prices and the consumer price inflation falls initially. As domestic prices respond to the demand stimulus over time inflation tends to rise and interest rates rise over time.

It appears that the inflation target accentuates the fluctuations in real output, although this depends importantly on the nature of the targeted inflation rate. If a domestic price had been used in the inflation rule, the outcome would have been more like the nominal income target.

The difference between the money target and the nominal income target can best be understood with reference to the money demand function in the model. Money demand in nominal terms is a function of the nominal income (with a unitary elasticity) and a negative function of the short-term nominal interest rate. Thus the difference between a nominal income target and a money target depends on what happens to the short-term interest rate in response to a shock. If interest rates rise with prices and output, then a money target will be more easily met (with less subsequent output contraction) than a nominal income target. This in illustrated in Figure 2.1 in which the GDP rise for a nominal income shock is less than the rise in GDP for a money target.

Figure 2.2: Inflation Under a Permanent Domestic Demand Shock

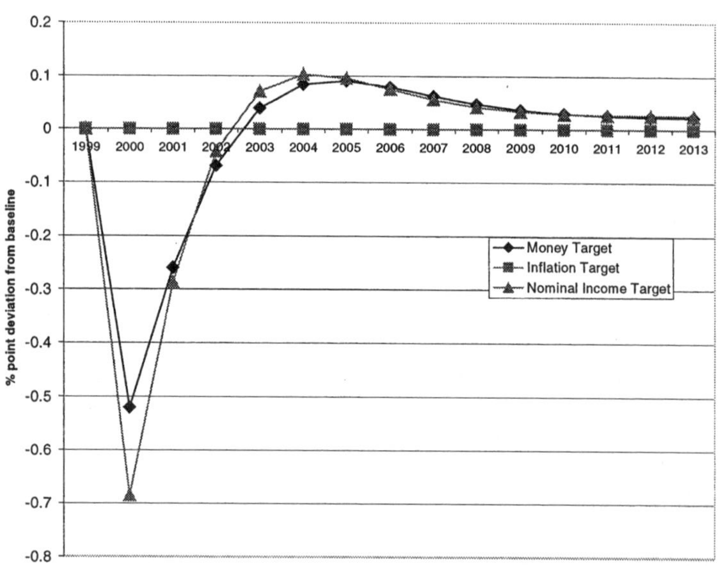

In terms of volatility of inflation, the opposite ranking of regimes is found. Under the inflation target, obviously the inflation rate does not deviate from baseline, whereas the nominal income target yields the largest deviation in inflation. The exchange rate changes as a result of the shock are driven by the interest rate responses. The nominal income target leads to the largest rise in interest rates as the central bank acts to reduce both the rise in real output as well as the rise in domestic prices. The higher interest rate causes a larger initial exchange rate appreciation. Note that the interest rate results in the long run are similar because the longer run inflation results are the same across regimes, and the higher nominal interest rate reflects the permanently higher real interest rate in India. The higher real interest rate reflects the fact that households and firms do not fully internalize the implications of higher exogenous consumption, due to the discount rate of future income being higher than the risk free government bond rate. Thus real interest rates must rise to crowd out other expenditure in order for the permanently higher exogenous spending to be maintained.

Figure 2.3: $US/Rupee Exchange Rate Under a Permanent Domestic Demand Shock

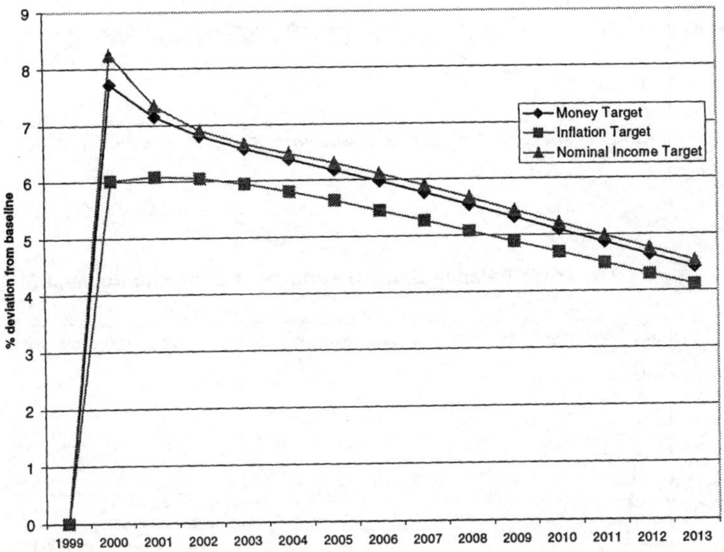

The effect of the monetary regime on the trade balance outcome is minor. This is consistent with the standard Mundell–Fleming results that the change in the trade balance due to any change in monetary policy under a flexible exchange rate and international capital mobility are insignificant. It is worth noting that Figure 2.5 shows that the rise in domestic demand is initially financed by borrowing from abroad reflected in a current account deficit. This capital inflow turn is achieved via an appreciation of the real exchange rate which increases imports and dampens exports and thus via a deterioration in the trade balance. Gradually over time the trade balance must move towards surplus in order to service the higher foreign debt.

Figure 2.4: Interest Rate Under a Permanent Domestic Demand Shock

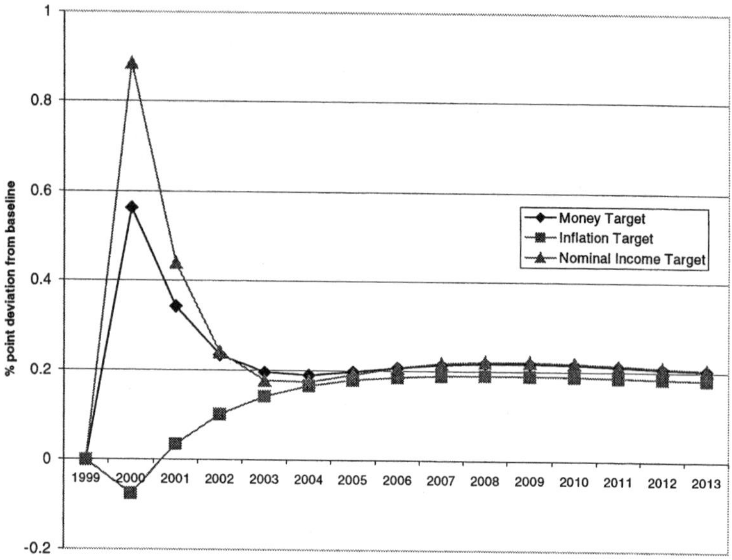

Figure 2.5: Trade Balance Under a Permanent Domestic Demand Shock

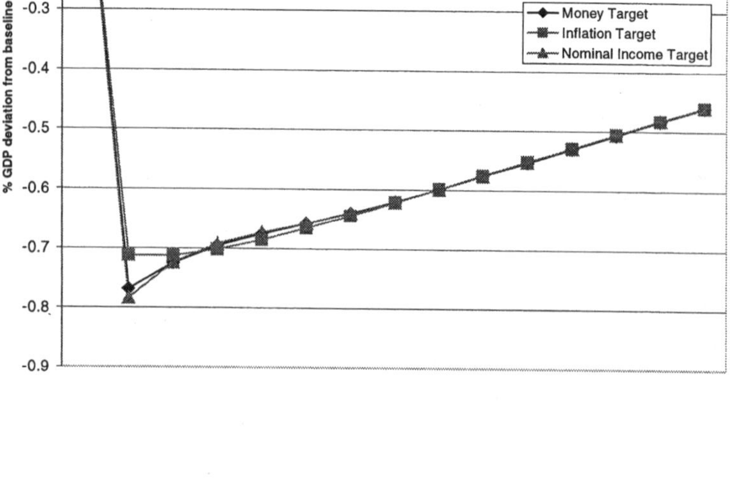

Figure 2.6: Stock Market Value Under a Permanent Domestic Demand Shock

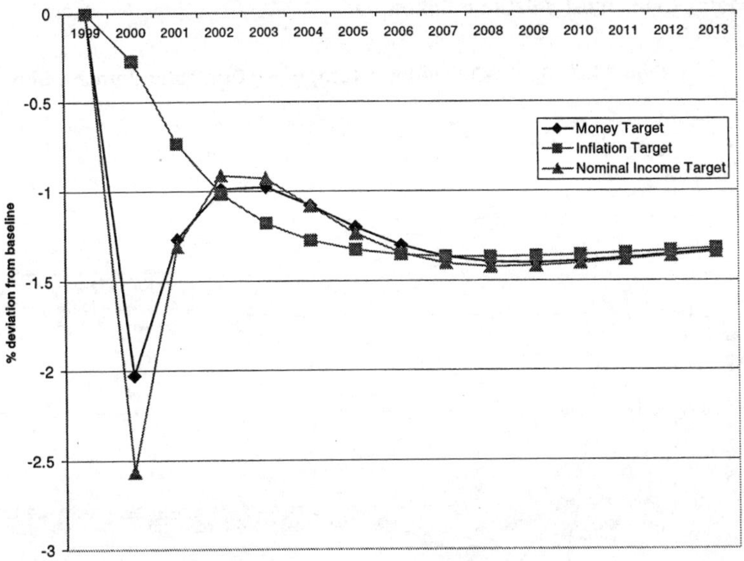

5.2 Temporary Demand Shock

Results for a temporary rise in domestic demand are shown in Figures 2.7 through 2.12. Because the shock is temporary, these figures are the impulse responses most often explored in the econometric literature on the monetary transmission mechanism (see McKibbin, et al. 1998).

It is clear that many of the insights are similar to those for the permanent demand shock although there are some important differences. It is useful to translate these impulse responses directly into volatility measures. As in Bryant, et al. (1993), the money target regime leads to the largest output volatility and the nominal income regime to lowest output volatility. Note that the ranking of regimes in terms of GDP volatility between inflation and money targets switches under the temporary versus the permanent shocks. The key difference is in the extent of appreciation of the exchange rate under the two shocks. For a temporary shock, the exchange rate appreciation is much less and therefore imported price effects are much smaller than under the permanent shock. Thus under the inflation target regime there is no longer an expansion of monetary policy induced by falling import prices because overall prices rise under the temporary demand shock (the fall in import prices is small because the exchange rate appreciation is small under a temporary shock). Thus the positive output effects from the inflation regime are smaller than for the money target regime. In terms of inflation, clearly the inflation target dominates with the nominal income target leading to the most volatile inflation.

Figure 2.7: Real GDP Under a Temporary Domestic Demand Shock

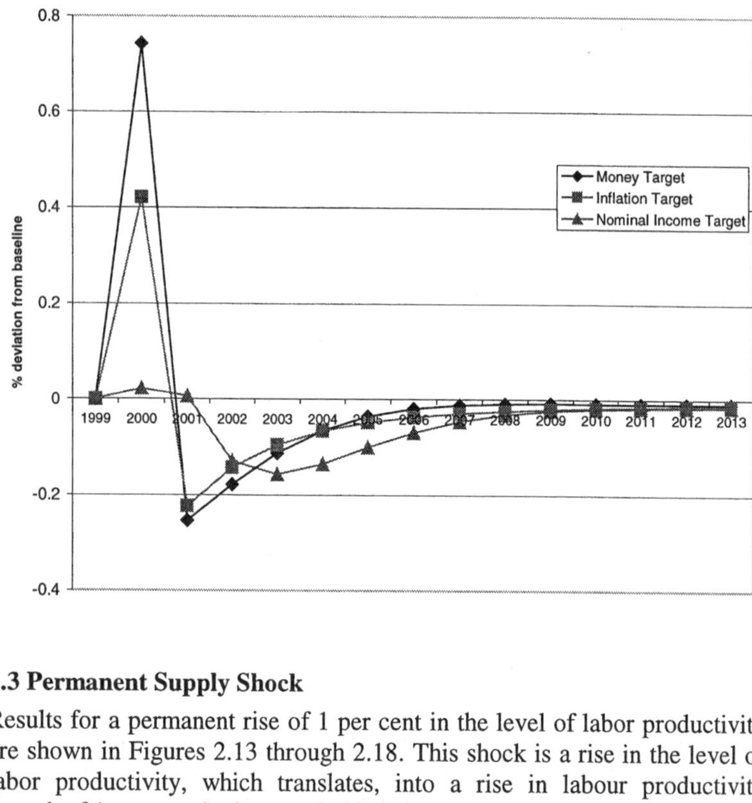

5.3 Permanent Supply Shock

Results for a permanent rise of 1 per cent in the level of labor productivity are shown in Figures 2.13 through 2.18. This shock is a rise in the level of labor productivity, which translates, into a rise in labour productivity growth of 1 per cent in the year 2000 and zero thereafter.

It is clear from Figure 2.13 that GDP fluctuates more under the inflation target than under the alternative regimes. This is a familiar result found in many other theoretical papers and modeling studies of industrial economies. The rise in productivity lowers prices (Figure 2.14), which induces a monetary relaxation (Figure 2.16). This monetary relaxation further increases the rise in output and thus leads to more output volatility than other regimes. Inflation targets work well for demand shocks but are counterproductive (in terms of output) for supply shocks. This is an important lesson for an economy such as India in which structural change and productivity shocks are likely to be important during a period of economic reform.

Figure 2.8: Inflation Under a Temporary Domestic Demand Shock

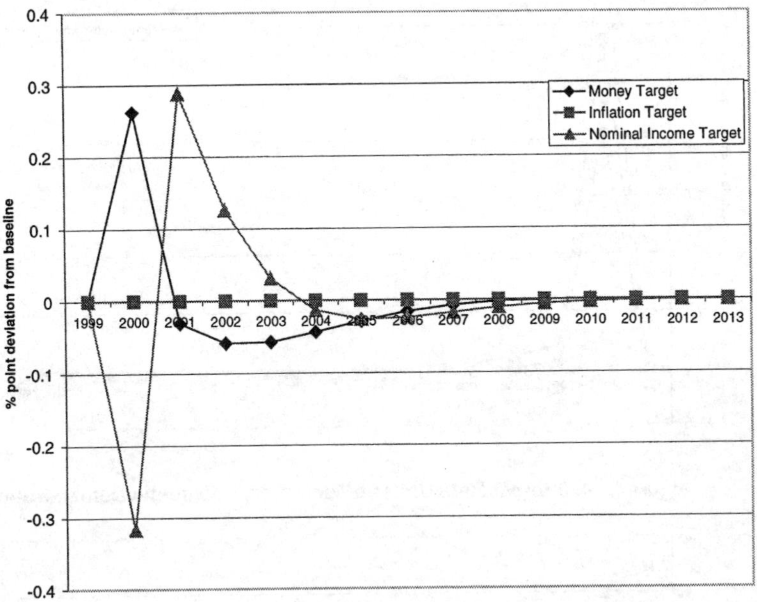

Note from Figure 2.18 that in contrast to the results for the demand shock in Fgure 2.6, a rise in GDP due to enhanced productivity has a much more positive effect on the stock market than a rise in GDP due to higher demand. The stock price is dominated by the higher expected future labour productivity.

5.4 Temporary Supply Shock

Results for a temporary supply shock are shown in Fgures 2.19 through 2.24. Although the profiles are very different to the permanent shock to supply, the rankings of regimes are very similar. Again the results for the temporary shock should be thought of in terms of volatility measures. The inflation-targeting regime causes greater volatility in real variables than the alternative regimes for the same reasons as it did for the permanent supply shock. As prices fall a monetary loosening further exacerbates the rise in real output.

Figure 2.9: $US/Rupee Exchange Rate Under a Temporary Domestic Demand Sh

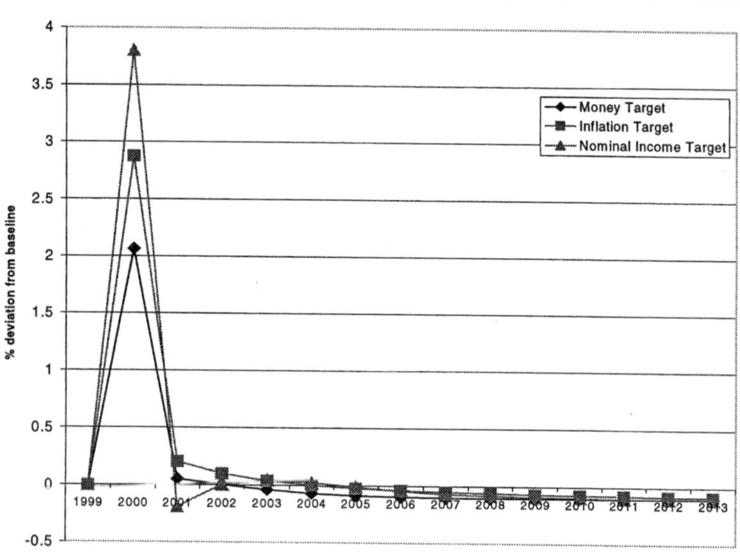

Figure 2.10: Interest Rate Under a Temporary Domestic Demand Shock

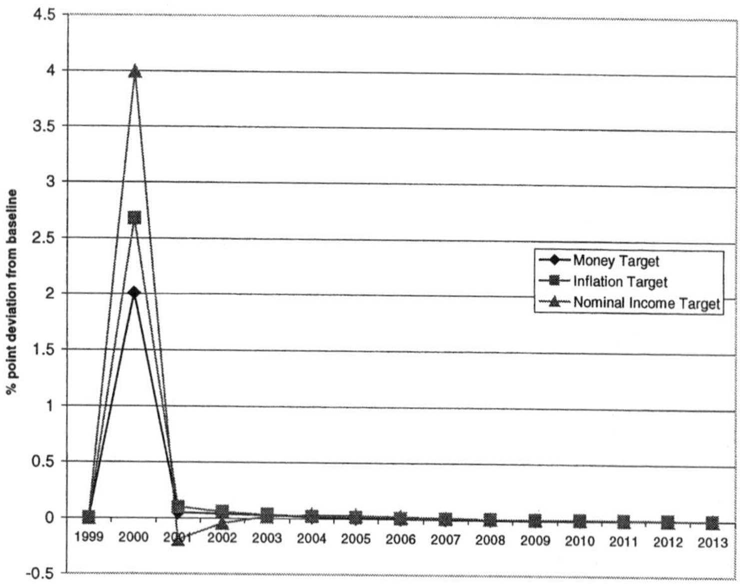

Figure 2.11: Trade Balance Under a Temporary Domestic Demand Shock

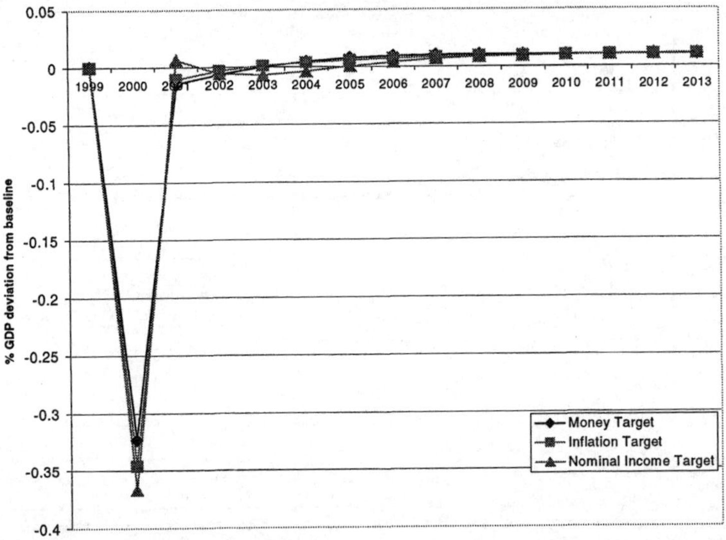

Figure 2.12: Stock Market Value Under a Temporary Domestic Demand Shock

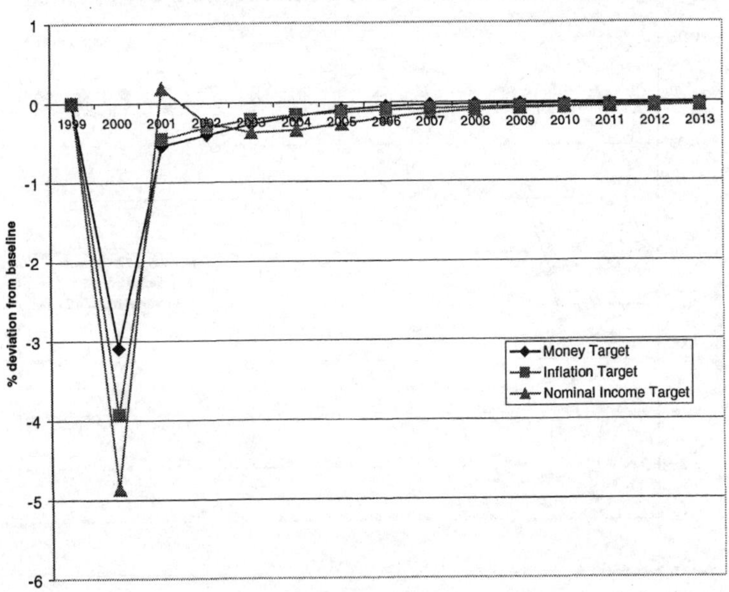

Figure 2.13: Real GDP Under a Permanent Domestic Supply Shock

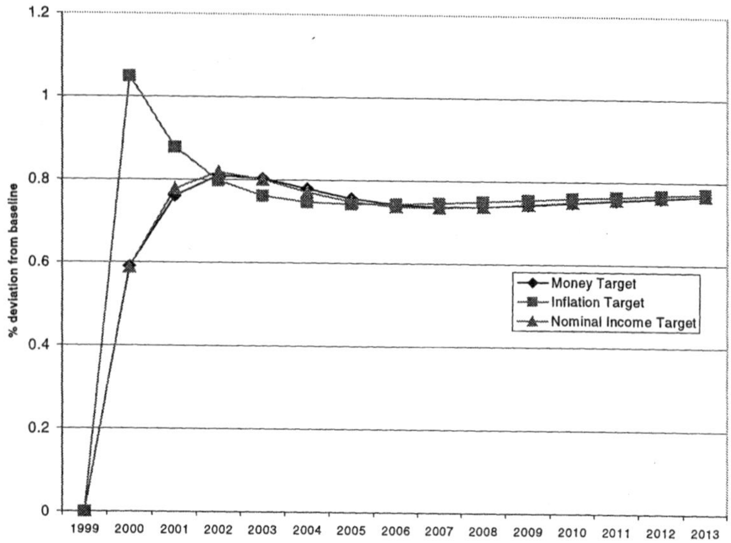

Figure 2.14: Inflation Under a Permanent Domestic Supply Shock

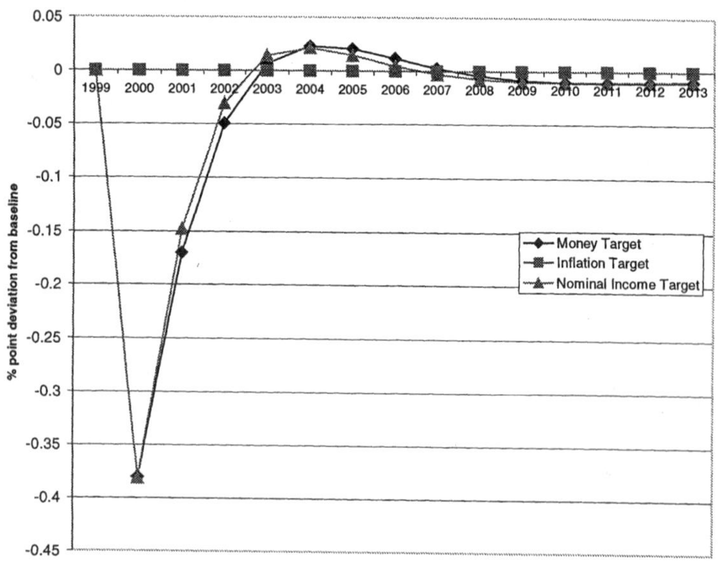

Figure 2.15: $US/Rupee Exchange Rate Under a Permanent Domestic Supply Shock

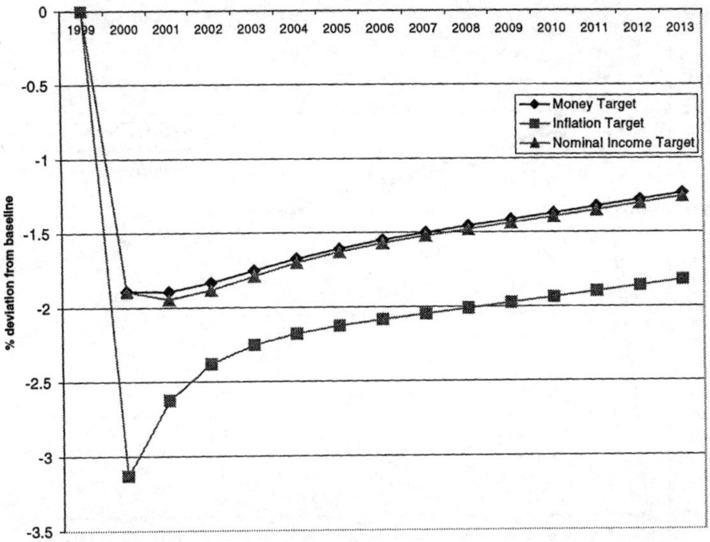

Figure 2.16: Interest Rate Under a Permanent Domestic Supply Shock

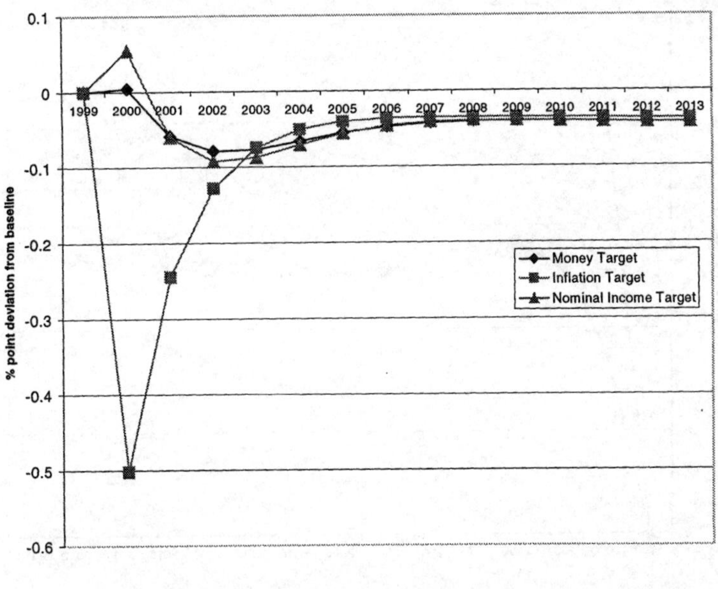

Figure 2.17: Trade Balance Under a Permanent Domestic Supply Shock

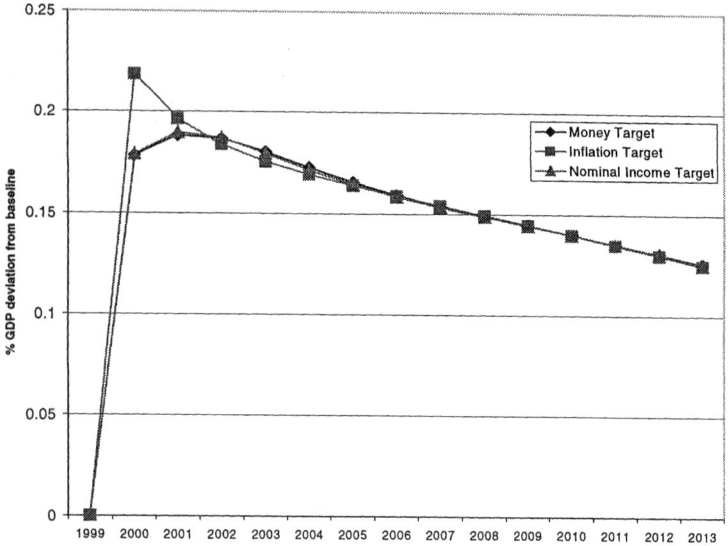

Figure 2.18: Stock Market Value Under a Permanent Domestic Supply Shock

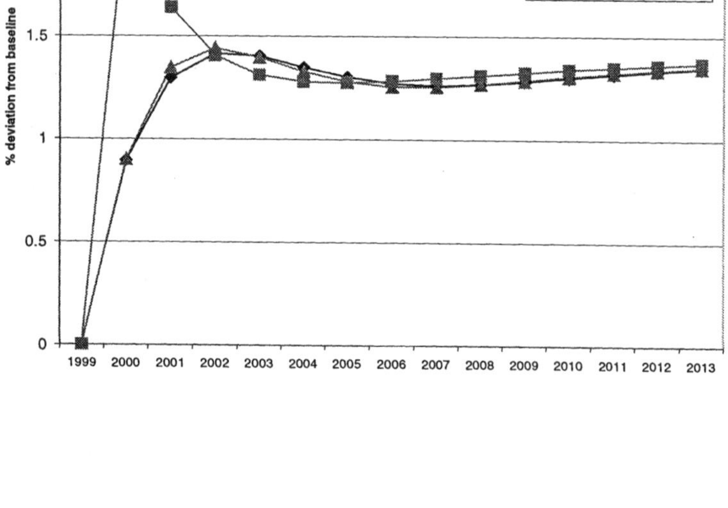

Figure 2.19: Real GDP Under a Temporary Domestic Supply Shock

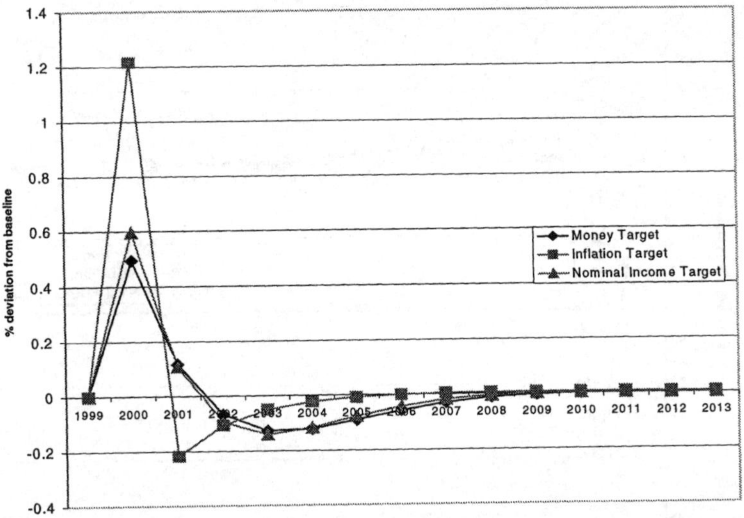

Figure 2.20: Inflation Under a Temporary Domestic Supply Shock

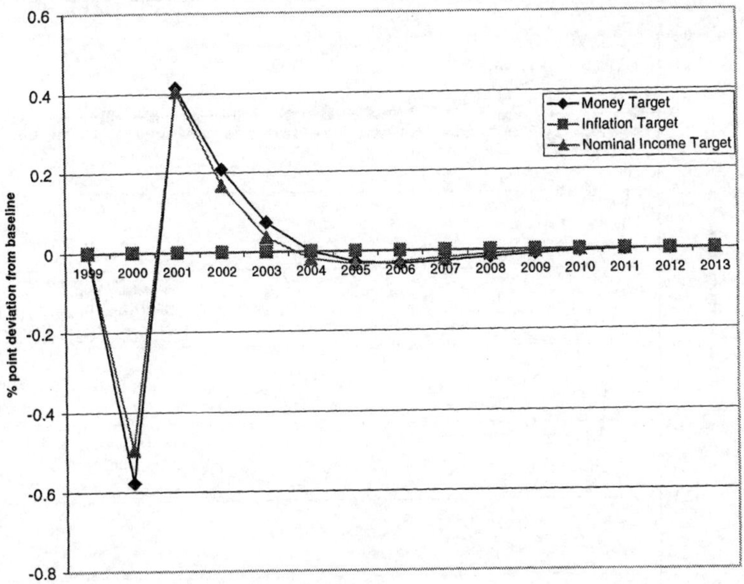

Figure 2.21: $US/Rupee Exchange Rate Under a Temporary Domestic Supply Sh

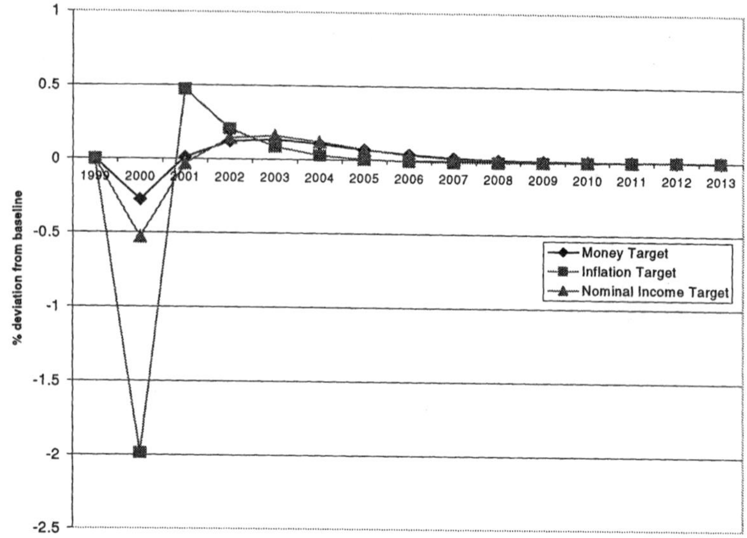

Figure 2.22: Interest Rate Under a Temporary Domestic Supply Shock

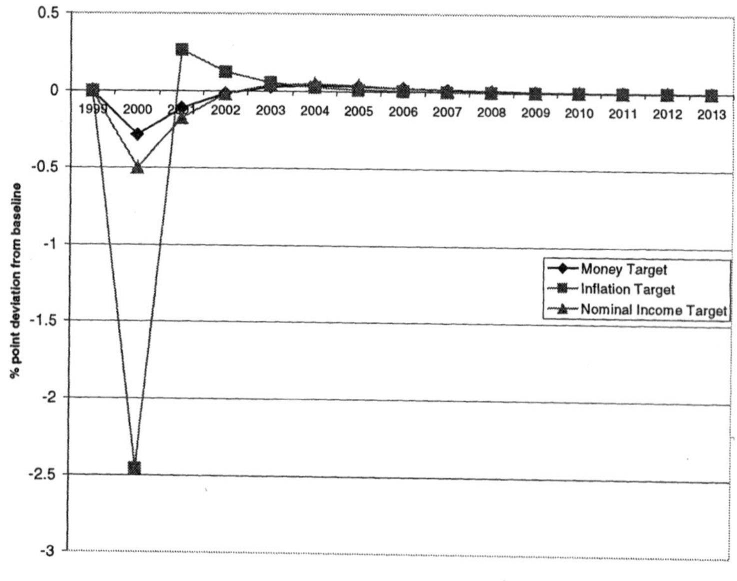

Figure 2.23: Trade Balance Under a Temporary Domestic Supply Shock

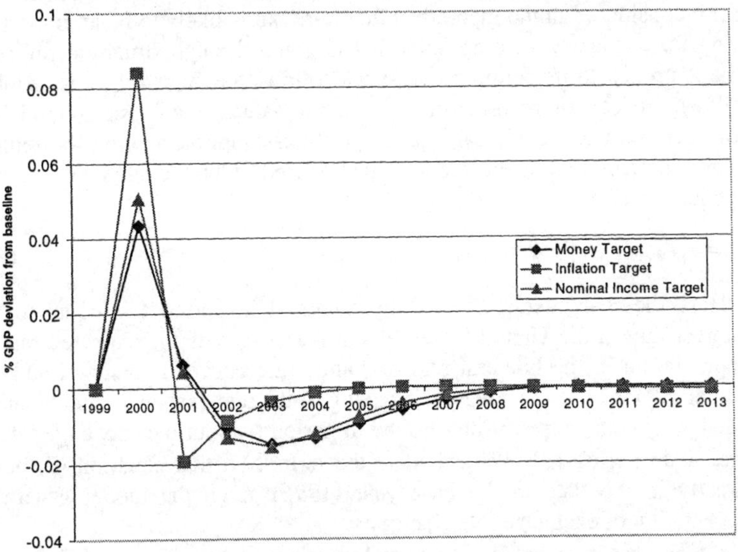

Figure 2.24: Stock Market Value Under a Temporary Domestic Supply Shock

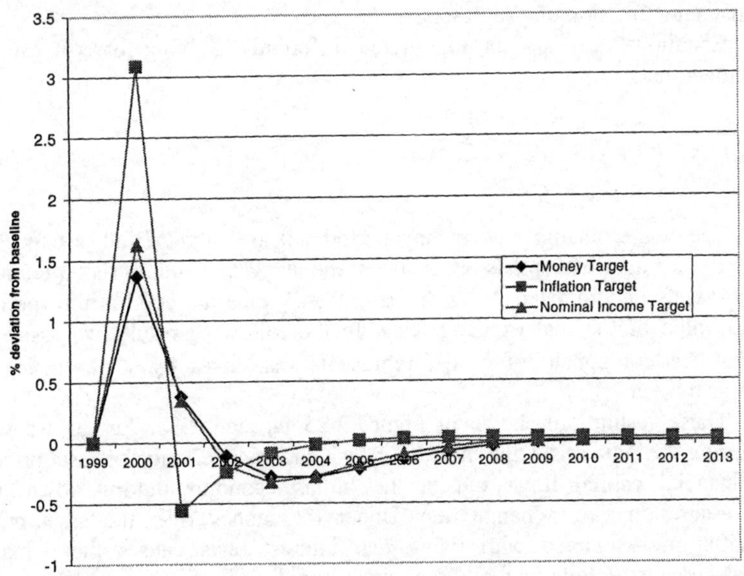

5.5 Permanent Increase in Risk of Investing in Indian Assets

In this section we model a rise in the risk of investing in Indian assets. This is not considered in the theoretical literature but is likely to be an important issue for a country such as India that is going through structural reforms. The approach to modeling a risk shock follows the approach in McKibbin (1998). To see more precisely how a re-evaluation of risk is modeled, consider the uncovered real interest parity assumption relating the returns to government debt in each country that is used in the model. This is shown in equation (7):

$$r_t^i = r_t^U + {}_t e_{t+1} - e_t + \xi_t \qquad (7)$$

Here the real interest rate (r) in country i in period t is equal to the interest rate in the United States (r^U) in period t, plus the expected rate of depreciation in the bilateral real exchange rate between country i and the United States (${}_t e_{t+1} - e_t$) where e_t is the log of the real exchange rate in period t and ${}_t e_{t+1}$ is the expectation, formed in period t, about the exchange rate to prevail in period t+1. We calculate the term ξ so that equation (7) holds exactly in the data in the base year (1996) given the model generated expectation of exchange rate changes.

ξ measures a range of factors including sovereign risk, impediments to financial flows, the degree of departure from rational expectations in actual data as well as a range of other factors. Suppose for expositional reasons that some fraction of ξ represents risk.

Equation 7 can also be interpreted differently. Solving for e_t it can be shown that:

$$e_t = \int_t^T (r_s^U - r_s + \xi_s)\, ds + {}_t e_T \qquad (8)$$

The real exchange rate in any period t is the sum of future expected interest rate differentials as well as the expected future risk premium on assets denominated in the home currency plus the equilibrium (period T) value of the real exchange rate. In the following results we assumed that the component of ξ that represents risk, rises by 1 per cent per year forever.

These results are shown in Figure 2.25 through 2.30. Just as we saw during the Asia crisis, the increase in risk causes a deflation of asset prices. Financial capital flows out of the Indian economy putting downward pressure on the exchange rate. Under the money rule, the asset price deflation associated with rising real interest rates causes the demand for money to fall, which for a given supply of money causes nominal interest rates to fall slightly (Figure 2.28). Falling prices for domestically produced goods and slowing economic activity also induces a relaxation of monetary policy in an effort to stabilize nominal income. Under the inflation target regime the exact opposite occurs. Because the exchange rate depreciates sharply, import prices rise quickly and the monetary authorities are forced to raise interest rates to prevent the exchange rate depreciation from feeding into domestic inflation. The effect of this is a sharp decline in real GDP relative to the other regimes. Indeed this is exactly the same policy mistake made by the New Zealand Reserve Bank during the Asia crisis that ultimately caused a recession during 1998. Just as we demonstrated above for a supply shock, an inflation target is not a good policy in the face of a shock to country risk.

It is important to note that this model and these results ignore the issue of credibility in policy that may be important in an actual situation of crisis. Nonetheless, there are some important lessons from these model results for Indian monetary policy during a structural reform period in which some shaking of confidence is likely to periodically accompany reform.

Note from the results, that the long run effect of a higher risk premium (which could also be interpreted as capital controls or taxes on capital inflow) is a permanently lower real output in the economy. This is not surprising because the higher risk premium artificially raises the marginal product of capital above the world interest rate so output must be lower. The monetary regime does make a real difference to the economy for up to 8 years from the start of the shock but then tends to peter out.

In terms of inflation (Figure 2.26), both the money target and nominal income target lead to a large positive inflation shock, primarily reflecting the larger exchange rate depreciation (Figure 2.27). The general deflation of asset prices and capital outflow is reflected in the improvement in the trade balance shown in Figure 2.29. This capital outflow is made consistent with the trade balance through the large depreciation in the real and nominal exchange rate and therefore strong rise in exports and fall in imports.

Finally the results for the stock market are shown in Figure 2.30. The general decline in asset prices in the Indian economy includes a collapse in the value of capital. Note that the stock market collapse is largest under the inflation target because of both a larger short-term fall in real GDP as well as a larger rise in real interest rates.

The ultimate choice of monetary regime for a risk shock depends on the relative weight policy makers place on the ultimate targets of inflation and real output. The problems with inflation targeting under a risk shock are similar to those faced under a supply shock.

Figure 2.25: Real GDP Under a Permanent Increase in Risk Premium on Indian As

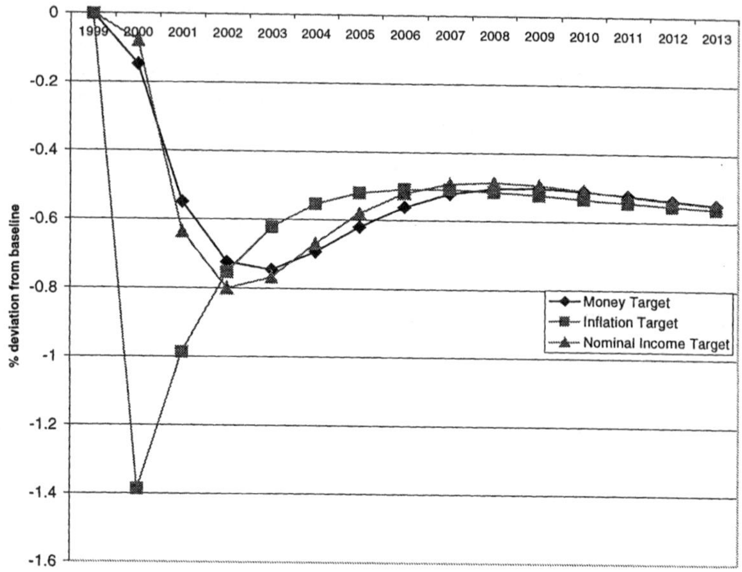

Figure 2.26: Inflation Under a Permanent Increase in Risk Premium on Indian A

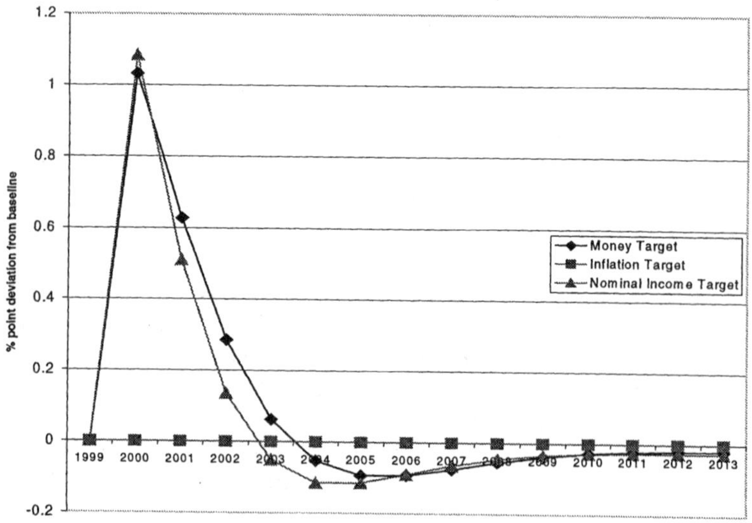

Figure 2.27: $US/Rupee Exchange Rate Under a Permanent Increase in Risk Premium on Indian Assets

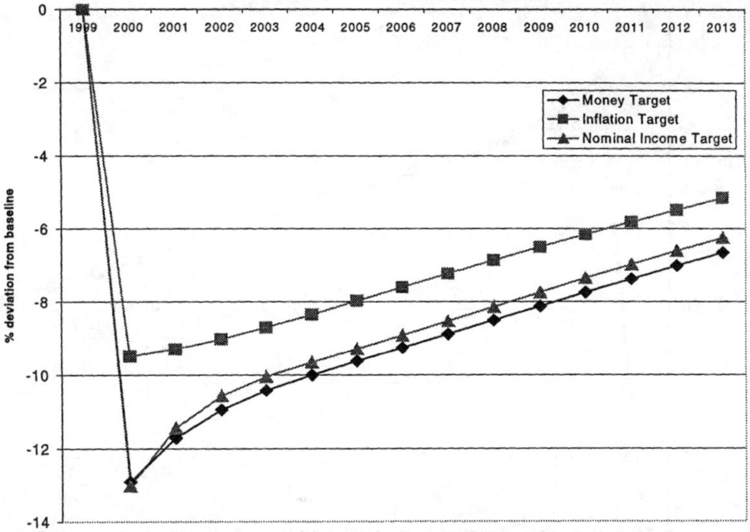

Figure 2.28: Interest Rate Under a Permanent Increase in Risk Premium on Indian Assets

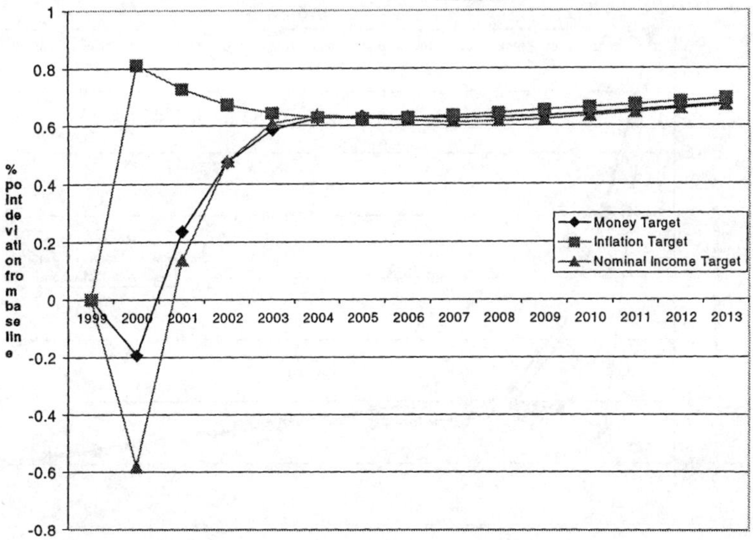

Figure 2.29: Trade Balance Under a Permanent Increase in Risk Premium on I Assets

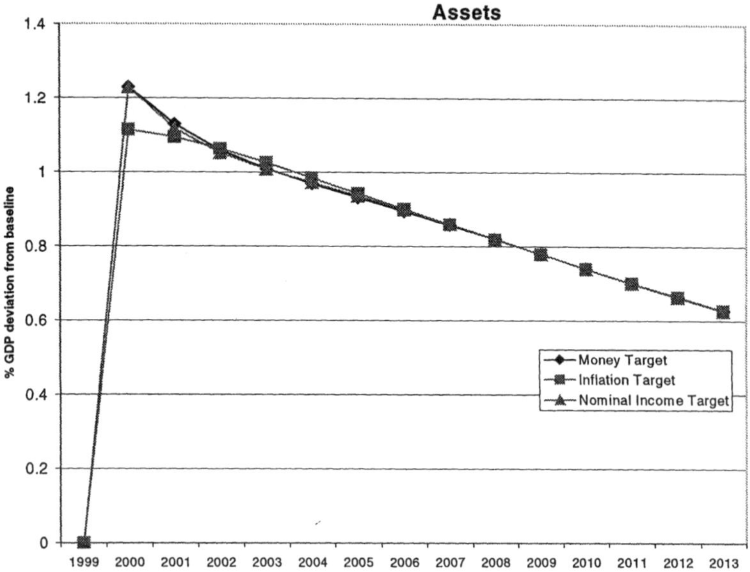

Figure 2.30: Stock Market Value Under a Permanent Increase in Risk Premiu Indian Assets

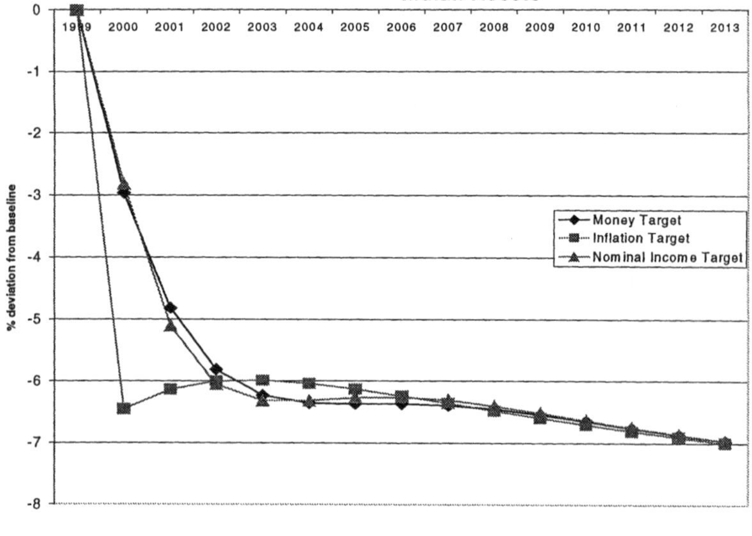

6. Conclusion

This chapter summarizes the current policy debate on selecting a monetary regime for India as well as draws some insights on the key issues from the burgeoning theoretical literature on policy regime choice. Many of the issues are ultimately empirical. To contribute to this aspect of the debate in India we have presented results from a new model of the Indian economy developed as part of the latest version of the McKibbin–Sachs Global (MSG2) simulation model. In exploring the impact of shocks to aggregate demand, supply and risk perceptions under the three policy regimes of a money target, inflation target and nominal income target we find a number of results. First in only considering the adjustment to shocks we find the inflation target regime works quite poorly in terms of output volatility for permanent demand shocks, both permanent and temporary supply shocks and shock to risk perceptions. This depends importantly on the concept of inflation used in the inflation rule and the degree to which exchange rate changes feed into prices. However, the results are consistent with the theoretical literature that in open economies, an inflation target can lead to an inappropriate response to supply side shocks. The risk shock explored in this paper has to our knowledge, not been explored in the theoretical literature on monetary regime choice but represents a real issue for many developing and developed economies.

Overall the money and nominal income rules seem to be very similar under the shocks considered here apart from money demand shocks. If the money demand function is unstable then the nominal income rule clearly dominates the money rule because it does not depend on stability of money demand. Clearly there is room for a great deal more empirical research over a wider range of possible scenarios and a wider set of rules for monetary policy in India.

It should also be stressed that we have not dealt with the issue of credibility in the analysis presented in the empirical part of this paper. It is clearly possible that the inflation target regime may have beneficial effects on credibility especially relative to the money rule. It is not clear why an inflation target would be more or less credible than a nominal income target. However, the actual implementation of the nominal income regime does rely on observing nominal income or at least having a reasonably good forecast of nominal income if used in the way specified in this paper. However if credibility is the argument for an inflation target relative to a nominal income target then the gains from this need to be large in order to offset the fundamental losses in following an inflation target for anything but temporary demand shocks.

References

Argy, V., McKibbin, W.J. and Siegloff, E., 'Exchange Rate Regimes for a Small Economy in a Multi-Country World', *Princeton Studies in International Finance* 67 (December 1989).

Barro, R.J. and Gordon, D.B., 'A Positive Theory of Monetary Policy in a Natural Rate Model', *The Journal of Political Economy* 91(4) (1983), 589–610.

Bean, C.R., 'Targeting Nominal Income: An Appraisal', *The Economic Journal,* 93(372) (1983), 806–819.

Bryant, R.C., Hooper, P. and Mann, C.L., *Evaluating policy regimes: new research in empirical macroeconomics* (Washington, D.C.: Brookings Institution, 1993).

Cecchetti, S.G., 'Policy Rules and Targets: Framing the Central Banker's Problem', *Federal Reserve Bank of New York Policy Review*, June 1998, 1–14.

Cukierman, A, *Central bank strategy, credibility, and independence : theory and evidence* (Cambridge, Mass.: MIT Press, 1992).

de Brouwer, G. and O'Regan, J., 'Evaluating Simple Monetary-Policy Rules for Australia', in P. Lowe (ed.) *Monetary Policy and Inflation Targeting*, Proceedings of a Conference (Reserve Bank of Australia, Sydney, 1997).

Friedman, B.M., 'Targets, Instruments, and Indicators of Monetary Policy', *Journal of Monetary Economics* 1 (1975), 443–73.

Friedman, B.M., 'The inefficiency of short-run monetary targets for Monetary Policy', *Brookings Papers on Economic Activity* 2 (1977), 293–335.

Friedman, B.M., 'Targets and instruments of Monetary policy', in B.M. Friedman and F. Hahn (eds) *Handbook of Monetary Economics*, Vol. II, 1990 Edition, Amsterdam: Elsevier Science Publishers B.V. (1990).

Hayashi, F. 'Tobins Marginal q and Average q: A Neoclassical Interpretation', *Econometrica* 50 (1982), 213–24.

Henderson, D.W. and McKibbin, W.J., 'An Assessment of Some Basic Monetary-Policy Regime Pairs: Analytical and Simulation Results from Simple Multiregion Macroeconomic Models', in R.C. Bryant, P. Hooper and C.L. Mann (eds) *Evaluating Policy Regimes: New Research in Empirical Macroeconomics* (Washington, D.C.: The Brookings Institution, 1993).

Henderson, D.W. and McKibbin, W.J., 'A Comparison of some basic Monetary Policy Regimes for Open Economies: Implications of different degree of Instrument Adjustment and Wage Persistence', *Carnegie–Rochester Conference Series on Public Policy* 39 (1993a), 221–317.

IMF, 'India: Recent Economic Developments' *IMF Staff Country Report No./98/120* (Washington D.C., 1998).

Joshi, V. and Little, I.M.D., *India : macroeconomics and political economy, 1964–1991* (Delhi: Oxford University Press, 1994).

Kannan, R., 'Inflation Targeting Issues and Relevance for India', *Economic and Political Weekly* XXXIV(3 and 4) (1999), 115–22.

Kareken, J.H., Muench, T. and Wallace, N., 'Optimal Open Market Strategy: The use of information variables', *American Economic Review* 63(1) (1973), 156–72.

Kydland, F.E. and Prescott, E.C., 'Rules rather than discretion: the inconsistency of optimal plans', *Journal of Political Economy* (85) (1977), 473–92.

Lucas, R., 'Econometric Policy Evaluation: A Critique', in B. Karl and A. Meltzer (eds), *The Phillips Curve and Labor Markets* (Amsterdam: North Holland, 1976).

Lucas, R.E. 'Adjustment Costs and the Theory of Supply', *Journal of Political Economy* 75(4) (1967), 321–34.

Masson, P.R., Savastano, M.A. and Sharma, S., 'The Scope for Inflation Targeting in Developing Countries', *IMF Working Paper WP/97/130*, Washington, D.C. (1997).

McCallum, B.T., 'Price Level Determinacy with an Interest rate Policy Rule and Rational Expectation', *Journal of Monetary Economics* 8 (1981), 319–29.

McCallum, B.T., 'Recent Developments in Monetary Policy Analysis: The Role of Theory and Evidence', *NBER Working Paper 7088*, Cambridge, MA (1999).

McKibbin, W., 'Perspective on the Australian Policy Framework', in P. Lowe (ed.) *Monetary Policy and Inflation Targeting*, Proceedings of a Conference (Sydney: Reserve Bank of Australia, 1997).

McKibbin, W., 'Risk Re-Evaluation, Capital Flows and the Crisis in Asia', in R. Garnaut and R. McLeod (eds) *East Asia in Crisis: From Being a Miracle to Needing One?*: Routledge, 1998a).

McKibbin, W.J., 'Stochastic Simulations of Alternative Monetary Regimes Using the McKibbin–Sachs Global (MSG2) Model', in R.C. Bryant, P. Hooper and C.L. Mann (eds) *Evaluating Policy Regimes: New Research in Empirical Macroeconomics* (Washington, D.C.: The Brookings Institution, 1993).

McKibbin, W.J., *The MSG Multi-Country Model version 44M: User Manual*: McKibbin Software Group Inc Arlington VA, USA (1998b).

McKibbin, W.J., Pagan, A.R. and Robertson, J.C., 'Some experiments in constructing a hybrid model for macroeconomic analysis', *Carnegie–Rochester Conference on Public Policy,* 49 (1998), 113–42.

McKibbin, W.J. and Sachs, J., *Global Linkages: Macroeconomic Interdependence and Cooperation in the World Economy* (Washington, D.C.: Brookings Institute, 1991).

McKibbin, W.J. and Sachs, J.D., 'Comparing the Global Performance of Alternative Exchange Rate Regimes', *Journal of International Money and Finance* 7 (1988), 387–410.

McKibbin, W.J. and K. Singh, 'Issues in the Choice of a Monetary Regime for India', in K.P. Kalirajan and U. Sankar (eds), *Economic Reform and the Liberalisation of the Indian Economy: Essays in Honour of Richard T Shand*, Cheltenhem: Edward Elgar, 2002).

Mishkin, F.S., 'International Experiences with Different Monetary Policy Regimes' *NBER Working Paper No. 6965*, Cambridge, MA, 1999).

Mohanty, D. and Mitra, A.K., 'Experience with Monetary Targeting in India', *Economic and Political Weekly* XXXIV (3 and 4) (1999), 123–32.

Poole, W., 'Optimal Choice of Monetary Policy Instruments in a Simple Stochastic Macro Model', *The Quarterly Journal of Economics,* 84(2) (1970), 197–216.

Rangarajan, C., *Indian Economy: Essays on Money and Finance* (New Delhi: UBSPD, 1998).

RBI, 'Report of the Committee to Review the Working of the Monetary System (Chairman, S. Chakravarty)' (Bombay: Reserve Bank of India, 1985).

RBI, 'The Annual Report on the Working of the Reserve Bank of India for the year July 1, 1997 to June 30, 1998' (Mumbai: Reserve Bank of India, 1998).

RBI, 'Annual Report on the Working of the Bank for the Year July 1, 1998 to June 30, 1999' (Mumbai: Reserve Bank of India 1999).

RBI, 'Monetary and Credit Policy for the Year 1999–2000', *Reserve Bank of India Bulletin* LIII(5) (1995b), 703–24.

Reddy, Y.V., 'Financial Sector Reform: Review and Prospects', *Reserve Bank of India Bulletin* LIII(1) (1999b), 33–94.

Reddy, Y.V., 'Monetary Policy in India: Objectives, Instruments, Operating Procedure and Dilemmas', *Reserve Bank of India Bulletin* LIII(7) (1999d), taken from web site http://www.rbi.org.in/index.dll/2?sectionhomepage?

Roper, D.E. and Turnovsky, S.J., 'Optimal Exchange Market Intervention in a Simple Stochastic Macro Model', *Canadian Journal of Economics* XIII (2) (1980), 296–309.

Sargent, T.J. and Wallace, N., '"Rational" Expectations, the optimal monetary instrument, and the optimal money rule', *Journal of Political Economy,* 83 (1975), 241–54.

Sen, K. and Vaidya, R.R., *The Process of Financial Liberalization in India* (Delhi: Oxford University Press, 1997).

Svensson, L.E.O., 'Inflation Forecast Targeting: Implementation and Monitoring Inflation Targets' *NBER Working Paper 5797*, Cambridge, MA (1996a).

Svensson, L.E.O., 'Open-Economy Inflation Targeting' *NBER Working Paper 6545*, Cambridge, MA (1988).

Svensson, L.E.O. 'Inflation Targeting as a Monetary Policy Rule' *NBER Working Paper 6790*, Cambridge, MA (1998a).

Treadway, A., 'On Rational Entrepreneurial Behavior and the Demand for Investment', *Review of Economic Studies,* 36(106), 1969, 227–239.

Vasudevan, A., 'Some Practical Issues in Monetary Policy Making', *Reserve Bank of India Bulletin* LIII (1) (January 1999), 121–8.

Walsh, C.E., *Monetary Theory and Policy* (Cambridge, Mass.: MIT Press, 1998).

West, K.D., 'Targeting Nominal Income: A Note', *The Economic Journal*, 96(384) (1986), 1077–83.

3
On the Endogeneity of the Money Multiplier in India

Raghbendra Jha and Deba Prasad Rath

1. Introduction

The conventional money multiplier model relates changes in broader money aggregates (primarily) to reserve money changes. It is argued that reserve money is exogenous since it is the monetary liability of the central bank. If the money multiplier is stable and predictable, the monetary authority could target the monetary/liquidity situation in the economy so long as reserve money is kept at a level consistent with desired broad money expansion. The stability of the money multiplier is, however, a testable empirical proposition.

Post-Keynesians, however, view money supply as an endogenous process. The financial system as a whole generates monetary liabilities, apart from the central bank's monetary stance reflected through reserve money creation. Financial liberalization is thought to generate new channels for monetary endogeneity as the financial system matures (Howells and Hussein 1998; Rath 2001).

In recent times, in countries receiving international capital (such as India) the money multiplier appears to have steadily risen. In India M_3 grew at the decadal average of 17.2 per cent in the 1990s as well as the 1980s whereas M_0 grew at only 14.5 per cent in the 1990s compared to 16.8 per cent in the 1980s. The money multiplier, has thus risen to 3.27 in the 1990s from 3.10 in the 1980s (RBI (1999)). In the 1990s India witnessed significant capital inflows as a result of the reforms. The RBI combined sterilization and foreign exchange market intervention in an attempt to contain the impact of such flows and to tackle periodic pressure on the Indian rupee. In response the rate of growth[1] in reserve money fell, indicating an upward drift in the money multiplier (Table 3.1).

---

1 In addition there were cash reserve ratio (CRR) reductions.

Table 3.1: Statistical Profile of Monetary Indicators

Item	*1980s*	*1990s*
Panel A: Monetary Aggregates		
1. Reserve Money (M_0)	16.8	14.5
2. Narrow Money (M_1)	15.1	15.6
3. Broad Money (M_3)	17.2	17.2
Panel B: Narrow Money Multiplier		
1. Maximum	1.2957	1.2702
2. Minimum	1.0205	1.0426
3. Mean	1.1614	1.1386
4. Standard Deviation	0.067325	0.053176
5. Coefficient of Variation	0.057968	0.46701

Stable money multipliers may obtain in a financial system with administratively controlled interest rates and few substitutes for money (Baghestani and Mott 1997). Papademos and Modigliani (1990) indicate interest rate deregulation can lead to money multiplier instability because: (i) a reduction in the private sector loan demand leads to increased reserves and an increase in the reserve-deposit ratio; (ii) as the opportunity cost of holding excess reserves rises with higher interest rates, banks may economise on excess reserves if the private sector loan demand is relatively interest-inelastic; and (iii) variations in households' portfolio between currency and deposits as well as various monetary assets *vis-à-vis* other non-monetary assets may lead to money multiplier instability. As deposit rates rise, people may move out of currency into deposit leading to a reduction in the currency-deposit ratio and increase in the money multiplier. See Tseng and Corker (1991) for some Asian evidence.

Free entry for banks and financial institutions into financial markets creates competitive pressure inducing financial institutions to become more innovative in their product design. Examples include flexibility in withdrawing from saving deposits, automatic transfer facilities combining features of current and savings accounts and automatic teller machines. Deposits become more liquid and increasingly perform the transaction functions of money. As the deregulated banking sector competes with other financial institutions for deposits, the distinction between banks and non-bank financial institutions becomes blurred. Thus financial innovation may lead to an increase in the money multiplier and a decline in the velocity of circulation.

Interest rate changes lead to changes in the substitution pattern among monetary assets. Davis and Gauger (1996); and Jha and Longjam (1999) argue that this pattern depends on substitution between monetary assets. Moreover as Moore, Porter and Small (1998) find, if interest rates adjust at varying speeds the associated spreads will be affected. If deposit rates adjust fast the opportunity costs, asset holdings and multipliers may remain the same. Slow adjustment affects opportunity costs and induces portfolio adjustments that affect the multipliers. Deposit rates respond more quickly to increases in market rates than to decreases.

Real income growth will increase demand for monetary assets. Asset holding ratios like the currency ratio depends on income and payments system (declines with rising income while rises with evolving payments system). The yield spread could also have a role to play since the steepness of yield curve is a good indicator of the source of asset shifts across or outside the monetary aggregates. Identification of the determinants of multipliers would facilitate identification of the sources of their endogeneity and variability. This chapter attempts this in the Indian case.

2. A Simplified Money-Multiplier Approach

Consider the following simple money multiplier model. There exists a system of reserves with a uniform CRR for both demand and time deposits. Thus

$$M^s = z\,(.)\,H \tag{1}$$

where M^s = Nominal money stock;
z (.) = Money multiplier.
Let
H = Nominal reserve money [Cash (C) + Reserves (R)],
D = demand deposits.
Thus

$$H = C + R \tag{2}$$

$$M = C + D \tag{3}$$

$$z = M/H = (C + D)/(C + R)$$
$$= (C/D + 1) / (C/D + R/D) \tag{4}$$

where *C/D* is currency-deposit ratio and *R/D* is reserve-deposit ratio. Thus the money multiplier is a function of two behavioural parameters: currency-deposit ratio and reserve-deposit ratio. Typically two types of reserves are recognised *i.e.*,

R = Required Reserves (RR) + Excess Reserves $(ER) = kD + ER$ (5)

where $ER/D = \varphi(r_{mkt})$ (6)

φ is a decreasing function of the market rate of interest (r_{mkt}) since banks may want to hold excess reserves beyond the required level in order to accommodate unexpected demands for cash payments to other banks. Since they earn no interest these excess reserves are costly to hold. Combining (5) and (6) we have

$$R/D = k + \varphi(r_{mkt}) \qquad (7)$$

Since $\varphi'(r) < 0$, reserve deposit ratio will be smaller, for a given value of statutorily determined k, the higher the r_{mkt}.

Substituting (7) in (4) yields:

$$M/H = (C/D + 1) / \{C/D + k + \varphi(r)\} \qquad (8)$$

i.e., $M/H = z(r, k, C/D)$ (9)

with $z_1 > 0$, $z_2 < 0$and $z_3 < 0$. Signs of z_1 and z_2 follow from (7). For z_3 we note that

$$k + \varphi(r) = R/D < 1 \qquad (10)$$

Now

$$\begin{aligned} M/H &= (C/D + 1) / (C/D + R/D) \\ &= (C/D + R/D - R/D + 1) / (C/D + R/D) \\ &= 1 + [1 - R/D] / [(C/D + R/D)] \qquad (11) \end{aligned}$$

The second term on the RHS of (11) (which is positive), decreases with any increase in *C/D* keeping *R/D* constant. Hence *m* varies inversely with *C/D*.

Borrowed reserves (*BR*) respond to central bank's discount rate (r_D) because *BR* would be positively related to the difference between the central bank's discount rate and the market rate ($r_D - r_{mkt}$). Thus we write the money multiplier as:

$$z = z(r_D, r_{mkt}, \sigma) \qquad (12)$$

where σ is the volatility in deposits.

Money supply (*M*) varies directly with the high-powered base (*H*) and inversely with the reserve deposit ratio chosen by banks and the currency-deposit ratio chosen by the public. (11) permits changes in money stock to be decomposed into changes in its 'proximate determinants': the exogenous monetary base (*H*) and two endogenous ratios (*C/D* and *R/D*). Over the very short run, monetary movements caused by changes in the multiplier dominate and precise control by the central bank is impossible. But over the long run, high-powered base is more important: changes in *H* have contributed about 90 per cent of the secular growth of the money supply in the US and UK, whereas changes in *C/D* and *R/D* have contributed about 10 per cent (Cagan 1965; Friedman and Schwartz 1963).

The wealth elasticity of currency is, typically, between zero and one. As national wealth increases the currency-deposit ratio decreases. In choosing between currency and deposits the non-bank public compares the expected return on these assets. Because currency yields no interest, an increase in interest paid on deposits reduces the demand for currency, thus decreasing the *C/D* ratio. During banking crises an increased *C/D* results from default risk being included in comparing currency with deposits. Currency enjoys an anonymity premium — it has higher value over deposits in certain types of (illegal) activities.

Banks' portfolio decisions on excess reserves and discount loans depend on expected return, which in turn influences the multiplier. Because reserves deposited with the central bank earn no interest, an increase in market interest rate increases the opportunity cost of holding excess reserves. Excess reserves tend to rise when the average level of deposit outflow or its variability rises, as banks require greater cushion against outflows. An increase in market interest rate, *ceteris paribus,* would raise banks' profit from discount borrowing.

3. Recent Advances in Money Multiplier Analysis

Johannes and Rasche (1987) use ARIMA models to forecast aggregate multipliers. Johannes and Rasche (1979; 1981) predict disaggregated money multiplier using a 'component' approach since events that influence the individual ratios might get masked in the aggregate model.

No conclusive evidence exists on the superiority of the components approach over the aggregate approach. Haffer and Hein (1998) find that the aggregate model yields quite accurate out of sample forecasts when compared with a components approach. Gauger and Black (1991) identify multiplier movements as a major source of volatility of aggregates but do not analyse underlying causal factors.

Ireland (1994) questioned the assumption that multipliers are unaffected by economic variables. Macroeconomic models incorporating financial innovations seem to provide better understanding of the monetary impacts on the economy. Freeman and Huffman (1991) and Manchester (1989) argue that nominal money supply variations are linked to multiplier changes and help predict innovations in real output.

In a SUR framework, Gauger (1998) found that *M1*, *M2*, *M3* multipliers (in the US) are impacted by income and interest rates and that the nature of multiplier responses to economic variables (particularly select opportunity costs, the yield curve and real income) changed in the 1990s. Davis and Gauger (1996) establish substitution between monetary assets and Jha and Longjam (1999) identify inter-monetary assets substitutability in India.

4. Stability of the Money Multiplier in India

We examine money multipliers in India using the Engle-Granger two-stage test for parameter instability with the pattern of instability unknown *a priori.* With stable multipliers there would be a (co-integrating) long-run relationship between money stock and reserve money and this relation should be independent of the period of analysis. We examine three time periods April 1980 to March 2000 (Period 1); April 1980 to March 1990 (Period 2) and April 1990 to March 2000 (Period 3) since deregulation in Indian financial markets came in the late 1980s. We expect the money multiplier to be stable in Period 2 but not Period 1.

Table 3.1 lists some basic statistics of the money multiplier.

All monetary variables in their log level form are I(1). Lags are chosen as per the SBC/AIC criteria (Table 3.2).

Table 3.3 reports on Engle–Granger co-integration tests using ADF test statistics. For period 1 neither M_3 nor M_1 is co-integrated with M_0. — indicating unstable multipliers. In period 2, however, broad money and narrow money are co-integrated with the reserve money, so that multipliers are stable.

5. Multiplier Movements in the Post-Reforms Period

During the reforms period (Period 3) financial liberalization led to instability of money multipliers. Portfolios of banks and non-bank households started responding to interest rates. There was a shift in monetary policy stance with greater reliance on market-based indirect measures and less on direct monetary control. The accompanying interest rate movements would impact upon money supply as variations in the interest rate may affect money multipliers. Financial deregulation initiated in the late 1980s entailed removal of interest rates ceilings which led to a reduction in statutory reserve requirements because otherwise the high interest rates that followed liberalisation would raise burden on banks since no interest is paid on reserves. Similarly RBI operations with government bonds in the open market impact on money multipliers.

We now test Gauger's hypothesis after adjusting for Indian monetary compilation procedures. We account for narrow and broad money (M_1 and

M_3) for which reliable data are available and which RBI uses for policy purposes.[2]

Table 3.2: Unit Root Tests

	Constant and No Trend		Constant and Trend	
Variable	*ADF (lag) Statistic*	*Critical Value*	*ADF (lag) Statistic*	*Critical Value*
1. M_0				
Original Level	3.2186 (12)	-2.8743	-0.3893 (12)	-3.4307
First Difference	-2.5643 (11)	-2.8743	-4.6907 (11)	-3.4307
Log Level	-1.1682 (12)	-2.8743	-0.3877 (12)	-3.4307
First Difference	-3.5129 (12)	-2.8743	-3.6693 (12)	-3.4307
2. M_1				
Original Level	2.6911 (8)	-2.8743	0.53942 (8)	-3.4307
First Difference	-1.3510 (11)	-2.8743	-3.5694 (11)	-3.4307
Log Level	-0.1138 (12)	-2.8743	-2.6753 (12)	-3.4307
First Difference	-3.6935 (11)	-2.8743	-3.6841 (11)	-3.4307
3. M_3				
Original Level	6.9707 (8)	-2.8741	5.5070 (8)	-3.4303
First Difference	0.6871 (12)	-2.8741	-1.6710 (12)	-3.4303
Log Level	-1.1682 (12)	-2.8743	-3.9630 (12)	-3.4307
First Difference	-5.0577 (11)	-2.8743	-5.0669 (11)	-3.4307
4. IIP				
Original Level	3.0634 (12)	-2.8743	0.34524 (12)	-3.4307
Log Level	-0.3652 (12)	-2.8743	-1.7350 (12)	-3.4307
First Difference	-4.7448 (12)	-2.8744	-4.7349 (12)	-3.4307
5. z_1				
Original Level	-1.0667 (4)	-2.8743	-0.6174 (4)	-3.4307
First Difference	-3.6430 (12)	-2.8743	-4.1093 (12)	-3.4307
6. z_3				
Original Level	-0.4373 (2)	-2.8743	-1.3255 (2)	-3.4299
First Difference	-3.5778 (12)	-2.8743	-3.9415 (12)	-3.4299
7. nz_3				
Original Level	-1.1089 (12)	-2.8743	-0.0347 (12)	-3.4307
First Difference	-3.2587 (12)	-2.8744	-3.5163 (12)	-3.4308
8. ryc				
Original Level	-2.4460 (1)	-2.8738	-2.3490 (1)	-3.4299
First Difference	-4.5424 (12)	-2.8744	-4.6485 (12)	-3.4299
9. rs1				
Original Level	-1.7172 (1)	-2.8738	-1.0231 (1)	-3.4299
First Difference	-3.5778 (12)	-2.8743	-3.9415 (12)	-3.4299
10. rs3				
Original Level	-3.1994 (5)	-2.8740	-3.2220 (5)	-3.4302
First Difference	-9.2578 (5)	-2.8740	-9.2398 (5)	-3.4303

Note: 1. Figures in parentheses are appropriate lag values based on AIC/SBC criteria.
2. Variables other than M_0, M_1 and M_3 have been used in the subsequent sections.

[2] There are serious limitations of postal and other savings included in the other two aggregates (M2 and M4).

Table 3.3: Stability Tests (OLS Engle-Granger Regression Results)

Particulars	*Regression Result*
Panel A: Period 1 Results	
1. Co-integration between M_3 and M_0	$LM_3 = 0.5528 + 1.0566\ LM_0$ (10.23) (218.78) Adj. $R^2 = 0.995$, DW = 0.2719, ADF (2 lags) = -1.5409 (-3.3630).
2. Co-integration between M_1 and M_0	$LM_1 = 0.32041 + 0.9837\ LM_0$ (10.23) (218.78) Adj. $R^2 = 0.9964$, DW = 0.3013, ADF (4 lags) = -0.68405 (-3.3633).
Panel B: Period 2 Results	
3. Co-integration between M_3 and M_0	$LM_3 = 1.0460 + 1.0566\ LM_0$ (13.076) (131.357) Adj. $R^2 = 0.9932$, DW = 0.9107, ADF (1 lag) = -4.1486 (-3.3889).
4. Co-integration between M_1 and M_0	$LM_1 = 1.3326 + 0.8862\ LM_0$ (22.8) (157.9) Adj. $R^2 = 0.9964$, DW = 0.3013, ADF (1 lag) = -3.8188 (-3.3889).

Note: Figures in parentheses are t-values, ADF lags decided on the basis of AIC/SBC criterion and critical values for the null of no co-integration respectively.

Given that narrow money aggregate: $M_1 = C + DD$; broad money aggregate: $M_3 = C + AD$ where $AD = DD + TD$; and $M_0 = C + R$ (assuming other deposits with RBI negligible), we write:

Narrow money multiplier:

$$\begin{aligned} z_1 &= M_1/M_0 \\ &= (C + DD)/M_0 \\ &= (C + AD - TD)/(C + R) \\ &= (C/AD + AD/AD - TD/AD)/(C/AD + R/AD) \\ &= (1 + c - t)/(c + r) \\ &= (1 + k)/\text{Denom where Denom} = (c + r) \text{ and } k = c - t \end{aligned} \tag{13}$$

Broad money multiplier:

$$\begin{aligned} z_3 &= M_3/M_0 \\ &= (C + AD)/(C + R) \\ &= (C/AD + AD/AD)/(C/AD + R/AD) \\ &= (1 + c)/(c + r) \\ &= (1 + c - t + t)/(c + r) \end{aligned}$$

$= (1 + k + t)/Denom$
$= (1 + k + \Sigma d_j^2)/\text{Denom}$
$= (1 + k)/\text{Denom} + \Sigma d_j^2/\text{Denom}$
$= z_1 + nz_3$
(where $nz3 = t/c{+}r = \Sigma d_j^2/\text{Denom}$) (14)

Where
C is currency with public,
DD is demand deposits,
TD is time deposits,
AD is aggregate deposits comprising both demand and time deposits,
R is the bank reserves,
M_0 is the reserve money comprising both C and R assuming other deposits with RBI to be negligible,
M_1 and M_3 are narrow and broad money aggregates respectively,
c (= C/AD) is the currency-deposits ratio,
t (=TD/AD) is the time deposits aggregate deposits ratio,
r (=R/AD) is the reserves-deposits ratio,
k (= c – t) is the difference between currency and time deposits ratio,
Denom (= c + r) is the denominator in the expressions for the multipliers,
d_j is the ratio of time deposits to aggregate deposits,
z1, z3 and nz3 are the narrow money, broad money and partial broad money multipliers.
Portfolio allocation impacts on the component ratios are given by:

$$dj = dj\ (rs1, rs2, rs3, \quad .., rsn, y) \tag{15}$$

where rs_i denote the opportunity cost of holding the respective monetary asset and *y* represents real income. Incorporating (15) into (13) and (14) we have the following specification in asset movements across monetary aggregates and to non-money financial asset:

$$z_1 = z_1\ (rs_1, rs_2, rs_3, \quad .., rs_n, y) \tag{16}$$

$$z_3 = z_1 + nz_3\ (rs_1, rs_2, rs_3, \quad .., rs_n, y) \tag{17}$$

Relative interest gaps and the yield curve measure are important for portfolio shifts. The former is based on own rates of return on M_1, M_3 and net M_3 *assets vis-à-vis* the return on assets outside the monetary aggregates (a short-term market interest rate). Currency, demand and time deposits being the three relevant assets for the monetary aggregates under consideration, calculation of returns on M_1, M_3 and net M_3 *assets* (r_{m1}, r_{m3} and r_{nm3} respectively) involves three corresponding returns. Return on currency is taken as zero, the Klein rate estimated by Jha and Longjam (1999) is applied to demand deposits. Return on time deposits has been proxied by 1-year time deposit rate. The own rates of return for various monetary categories (r_{m1}, r_{nm3} and r_{m3}) are measured by quantity-weighted averages of returns on related component assets for which data are available in the Report of the Working Group on Money Supply, RBI (1998) and various issues of the monthly RBI Bulletin. The own rates for narrow money and broad money are:

r_{m1} = (Return on currency * Currency share in M_1) + (Klein rate * Demand deposits share in M_1);

r_{m3} = (Return on currency * Currency share in M_3) + (Klein rate * Demand deposits share in M_3) + Return on time deposits * Time deposit share in M_3).

The relative interest rate terms considered are the interest rate spread (rs_1) between net M_3 assets and M_1 asset ($rs_1 = r_{nm3} - r_{m1}$); the interest rate spread (rs_3) between a short-term market interest rate and net M_3 asset (*i.e.*, $rs_3 = r_{mkt} - r_{nm3}$). *rs1* being the lowest level opportunity cost is also the primary opportunity cost affecting all multipliers. *rs3* — the higher level opportunity cost — may significantly affect only the broader multipliers. Real income growth may exert positive impacts on the z_1 multiplier through declining currency ratio. Since time deposits have high income elasticities, the nz_3 impact may be positive. Steepness of the yield curve is proxied by the difference between the yields of a long-dated government security (10-year bond) and 91-day Treasury bill. Secondary market data for yield spread has been used for the period since 1995–96. For the period prior to 1995–96, primary market data are used. A steeper yield curve may induce shifts to higher return substitute assets and if transaction balances decline so will z_1. If funds flow over to broader aggregates, the broad money multiplier will rise.

With new asset alternatives, funds may flow to non-monetary assets so that *ryc* impacts on the broad money multiplier sub-components may turn out to be negative. Slow adjustment of deposit rates affects opportunity costs and induces portfolio adjustments thus affecting the multipliers.

Real income growth may raise z_1 through declining currency ratio. Easier transfer to cash will lead to a rising currency ratio and the z_1 impact may be negative. Real income growth may raise the nz_3 multiplier since the non-transaction assets in net M_3 are less closely related to transactions and income than are checkable deposits. However the nz_3 impact may turn out to be positive for the time deposit ratio because of their high income elasticity. To empirically assess these patterns write the estimable forms of (16) and (17) as:

$$z_{1t} = \alpha_0 + \Sigma\alpha_1\, rs_{1t} + \Sigma\alpha_2\, rs_{3t} + \alpha_3\, r_{yc} + \alpha_4\, y_t + e_{1t} \qquad (18)$$

$$z_{3t} = z_{1t} + \beta_0 + \Sigma\beta_1\, rs_{1t} + \Sigma\beta_2\, rs_{3t} + \beta_3\, r_{yc} + \beta_4\, y_t + e_{2t} \qquad (19)$$

Other multipliers can affect each multiplier. Further broad money contains narrow money within itself. Thus the error terms in the two equations could be both contemporaneously and serially correlated requiring the use of Seemingly Unrelated Regression (SUR) methods. Serial correlation of the individual error terms is modelled in two alternative forms.

Auto-correlation Model 1: $e_{i,t} = \rho_i \, e_{i,t-1} + u_{i,t}$ (20)

Auto-correlation Model 2: $e_{i,t} = \rho \, e_{i,t-1} + u_{i,t}$ (21)

The use of Zellner's feasible generalised least squares (FGLS) assures consistent and asymptotically efficient estimates. In model 1, the auto-correlation coefficients are estimated by using $\rho_i = 1 - DW_i/2$ where DW_i is the Durbin–Watson statistic computed using OLS; whereas in model 2, the common estimate is the simple average of the individual estimates. We prefer model 1 for using the SURE approach for the simultaneous estimation of z1 and nz3 as well as z1 and z3 multipliers and report results in Tables 3.4 and 3.5.

The SURE results are limited because they presume one-way direction of causality: from interest rate spreads, real income and yield curve measures to money multipliers. But this is an empirical proposition to be tested. To augment the SURE results[3], we analyze the mutual dependence of select macroeconomic variables and money multipliers using VAR methods without imposing any prior direction of causality.

Tables 3.6 to 3.10 report the results of co-integration for the multipliers (z1, z3 and nz3) as well as hypotheses on causation of the relevant variables for the multipliers for periods 1, 2 and 3. The likelihood ratio based chi-squared tests from Tables 3.6 to 3.8 show that the null hypothesis of non-causality of rs1 cannot be rejected in Period 3 or period 1 whereas it is rejected for period 2. The non-causality of rs3 can be rejected for all periods. The yield curve measure causes the narrow money multiplier only in period 3 and real income causes the narrow money multiplier in periods 2 and 3 but not for period 1. For period 1 only rs3 causes z1 while all other variables are non-causing z1.

The null hypothesis of non-causality of each of the variables in the broad money multiplier can be rejected for period 1 (Tables 3.6, 3.7 and 3.9). For period 2 while the null of non-causality of yield curve measure cannot be rejected, others can be. For period 3, while the null of non-causality of lower-level interest rate spread cannot be rejected, others can be.

---

[3] This is the first such attempt for India and only second for any country.

Table 3.4: FGLS Estimates
(z_1 and nz_3 for Periods 1, 2 and 3 using Model 1 of the SURE Approach)

Variable	*Estimate*	*Std. Error*	*Z-Statistic*	*P-Value*
1. Period 1: z_1 Equation				
constant	1.3124	0.75044E-01	17.488	0.00000
rs1	-0.55446E-01	0.43191E-02	-2.838	0.00000
rs3	-0.53485E-03	0.42352E-03	-1.263	0.20664
ryc	0.87634E-02	0.27656E-02	3.169	0.00153
logiip	0.24763E-01	0.33266E-01	0.744	0.45665
Adjusted R^2 = 0.83621 ; D-W statistic = 2.3731				
2. Period 1: nz_3 Equation				
constant	0.41090	0.23011	1.786	0.07415
rs1	-0.83727E-01	0.13244E-01	-6.322	0.00000
rs3	-0.36680E-02	0.12987E-02	-2.825	0.00474
ryc	0.26179E-01	0.84800E-02	3.087	0.00202
Logiip	0.86391	0.10200	8.469	0.00000
Adjusted R^2 = 0.91219 ; D-W statistic = 1.9858				
3. Period 2: z_1 Equation				
constant	1.4446	0.78620E-01	18.374	0.00000
rs1	-0.12339	0.55993E-02	-2.037	0.00000
rs3	-0.15269E-02	0.95968E-03	-1.591	0.11160
ryc	0.28511E-01	0.31106E-02	9.166	0.00000
Logiip	0.42638E-01	0.43798E-01	0.974	0.33030
Adjusted R^2 = 0.95231 ; D-W statistic = 1.9409				
4. Period 2: nz_3 Equation				
constant	1.6514	0.34796	4.746	0.00000
rs1	-0.11758	0.25761E-01	-4.564	0.00001
rs3	-0.95397E-02	0.42628E-02	-2.238	0.02523
ryc	0.10365	0.15337E-01	6.758	0.00000
logiip	0.17593	0.19090	0.922	0.35675
Adjusted R^2 = 0.71203 ; D-W statistic = 1.8986				
5. Period 3: z_1 Equation				
constant	0.22076	0.10953	2.016	0.04385
rs1	-0.11830E-01	0.31727E-02	-3.729	0.00019
rs3	0.19471E-03	0.40659E-03	0.479	0.63203
ryc	0.77569E-02	0.16882E-02	4.595	0.00000
logiip	0.38877	0.41189E-01	9.439	0.00000
Adjusted R^2 = 0.77252; D-W statistic = 1.7502				
6. Period 3: nz_3 Equation				
constant	-0.38369	0.48980	-0.783	0.43341
rs1	-0.35313E-01	0.14408E-01	-2.451	0.01425
rs3	-0.19591E-02	0.12499E-02	-1.567	0.11701
ryc	0.15350E-01	0.83840E-02	1.831	0.06712
logiip	1.1289	0.18885	5.978	0.00000
Adjusted R^2 = 0.9280 ; D-W statistic = 1.5171				

Table 3.5: Impacts on Multipliers (z1 and z3) Using Model 1 of SURE Approach

Variable	*Estimate*	*Std. Error*	*Z-Statistic*	*P-Value*
Period 1: z_1 Equation				
cons	1.2659	0.78474E-01	16.131	0.00000
rs1	-0.58436E-01	0.43434E-02	-13.454	0.00000
rs3	-0.59968E-03	0.41867E-03	-1.432	0.15205
ryc	0.10529E-01	0.27942E-02	3.768	0.00016
Logiip	0.48071E-01	0.34499E-01	1.393	0.16350
Adjusted R^2 = 0.83766 ; D-W statistic = 2.4322				
Period 1: z_3 Equation:				
Cons	1.3941	0.26629	5.235	0.00000
rs1	-0.14944	0.16062E-01	-9.304	0.00000
rs3	-0.46180E-02	0.16233E-02	-2.845	0.00444
ryc	0.40145E-01	0.10176E-01	3.945	0.00008
logiip	1.0450	0.11924	8.763	0.00000
Adjusted R^2 = 0.88301 ; D-W statistic = 2.1645				
Period 2: z_1 Equation				
Cons	1.4469	0.78666E-01	18.393	0.00000
rs1	-0.12346	0.56070E-02	-22.020	0.00000
rs3	-0.15152E-02	0.96033E-03	-1.578	0.11462
ryc	0.28633E-01	0.31160E-02	9.189	0.00000
logiip	0.41414E-01	0.43820E-01	0.945	0.34461
Adjusted R^2 = 0.95233 ; D-W statistic = 1.9352				
Period 2: z_3 Equation				
cons	3.0959	0.41494	7.461	0.00000
rs1	-0.24426	0.30493E-01	-8.010	0.00000
rs3	-0.11013E-01	0.50821E-02	-2.167	0.03023
ryc	0.13409	0.17857E-01	7.509	0.00000
logiip	0.22084	0.22855	0.966	0.33390
Adjusted R^2 = 0.58861 ; D-W statistic = 1.9212				
Period 3: z_1 Equation				
cons	0.23232	0.10702	2.171	0.02994
rs1	-0.11370E-01	0.31036E-02	-3.663	0.00025
rs3	0.20990E-03	0.39685E-03	0.529	0.59686
ryc	0.74206E-02	0.16573E-02	4.477	0.00001
Logiip	0.38360	0.40300E-01	9.519	0.00000
Adjusted R^2 = 0.77039 ; D-W statistic = 1.7336				
Period 3: z_3 Equation				
Cons	-0.14148	0.58669	-0.241	0.80944
rs1	-0.58502E-01	0.17307E-01	-3.380	0.00072
rs3	-0.18425E-02	0.15717E-02	-1.172	0.24107
ryc	0.23158E-01	0.99497E-02	2.328	0.01994
logiip	1.5326	0.22531	6.802	0.00000
Adjusted R^2 = 0.91242 ; D-W statistic = 1.6379				

Table 3.6: Period 1 Multipliers — Restricted Co-integrated Vectors in Johansen Estimation (Normalised in Brackets)

Panel A: Co-integrating Vector for z_1 Order of VAR = 1, chosen r =2.		
Variables	Vector 1	
z_1	-0.4968 (-1.0000)	
rs1	0.001998 (0.00402)	
rs3	-0.013566 (-0.27309)	
ryc	-0.0037548 (-0.007559)	
Liip	-0.3018 (-0.060753)	
Intercept	0.80525 (1.6210)	
Panel B: Co-integrating Vector for z3 Order of VAR = 1, chosen r =2.		
Variables	Vector 1	Vector 2
z3	-0.13538 (-1.0000)	0.39589 (-1.0000)
rs1	-0.0084037 (-0.062075)	.085596 (-0.21621)
rs3	-0.014078 (-0.10399)	-0.4906E-3 (0.0012393)
ryc	0.0047227 (0.034885)	-0.020897 (0.052785)
Liip	0.058873 (0.43487)	-0.30856 (0.77939)
Intercept	0.21923 (1.6194)	0.039955 (-0.10092)
Panel C: Co-integrating Vector for nz3 Order of VAR = 1, chosen r =2.		
Variables	Vector 1	Vector 2
nz3	-0.11359 (-1.0000)	-0.47722 (-1.0000)
rs1	-0.9516E-3 (-0.0083776)	-0.085978 (-0.18016)
rs3	-0.014030 (-0.12351)	-0.7343E-3 (-0.0015387)
ryc	0.0044556 (0.039226)	0.026714(0 .055978)
Liip	0.040627 (0.35767)	0.35842 (0.75107)
Intercept	0.081276 (0.71554)	-0.60479 (-1.2673)

From Tables 3.6, 3.7 and 3.10 for the partial broad money multipliers it can be seen that null hypothesis of non-causality of each of the variable in the net broad money multiplier can be rejected for period 1. For period 2 while the null of non-causality of yield curve measure is not rejected, others are. For period 3 while the null of non-causality of lower-level interest rate spread cannot be rejected, others can be rejected.

Table 3.7: LR Test of Restrictions on Multipliers

Panel A: z1 equation	
A1=0	CHSQ (1) = 4.0554 [0.044]
A2=0	CHSQ (1) = 0.02182 [0.883]
A3=0	CHSQ (1) = 30.7604 [0.000]
A4=0	CHSQ (1) = 0.37042 [0.543]
A5=0	CHSQ (1) = 1.2880 [0.256]
Panel B: z3 equation	
A1=0	CHSQ (2) = 27.348 [.000]
A2=0	CHSQ (2) = 17.0823 [.000]
A3=0	CHSQ (2) = 46.3510 [.000]
A4=0	CHSQ (2) = 5.6523 [.000]
A5=0	*CHSQ (2) = 25.4097 [.000]*
Panel C: nz3 equation	
A1=0	CHSQ (2) = 29.432 [0.000]
A2=0	CHSQ (2) = 21.1021 [0.000]
A3=0	CHSQ (2) = 46.0262 [0.000]
A4=0	CHSQ (2) = 9.5759 [0.008]
A5=0	*CHSQ (2) = 29.1841 [0.000]*

Table 3.11 summarises our SURE and VAR findings. Parameter changes have occurred across periods and VAR results are somewhat different from SURE.

Table 3.8: Restricted Co-integrated Vectors for z1 for Part Periods in Johansen Estimation (Normalised in Brackets)

Panel A: Period 2 Order of VAR = 1, chosen r =2.		
Variables	*Vector 1*	*Vector 2*
z1	-4.7478 (-1.0000)	1.1174 (-1.0000)
rs1	-0.51475 (-0.10842)	-0.13984 (0.12515)
rs3	-.022806 (-0.0048036)	-.029295 (0.026217)
Ryc	0.035829 (0.0075464)	-0.012332 (0.011036)
Liip	0.59913 (0.12619)	1.0087 (-0.90276)
Intercept	4.5524 (0.95883)	-5.5095 (4.9306)
Panel B: LR Test of Restrictions		
A1=0	CHSQ (2) = 28.442 [0.000]	
A2=0	CHSQ (2) = 24.9900 [0.000]	
A3=0	CHSQ (2) = 11.7017 [0.003]	
A4=0	CHSQ (2) = 1.8748 [0.392]	
A5=0	*CHSQ (2) = 26.1493 [0.000]*	
Panel C: Period 3 Order of VAR = 1, chosen r =2.		
Variables	*Vector 1*	*Vector 2*
z1	3.0367 (-1.0000)	.82679 (-1.0000)
rs1	0.015306 (-0.0050405)	0.0050319 (-0.0060861)
rs3	-.0040112 (0.0013209)	0.014464 (-0.017494)
Ryc	-0.037953 (0.012498)	-.0012947 (0.0015660)
Liip	-.85151 (0.28041)	0.0070351 (-0.0085089)
Intercept	1.4130 (-0.46531)	-1.0746 (1.2997)
Panel D: LR Test of Restrictions		
A1=0	CHSQ (2) = 59.339 [0.000]	
A2=0	CHSQ (2) = 1.7080 [0.426]	
A3=0	CHSQ (2) = 29.019 [0.000]	
A4=0	CHSQ (2) = 27.111 [0.000]	
A5=0	CHSQ (2) = 57.051 [0.000]	

Table 3.9: Restricted Co-integrated Vectors in z3 for Periods 2 and 3 Johansen Estimation (Normalised in Brackets)

Panel A: Period 2 Order of VAR = 1, chosen r =3.			
Variable	*Vector 1*	*Vector 2*	*Vector 3*
z3	0.48084 (-1.0000)	-0.76483 (-1.0000)	0.26049 (-1.0000)
rs1	0.29229 (-0.60787)	0.027806 (0.036356)	0.12439 (-0.47751)
rs3	0.038339 (-0.079733)	0.0015101 (0.0019745)	-0.011517 (0.044214)
Ryc	-0.018330 (0.038122)	0.027052 (0.035370)	-0.077017 (0.29566)
Liip	-1.1704 (2.4341)	-0.23750 (-0.31053)	0.14680 (-0.56354)
Intercept	3.0025 (-6.2443)	3.3155 (4.3350)	-1.7235 (6.6165)

Panel B: LR Test of Restrictions	
A1=0	CHSQ (3) = 25.5259 [0.000]
A2=0	CHSQ (3) = 26.4468 [0.000]
A3=0	CHSQ (3) = 14.4198 [0.002]
A4=0	CHSQ (3) = 3.5118 [0.319]
A5=0	CHSQ (3) = 35.7018 [0.000]

Panel C: Part Period (1990M4 – 2000M3) Order of VAR = 1, chosen r =1.	
Variables	*Vector 1*
z3	0.32924 (-1.0000)
rs1	0.027073 (-0.082228)
rs3	-0.010606 (0.032214)
Ryc	-0.032431 (0.098501)
Liip	-0.69538 (2.1121)
Intercept	2.8370 (-8.6167)

Panel D: LR Test of Restrictions	
A1=0	CHSQ (1) = 5.7299 [0.017]
A2=0	CHSQ (1) = 1.6135 [0.204]
A3=0	CHSQ (1) = 7.3419 [0.007]
A4=0	CHSQ (1) = 6.2616 [0.012]
A5=0	CHSQ (1) = 9.5502 [0.002]

Table 3.10: Restricted Co-integrated Vectors in nz3 for Period 2 Johansen Estimation (Normalised in Brackets)

Panel A: Period 2 Order of VAR = 1, chosen r =3.			
Variable	Vector 1	Vector 2	Vector 3
nz3	0.51486 (-1.0000)	0.95099 (-1.0000)	0.25549 (-1.0000)
rs1	0.25443 (-0.49417)	-.074547 (0 .078389)	0.11672 (-0.45686)
rs3	0.038213 (-.074221)	0.7670E-3 (-0.8065E-3)	-0.0095410 (0.037344)
ryc	-0.015007 (0.029148)	-0.030960 (0 .032555)	-0.083060 (0.32510)
Liip	-1.1829 (2.2976)	0.18538 (-0.19493)	0.15190 (-0.59454)
Intercept	3.6925 (-7.1718)	-2.3492 (2.4703)	-1.3875 (5.4310)

Panel B: LR Test of Restrictions	
A1=0	CHSQ (3) = 22.7879 [0.000]
A2=0	CHSQ (3) = 26.4705 [0.000]
A3=0	CHSQ (3) = 14.2398 [0.003]
A4=0	CHSQ (3) = 4.0019 [0.261]
A5=0	CHSQ (3) = 35.8161 [0.000]

Panel C: Part Period (1990M4 – 2000M3) Order of VAR = 1, chosen r =1.	
Variables	Vector 1
nz3	0.25331 (-1.0000)
rs1	0.018493 (-0.073005)
rs3	-0.012620 (0.049820)
Ryc	-0.024015 (0.094806)
Liip	-0.54363 (2.1461)
Intercept	2.5511 (-10.0711)

Panel D: LR Test of Restrictions	
A1=0	CHSQ (1) = 3.0501 [0.081]
A2=0	CHSQ (1) = 0.6822 [0.409]
A3=0	CHSQ (1) = 10.914 [0.001]
A4=0	CHSQ (1) = 3.4997 [0.061]
A5=0	CHSQ (1) = 7.1091 [0.008]

Table 3.11: Summary Results from SURE/VAR Exercises

Variable	*1980–90*	*1990–00*	*1980–00*
Panel A: Full Multiplier z_1			
rs1	-S (-S)	-S (-NS)	-S (+NS)
rs3	-NS (-S)	+NS (+S)	-NS (-S)
ryc	+S (+NS)	+S (+S)	+S (-NS)
Real Y	+NS (+S)	+S (+S)	+NS (-NS)
Panel B: Partial Multiplier nz3			
rs1	-S (-S)	-S (-NS)	-S (-S)
rs3	-S (-S)	-NS (+S)	-S (-S)
ryc	+S (+NS)	+S (+S)	+S (+S)
Real Y	+NS (+S)	+S (+S)	+S (+S)
Panel C: Full Multiplier z_3			
rs1	-S (-S)	-S (-NS)	-S (-S)
rs3	-S (-S)	-NS (-S)	-S (-S)
ryc	+S (+NS)	+S (+S)	+S (+S)
Real Y	+NS (+S)	+S (+S)	+NS (+S)

Note: 1. -/+ Stand for negative/positive values respectively for the parameters. S and NS represent significance and non-significance of the variable in the concerned equations.

2. The parenthetic representations relate to VAR results. S and NS represent significant and non-significant chi-square statistics.

The rate spread (*rs1*) being the lowest level of opportunity costs turns is expected to be a key primary opportunity cost for narrow broad as well as net broad multipliers. An increase in *rs1* should trigger an outflow from transaction deposits so that the coefficient is expected to be negative and significant. This impact alone may be sufficient to cause all other component ratios to increase for other multipliers as well, given that transactions deposits are the denominator in each of the component ratios. This is the case with SURE results for all reference periods. As for VAR, *rs1* is insignificant in Period 3 perhaps because saving deployment in high-yielding monetary assets does not result from outflow of money from transaction deposits, but directly from cash. A contributory factor could be a reduction in the minimum maturity period over the post reform period for term and better rates of interest.

Secondly, although we expect that the higher-level opportunity cost (*rs3*) would be insignificant in the narrow multiplier, VAR results indicate otherwise in both narrow as well as broad money multipliers. When agents expect the short-term market interest rate to increase (for example in the call money sector), there is an outflow from the shortest maturity term deposits. Agents may park funds as demand deposits for eventual transmission to the targeted instrument. Such a *rs3* impact on the multipliers could be because the returns entering into this rate spread are not tracking each other quite well even in period 3. Had the deposit rate tracked the money market rate, the incentive for asset shifting would have been much lower. With greater financial sector integration, increased interest rate alignment would ensure improved responsiveness of deposit rates to general interest rate movements.

The VAR analysis indicates that the yield curve measure exerts a positive and significant impact for the broad money multiplier in all time periods. For period 1 it is negative and significant. The positive and significant coefficient indicates that the outflow of funds from average transactions balances in response to a steepening of the yield curve is not high. This reduces the possibility of the negative impact on the *z1* multiplier. However, a steeper yield curve causes inflow to higher yield assets within nz_3. The incentives to move away to higher return non-monetary assets may be somewhat dampened by the illiquidity of long-dated government securities.

The coefficient on real income is uniformly positive and significant for the broad money multiplier in all periods. Results from VAR differ significantly from SURE. The VAR results point to the importance of income in the asset holding decisions of the agents encompassing the broad spectrum of monetary assets. Thus even in the post-reforms period where relative rates should gain prominence *vis-à-vis* income factors, the latter still remain important determinants of multipliers. This is partly explained by the fact that the reforms period has experienced high economic and monetary growth leading to an upward drift in the money multipliers.

6. Conclusions

This chapter has examined the behavior of alternative money multipliers in India and the related issue of endogeneity of money multipliers and the money supply.

We conclude that money multipliers in India have been endogenous — particularly since the reforms. We examined narrow and broad money multipliers in a simultaneous equation and VAR frameworks and found significant impacts on them from select opportunity costs as also measures of the yield curve and real income. Changing significance of determinants of alternative multipliers across periods appears to contribute towards their greater variability and instability.

References

Baghestani, H. and T. Mott, 'A Co-integration Analysis of the U.S. Money Supply Process', *Journal of Macroeconomics*, 19(2) (1997).

Cagan, P., *Determinants and Effects of Changes in the Stock of Money, 1875–1960*, Columbia University Press for the National Bureau of Economic Research (New York, 1965).

Davis, G. and Gauger, J., 'Measuring Substitution in Monetary Asset Demand Systems', *Journal of Business and Economic Statistics*, 14 (April 1996).

Freeman, S. and G. Huffman, 'Inside Money, Output and Causality', *International Economic Review*, 32 (August 1991).

Friedman, M. and, A.J. Schwartz, *A Monetary History of United States, 1867–1960* (Princeton, NJ: Princeton University Press, 1963).

Gauger, J., 'Economic Impacts on the Money Supply Process', *Journal of Macroeconomics*, 20(3) (Summer 1998).

Gauger, J. and H. Black, 'Asset Substitution and Monetary Volatility', *Journal of Money, Credit and Banking* 23 (November 1991).

Howells, P. and K. Hussein, 'The Endogeneity of Money: Evidence from the G-7', *Scottish Journal of Political Economy*, 45(3) (1998).

Ireland, P., 'Money and Growth: An Alternative Approach', *American Economic Review* 84 (March 1994).

Jha, R. and I.S. Longjam, 'Will the Right Monetary Aggregate for India Please Stand Up', *Economic and Political Weekly* 34(10&11) (6–13 March 1999).

Johannes, J. and R. Rasche, 'Predicting the Money Multiplier', *Journal of Monetary Economics* 5 (March 1979).

Johannes, J. and R. Rasche, 'Can the Reserves Approach to Monetary Control Really Work', *Journal of Money, Credit and Banking*, 13 (1981).

Johannes, J. and R. Rasche, 'Controlling the Growth of Monetary Aggregates', *Rochester Studies in Economic and Policy Issues* (Boston: Kluwer Academic Publishers, 1987).

Manchester, J., 'How Money Affects Real Output', *Journal of Money, Credit and Banking* 21 (February 1989).

Moore, G., R. Porter and D. Small, Modelling the Disaggregated Demand for M2 in the 1980s, Federal Reserve Board of Governors, Mimeo (1988).

Papademos, L. and, F. Modigliani, 'The Supply of Money and Control of National Income', in *Handbook of Monetary Economics*, B.M. Friedman and F.H. Hahn (eds), Vol. 1 (I) (Amsterdam: North-Holland, 1990).

Rath, D.P., *Endogeneity Issues in the Money Supply Process of India*, Ph.D. Thesis (Mumbai: IGIDR, September 2001).

Reserve Bank of India, *Report of the Working Group on Money Supply* (June 1998).

Tseng, W. and R. Corker, 'Financial Liberalisation, Money Demand and Monetary Policy in Asian Countries', *IMF Occasional Paper* No. 84 (1991), Washington D.C.

4

Financial Fragility in Indian Stock Markets: the decade of the 1990s — a time series study

Amitava Sarkar, Kalyan K. Roy and Soumitra Kumar Mallick

1. Introduction

A major plank in a non-fragile financial infrastructure is an efficiently performing stock market. Optimal stock market operations imply, among other factors, stock prices moving in tandem with fundamentals thus ensuring optimal returns (i.e. risk free rate plus premium for risk borne) for investors and raising required capital at least cost for borrowing firms. At any given point in time or during any given period of time, stock prices will move in an attempt to find levels commensurate with fundamental explanatory variables. Fundamental explanatory variables include financial as well as economic variables. In an efficient market the deviation of actual market price from fundamentally explained price of a stock should be random. Conversely, the non-random behavior of errors points to existence of and building up of bubbles (with possibilities of boom and subsequent bust) leading to financial fragility.

Fama's (1970) original work indicated that stock prices moved according to fundamentals. However, empirical research since then has raised serious doubts. Shiller (1981) found stock prices to be more volatile than what would be warranted by economic events. Blanchard and Watson (1982) show that when a bubble is present, the proportional change in stock prices is an increasing function of time and therefore predictable; further, with the passage of time the bubble starts dominating fundamentals. This can be tested by regressing the proportional change in stock prices on time. Summers (1986) opined that financial markets were not efficient in the sense of rationally reflecting fundamentals. Fama and French (1988) found returns to possess large predictable components casting doubts about the efficiency of the stock market. Dwyer and Hafer (1990) examined the behavior of stock prices in a cross-section of countries and found no support for either 'bubbles' in or the fundamentals in explaining the stock prices. Froot and Obstfeld's (1991) study on 'Intrinsic Bubbles — the Case of Stock Prices' once again raises doubts about the stock prices being determined by the fundamentals.

For Indian stock markets, there have been a number of studies examining efficiency. Barua (1981), Sharma (1983), Gupta (1985) and others confirm a weak form of market efficiency. Sharma (1983) uses data of 23 stocks listed in the BSE for the period 1973–78 and confirms a weak form of random walk holding for the BSE during the period. Dixit (1986) and others regressed stock prices on dividends to test the role of fundamentals. These tests also found support for efficiency hypothesis. However, evidence in the recent period, particularly in the 1990s (Barua and Raghunathan 1990; Sundaram 1991; Obaidullah 1991) raise doubts about this hypothesis. Barua and Raghunathan (1990) used 23 leading company stock prices. They estimated Price Earning (P/E) ratio based on fundamentals and compared them with actual P/E data. The result indicated shares to be overvalued. Obaidullah (1991) used sensex data from 1979–1991 and found that stock price adjustment to release of relevant information (fundamentals) is not in the right direction again implying wrong valuation by the stock market. Barman and Madhusoodan (1993) found that stock returns do not exhibit efficiency in the short or medium term, though appear to be efficient over a longer period. Barman (1999) finds that fundamentals rather than bubbles are more important in the determination of stock prices in the long run. He discerns contribution of bubbles (although mild) toward stock prices in the short run.

The 1990s have seen significant structural changes with the opening up of financial markets through privatising a large part of the public sector and the opening of the national stock exchange with the introduction of online trading. The purpose of this chapter is to bring out the long run properties of the Indian stock market by relating a) the relation of stock prices to fundamentals; and b) by estimating the extent to which bubbles are present in the stock market data. This study differs from other studies for another reason. We analyze the properties of the stock prices as opposed to returns in the section on cross-sectional analysis. Since financial capital is to a large extent independent of the structure of the firm, cross-sectional analysis can estimate the stationary properties of stock prices at least around that date. In a section on time series analysis, we examine price differentials over various time periods.

2. The Data

Data for the analysis is obtained from the Prowess database of Centre for Monitoring the Indian Economy (CMIE). The data is pooled and covers the period 1988–2001. Prowess provides information on around 7638 companies and covers public, private, co-operative and joint sector companies, listed or otherwise. These account for more than seventy per cent of the economic activity in the organised industrial sector of India. These data have been compiled from the audited annual accounts of all public limited companies in India which furnish annual returns with the Registrar of Companies and are listed on the Bombay Stock Exchange. The database provides financial statements, ratio analysis, funds flows, product profiles, returns and risks on the stock markets, etc. Also, it provides information from scores of other reliable sources, such as the stock exchanges, associations, etc.

In estimating the time series properties of price formation in stock markets, the historical data can be divided into instantaneous, short-run, medium-run and long–run. Instantaneous analysis requires data generated in continuous time for all variables whether relating to price formation or fundamentals. This study however, uses discrete time data organised annually into a decade. Hence, this study is both a short-run, as well as, a medium-run study of the stock market system. Long-run analysis of stock market data however, requires analysis of historical epochs, which in a semi-planned economy such as India ought to cover more than two consecutive plan periods. This study covers a segment of the 7th Five Year Plan Period, the 8th Five Year Plan Period in full and the first half of the 9th Five Year Plan Period. This period also witnessed two significant stock market crashes (in 1993 and 1997) and the 'Harshad Mehta scam' in 1992. The time series results have to be analyzed against this background (Bagchi 1998).

2.1 Time Series Dataset

Data for the time series regression are obtained from the Prowess database of CMIE. The database covers the period 1988 to 2000.

In our time series analysis we used annual series of all the variables, listed below, for the period 1990–2000. While higher frequency series for some of the variables are available, since matching series for all the variables are not contained in the database, we have analyzed data for years ending 31 December for all variables.

2.1.1 'Average Growth' Data

The total market set of companies has been pooled for 10 years from 1990 to 2000, working backwards. The common set of firms which have 'survived' in the period 1990 to 2000 number 582 which after adjustment for missing data is pruned to 573 firms. This is the 'bootstrap' average growth data set. (The graphs for the raw variables are available on request.)

2.1.2 Annual Price Differential Data

One period annual price differential (Return) datasets for the annual growth models 1999–2000 to 1990–1991 are presented in the form of the correlation matrix in Table 4.1.

Table 4.1: Annual Differential Return

	RET 1Y	RET 2Y	RET 3Y	RET 4Y	RET 5Y	RET 6Y	RET 7Y	RET 8Y	RET 9Y	RET 10Y
RET 1Y	1.00	.04	.00	.02	-.01	-.01	.01	.00	.01	.00
RET 2Y	-.04	1.00	-.05	.01	.01	.02	-.00	-.01	-.01	-.03
RET 3Y	.00	-.05	1.00	.03	-.02	.01	.02	.05	.02	-.01
RET 4Y	.02	.01	.03	1.00	.01	-.02	.01	.01	-.01	-.04
RET 5Y	-.01	.01	-.02	.01	1.00	-.03	.00	-.02	.00	.05
RET 6Y	-.01	.02	.01	-.02	-.03	1.00	.02	.02	.04	.01
RET 7Y	.01	-.00	.02	.01	.00	.02	1.00	-.00	-.01	-.01
RET 8Y	.00	-.01	.05	.01	-.02	.02	-.00	1.00	-.03	-.01
RET 9Y	.01	-.01	.02	-.01	.00	.04	-.01	-.03	1.00	-.01
RET 10Y	.00	-.03	-.01	-.04	.05	.01	-.01	-.01	-.01	1.00

No correlations are significant at $p < .05000$

2.2 Manufacturing Sector Data

The only industry that has been considered in isolation from the market dataset is the manufacturing sector. This is because this is the only sector having a large number of surviving firms between 1990 and 2000. Three stages in the algorithm are carried out with respect to this dataset. The 1990–2000 and the 1999–2000 growth rates are fitted. The fits, as well as the errors, are then compared to ensure that the errors are uncorrelated. The total number of firms in the first data set is 517 and in the other case is 1925. The correlation matrices with respect to the two growth models are given in Tables 4.2 and 4.3.

Table 4.2: Correrlation Matrix for Returns — Growth Model 1

	NW_SH90	DE_SH90	PT_SH90	DIV_SH90	GNW_S10Y	GDE_S10Y	GPT_S10Y	GDV_S10Y	RET10Y
NW_SH90	1.000000	.025183	.740111	.851955	.114692	-.032914	-.100677	-.429485	.210495
DE_SH90	.025183	1.000000	.018750	.010412	.019033	-.777652	.012947	.008249	.014449
PT_SH90	.740111	.018750	1.000000	.706037	.139353	-.038373	-.218449	-.450747	.071874
DIV_SH90	.851955	.010412	.706037	1.000000	-.113054	-.009213	-.306639	-.658594	.062606
GNW_S10Y	.114692	.019033	.139353	-.113054	1.000000	-.008633	.881516	.413916	.355693
GDE_S10Y	-.032914	-.777652	-.038373	-.009213	-.008633	1.000000	.006541	-.015088	-.016135
GPT_S10Y	-.100677	.012947	-.218449	-.306639	.881516	.006541	1.000000	.463758	.339531
GDV_S10Y	-.429485	.008249	-.450747	-.658594	.413916	-.015088	.463758	1.000000	.439172
RET10Y	.210495	.014449	.071874	.062606	.355693	-.016135	.339531	.439172	1.000000

Table 4.3: Results for Market Data — Growth Model 2

	NW_SH99	DE_SH99	PT_SH99	DIV_SH99	GNW_S1Y	GDE_S1Y	GPT_S1Y	GDV_S1Y	RET_1Y
NW_SH99	1.000000	.006132	.732348	.440819	.618084	-.000103	.285385	-.010703	-.212520
DE_SH99	.006132	1.000000	.014161	-.001055	.012673	-.339267	.004004	.000673	.003175
PT_SH99	.732348	.014161	1.000000	.289349	.526261	-.008514	-.206490	-.017957	-.157580
DIV_SH99	.440819	-.001055	.289349	1.000000	.035746	-.001292	-.072465	-.565834	-.382219
GNW_S1Y	.618084	.012673	.526261	.035746	1.000000	-.007056	.427272	.287532	-.107605
GDE_S1Y	-.000103	-.339267	-.008514	-.001292	-.007056	1.000000	-.002271	-.000435	.001055
GPT_S1Y	.285385	.004004	-.206490	-.072465	.427272	-.002271	1.000000	.163399	.063614
GDV_S1Y	-.010703	.000673	-.017957	-.565834	.287532	-.000435	.163399	1.000000	-.019667
RET_1Y	-.212520	.003175	-.157580	-.382219	-.107605	.001055	.063614	-.019667	1.000000

3. Time Series Model

We consider the following time series model for dynamic price formation in Indian stock markets.

$$P_{t+1} - P_t = A_t + B_{1t} NW_t + B_{2t} DE_t + B_{3t} PT_t + B_{4t} DIV_t$$
$$B_{5t} E_t \Delta NW_t + B_{6t} E_t \Delta DE_t + B_{7t} E_t \Delta PT_t + B_{8t} E_t \Delta DIV_t$$
$$+ \tilde{\eta}_t,\ \tilde{\eta}_t \sim N(0, \sigma^2_{\eta_t})$$

where, P_t = closing price of shares at 31 December of the year t,

NW_t = net worth per outstanding equity share at 31 December of the year t,

PT_t = profit for the year t per outstanding equity share at 31 December of the year t,

DE_t = debt equity ratio at 31 December of the year t,

DIV_t = dividend declared during year t per outstanding equity share at 31December of year *t*

$\Delta NW_t = NW_{t+1} - NW_t$, is the first forward difference in NW,

$\Delta PT_t = PT_{t+1} - PT_t$, is the first forward difference in PT,

$\Delta DE_t = DE_{t+1} - DE_t$, is the first forward difference in DE,

$\Delta DIV_t = DIV_{t+1} - DIV_t$ is the first forward difference in DIV

E_t is the forward looking rational expectations operator with respect to 31 December of year *t*.

η_t is a random error term normally distributed with mean 0 and variance matrix $\sigma^2_{\eta_t} > 0$

We shall jointly test for the fit of the model as well as the properties of the error terms hypothesized, with annual data over the period 1990–2000. The econometric testing of a time series model of this form consisting of a large cross section of companies at any given *t*, can be carried out along two directions. The first method is the traditional Vector Auto Regression method of the Box Jenkins type. In such a method the entire data pooled across firms and time periods has to be studied in integrated form to give GLS estimates by the ARIMA model. This has the cost of there being around 2500 firms for each of the years 1990–2000 with twelve variables, which could become a 2500 X 10 X 12 matrix requiring high computing time and memory costs. Besides, with a linear model specification, such as ours, the nonlinearity involved in the historical behavior of stock prices would not be readily evident till we change our specification and fit a nonlinear model. This prompts us to carry out the Time-Series GLS regression in a 'nested' procedure similar in many respects with that suggested by Granger & Newbold (1977). The algorithm used models the residual matrix of nested models to set up an objective function based on correlations amongst nested residuals. While this procedure helps in time series estimation of the parameters along the Granger et al. approach, it also provides a procedure for estimating TVP (Time Varying Parameter) problems as discussed in Rao (2000), without using any exogenous cost minimisation objectives.

In the first step we break up the pooled time series ARIMA model into nested models, identified by years, as follows:

$$[\ P_{t+1} - P_t\ ] = [\ A_t + \sum_{i=1}^{4} B_{it} \text{ historical variable }_{it} + \sum_{i=5}^{8} B_{it} \text{ expectation variable }_{it} + \eta_t]\ _{C} \otimes _{T}$$

where C is the number of companies in the data set, T is the time 'horizon' which in this case is 1990–2000 and B_{it} is the coefficient on historical variable i at time t where *i* is the indicator as follows:

$i=1 \Rightarrow NW$

$i=2 \Rightarrow DE$

$i=3 \Rightarrow PT$

$i=4 \Rightarrow DIV$

The historical variables are as given above, the expectation variables follow exactly the same identification, i.e.:

$i=5 \Rightarrow E_t \Delta\ NW$

$i=6 \Rightarrow E_t \Delta\ DE$

$i=7 \Rightarrow E_t \Delta\ PT$

$i=8 \Rightarrow E_t \Delta\ DIV$

This is the basic time series model.

We then break up this general ARIMA (1,1,1) specification into first a 'bootstrap' average growth model as follows:

$$P_{2000}\ \ P_{1990} = A + B_1\, NW_{1990} + B_2\, DE_{1990} + B_3\, PT_{1990} + B_4\, DIV_{1990} + B_5\, E_{1990}\, \Delta\, NW_{1990 \text{ to } 2000}$$

$$+ B_6\, E_{1990}\, \Delta\ DE_{\ 2000\ 1990} + B_7\, E_{1990}\, \Delta PT_{\ 2000\ 1990} + B_8\, E_{1990}\, \Delta DIV_{2000\ 1990} + \tilde{\eta}$$

where, $E_{1990}\ \Delta NW_{2000\ 1990} = NW_{2000} - NW_{1990}$,

$E_{1990}\ \Delta DE_{2000\ 1990} = DE_{2000} - DE_{1990}$,

$E_{1990}\ \Delta PT_{2000\ 1990} = PT_{2000} - PT_{1990}$

$E_{1990}\ \Delta DIV_{2000\ 1990} = DIV_{2000} - DIV_{1990}$

Thus, here the dependant variable is the total price differential over the decade. Any of the coefficients B_5 to B_8 is the 'average growth' coefficient. For example:

$$B_5\ E_{1990}\ \Delta\ NW_{2000\ 1990} = 10\ B_5\ E_{1990}\ \underline{\Delta NW_{2000\ 1990}}10$$

This model seems as the benchmark 'bootstrap' model for the decade of the nineties.

In the third step the linear growth assumption along with the 10-year horizon assumption is relaxed to test a set of ten 'nested' models, one for each year as follows:

$$Ret_n = A_n + \sum_{i=1}^{4} B_{in} \text{ historical variable i} + \sum_{i=5}^{8} B_{in} \text{ expectation variable i}$$

$$+ \tilde{\varepsilon}_n\ ,\ \tilde{\varepsilon}_n \sim N(0, \sigma_{\varepsilon_t}^2),\ n = 1999\ .....\ 1990$$

and growth is taken over 1 year periods working back from 2000 for each n, while expectations is forward looking over the one year. For example:

$B_{15}\ E_1\ \Delta NW_1 = B_{1999,5}\ (NW_{2000}\text{-}NW_{1999})$ and so on

$Ret_n = P_{n+1}\ P_n$

Granger & Newbold (1977) argue, this is a valid procedure for obtaining the time series properties of stock price, provided the residual matrix [ϵ_n] does not show significant serial correlation. Therefore the final step in this algorithm is to check for the correlation in the [ϵ_n] matrix from the ten nested models obtained in step 3. If the significance of serial correlation is low then this is also a algorithmic procedure for cointegration of stock price variables. We test these hypotheses in the following sections.

3.1 Time Series Results (Goodness-of-Fit)

3.1.1 The 'Average Growth' Model

The average growth model for the ten year period 1990–2000 is presented. The dataset consists of the entire market data and the partitioned manufacturing data. Both sets of results serve as a bootstrapping benchmark for the linear model specification in stage 1 of the modeling algorithm.

3.1.2 The Market Data

The total number of 'surviving' firms between the decade 31 December 1990 and 31 December 2000 is 573 in the total market dataset. The average growth model was run on the set taking the annual series as has been discussed. The results are summarised in Table 4.4.

Table 4.4: Estimates of Growth Model

Variable	B	t (573)	Level of significance
Intercept	-16.47	-1.298	Insignificant
NW_{1990}	- 0.165	-1.225	Insignificant
DE_{1990}	0.085	0.079	Insignificant
PT_{1990}	2.819	4.33	1%
DIV_{1990}	23.30	6.823	0%
$GNW_{1990\ to\ 2000}$	-2.909	-3.227	1%
$GDE_{1990\ to\ 2000}$	0.875	0.106	Insignificant
$GPT_{1990\ to\ 2000}$	21.355	4.415	1%
$GDV_{1990\ to\ 2000}$	326.194	14.356	0%

Thus, the estimated equation becomes:

$P_{2000} - P_{1990} = -16.47 - 0.165NW_{1990} + 0.085\ DE_{1990} + 2.819\ PT_{1990} + 23.30\ DIV_{1990}$

(-1.298) (-1.225) (0.079) (4.33) (6.823)

$-2.909\ GNW_{1990\ to\ 2000} + 0.875\ GDE_{1990\ to\ 2000} + 21.355\ GPT_{1990\ to\ 2000} + 326.194\ GDV_{1990\ to\ 2000}$

(-3.227)(0.106) (4.415) (14.356)

The R^2 is high at 0.36 and the F-statistic is high at 42.09366 which is significant at the 0 per cent level and the serial correlation of the residuals is low at 0.05 suggesting a good fit for the model.

The signs of the significant weights on the initial profit (PT_{1990}), initial dividend (DIV_{1990}) and in their growth, is substantiated by the model, while the negative weightage on $GNW_{2000\ 1990}$ seems to be arising due to the predominance of the supply factors over demand in the fixed point equation of the model. The fitted 'price differential' line is plotted in Figure 4.1 as RET 10Y.

3.2 Manufacturing Sector Data

The total number of 'surviving ' firms in the manufacturing sector dataset over the period 1990 to 2000 is 517. The average growth linear model was run on the dataset taking annual series, as has been discussed, to obtain the GLS estimates. The results are presented in the Table 4.5.

Figure 4.1: Predicted vs Observed Values — Dependent Variables RET10Y

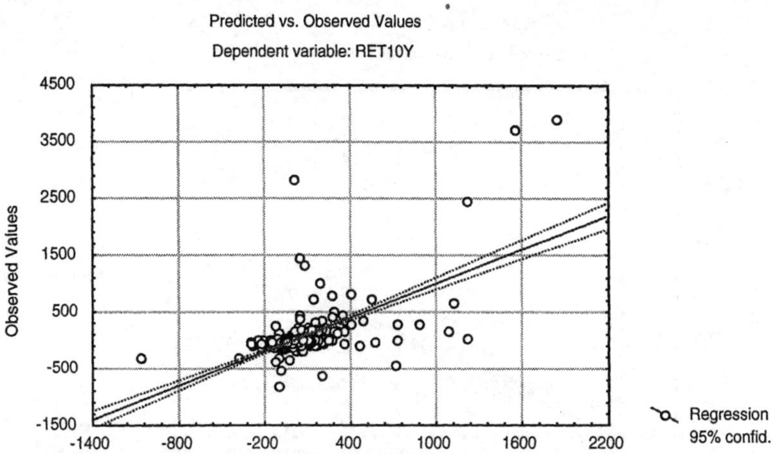

Figure 1

Table 4.5: GLS Estimates for Average Growth

Variable	*B*	*t (573)*	*Level of significance*
Intercept	-20.47	-1.425	Insignificant
NW_{1990}	0.215	1.003	Insignificant
DE_{1990}	0.069	0.061	Insignificant
PT_{1990}	2.967	4.04	1%
DIV_{1990}	30.885	6.504	0%
$GNW_{1990\ to\ 2000}$	-5.987	-5.586	0%
$GDE_{1990\ to\ 2000}$	1.273	0.146	Insignificant
$GPT_{1990\ to\ 2000}$	37.317	6.716	0%
$GDV_{1990\ to\ 2000}$	441.713	16.69	0%

The R^2 is high at 0.46.
The graph of the plot of the fitted price differential is shown in Figure 4.2.

3.3 Annual Price Differential Data

In keeping with the algorithmic approach to the time series analysis of this paper we regress the model on annual data for the periods 1990–2001. The results of the regression for the various periods within the decade are summarized in Table 4.6.

Figure 4.2: Predicted vs Observed Values — Dependent Variable RET10Y

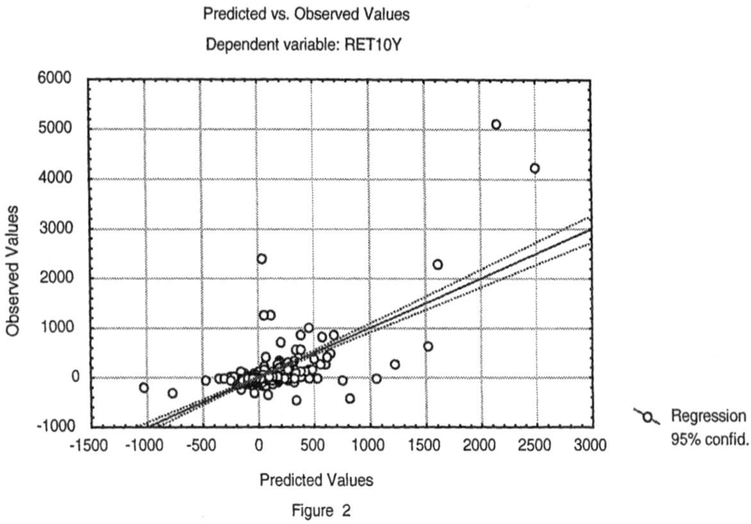

The fit of the ten annual models never perform better than the average growth model over the 10-year horizon in terms of R^2, which has a significantly high R^2 at 0.36. Besides, the F-statistic is significant for the average growth rational expectations model over 10 years and the serial correlation of residuals is also low, rejecting a non-linear fit to the pricing equation through annual series in favour of a linear fit. This inference is correct based on the comparison of the two sets of models, because as required by Granger & Newbold (1977), the error correlation matrix among the nested residuals as given in Table 4.7 does not show significant serial correlation.

This rejects the hypothesis of significant correlation with only 3 out of 45 correlations being significant and that too with a maximum magnitude of 0.16. This inference is also true when one compares the manufacturing sector for its fit over 1990 to 2000 with 1999 to 2000 the most recent one year. The results for the 1990 to 2000 period are given in Table 4.8.

Here also the average growth ten-year model obtains a better fit, suggesting that the longer-term linear rational expectations model performs better. In other words, the cointegrated price variables fit better in both cases with a linear average growth trend. Both these observations are somewhat incongruous with a high and significant weightage on historical dividends and dividend growths, which suggest high liquidity preference and therefore 'myopia'.

Table 4.6: Regression Results on Bill Differentials

period	Intercept	NW	DE	PT	DIV	GNW	GDE	GPT	GDIV	R^2	F	DW
00–99	-4.2 (-1.39)	-0.021 (-0.46)	0.023 (0.163)	0.419 (2.30)	-16.87 (-19.14)	-0.33 (-3.54)	0.01 (0.11)	0.977 (5.01)	-13.49 (-11.40)	0.19	73.24	1.80
99–98	22.88 (5.74)	0.098 (2.79)	-0.05 (-0.14)	1.02 (7.15)	7.54 (6.78)	0.21 (3.44)	-0.04 (-0.24)	1.15 (6.45)	6.29 (5.04)	0.08	34.38	1.76
98–97	3.38 (3.84)	0.019 (4.57)	-0.01 (-0.11)	0.18 (3.47)	-3.16 (11.86)	0.34 (-8.14)	0.00 (0.08)	0.61 (8.4)	1.28 (4.07)	0.08	39.18	1.97
97–96	7.52 (5.72)	0.04 (6.08)	-0.15 (-1.06)	-0.39 (-8.02)	-11.21 (-28.23)	-0.56 (-25.18)	0.01 (0.17)	-0.5 (-5.3)	7.02 (9.03)	0.34	226.20	1.97
96–95	3.01 (1.71)	-0.31 (-11.24)	-0.00 (-0.001)	1.13 (9.61)	-7.52 (-10.20)	-0.55 (-8.23)	-0.01 (-0.05)	-0.63 (-6.92)	4.04 (3.03)	0.27	147.86	2.02
95–94	-13.15 (-3.45)	-0.68 (-11.48)	0.01 (0.07)	1.35 (6.19)	-5.13 (-3.54)	-0.53 (-7.21)	-0.02 (-0.16)	2.14 (11.78)	-14.11 (-6.73)	0.24	89.38	1.99
94–93	37.6 (3.75)	1.19 (8.85)	-0.07 (-0.11)	-1.58 (-3.61)	-14.11 (-4.61)	0.13 (0.68)	-0.05 (0.09)	0.36 (0.85)	-11.4 (-1.99)	0.09	19.29	1.97
93–92	6.55 (2.50)	0.07 (2.44)	-0.16 (-0.44)	-0.07 (-0.66)	0.699 (1.16)	-0.06 (-1.71)	-0.005 (0.06)	0.323 (4.23)	4.962 (3.385)	0.07	11.67	2.02
91–90	20.12 (3.86)	0.09 (1.67)	0.04 (0.07)	-0.53 (-2.43)	8.84 (6.36)	-0.29 (-2.33)	0.034 (0.07)	0.64 (3.074)	2.883 (2.98)	0.14	17.40	2.11

Table 4.7: Error Correlation Matrix

	E1	E2	E3	E4	E5	E6	E7	E8	E9	E10
E1	1.00	-.04	-.01	.01	-.07*	.01	.04	.07*	-.01	-.00
E2	-.04	1.00	-.03	-.04	-.04	.01	.02	-.02	-.00	-.00
E3	-.01	-.03	1.00	-.01	-.01	-.03	-.03	-.02	-.00	.04
E4	.01	-.04	-.01	1.00	.00	.00	.01	-.02	.01	.02
E5	-.07*	-.04	-.01	.00	1.00	-.03	.02	.02	-.02	.00
E6	.01	.01	-.03	.00	-.03	1.00	.02	.05	-.01	-.01
E7	.04	.02	-.03	.01	.02	.02	1.00	.03	.01	.16*
E8	.07*	-.02	-.02	-.02	.02	.05	.03	1.00	-.04	-.02
E9	-.01	-.00	-.00	.01	-.02	-.01	.01	-.04	1.00	.00
E10	-.00	-.00	.04	.02	.00	-.01	.16*	-.02	.00	1.00

Marked correlations are significant at $p < 0.05000$

The fitted lines for the ten year average growth model and for the1999 to 2000 model for the entire market data set are presented in figures 3 and 4.

Table 4.8: Manufacturing Sector Results

Variable	B	t-statistic	Level of significance
Intercept	-3.91	-1.057	Insignificant
NW_{99}	0.007	0.183	Insignificant
DE_{99}	0.02	0.129	Insignificant
PT_{99}	0.327	1.564	Insignificant
DIV_{99}	-21.09	-19.967	0%
GNW	-0.27	-2.483	2%
GDE	0.005	0.065	Insignificant
GPT	0.832	3.733	1%
GDV	-18.197	-13.214	0%

Adjusted R^2 is 0.23.

Figure 4.3: Predicted vs Obsereved Values — Dependent Variable RET_10Y

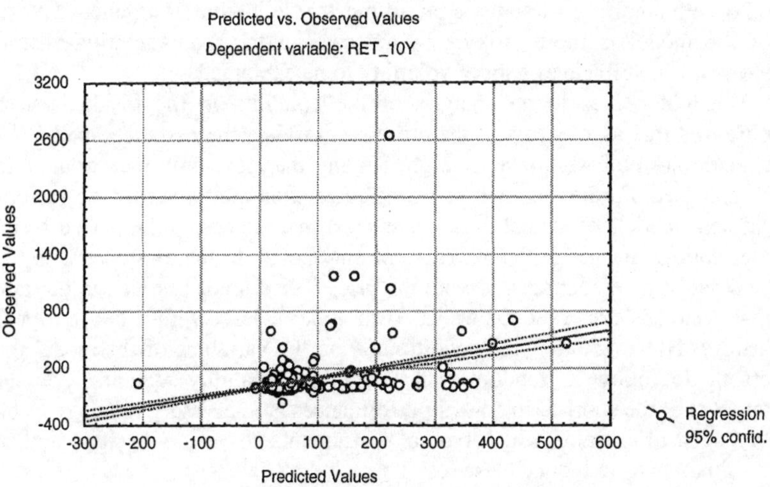

Figure 3

Figure 4.4: Predicted vs Observed Values — Dependent Variable RET_1Y

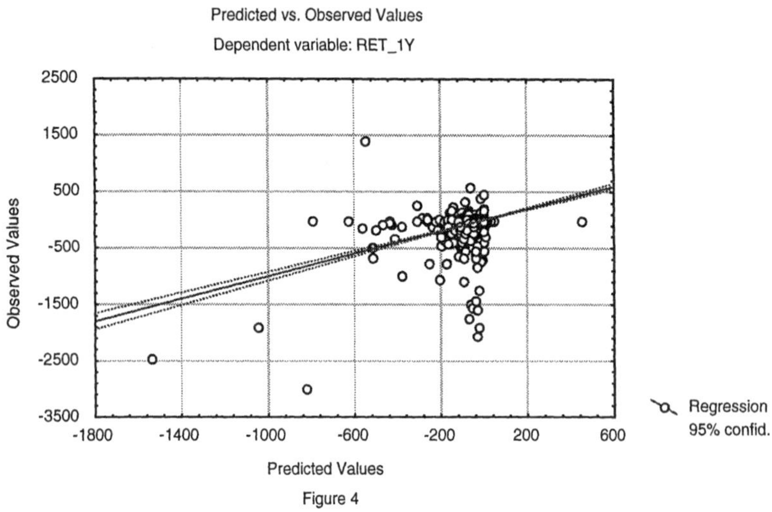

3.4 Time Series Results (Volatility)

An analysis-of-fit of the model to the time series data reveals that on average a good part of the dynamic price differential is explained by the set of historical and rational expectations variables. The result shows an overall R^2 (adjusted for serial autocorrelation and heteroskedasticity) of 0.36 with significant t-statistic on all but the debt-equity variables. The fit of the model is more striking in the case of the manufacturing sector. However, it still leaves a lot of volatility to be explained.

When it comes to an analysis of the volatility in the residuals it is observed that as was true in the cross-section data the F-statistic and DW-statistic are both significantly high, leaving therefore only the variance to be analysed. Further an analysis of the correlation matrix across the various 'nested' models of annual duration suggest that the across the period serial correlations are insignificant. This not only points to the existence of a ten year set of data cointegrated with the price differentials but also to the fact that residuals are 'random walks' over time at least within this ten year history. However, after the conditioning on the variables of the model the errors do follow a 'random walk' pattern. Variability reducing policies targeted at the short-term annual performances are necessary in this respect. We need to examine which type of instruments co-vary with these annual residuals so as to reduce these residuals.

Figures 4.5: Distribution of Raw Residuals

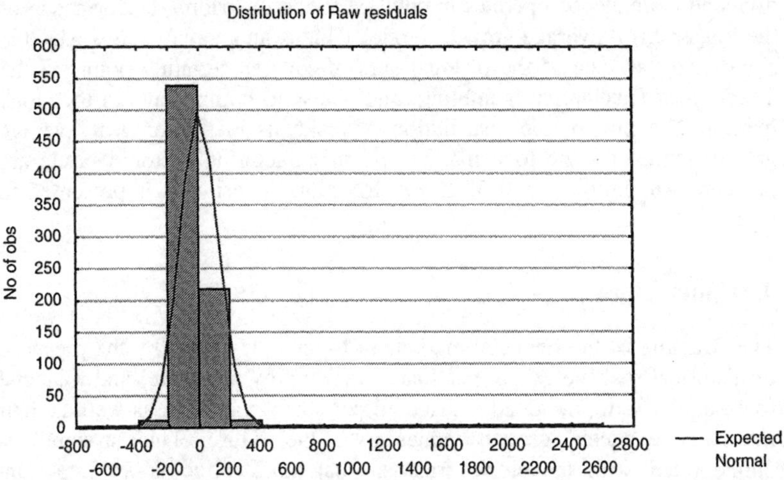

Figure 5

Figure 4.6: Distribution of Raw Residuals

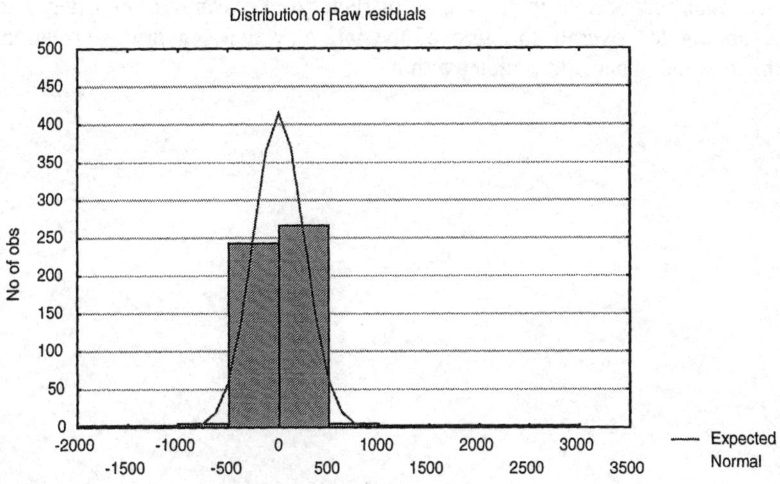

Figure 6

Behaviourally speaking 'myopia' through dividend and expected dividend dependence operates in contrast to the overriding performance of the longer term 'average growth' model. This is an anomaly. However, the significant variance of the residual sum of squares certainly points in the direction of speculative 'gambling' and 'sunspot' components in the stock market. The plot of the distribution of residuals in the ten-year average growth model for the total market and manufacturing sector datasets are presented in figures 4 and 5. The distribution of residuals is presented in figure 6.

4. Conclusions

The structure of the financial markets in India is described by the presence of historical real (net worth per share, profitability per share) and financial (debt-equity ratio, dividend distributed per share) variables as well as their rationally expected growth values over the future. This structure is cointegrated with the stock price so that stock price is an important consideration in making corporate decisions. This is in the light of the fact that although there is considerable residual volatility, lack of explosive components makes cointegration possible. If one compares it with the fact that the relationships within the model are stronger in the annual data in periods distant from 1993 and 1997, the two periods of crashes and other significant events, as discussed in the beginning (which therefore opens up areas of further analysis of structural breaks), then the linear fit, on average, suggests that, albeit with a high degree of volatility, 'planned competition' has been responsible in preventing markets from crashing more often, and changing the overall structure of the interplay between price formation, history and expectations along with it.

References

Bagchi, A. K., *History of the State Bank of India* (State Bank of India, 1998).

Barman, R.B., 'What Determines the Price of Indian Stock; Fundamentals or Bubbles?', ICFAI *Journal of Applied Finance*, (December 1999).

Barman, R.B. and T. P.Madhusoodan, 'Permanent and Temporary Components of Indian Stock Market Returns', *RBI Occasional Papers* (June 1993).

Barua, S.K., ' The Short Run Price Behaviour of Securities: Some Evidence of Indian Capital Market', *Vikalpa* (April 1981).

Barua, S.K. and Raghunathan, 'Soaring Stock Prices Defying Fundamentals', *Economic & Political Weekly*, Nov.17, (1990).

Blanchard O. and M. Watson, 'Bubbles, Rational Expectation & Financial Markets', *Crisis in the Economic & Financial Structure* (MA: Lexington Books, 1982).

Dixit, R.K., *Share Price and Investment in India* (New Delhi: Deep & Deep, 1986).

Dwyer G.P. and R.W. Hafer, 'Do Fundamentals, Bubbles or Neither Determine Stock Prices? Some International Evidence', in Dwyer & Hafer (eds), *The Stock Market: Bubbles, Volatility & Chaos* (Boston: Kluwer Academic Publishers, 1990).

Engle, R. F. and C. W. J. Granger, 'Cointegration and Error Correction: Representation, Estimation and Testing', *Econometrica*, 55 (1987).

Fama, E., 'Efficient Capital Markets', Journal of Finance, 1970.

Fama, E. and K. French, 'Permanent and Temporary Components of Stock Prices', *Journal of Political Economy*, 96(2) (1988).

Froot K.A. and M. Obstfeld, 'Intrinsic Bubbles: The Case of Stock Prices', *American Economic Review*, 81(5), (1991).

Granger, C.W.J. and P. Newbold, *Forecasting Economic Time Series* (N.Y.: Academic Press, 1977).

Gupta, O.P., 'Behaviour of Share Price in India: a Test of Market Efficiencies', New Delhi, 1985.

Obaidullah, M., 'The Price-Earnings Ratio Anatomy in Indian Stock Markets', *Decisions*, (July–September 1991).

Rao, M.J.M., 'Estimating Time-Varying Parameters in Linear Regression Models using a Two-Part Decomposition of the Optimal Control Formulation', *Sankhya*, Series B, 62(3), 2000.

Sarkar, A., K.K. Roy, S.K. Mallick, A. Chakraborti and T. Datta Chaudhuri, *Financial Fragility, Asset Bubbles, Capital Structure and Real Rate of Growth — A Study of the Indian Economy During 1970–99* (The Planning Commission, Govt. of India, 2000–2001)..

Sharma, J.L., 'Efficient Capital Market and Random Character of Stock Price Behavior in a Developing Economy', *Indian Journal of Economics*, October December 1983.

Shiller, R.J., 'Do Stock Prices Move too Much to be Justified by Subsequent Changes in Dividends', *American Economic Review*, 74(3) 1981.

Sundaram, S. M., 'Soaring Stock Prices', *Economic & Political Weekly*, May 04, 1991.

5

A Perspective on Saving, Investment and Macroeconomic Policies in India in the 1990s

Mridul Saggar

1. Introduction

The decade of the 1990s was a different experience for the Indian economy in many ways. First, it started with one of the severest external payments crises. The fiscal profligacy of the 1980s coupled with the oil shock emanating from the Gulf War precipitated a run on the foreign exchange reserves that were depleted to less than a month's level of import financing. Second, there were two clear credit slow-downs at least one of which, and perhaps both, were induced, or at least accommodated by macroeconomic policy stances. Third, the decade was marked by severe exogenous shocks transmitted by the world economy amidst growing cross-border integration. Apart from the Gulf War, the East Asian financial crisis of 1997–98 and the impact of sanctions in the aftermath of the nuclear tests had significant impact on the Indian economy. Fourth, the 1990s were marked by wide-ranging reforms covering both the real and financial sectors. Financial liberalization and financial sector reforms perhaps outstripped the transformation of the real economy. Fifth, there were real gains: the real GDP growth moved to a higher trajectory with lower variance. Finally, saving and investment rates touched new highs raising the spectre of permanently high growth rates that could facilitate India catching-up with Newly Industrialized Countries (NICs) and possibly even with advanced economies. However, some of these gains have since begun to wane.

This chapter seeks to study the trends in saving and investment with a view to improving our understanding of their behaviour in the reforms period. The period of investigation stretches from 1950–51 to 2000–01, though the focus is on 10-years of reforms starting 1992–93.

2. Trends in Aggregate Saving

Saving rates in India have risen impressively over successive decades (Figure 5.1). Gross Domestic Saving (GDS) rate averaged 10.0 per cent in the 1950s, 12.6 per cent in the 1960s, 17.5 per cent in the 1970s, 19.4 per cent in the 1980s and 23.1 per cent in the 1990s. The last decade notched up a 3.7 per cent increment in the gross saving rate on a decadal average basis, that was next only to a 4.9 per cent gain recorded in the 1970s and clearly reversed the deceleration in saving witnessed in the 1980s. In terms of Net Domestic Saving (NDS) rates, the average saving rate improved from 5.6 per cent in the 1950s to 7.1 per cent, 11.0 per cent, 11.2 per cent and 14.8 per cent in the 1960s, 1970s, 1980s and 1990s, respectively.[1] So in net terms, the increment in decadal average for the 1990s at 3.6 per cent was only somewhat less than 3.9 per cent gain in the 1970s and very much higher than the mere 0.2 per cent rise in the 1980s. *Prima-facie*, the reforms of the 1990s have been accompanied by higher saving rates.

Figure 5.1: GROSS & NET DOMESTIC SAVING RATES

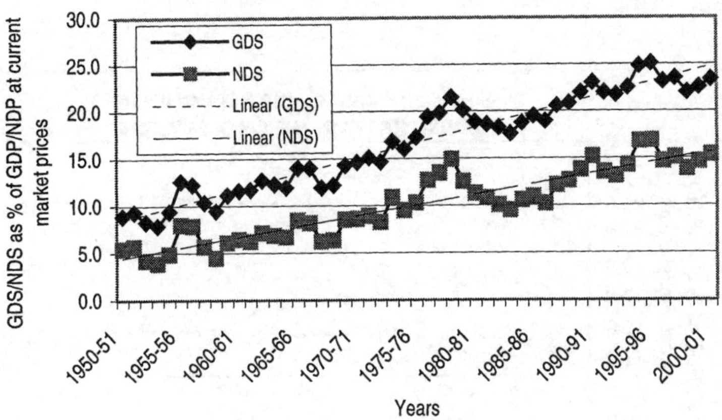

However, although average saving rate has been distinctly higher in the 1990s than the 1980s, the underlying linear trend has been fairly flat in the 10 reform years (Figure 5.2(b)). This is in contrast to the upward sloping linear trend in the pre-reform period 1980–81 to 1990–91 (Figure 5.2(a)).

---

[1] The average GDS and NDS rates for the 10-years of reform period 1991–92 to 2000–01 works out to be the same as that in the decade 1990s.

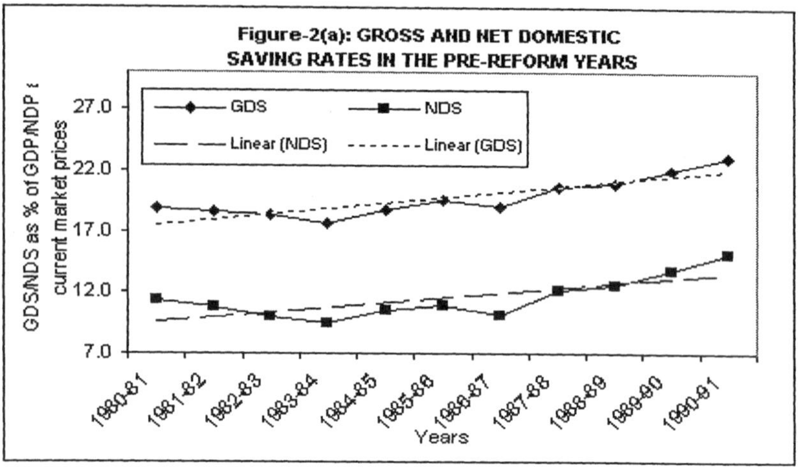
Figure-2(a): GROSS AND NET DOMESTIC SAVING RATES IN THE PRE-REFORM YEARS
GDS
NDS
Linear (NDS)
Linear (GDS)
GDS/NDS as % of GDP/NDP at current market prices
27.0
22.0
17.0
12.0
7.0
1980-81
1981-82
1982-83
1983-84
1984-85
1985-86
1986-87
1987-88
1988-89
1989-90
1990-91
Years

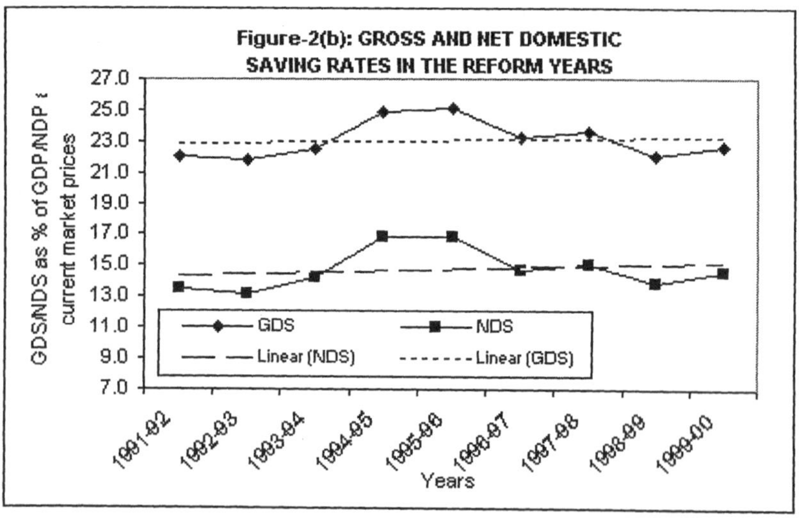
Figure-2(b): GROSS AND NET DOMESTIC SAVING RATES IN THE REFORM YEARS
GDS/NDS as % of GDP/NDP at current market prices
27.0
25.0
23.0
21.0
19.0
17.0
15.0
13.0
11.0
9.0
7.0
GDS
NDS
Linear (NDS)
Linear (GDS)
1991-92
1992-93
1993-94
1994-95
1995-96
1996-97
1997-98
1998-99
1999-00
Years

The saving rate dropped in the early 1990s at the onset of the external payments crisis set in 1991–92, and it started to recover from 1993–94 onwards, reaching the peak of 25.1 per cent in 1995–96 in gross terms[2] surpassing the earlier peak of 23.1 per cent in 1990–91. The saving rate dropped to 22.0 per cent by 1998–99 but recovered to 23.4 per cent in 2000–01. This quick estimate for 2000–01 is not very different from the saving rate in 1990–91, so that in broad terms, the initial gains on the saving front after initiation of reforms appear to have been lost.

The rise in the savings rates in the 1990s over the 1980s has been magnified by the fact that the saving rate averages for the 1980s were lowered by an unprecedented five-year decline in gross and net saving rates during 1979–80 to 1983–84 consequent on the drought of 1979. Saving rates improved during 1984–85 to 1990–91.

To a large extent the failure to sustain the initial gains in aggregate saving in the reform period has been the result of the dismal saving performance of public sector. The gross domestic private saving rate recorded an impressive rise from 20.1 per cent in 1991–92 to 23.2 per cent in 1994–95. Though it fell back to 21.5 per cent in 1996–97, it hit the peak of 25.0 per cent in 1999–00. Public sector saving rate (PSSR) has deteriorated through the 1980s and the 1990s. From a peak of 4.9 per cent in 1976–77, the PSSR began falling since 1983–84, when it dropped 1-percentage point of GDP from 4.4 per cent in 1982–83. It dropped to 1.1 per cent of GDP in 1990–91 — the ninth successive year of this fall. The gross public sector saving rate oscillated in the range of 0.6 per cent to 2.0 per cent, thereafter, before turning negative in 1998–99 and dropping to -1.7 per cent of GDP in 2000–01 (Figure 5.3).

PSSR in the 1990s has averaged a mere 1.0 per cent of GDP against 3.0 per cent in the 1980s. The average for the 10-year reform period 1991–92 to 2000–01 is still lower at 0.7 per cent of GDP and this, to a large extent, explains the puzzle of poorer than expected saving performance in the reform period. In net terms the public sector has been dissaving since 1983–84. By 2000–01, NDS of the public sector was -5.9 per cent of NDP at current market prices. This is a position far away from what proponents of Lawson doctrine would be happy with.[3]

The public sector no longer contributes to domestic saving. Its share in GDS has declined from 21.2 per cent in the 1970s to 15.9 per cent in the 1980s and then to a mere 4.3 per cent in the 1990s (Figure 5.4). The loss of public sector's share in the 1980s was more than compensated for by

---

2 The peak saving rate in net terms of 16.8 per cent was registered in 1994–95 and 1995–96.

3 The Lawson doctrine states that as long as public sector accounts are balanced, private saving reflects the inter-temporal consumption smoothing choices of the individuals and public policy should have no role in this.

saving from the household sector comprising of households, trusts and unincorporated enterprises. The share of this sector improved from 69.8 per cent to 75 per cent. In the 1990s, the loss of the share of the public sector resulted in higher shares for both household sector and private corporate sector, with the former improving its share to 79.9 per cent, while the latter improving its share to 15.7 per cent — up from 9.1 per cent a decade ago.

Figure 5.3: PRIVATE AND PUBLIC GROSS DOMESTIC SAVING

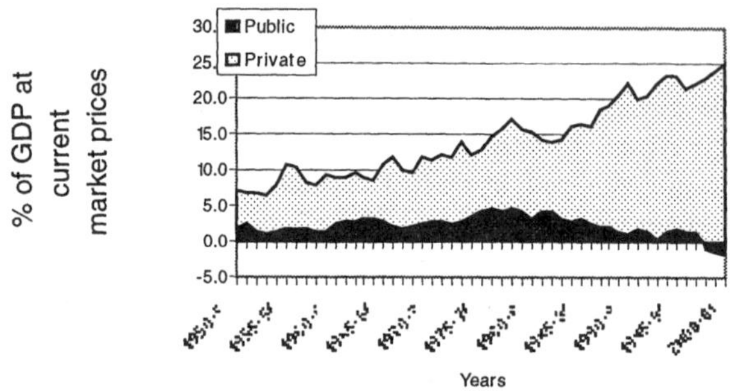

Figure 5.4: SECTORAL SHARES IN GROSS DOMESTIC SAVING

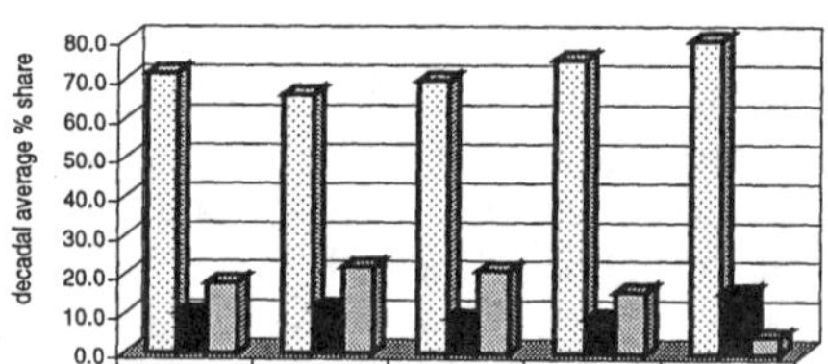

Period	1950/51 to 1959/60	1960/61 to 1969/70	1970/71 to 1979/80	1980/81 to 1989/90	1990/91 to 1999/00
Household	71.7	66.2	69.8	75.0	79.9
Private Corp	10.2	11.8	9.1	9.1	15.7
Public	18.1	22.1	21.2	15.9	4.3

3. Household Saving

Household sector saving is clearly the mainstay of the saving in India, accounting for as much as four-fifths of the aggregate GDS and a fifth of the GDP today. However, improvement in household sector saving rate has been much less in the reforms period beginning 1991–92 than it was during 1982–83 to 1990–91, when in gross terms it improved from 12.3 per cent of GDP to 19.3 per cent of GDP (Figure 5.5). In 2000–01, the household saving rate stood at 20.9 per cent, only marginally above the 1990–91 level and after being lower than that level for seven of the ten of the reform period years for which estimates are available.

Figure 5.5: HOUSEHOLD GROSS DOMESTIC SAVING RATES

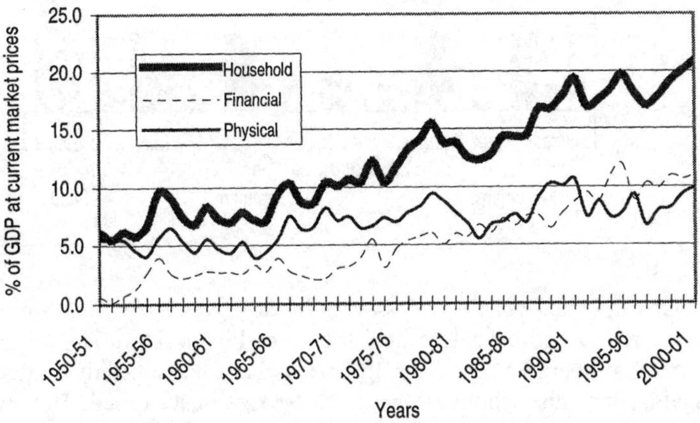

Household saving comprises of saving in the form of financial assets (that is calculated net of accretion to their liabilities) and in the form of physical assets that may take the form of construction, machinery and equipment and changes in stocks. Household saving rate may have stagnated in the reform period beginning 1991–92. However, their saving in financial assets showed a distinct improvement averaging 10.1 per cent in the 1990s against 6.8 per cent in the 1980s.[4] Household saving in physical assets recorded a small rise from an average of 7.8 per cent of GDP in the 1980s to 8.4 per cent in the 1990s. In fact, compared with the

4 The household financial saving rate and physical saving rate averaged 10.3 per cent and 8.3 per cent, respectively in the reform period 1991–92 to 2000–01.

rate of 10.6 per cent in 1990–91, household physical assets saving rate was lower in each of the 10 years of reforms that followed. It was also lower than the household financial saving in each of these years, with the exception of 1995–96. With financial saving outstripping physical saving, a scissors pattern appears to be in place.

Figure 5.6: HOUSEHOLD SAVING IN FINANCIAL INSTRUMENTS

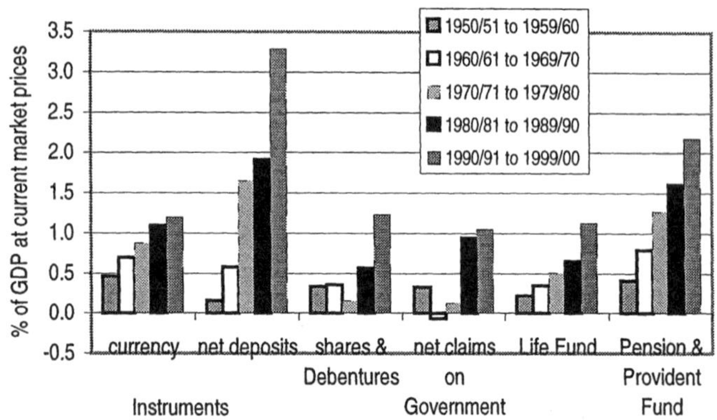

The gains in household financial saving in the 1990s have come from net deposits, shares and debentures and life fund (Figure 5.6).[5] This indicates that financial liberalization in the 1990s may have had a positive influence on saving, but this hypothesis needs to be rigorously tested. Household saving in net deposits increased from 1.9 per cent of GDP in the 1980s to 3.3 per cent of GDP in the 1990s. Household saving in shares and debentures as percentage of GDP doubled from 0.6 per cent to 1.2 per cent over the same period. Household saving in life funds improved from 0.7 per cent of GDP to 1.1 per cent. Net claims on government that includes small saving instruments had witnessed a jump in the 1980s to 0.9 per cent of GDP from a mere 0.1 per cent of GDP in the 1970s. These recorded only a small rise in the 1990s to touch 1.0 per cent of GDP. Contractual saving rates in the form of pension and provident funds continued its step-wise

[5] While aggregate and sectoral saving rates estimates for 2000–01 are available as CSO's quick estimates, there instrument-wise details are not available as yet. Data for earlier years are not revised as per Quick Estimates released on 31 January 2002 in this article as the break-ups are not available.

growth to average 2.2 per cent of GDP in the 1990s compared with 1.6 per cent in the preceding decade, while currency holdings as a percentage of GDP declined marginally in the latter half of the 1990s to 1.1 per cent from 1.3 per cent in the first half.

4. Private Corporate Saving

The private cooperate sector has contributed significantly to the improvement in saving rate in the nineties. Gross private corporate saving rate that had hovered between 0.6 per cent and 2.0 per cent of GDP during 1950–51 to 1988–89, began showing an upward trend improving from 1.7 per cent of GDP in 1987–88 to a peak of 4.9 per cent in 1995–96. It has, however, declined subsequently to 3.7 per cent of GDP in the last two years of the 1990s, before improving to 4.2 per cent 2000–01. The private corporate saving rate in 2000–01 was a clear 1.5-percentage of GDP above the earlier peak of 2.7 pre-reform period, registered in 1990–91. On an average basis, the private corporate saving rate at 3.8 per cent in the 10-years of reforms starting 1991–92 was more than double that of 1.8 per cent in the 1980s.

Non-financial joint stock companies contribute the bulk of private corporate savings, accounting for 85.0 per cent share of the total private corporate saving. These companies improved their saving rate from 1.6 per cent of GDP in the 1980s to 3.1 per cent of GDP in the 1990s (Figure 5.7). Non-financial joint stock companies also improved their saving rate from 0.1 per cent to 0.4 per cent over the same periods. Cooperative banks and credit societies contributed savings equal to nearly 2 per cent of GDP, almost the same as in the 1970s.

Figure 5.7: PRIVATE CORPORATE SAVING

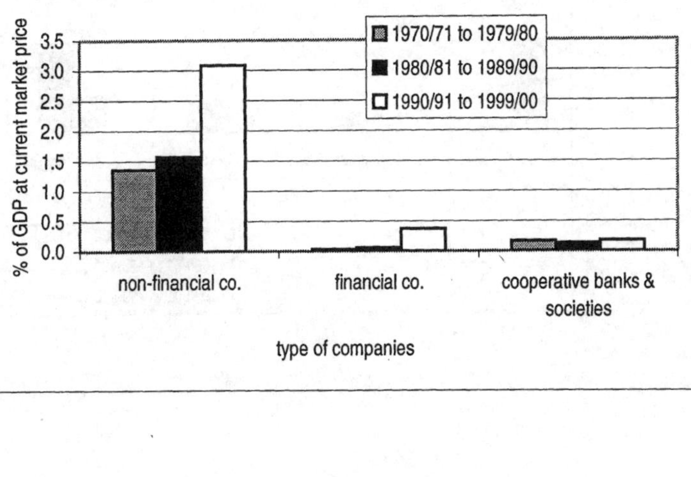

5. Public Saving

The deterioration in public sector saving is really a story of deteriorating current account fiscal position of the general administration of central and sub-national governments that is reflected in large revenue deficits. Reforms in India have not been even paced. Temporally the reforms were loaded upfront, but phased thereafter. Sector-wise, the reforms on the financial sector side have outdone real sector reforms. The real sector reforms have in turn outperformed fiscal and labour sector reforms. Failure to push labour sector reforms has affected the saving of both, the government administration and that of public sector enterprises. The latter has also been affected by unsatisfactory progress on exit policies and disinvestments (privatisation).

Gross saving of the government administration as percentage of GDP declined from the peak of 2.5 per cent in 1978–97 to a trough of -2.5 per cent in 1990–91, when centre's revenue deficit touched 3.3 per cent of GDP (Figure 5.8). It recorded a marginal improvement in next two years before slipping to a new low of -3.0 per cent in 1993–94 with centre's revenue deficit being placed at a whopping 3.8 per cent of GDP. In 1995–96 the dissaving was contained with the rate of -2.0 per cent. But a sharp deterioration followed and in the three-year period 1998–99 to 2000–01, the rate averaged -5.2 per cent, touching -5.5 per cent and of GDP in 1999–00. This deterioration was partly due to slippage on central government's current account and a sharp deterioration in current accounts

Figure 5.8: PUBLIC SAVING

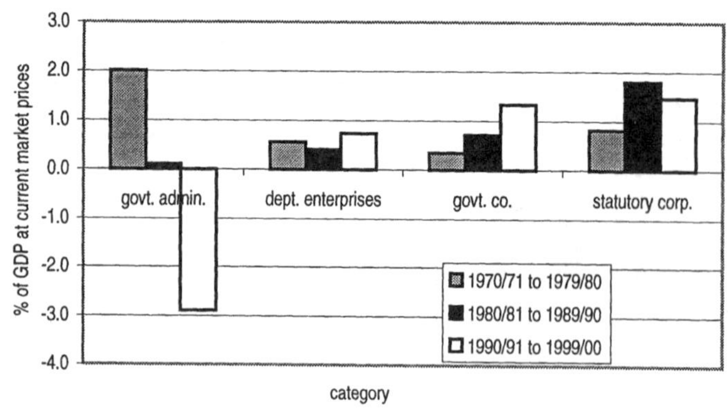

of state governments. Revenue deficit of the states as a percentage of GDP shot up from 1.1 per cent of GDP in 1997–98 to 2.5 per cent of GDP in 1998–99 and may have only marginally improved from that level in 1999–00. Revenue deficit of the centre reattained the high of 3.8 per cent of GDP set in 1998–99. Combined revenue deficit of centre and state governments had bludgeoned to 6.3 per cent of GDP in 1998–99. Up from an average of mere 0.6 per cent in the first half of 1980s, this shows a disquieting position of public finances in the country.

Gross saving of the departmental enterprises averaged 0.7 per cent of GDP in the 1990s compared with 0.4 per cent in the 1980s and 0.6 per cent in the 1970s. Saving of the non-departmental enterprises, especially of government companies improved during the reform period. Government companies' saving averaged 1.3 per cent of GDP in the 1990s compared with 0.7 per cent in the 1980s and 0.3 per cent in the 1970s. Saving of statutory corporations jumped from 0.8 per cent in the 1970s to 1.8 per cent in the 1980s, but declined somewhat to 1.5 per cent of GDP in the 1990s.[6]. Thus reforms helped public enterprises improve their operating surpluses, somewhat. A similar conclusion holds for private sector enterprises, but fiscal imbalances in budgetary operations have wiped away public sector saving. Public sector in India is characterised by sizable disguised unemployment, quite like the phenomenon seen in the agricultural sector. As such, the gains would have been larger if labour sector reforms permitting flexibility in hiring and firing labour were instituted. Labour training and redeployment could accompany such reforms. Lower wage bills would have helped public enterprises improve their surpluses and general government lower its current expenditure. In practice, higher wage settlements added to the wage bills of the central and state governments and contributed to public sector saving rate turning negative

6. Private Corporate Investment

Private corporate fixed investments picked up markedly in the reform years, while inventory rates declined (Figure 5.9).

Most of this investment was in machinery and equipment, and increased from an average of 2.8 per cent in the 1980s to 5.8 per cent in the 1990s. Private corporate sector's GCF in construction as a percentage of GDP doubled from 0.5 per cent to 1.0 per cent over the same period, while inventories declined from 0.9 per cent to 0.4 per cent. Overall, the private

---

6 Saving of the non-departmental enterprises comprising of both, government companies and statutory corporations improved from 1.2 per cent of GDP in the 1970s to 2.5 per cent in the 1980s and further to 3.2 per cent in the 1990s.

sector investment rate increased in four of the first five years of reforms till 1995–96, when it touched a peak of 9.6 per cent, but it declined in each of the years, thereafter to reach 5.9 per cent of GDP in 2000–01. Even after this drop the sector's investment rate is distinctly higher than the pre-reform years.

Figure 5.9: PRIVATE CORPORATE INVESTMENT RATES

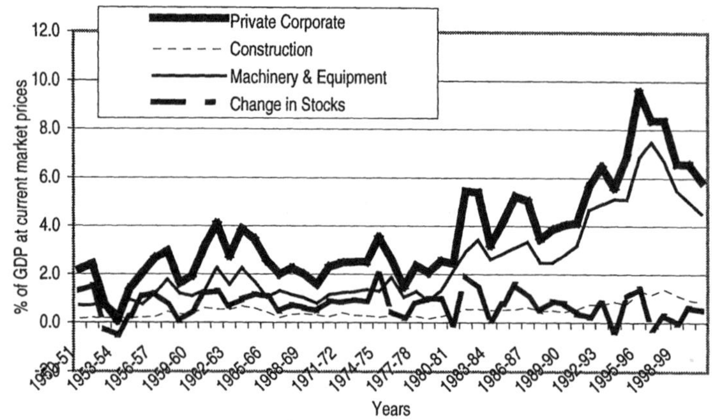

7. Public Investment

Public sector investment rate suffered a steep fall in the reform years (Figure 5.10). Compared to an average of 10.0 per cent of GDP in the 1990s, GCF in public sector averaged only 7.8 per cent in the 1990s and 7.6 per cent of GDP in the 10-year reform period. Public sector investment rates for both, construction and machinery & equipment suffered declines of similar magnitude (Figure 5.10).

Public sector investment rates have declined since 1986–87, when they reached the peak of 11.2 per cent of GDP, up from 5.5 per cent in 1969–70. The decline in public sector investment since mid-1980s has been sustained and more prolonged than the decline that was registered in the latter half of 1960s. Reforms only accelerated the trend of falling public investment rates, raising the importance of knowing the nature of complementarities and substitutability between public and private investments.

Figure 5.10: PUBLIC INVESTMENT RATES

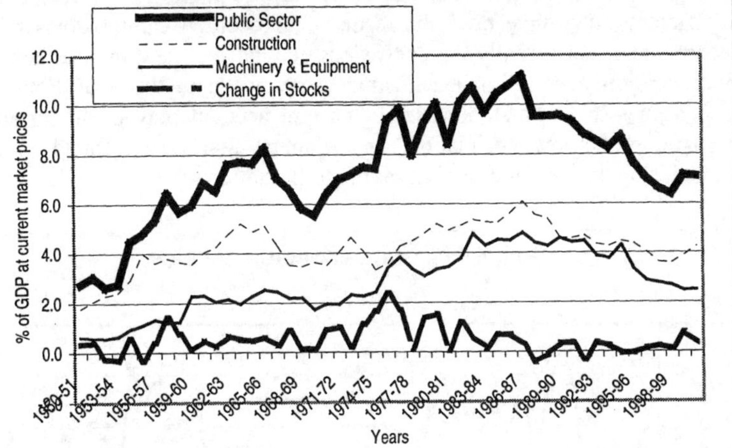

8. Saving-Investment Gaps

The gap between aggregate investment and aggregate saving measures the recourse to foreign saving and is measured by net capital inflows from abroad. Given the balance of payments accounting practices, this is equal to the Current Account Deficit (CAD) with minor adjustments. Thus, foreign saving rate measured formally in national accounts by and large mirrors CAD/GDP ratio. A small opening economy that lags in development, has capital scarcity but is abundant in labour would expect to see increased recourse to foreign saving as the economy liberalizes its capital account as part of the reforms process. This suggests that the 10-years of reform for the Indian economy would be associated with a widening of sustainable CAD/GDP ratio, as also the actual CAD/GDP ratio. However, it is not very clear whether the sustainable CAD/GDP ratio for the Indian economy now is higher than it was 10-years ago, though there are some indications that a CAD/GDP ratio of 2.0 per cent or a little higher should pose no difficulties. What is most striking is that the actual CAD/GDP ratio has fallen after reforms. The foreign saving rate that averaged 1.9 per cent in the 10-years prior to reforms declined to 1.3 per cent in the 10-years of reforms starting 1992–93 (Figure 5.11).

Schneider (1999) found that saving-investment correlation was low for India, which in the context of Feldstein–Horioka (1980) hypothesis implies that capital may be mobile. This is surprising given that foreign saving rates have declined in the 10-years of reforms, when total and private saving rates have increased. Schneider argues that the low correlation coefficients may have been the result of unrecorded capital flows before reforms and that actually the coefficient may have gone down further after liberalization once suitable adjustments are made in the data. Schneider also argues that non-stationarity of current account may be important in explaining the low correlation, an argument that is not found to hold considering that we find foreign saving to be stationary.

Figure 5.11: GROSS FOREIGN SAVINGS

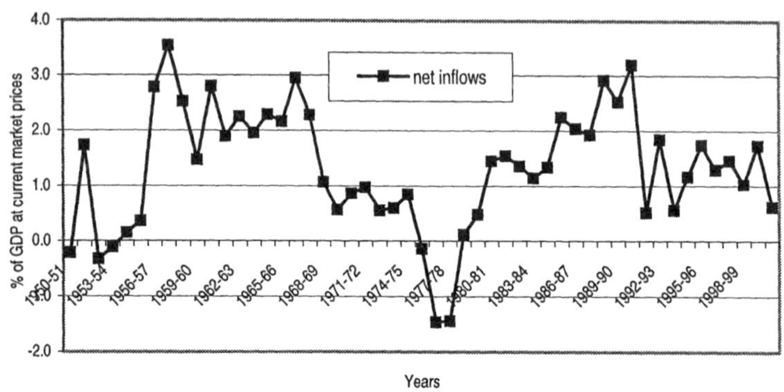

9. Measurement Problems and the Estimates

In drawing any meaningful interpretations from the saving and investment estimates, it is important that due recognition is given to possible measurement problems. Some important indicators are available that measurement problems in saving and investment estimates might have increased in the 1990s. First, a clear reflection of this is available in the form of larger absolute size of errors and omissions shown in the official data in estimates of gross and net investments. In gross terms these errors and omissions were averaged 1.5 per cent of GDP in the 1990s, compared with averages of -0.6 to -0.8 per cent of GDP in the earlier three decades (Figure 5.12). In terms of net investment, the errors and omissions were 1.6 per cent of NDP in the 1990s as against averages of -0.7 to -0.9 per cent of GDP for the earlier three decades. Second, the change in sign of the errors and omissions from negative to a large positive itself may be of some significance.

Figure 5.12: ERRORS AND OMISSIONS IN ESTIMATES OF GROSS AND NET INVESTMENT RATES

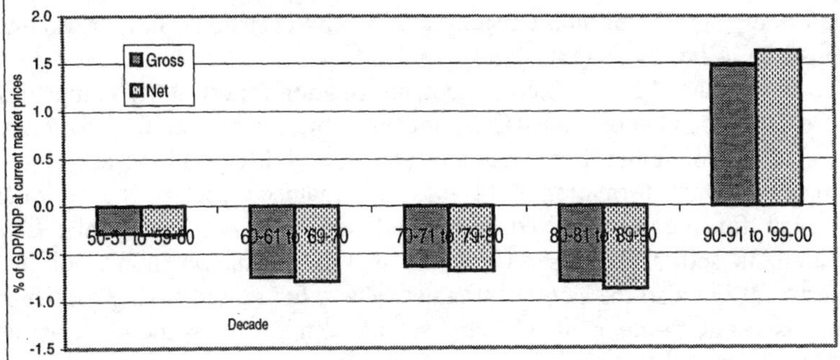

The large errors and omissions are, to an extent, a weakness of the statistical compilation procedures and also reflect structural changes that may have taken place as a result of reforms. The latter too could have biased the estimates.

The estimation problems are inherent in the procedure of compiling household physical asset formation being captured as a residual. Estimates for household capital formation are arrived at by first estimating the capital formation for the country as a whole using the commodity-flow approach, and then netting the independent capital formation estimates for the organised sectors, *viz.*, public and private corporate sectors, for whom the accounts data are available. Capital formation data for the government administration and departmental commercial undertakings (DCUs) is available from expenditure data contained in the government budgets. The expenditures are susceptible to large leakages and do not necessarily constitute the best basis for investment estimation. For the non-departmental commercial undertakings (NDCUs) annual accounts provide the information on investments and are more reliable, though lack of information on enterprises of sub-national governments does affect the reliability of the estimates.

A more serious problem arises in relation to estimates of investments of the private corporate business enterprises. Both saving and capital formation estimates for this sector are affected by lack of information on a population basis. These estimates are generated by the Reserve Bank of India (RBI) on the basis of annual accounts of a sample of large and medium firms by blowing up the sample estimates by a multiplier arrived at by dividing the total paid-up-capital (p.u.c.) as obtained from data available with the Department of Company Affairs (DCA) by the p.u.c. of the RBI sample study that forms the basis of investment estimation. DCA's total population figure for p.u.c. is itself subject to large errors with a number of listed companies being non-existent and also by occasional large revisions that the DCA has made in its data.

To compound these problems, poor information reporting by companies to Registrar of Companies (ROCs) makes it impossible for RBI to adopt any scientific sampling frame. As a result of reliability problems associated with the capital formation data for the organised sector, the residual obtained for the unorganised household sector is also unreliable. The problem is serious because the errors in this estimation affect not just investment but also the saving estimates, where household saving estimates are biased one-to-one as its physical saving components is the same as the household capital formation.

Household financial saving that is estimated by RBI are more reliable, but financial innovations in the 1990s may have affected their quality to a degree as several new instruments and practices came into place that were not immediately and correctly captured with the existing estimation methodology. For instance, estimates of household investment in shares and debentures may have been biased, as theses are calculated by deducting from total primary market mobilisations the shares and debentures accretion of the organised sectors, as is available from the flow of funds account. As the flow of funds accounts are not available after 1993–94, the estimates may be subject to revisions once more complete information becomes available. Financial saving may also have been downward biased for some initial period as a system to collect information on innovative instruments, such as warrants that may have got converted did not exist and data on investments in mutual funds instruments was not fully collected for some time. Many of these problems have been recognised in official reports, specially the Expert Group set up under the chairmanship of Chelliah (GOI 1996) and the National Statistical Commission set up under the chairmanship of Rangarajan (GOI 2001). Several private researchers or research bodies have also raised issues of methodology or data reliability.[7] In view of the above some circumspection is necessary for drawing any inferences from the data on trends in saving and investment.

9.1 Saving, Investment and Growth

Development and growth theories are replete with examples of how saving and investment play a critical role in fostering economic growth. However,

[7] These include EPW Research Foundation (1995), Goyal (1996) and Mühleisen (1997).

statistical evidence on this issue is not so forthcoming. In this section, we look at the statistical evidence formally.

9.2 Saving-Growth Causality

Cross-country econometric evidence overwhelmingly supports the hypothesis that saving does not cause growth, but growth does cause saving — a hypothesis that has come to be known as the Carroll–Weil hypothesis (Carroll and Weil, 1994). These results are generally based on Granger causality tests. Existing evidence in respect of India supports the presence of Carroll–Weil hypothesis. Mühleisen (1997), provides Granger causality results for the saving rate and growth rate relationship for the Indian economy for the period 1950–51 to 1994–95 showing that generally growth causes saving, but saving does not cause growth. These results of Mühleisen are arrived at from bivariate VARs and consistently rejected causality from saving to growth irrespective of whether aggregate, public or private saving rates are considered and whether the VARs are run in levels or first difference. Mühleisen also asserts that this outcome was robust to variations in VAR length. In this paper, Mühleisen's investigation is revisited for a longer period, *viz*, 1950–51 to 2000–01. The results are summarized in Table 5.1(a) & 5.1(b).

Table 5.1(a) Saving-Output Causality, 1950–51

Saving Rate	Direction of Granger Causality (VARs in levels)			
	Saving → Output		Output → Saving	
	F	Significance	F	Significance
Lag=1				
Total	0.37	54.7	7.34**	0.9
Public	0.52	47.2	3.47*	6.8
Private	0.0001	99.0	15.68**	0.03
Foreign	0.05	82.7	1.06	30.9
Lag=2				
Total	0.51	60.2	5.46**	0.8
Public	0.42	65.8	4.92**	1.2
Private	0.15	86.3	9.59**	0.04
Foreign	1.26	44.8	1.16	32.4

Notes: (1) Granger F-statistics are based on bivariate VARs between output measured as log of real GDP and total, public or private saving rates and output measured by real GDP growth and foreign saving rate.
(2) Significance level is given in percentage. ** denotes significance at 1% level; * denotes significance at 5% level.
(3) Shaded cells relate to chosen order of the VAR based on multiple criteria, viz., AIC, SBC, LR & Adjusted LR Tests. In this case, invariably the AIC & SBC select a lag length of 1.

Table 5.1(b): Saving-Output Causality, 2000–01

Saving Rate	Direction of Granger Causality (VARs in first difference)			
	Saving → Output		Output → Saving	
	F	Significance	F	Significance
Lag=1				
Total	0.70	40.8	3.35*	7.4
Public	0.76	38.9	1.76	19.2
Private	0.17	67.8	1.52	22.5
Foreign	1.32	25.7	2.06	15.8
Lag=2				
Total	0.24	78.7	1.26	29.3
Public	0.24	78.9	4.49**	1.7
Private	0.08	92.6	2.10	13.5
Foreign	1.27	29.1	0.99	37.8

Notes: (1) Granger F-statistics are based on bivariate VARs between output measured as log of real GDP and total, public or private saving rates and output measured by real GDP growth and foreign saving rate.
(2) Significance level is given in percentage. ** denotes significance at 1% level; * denotes significance at 5% level.
(3) Shaded cells relate to chosen order of the VAR based on multiple criteria, viz., AIC, SBC, LR & Adjusted LR Tests. In this case, invariably the AIC & SBC select a lag length of 1.

The results obtained have important differences with that in the IMF study by Mühleisen. First, Mühleisen runs bivariate causality between saving rates and growth rate. This is surprising because real GDP growth rate was found to be level stationary I(0) process, while total, public and private saving rates are observed to be unit root or difference stationary I(1) process. Considering the results of Augmented Dickey–Fuller (ADF) and Phillip–Peron (PP) tests we run bivariate VARs between log of real GDP and the total, public or private saving rates, as log of GDP is a unit root process. Second, Mühleisen's outcome for Carroll and Weil hypothesis was robust to variations in VAR length and the specification of variables in levels or differences. However, it is not at all clear from Mühleisen's paper what lag lengths were considered. His paper does not provide much empirical evidence and only reports the significance levels of Granger F-test without any accompanying information on F-statistics or the chosen lag lengths. In our more formal approach, we select VAR lengths based on Akaike Information Criteria (AIC) and the Schwarz Bayesian Criteria (SBC). In our case, both AIC and SBC select one lag for bivariate VARs of real GDP with total saving, private saving, public saving and foreign saving. A short lag is also justified for annual data. Besides, with a sample size of 50 observations, we explicitly recognise that the choice of long lags may lead to over-parametrization. We, nevertheless, present results for both one and two lags to demonstrate that the results are robust to lag length selection. Third, unlike Mühleisen, we do not obtain neat Carroll–Weil type results when VARs are run in levels or first difference of the variables between saving rates and growth rates. However, essential elements of Mühleisen's results are found to hold when bivariate VARs are run between saving rates and log of real GDP. Causality runs from output to saving and not the other way round. We do not consider running VAR in first difference as necessary or even advisable. There is a good amount of econometric theory that suggests that such transformation is best avoided. However, there is a school of thought that believes in VAR estimation with stationary variables alone and in this case the VAR in first difference is relevant for causality inferences. However, under this belief causation between saving rates and output is rather poor and causality does not seem to be running in any direction. In case of level VARs, while Mühleisen finds that GDP to saving rates Granger F-statistics are significant at 1 per cent level for all saving rates, in our exercise the output to public saving rate causality holds only at 5 per cent level. Fourth, Mühleisen does not consider the possible role of foreign saving. We find foreign saving rate to be level stationary process and consider Granger causality from a bivariate VAR of foreign saving rate and real GDP growth rate. The results obtained show that causality does not run in any direction between foreign saving rate and real GDP growth rate. This is important as capital inflows are known to have caused real appreciation and a significant adverse impact on monetary control (Kohli 2001).

However, one needs to interpret the causality results with some caution. VAR specifications are more useful for data sets spanning a long period. Second, it is best to infer that Granger causality tests are more indicative of whether the inclusion of lags of a variable improves the forecasting performance of the other variable, rather than being a solid evidence of causation. Bivariate VARs also have the limitation that they are unable to model interactions with other macro-economic variables. For instance, the saving rate may be raised by financial deepening or financial reforms instead of real GDP. The interest sensitivity and inflation sensitivity of saving also require attention. We undertake supplementary exercise later in this chapter through cointegrating VARs between some such variables. The results in this section, therefore, must be interpreted with caution and in conjunction with theoretical reasoning that saving and investment do have a role to play in economic growth.

10. Investment-Growth Causality

Mühleisen does not examine lead/lag relationship between investment and growth. The results in this paper show that it is not easy to infer on direction of causality between investment and output. Based on ADF and

PP tests we find that rate of public sector investment (GCF/GDP at current market prices) is unit root I(1) processes. However, total GCF and private investments were observed to be trend series and level stationary I(0) processes based on the two unit root tests.

Granger causality results based on bivariate VARs between investment and output show that while private and total investment rate does Granger cause real GDP growth rate, the same cannot be said of public investment rates (Table 5.2). This result seemed to hold even when VAR lag length was increased to two lags, though given the annual data and formal lag length selection of based on SBC, one lag could be considered as justified. Real output growth does not appear to Granger cause investment in any case.

Table 5.2: Investment-Output Causality

Investment Rate	Direction of Granger Causality (VARs in levels)			
	Investment → Output		Output → Investment	
	F	Significance	F	Significance
Lag=1				
Total	5.27**	2.5	0.08	78.0
Public	0.39	53.7	0.01	90.9
Private	4.43**	4.1	0.16	58.8
Lag=2				
Total	2.98*	6.1	2.57*	8.8
Public	1.49	23.6	0.80	45.6
Private	3.92**	2.7	1.10	34.2

Notes: (1) Granger F-statistics are based on bivariate VARs between output measured as log of real GDP and public investment rate and output measured by real GDP growth and total GCF and private investment rates.

(2) Significance level is given in percentage. ** denotes significance at 1% level; * denotes significance at 5% level.

(3) Shaded cells relate to chosen order of the VAR based on multiple criteria, viz., AIC, SBC, LR & Adjusted LR Tests. In event of conflicting signals from AIC & SBC, the LR-test & Adjusted LR-tests in this case are found to invariably provide the same lag selection. Therefore, SBC is preferred. SBC is also preferred for its short lag length selection, considering the limited number of total observations.

It is interesting to note that ten years of reforms have seen a sharp drop in public investment rates accompanied by an impressive increase in private investment rates. During this period the private investment rate averaged 15.3 per cent in comparison with 12.6 per cent in the ten years prior to reforms. The public sector investment rate dropped to an average of 7.6 per cent compared with an average of 10.0 per cent in the ten years prior to reforms. The direction of Granger causality from private investment to growth, this augurs well for the Indian economy.

However, the results obtained on saving-output causality and investment-output causality are somewhat paradoxical and point to the need for extreme caution in deriving conclusions. They also indicate need for further investigation, perhaps in a multivariate setting.

Financial Development and Saving

We consider modeling cointegrated VARs between saving rates and other variables that might have a long-run relationship with them and set up a cointegrating VAR between private, public saving and foreign saving rates, log of real GDP and finance ratio as a financial deepening variable. All these variables, except foreign saving are I(1) processes. Foreign saving rate is I(0) and is introduced as an exogenous variable in the cointegrating VAR. Other studies have attempted to capture financial development through variables such as income velocity of money or by money/GDP ratio as a financial deepening variable. These are, however, poor proxies for financial development as they capture monetary behaviour rather than the role of finance in development. Fortunately, a rich time series of flow of funds accounts are available for the Indian economy starting 1951–52. We compute the Finance Ratio (FR) from these accounts as total financial issues by all sectors of the economy divided by Net National Product (NNP) at current market prices.[8]

Using the computed data on FR, formal Johansen Maximum likelihood procedure was adopted to test for cointegration between public and private foreign saving rates, log of real GDP and the FR. Other variables were not introduced in this VAR as it would have lowered degrees of freedom inordinately since we had only 50 observations. Alternative VAR specifications were considered later for inflation and real interest rate as determinants of private saving. The use of Full Information Maximum Likelihood (FIML) procedure makes the results more reliable, as they are not order sensitive except in case of impulse response analysis.

Johansen's multivariate procedure for cointegration employs a p-dimensional vector autoregressive (VAR) model with Gaussian errors:

$$z_t = A_1 z_{t-1} + \ldots + A_k z_{t-k} + \mu + \psi D_t + \varepsilon_t, \; t=1, \ldots T \qquad (1)$$

[8] The RBI monograph on flow of funds accounts (RBI 2000) computes Finance Ratio as the ratio of primary issues (i.e. issues by all sectors other than banks and other financial institutions) to National Income. This, however, is not the most appropriate definition of Finance Ratio, as it does not capture the overall financial deepening as it captures direct market-based finance and ignores financial intermediation. Therefore, Finance Ratio is recomputed as total financial issues by all sectors as ratio of NNP at current market prices. As flow of funds accounts are available up to 1995–96, data for subsequent years has been extrapolated.

where z_t is a p X 1 vector of stochastic variables, $z_{-k+1}, \ldots, z_0$ are fixed, $\varepsilon 1, \ldots \varepsilon_T$ are niid(0,Σ) D_t is a vector of non-stochastic variables, such as seasonal dummies or intervention dummies. In its general form, D_t can also contain stochastic variables that are weakly exogenous and are excluded from the cointegration space. Z_{ts} are mostly I(1) variables, but technically speaking only two of the variables need be I(1) for the cointegration to exist with unit root variables.

The Error correction model (ECM) is

$$\Delta z_t = \Gamma_1 \Delta z_{t-1} + \ldots + \Gamma_{k-1} \Delta z_{t-k+1} + \Pi z_{t-1} + \mu + \psi D_t + \varepsilon_t \tag{2}$$

The cointegration hypothesis is based on the reduced rank of Π matrix:

$$H1[r]: \Pi = \alpha\beta' \tag{3}$$

Where α and β are p X r matrices of full rank. The null hypothesis implies that process Δz_t is stationary, zt is non-stationary, but β' z_t is stationary (Johansen, 1991).

Decomposing the deterministic term, the model can be reformulated as:

$$\Delta z_t = \Gamma_1 \Delta z_{t-1} + \alpha \left(\begin{bmatrix} \beta \\ \mu_1 \\ \delta_1 \end{bmatrix} \right) \tilde{z}_{t-1} + \alpha_{\perp}\mu_2 + \alpha_{\perp}\delta_2 t + \varepsilon_t \tag{4}$$

where the third term pertain to linear trend slopes in data and the last term pertain to quadratic trend coefficients. For details, Johansen (1995) may be cited. Five different models restricting deterministic components are developed. The model with unrestricted intercept and allowing linear trend in data, though not in cointegrating relation, suits our analysis. The choice of this VAR specification was made considering that no *a-priori* theoretical reason exist to for a constant to appear in a set of cointegrationg relationship among the chosen variables that may prompt us to constrain the intercept or to for us to expect a trend in the cointegrating relation between these variables. We introduce foreign saving as an I(0) exogenous variable in our long-run relationship.

The results of the Maximum Eigenvalue and the Trace tests are reported in Tables 5.3(a) and 5.3(b), respectively.

The Eigenvalue tests for the null of the at most *r* cointegration vectors against the alternative of *r* cointergrating vectors. The Trace test provides the LM statistic for at most *r* cointegrating vectors against an alternative of r+1 or more cointegrating vectors. Both tests show presence of one cointegrating vector for the chosen set of variables.

The cointegrating vector normalised and expressed in terms of private saving takes the form:

Sp=-0.35807Sg-2.7702logY+0.54794FR (5)
(0.2003) (3.0450) (0.1455)

Figures in bracket below the coefficients in equation (5) are asymptotic standard errors. Given the high standard error for log of real GDP (log Y), we reestimate the long-run cointegrating relationship by imposing the over-identifying restriction and forcing the log real GDP coefficient to zero. The log-likelihood ratio statistics for this restriction provides justification for the restriction. The resultant cointegrating vector is reported as equation (6) below:

Sp=-0.33557Sg-0.0000logY+0.41701FR (6)
(0.1733) (0.0182)

Table 5.3(a): Cointegration with unrestricted intercepts and no trends in the VAR: LR Test Based on Maximal Eigenvalue of the Stochastic Matrix

Null	Alternative	Statistic	95% Critical Value	90% Critical Value
r = 0	r = 1	39.0878	27.4200	24.9900
r<= 1	r = 2	13.1866	21.1200	19.0200
r<= 2	r = 3	4.4067	14.8800	12.9800
r<= 3	r = 4	1.0358	8.0700	6.5000

Table 5.3(b): Cointegration with unrestricted intercepts and no trends in the VAR Cointegration LR Test Based on Trace of the Stochastic Matrix

Nul	lAlternative	Statistic	95% Critical Value	90% Critical Value
r = 0	r>= 1	57.7169	48.8800	45.7000
r<= 1	r>= 2	18.6291	31.5400	28.7800
r<= 2	r>= 3	5.4425	17.8600	15.7500
r<= 3	r = 4	1.0358	8.0700	6.5000

It is obvious from the equation that public saving crowds out private saving in the long-run and that private saving is largely determined by financial deepening in the long-run. This provides credence to the belief that financial liberalization that may have helped the deepening and widening of various financial markets in the reforms period may have supported the rise in private saving rates for the Indian economy during 1990s.

To study the impact of short-run dynamics we construct the ECM as OLS regression in first difference with the residuals of cointegrating equation being stationary. We also introduce tax rate defined as tax revenue as a ratio of GDP as a stationary variable to provide additional information from the ECM. The estimated ECM is:

$$\Delta Sp = \underset{(4.50)}{3.2180} - \underset{(-2.67)}{0.3778}\Delta Sf - \underset{(-1.91)}{0.1113}\Delta Sg - \underset{(-1.88)}{0.4815}\Delta t - \underset{(-3.74)}{0.3798}ECM(-1) \qquad (7)$$

The joint modeling of the long-run relationship between private and public saving rates with financial deepening show that public saving does crowd out private saving. However, the coefficient restriction of -1 for the Ricardian equivalence test is rejected. The coefficient of -0.34 obtained implies that for a 1-percentage point increase in public saving rate, the private saving rate falls by a third. This means that the sharp decline in public saving rate in the reforms period may have contributed to a rise in private saving rate, but the rise failed to fully compensate for the fall in public saving and resulted in lowering the overall GDS rate from the level it could have attained if fiscal reforms had progressed at a desired pace. On the other hand, financial deepening seemed to have contributed favourably to improved domestic saving performance in India over the long-run. The Finance Ratio seemed to have improved to an average of nearly 40 per cent in the first four years of reform (1992–93 to 1995–96) for which the data is available so far from an average of 31.7 per cent in the six years prior to reforms (1985–86 to 1991–92). It is, therefore, reasonable to presume that financial development had a crucial role to play in improving the saving performance in the reform years. Several new instruments and new institutions emerged to improve the choice of saving vehicles for the households and corporates.

The ECM equations throw some added insights. In the equation for private saving one finds that the exogenous I(0) foreign saving variable has a significant negative coefficient. The short-run dynamics of private saving are such that a rise in foreign saving rate by 1.0 per cent leads to a fall in private saving rate by 0.38 per cent. The short-run impact of fiscal policy on private saving is reflected in the negative relationship between public saving (Sg) and the tax rate (t) on private saving. Incorporation of tax rate for ECM in first difference using residuals of the cointegrating equation is justified as the variables are stationary and other stationary variables could be included in the OLS equation.

The impulse response functions (Figure 5.13) show fairly quick adjustment to shocks in the variables. As an example, the generalized impulse response to unit standard error shock to public saving is reported below:

Figure 5.13: GENERALIZED IMPULSE RESPONSE(S) TO ONE S.E. SHOCK IN THE EQUATION FOR SG

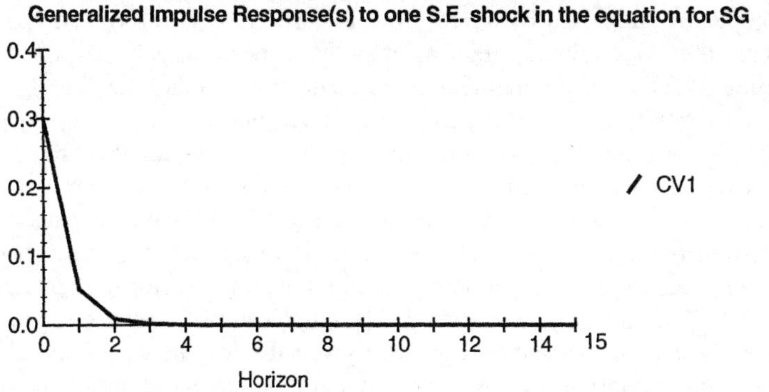

The persistence profile also shows fairly quick adjustment. The quick adjustment to shocks is understandable as agents make most of their portfolio adjustments within a year to changing macroeconomic and financial environment, with balance of adjustment following through in the succeeding year.

A parallel analysis was conducted for cointegration between private saving, WPI inflation rate and real interest rate computed as SBI advance rate minus the WPI inflation rate. While trace and eigenvalue tests revealed existence of two cointegration vectors, meaningful signs were obtained only in one of the case and asymptotic standard errors were high enough to conclude that saving rate was not sensitive to inflation and real interest rates.

5. Conclusions

The narrative, descriptive and econometric evidence provided in this chapter lead us to conclude that reforms brought about some gains on the saving-investment front but these were limited. The initial gains may have been supported partly by asset boom. However, the stock prices declined sharply and resulted in lower mobilization of saving from the households by the corporates directly in the form of primary issues or intermediated through mutual funds or other financial institutions. To that extent the lowering of the saving rate in later years of the reform period can be considered to be the result of dampening of the wealth effect that brought about the initial gains.

The gains in private saving were largely supported by financial deepening supported by the reforms. Failure of fiscal reforms to keep pace with the wide-ranging reforms may have been largely responsible for limited gains on saving and investment front. Sharp decline in public saving rate in the reforms period may have contributed to a rise in private saving rate, but the rise failed to fully compensate for the fall in public saving rate and resulted in lowering the overall GDS rate from the level it could have attained, if the fiscal reforms would have progressed at a desired pace. The econometric evidence in this paper suggests that private saving rate rises by only a third of the loss in public sector saving rate.

We find that it is not easy to decipher causality between saving and growth and investment and growth, given the low power of the unit root tests and limitations of VAR and cointegration methodologies in the face of relatively small sample sizes. The Carroll–Weil hypothesis is upheld, perhaps more as a statistical quirk and it is best to interpret these results with caution and in conjunction with theoretical logic. While this paper has provided new evidence and added perspectives on saving and investment in Indian economy, further theoretical and empirical work is necessary to improve our understanding of the saving and investment behaviour in the reforms period.

References

Carroll, C. and D. Weil, 'Saving and Growth: A Reinterpretation', *Carnegie–Rochester Conference Series on Public Policy*, 40 (1994), 133–92.

EPW Research Foundation, 'Economic Reforms and Rate of Saving', *Economic and Political Weekly*, 27 (April 1995), 893–9.

Feldstein, Martin and Charles Horoika, 'Domestic Saving and International Capital Flows', *Economic Journal*, 90 (1980), 314–29.

Government of India, *Saving and Capital Formation in India: 1950–51 to 1994–95: Report of the Expert Group on Saving and Capital Formation* (Chairman: Raja Chelliah) (New Delhi: Department of Statistics, Government of India, (1996).

Goyal, Ashima, 'Savings: When Data is Doubted Can Theory Help?', *Economic and Political Weekly* (1996).

Johansen, S., *Likelihood Based Inference on Cointegration in the Vector Autoregressive Model* (Oxford: Oxford University Press, 1995).

Kochar, A., 'Smoothing Consumption by Smoothing Income: Hours-of-Work Response to Indiosyncratic Agricultural Shocks in Rural India', *Review of Economics and Statistics*, 81 (1999), 50–61.

Kohli, Renu, 'Capital Flows and Their Macroeconomic Effects in India', *IMF Working Paper, WP/01/192* (Washington, D.C.: International Monetary Fund, 2001).

Lahiri, Ashok K., 'Dynamics of Asian Saving: The Role of Growth and Age Structure', *IMF Staff Paper*, 36 (1989), 228–61.

Ludvigson, S. and C. Steindel, 'How Important is the Stock Market Effect on Consumption?', *Federal Reserve Bank of New York Economic Policy Review*, 5 (1999), 29–52.

Mühleisen, Martin, 'Improving India's saving Performance', *IMF Working Paper, WP/97/4* (Washington, D.C.: International Monetary Fund, 1997).

RBI (Reserve Bank of India), *Flow of Funds Accounts of the Indian Economy: 1951–52 to 1995–96* (Mumbai: Reserve Bank of India, 2000).

Rosenzweig, Mark R., 'Saving Behaviour in Low Income Countries', *Oxford Review of Economic Policy*, 17(1) (2001), 40–54

Saggar, Mridul and Partha Ray, 'Inflation, Saving and Public Policies in India: Will Indexation Help?', in T. Hansen, and M. Griffith (eds), *Inflation, Growth and Development*, EDAP Joint Policy Studies No. 3 (Korean Development Institute & the Australian National University for UNDP, 1998).

Schneider, Benu, 'Saving-Investment Correlations and Capital Mobility in Developing Countries with Special Reference to India', *Working Paper No. 48* (New Delhi: International Council for Research on International Economic Relations, 1999).

Schmidt–Hebbel, K., Luis Serven and Andres Soliamno, 'Saving and Investment: Paradigms, Puzzles and Policies', *The World Bank Research Observer*, 11(1) (1996), 87–117.

6

Exchange Rate Policy in India

Partha Sen

1. Introduction

This chapter examines the Indian exchange rate experience since the start of the liberalization process in 1991. I analyze macroeconomic data pertaining to the external sector and the relationship between foreign capital flows and the exchange rate. In the last decade, the various items in the capital account of the balance of payments have had governmental controls removed. The exchange rate can be said to be increasingly 'determined' by these flows (and, of course, the policy stance in response to them).

I also survey the debate on full convertibility of the capital account among Indian policymakers in particular and developing countries in general. Should capital account liberalization be ordained in a phased manner or instantaneously? I will evaluate these arguments and briefly analyze where India stands today.

This chapter brings together two strands: the exchange rate experience in India in the last decade, and the lessons that Indian policy-makers may draw in charting the future course of the economy (in the area of monetary policy and the external sector) from the experience of those economies in Asia and Latin America that opened up their capital accounts.

2. The Macroeconomics of the External Sector since Liberalization

The Indian financial system was rigidly controlled — as was the industrial sector — until the balance of payments crisis of 1990–91. In spite of this it did not necessarily perfectly fit the description of a common feature of a developing economy — financial repression. Financial repression is not a structural feature but arises due to populist pressures. It involves keeping interest rates artificially low and appropriating funds for financing the government deficit. India has had banks and a stock market for over a century and it has a diversified production structure. Since Indira Gandhi's ascent to power, however, the financial system was used for populist ends. Banks were nationalized and a vast network of branches created. The system was very successful in mobilizing savings but the asset side of the banks' ledgers told a sorry story. A high cash-reserve ratio (CRR) and statutory liquidity ratio (SLR) meant that very little was left for lending on commercial terms. The stock market was regulated with the Controller of Issues calling the shots. A superficial reading of the statistics — say the money to GDP ratio — would give a misleading picture about how developed India was in financial terms at the end of the eighties.

Some tentative steps had been taken to unshackle the financial sector in the light of the recommendations of the Chakravarty Committee in 1985. From the viewpoint of exchange rate policy, the second half of the 1980s was different from the period 1947–84 in that real exchange rate targeting was practiced with a view to improve the country's export performance. The real effective exchange rate depreciated by 30 per cent between 1985–86 and 1989–90 due to nominal depreciation of about 45 per cent. If allowance is made for tax breaks and other subsidies to exporters, the real depreciation could be as high as 40 per cent.[1] But such was the centralized process of decision-making in the country (and the inconsequential nature of the Reserve Bank of India (RBI)) that this decision on real depreciation was taken by the Union Cabinet!

During this period exports rose at an annual rate of five percent and imports (also liberalized somewhat) at eight per cent.[2] The fiscal deficit had ballooned to 8.4 per cent of GDP and the current account deficit was 3.1 per cent of GDP (in 1990–91). The Gulf War exposed the fragility of the macroeconomic balance in India — the shock was temporary and at most amounted to one per cent of GDP but caused a full-blown balance of payments crisis.

After the damage control exercise and a general election, the new government at the Centre started pursuing a policy of liberalization — mainly in international trade and the financial system.[3] In the financial sector entry of foreign banks, deregulation of interest rates, reduction of CRR and SLR etc., occurred in quick succession and rather painlessly.

---

1 See Joshi and Little (1994), for an account of the macroeconomic developments in this period.

2 There is some discrepancy about the foreign trade figures depending on the source — see Joshi and Little (1994), Chapter 7.

3 See Sen (2001) for an account.

Following the crisis of 1990–91, the RBI moved swiftly towards liberalizing the current account. The rupee was devalued by 18 per cent in July 1991. Between 1991 and 1993 it replaced exim scrips with a dual exchange rate where the market exchange rate had a 60 per cent weight. The Report of the Rangarajan Committee in 1993 recommended, *inter alia*, the introduction of market determined exchange rates and current account convertibility. India signed Article VIII of IMF's Articles of Agreement in 1994 and decontrolled several capital account transactions. It kept a lid on short-term volatile flows but gave permission for full outflows associated with inflows (i.e., principal, interest, dividends, profits and sale proceeds).

Table 6.1 provides data on foreign capital inflows into India in the decade since the reform process began, and the break-up into FDI and portfolio investment.

FDI increased steadily from US$129 million in 1991–92 to peak at US$3557 million in 1997–98 and then declined to about a third of its peak value. Portfolio investment, on the other hand, has been much more volatile. It increased from almost nothing in 1991–92 to US$3.8 billion in 1994–95, became negative in 1998–99 but rebounded strongly to US$2.7b in 2000–2001. New (net), non-resident Indian deposits, quantitatively, have been as important and certainly less volatile than portfolio investment. The same is true for commercial borrowing. External assistance has been declining over time as a contribution to the capital account but its level is still significant.[4]

To anticipate the analysis of the response to these flows, one can say that overall in the last ten years the RBI has been very successful in managing capital flows without letting them cause real appreciation or increasing the money supply so much that inflation results. It has been continuously accumulating reserves. Why it does so is a mystery (to us and, I suspect, even to them!). However, over this period the central government's deficit has been way out of control.[5]

The RBI has, by and large, used CRR to 'sterilize' the money supply. The usual channel of conducting an 'exchange market operation' to mop up excess liquidity is not an option in India since government securities markets are thin. I now turn to analyzing the behaviour of exchange rates (real and nominal) and base money in the last decade.

---

4 Over time the access of Indian firms to foreign credit markets (through GDRs, ADRs and ECBs) has also been liberalized but this is still restricted and small compared to inflows.

5 See the figures in Table 6.2 for the Centre and the combined Centre and States budget deficit.

Table 6.1: Macroeconomic Data for India

Item	*1991–92*	*1992–93*	*1993–94*	*1994–95*	*1995–96*	*1996–97*	*1997–98*	*1998–99*	*1999–00*	*2000–01*
Trade Balance	-2798	-5447	-4056	-9049	-11349	-14815	-15507	-13246	-17841	-14370
Foreign investment	133	557	4235	4807	6153	5390	2412	5191	5191	5102
Foreign investment (i) Direct Investment	129	315	386	1314	2144	2821	3557	2462	2155	2339
Foreign investment (ii) Portfolio investment	4	244	3567	3824	2748	3312	1828	-61	3026	2760
External Assistance.net	3037	1859	1901	1526	883	1109	907	820	901	427
Commercial Borrowings.net	1456	.358	607	1030	1275	2848	3999	4362	313	4011
NRI Deposits.net	290	2001	1205	172	1103	3350	1125	960	1540	2317
Reserves (increase/ Decrease+)	-3385	-698	-8724	-4644	2936	-5818	-3893	-3829	-6142	-5830

Source: Reserve Bank of India (2001)

Table 6.2: Balance of Payments Data for India

Item	*1991–92*	*1992–93*	*1993–94*	*1994–95*	*1995–96*	*1996–97*	*1997–98*	*1999–00*	*2000–01*	
REER	64.20	57.08	61.59	66.04	63.62	63.81	67.02	63.44	66.29	66.53
NEER	52.51	43.46	44.69	43.37	39.73	38.97	40.01	36.34	35.46	35.52
Current Acc/GDP	-0.3	-1.7	-0.4	-1.7	-1.2	-1.4	-1.0	-1.0	-1.0	-1.5
Gross Fiscal Def/GDP	5.6	5.4	7.0	5.7	5.1	4.9	5.8	6.5	5.4	5.1
States+Central Def./GDP	7.0	7.0	8.3	7.1	6.5	6.4	7.3	8.9	9.4	9.1
M0 Growth rate	16.4	14.6	16.1	21.5	16.4	6.4	10.2	12.3	11.7	7.7
WPI Inflation rate	13.7	10.0	8.4	12.5	8.1	4.6	4.4	5.9	3.3	7.2

Source: Reserve Bank of India (2001)

The multilateral (trade weighted) nominal exchange rate (NEER) depreciated by about 30 per cent over the period, while the real (trade-weighted) exchange rate (REER) stayed more or less constant (Table 6.2, Figure 6.1). The REER series records appreciations in 1993–94, 1994–95 and 1997–98, when capital flows were particularly strong. This constancy of the real exchange rate also kept the current account deficit under control — India's current account deficits have remained below two per cent of GDP over the decade. For instance until 1996–97 it was never more than 1.7 per cent of GDP (currently under one per cent of GDP, see Table 6.2), whereas for Thailand it was 8.3 per cent of GDP and 8.1 per cent in 1995 and 1996 respectively.

Figure 6.1: Multilateral Nominal Exchange Rate

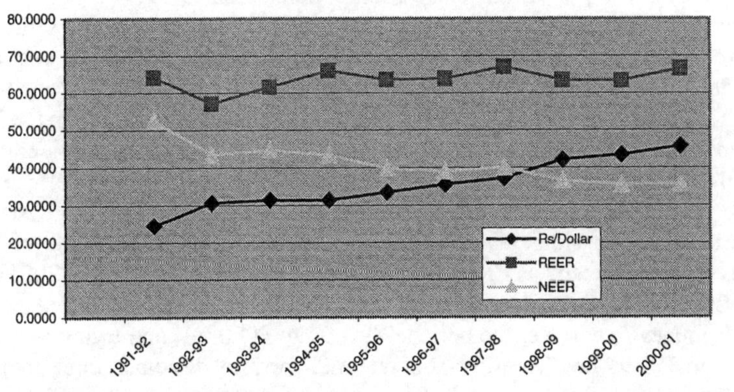

The Indian experience of limited nominal appreciation in response to capital flows is similar to that in east and south-east Asian countries. Exchange rates are more flexible in Latin America although there are exceptions (Argentina was on a currency board). Also capital flows to India were but a fraction of those received by the east and south-east Asian countries (and Latin America). Even at its peak in 1993–94 the figure was below four per cent of GNP compared to 10 to 20 per cent for the south-east Asian economics.

However, not just the magnitude of total flows but also their composition is crucial — Thailand's short term debt as a proportion of total external debt climbed from 35.2 per cent to 49.4 per cent between 1992 to 1995, before falling back somewhat to 41.4 per cent in 1996. For Indonesia, the figures varied between 18 per cent and 25 per cent. India, on the other hand, never let the figure climb above 7.5 per cent in that period.[6] Hence credit expansion in India stayed between 11 to 17 per cent, whereas for Thailand the usual range was 23 to 32 per cent, hitting 98.3 per cent in 1996![7]

On the fiscal front though, the south-east Asian countries which were hit by the crisis of 1997, fared significantly better. Thailand ran a budget surplus between 1992–96 of between 3 per cent of GDP to 0.9 per cent of GDP. The Indonesian budget was on average balanced during this period, while India's Union government deficits alone ranged between 7.4 per cent and 5 per cent.

Table 6.1 documents the steady growth of the RBI's foreign assets. The RBI's foreign exchange reserves accounted for about a fifth (Rs. 18838 crores) of the reserve money stock in 1991–92 (Rs 94090 crores) but accounted for over two third (Rs. 197175 crores out of Rs. 282683 crores in 2000–01). The rise of this share has accelerated since 1997–98. In the 40 quarters between 1991–92 to 2000–01, the RBI has been a net seller of foreign exchange in only twelve. This reflects itself as only in one year out of ten (1995–96) has the RBI decumulated foreign exchange reserves.

The growth rate of M0 (Table 6.2) does not show acceleration. In the last two years of the decade under consideration it slowed down considerably. This implies that the RBI has been successful in sterilizing the effects of the foreign reserve accumulation on the money supply (M0). The RBI has varied CRR considerably over the last decade. As the growth rate of M0 has come down, so has CRR (it stood at 5.50 per cent at the end of 2001).

Looking at the behavior of Indian interest rates (annual averages of call money rates) over the period 1993–94 to 2000–01, and trying to relate this to US 91-day Treasury Bill rate and forward discount (three month) on the rupee over the period.[8] This is only indicative since the call money rate is not the representative short rate,[9] annual averages are not what arbitrage (or the lack of it) hold over etc. But the columns of Table 6.3 reveal that the return on US treasury bills in Indian rupees were above Indian rates till 1995–96 — when Indian rates were high — but since then over-predict the Indian interest rate — often by over 4 per cent! The evidence since 1996–97 is consistent with restrictions on outflows on the capital account. If Indian capital controls were not in place, the US rates should be lower signifying a developing country risk premium.

6 See Asian Development Bank (1997) and Gokarn (1999) for more details.

7 For Indonesia it was in the range of 20 per cent to 26 per cent but hit 42.1 per cent in 1996 — see Asian Development Bank (1997).

8 The series on forward premia begin in 1993.

9 The market for treasury bills in India is still very thin to use that rate as a representative short rate.

Table 6.3: Return on Financial Assets

Item	*1993–94*	*1994–95*	*1995–96*	*1996–97*	*1997–98*	*1998–99*	*1999–00*	*2000–01*
3-Month Forward Discount	3.74	3.42	11.43	9.08	7.45	7.07	4.51	3.88
91-day US Treasury Bill Rate	3.14	5.02	5.45	5.18	5.20	4.74	5.07	5.81
Average Call Money Rates	6.99	9.40	17.73	7.84	8.69	7.83	8.87	9.15

Source: Reserve Bank of India (2001), and IMF International Financial Statistics.

Overall, monetary policy since liberalization has been successful in handling the capital flows by preventing a real appreciation, keeping the current account deficit under control and sterilizing the effect of capital flows. There are costs in terms of reserve accumulation and slowdown in credit demand. I have not discussed the domestic constraints on monetary policy.

3. Issues in Capital Account Convertibility

This is a much-surveyed area — see for example, Gilbert, Irwin and Vines (2001), Johnston and Sundarajan (1999), Kletzer (1999), Schneider (2001), and Williamson (2001). Here I bring together three strands of the literature that may help make sense of the capital account convertibility issue in the Indian context. First, we will look at the types of capital flows to developing countries (these are restricted or closed under a less-than-full capital account convertibility) and assess which of these are likely to pose a policy problem if a partially closed capital account is opened up. In the light of the east Asian experience, short-term borrowing (other than trade credits) is the most problematic. The theoretical results are even more driven by the actual macroeconomic experience of countries than is usual for theoretical models in macroeconomics. The evidence suggests that a large number of prerequisites must be satisfied before we embark on capital account liberalization. An advantage of being a latecomer in the field is that we can learn from failed or costly attempts at liberalization.

Some preliminary observations are in order. First, for the capital inflow episode beginning in 1989, it has been debated whether the flows were due to push factors — that is, due to excess savings in the industrialized countries looking for high returns in developing economies — or, whether, the latter had turned the corner as far reforms were concerned and the flows were in response to pull factors. No clear answers have emerged but (at the global level) I find the push arguments more convincing. This is because there was contagion in inflows — countries which had not undertaken significant reforms also received inflows because they happened to be in the same region — as there was when in 1997 we witnessed outflows.[10] Second, it is often alleged that capital controls do not work because people by-pass them via a porous current account. If this were true then there is nothing to debate — we have a de facto regime of capital account convertibility although there might some costs of DUP activities in by-passing governmental regulations. It is true the discrepancies in current account transactions are large and need explaining. A third point, (often overlooked) is that capital account convertibility is neither a necessary nor a sufficient condition for a crisis. There is no crisis if the capital account is open but there are no inflows or there are inflows but the domestic financial system is able to cope with them. Malaysia and Thailand had relatively open capital accounts for about two decades before the crises erupted. Thus we need a combination of actual flows (which are facilitated by the removal of capital controls) and bad macroeconomic and/or financial policies. The experience of the crisis of 1990–91 in India should remind us that we could have a crisis even in the absence of capital flows — capital controls are not a substitute for good macroeconomic policies (Kaminsky, Lizondo and Reinhart 1998).

In the early stages of development, an economy with relatively underdeveloped capital markets imposes controls fearing an outflow if it did not do so. The only capital flows in these underdeveloped economies, both in manufacturing and financial terms, takes the form of FDI in mining etc., and trade credit for which readily seizable collateral is available. As the economy develops inflows are liberalized and take the form of syndicated bank loans to the government. Only much later do other forms of capital for example, investment in equity, bank lending to the private sector, flow in. The surge of capital inflows to the emerging economies which began in 1989 was supposed to be different from the one in the late 1970s in that in the previous episode almost all the lending was syndicated bank loans where as the later inflows were more diversified. Not enough, as we shall see below. One feature of an immature financial market is that banking is the main form of financial intermediation. Since banks engage in maturity transformation, they are fragile (that is, prone to crises). This is

---

[10] The data on aggregate private investment flows to India do not lend support to the hypothesis that push factors in the OECD economies are the cause of these flows. Barring, the year 1998–99 — the year following the Asian crisis and the year India exploded nuclear devices — capital flows have been strong (although well below the peak of 1995–96). Chakrabarti (2001) finds that FII investment is more sensitive to returns in India in the post-Asian crisis period than they were before.

true of the rich countries as well. But they are able to cope with idiosyncratic shocks better since their production structures are more diversified and banks constitute a smaller proportion of the financial sector.

Given their underdeveloped financial markets, developing economies typically have (not unrealistically) a fear of outflow of capital if flows are liberalized. The two major types of outflows are (i) capital flight,[11] and (ii) outflows for portfolio diversification. Both kinds of outflows take place even in the presence of controls through a porous current account, through under-invoicing of exports and over-invoicing of imports.

The case for liberalization treats goods and assets symmetrically and would leave everything to an (efficient) marketplace (subject to supervision). Proponents of capital account liberalization point to the loss of opportunities for a small economy that the international market provides for diversification of idiosyncratic risk.[12] Presumably, by holding a diversified portfolio one can buy insurance against country specific (temporary) shocks. Caballero (2000) points out that in the case of Chile — which is regarded as a resounding success story in terms of the liberalization of its financial sector — all the major macroeconomic series move, more or less, in tandem with the price of copper (Chile's main export).

Some economists believe that the losses from the lack of diversification are so large that there should be a 'big-bang' or 'cold turkey' approach to financial liberalization. But if we are agreed that capital account liberalization should be a phased exercise how should this be done? The bulk of the literature seems to have its origins in the aborted attempts at liberalization in Latin America in the 1980s. The lesson from that experience suggested the capital account liberalization exercise had to follow convertibility on current account. Domestic financial liberalization should precede capital account convertibility.

Capital inflows were expected to generate large real appreciation, which would squeeze the domestic tradeables sector and subject the whole liberalization process to risk. The financial system was not developed enough to handle large inflows and outflows of capital. So capital controls were to remain in place initially to provide time for the domestic financial sector to prepare for the challenge of opening up.

I note, *en passant*, that usually there are some items in the capital account, which depend on whether the current account is liberalized. FDI, for instance, is attracted to a liberal trade regime, although there is a large

---

[11] Capital flight may take place due to arbitrage opportunities presented by different tax rates for domestic residents and foreigners and in response to economic and political uncertainty.

[12] Capital account convertibility is also seen to be bringing in new technology and also access to innovations when they take place. Moreover competition from foreign financial intermediaries helps to break up an oligopolistic market structure.

theoretical and empirical literature associated with 'tariff-jumping FDI' (and the so-called Brecher-Diaz-Alejandro set-up). Similarly trade credits are also related to trade flows. It is interesting to note that trade credit is a really short-term capital item and FDI is really long term. But both of these are very stable components of capital flows and not prone to sudden reversals or subject to contagion. This is not an unimportant point because regressions have been run with regressors that include all short-term maturity liabilities and then find no predictive power of short-term capital flows for a crisis.

In the data on international capital flows FDI and portfolio investment flows are not correlated. Among developing counties, China is the single-largest recipient of FDI — its capital account is completely closed — while Brazil was the largest recipient of portfolio investment (for the first half of the 1990s).[13] Every rupee of FDI is seen to generate a fixed investment of the same amount. The investment generation ability of portfolio investment is much lower. In India some have asked for capital account convertibility because of the need for large capital flows to the infrastructure sector.[14] However these flows can be treated as FDI is treated — of course recognizing that the returns to such investment may often not generate foreign exchange.[15]

Countries restricting the flow of capital have used two broad types of control mechanisms: (a) which distinguish between transactions — implemented for example, in Chile, Argentina, and (b) which differentiate between domestic residents and others, with domestic residents being forbidden from participating in certain transactions — almost inevitably this translates in liberalizing inflows first, and then outflows. This is the strategy followed in India and South Africa.

Table 6.4 gives some figure on net capital inflows to emerging markets for the five years 1996 to 2000. Of the private flows, FDI has the lowest variance, bank lending the highest with portfolio investment, in between. Official flows include disbursement by the multilateral agencies and, therefore, tend to be high in years of crises.

Table 6.4 reveals that in east Asia, there was a shutdown of capital flows mainly due a change in direction of bank lending, which constituted an inflow of $114 billion in 1996 to an outflow of $54 billion in 1998, the estimate for 2000 being an outflow of $13 billion. Portfolio investment declined from $17 billion to $5 billion. Similarly, in Latin America during

---

13 This may have been due to the high real interest rates in Brazil due to the government's budget problems. It is not surprising that Brazil attracted very little FDI in this period — see Bosworth and Collins (1999).

14 See Srinivasan (2000) for a discussion on the urgent need for capital in this sector.

15 That is, are non-tradeable in nature.

1996–99 bank loans fell from $49 billion to -$7 billion. For all emerging markets during 1996–2000 bank loans fell from about 56 per cent of all inflows to about a fifth.

4. Prerequisites for Full Convertibility

Some of the prerequisites for a liberalized capital account highlighted in the literature are (a) financial sector reforms, (b) fiscal balance; and (c) properly designed monetary (and exchange rate) policy. I now discuss these.

4.1 Financial sector reforms

Domestic financial sector reforms can be painful even in the absence of capital flows. Often financial crises result, as in Argentina and Chile in the early 1980s. This can induce major contractionary effect on real activity.

Table 6.4: Net capital inflows to emerging markets (US$ bn)

	1996	*1997*	*1998*	*1999*	*2000*
Emerging markets					
Total Private capital inflows	327.9	265.7	147.8	148.	193.1
Bank loans and other	202.5	124.7	16.2	-7.1	39.6
Portfolio investment	33.7	25.7	13.7	17.	33.7
FDI	91.7	115.3	117.9	138.8	119.8
Net official in	7.6	38.9	52.8	11.9	9.1
Total inflows	**335.5**	**304.6**	**200.6**	**160.6**	**202.2**
Asia and the Pacific					
Total private capital inflows	176.3	67.9	5.8	39.3	59.4
Bank loans and other	113.7	10.0	-54.3	-30.2	-12.6
Portfolio investment	17.2	6.0	4.9	14.9	18.4
FDI	45.4	51.9	55.2	54.6	53.6
Net official inflows	5.0	36.7	31.2	4.3	8.3
Total inflows	**181.3**	**104.6**	**37.0**	**43.6**	**67.7**
Latin America					
Total private capital inflows	97.3	107.7	97.5	68.8	89.6
Bank loans and other	48.9	45.6	47.0	7.3	34.3
Portfolio investment	12.7	13.2	1.6	-5.0	7.8
FDI	35.8	48.8	48.9	66.5	47.6
Net official inflows	-10.5	-2.6	15.7	5.5	-1.9
Total inflows	**86.8**	**105.1**	**113.2**	**74.3**	**87.7**

Source: Williamson (2001).

To absorb capital inflows, most of which tend to be short term, what is needed is a strong domestic financial system resilient enough to cope with inflows and outflows. A movement away from quantitative restrictions to more market determined interest rates, prudential norms, development of a money market, a market for government securities, a foreign exchange market, the existence of a yield curve for pricing floating rate instruments etc., need to be in place. The Basle prudential norms, which have been criticized (correctly) for other reasons, have helped set some standards in the banking sector.[16] In addition to currency mismatch there could also be maturity mismatch. It is only after financial liberalization that the banking sector's non-performing assets (NPAs) have been recognized as problem — in the past they were just swept under the carpet. The definition, provisioning etc., are norms that are still evolving in developing economies. The figure for 2000–01 was 7.2 per cent for Indian public sector banks,[17] which is too high for these institutions to be called healthy.

Bank credit tends to grow quickly following financial sector liberalization. This is exacerbated by capital inflows leading to funding of high-risk projects. Because of the inadequate monitoring and information, banks' balance sheets become strained. Excessive risk taking is more likely in a regime where there are implicit or explicit government guarantees. In these situations it is important that banks should not have access to foreign borrowing, because excessive lending takes place without adequate monitoring or hedging of foreign currency. Corrective action takes place only after a crisis erupts (as in Thailand). The Thai banking crisis, which heralded the Asian crisis in 1997, is widely believed to be due to poor monitoring by the Thai Central Bank. About half of the (unhedged) foreign exchange loans were made to firms located in the non-traded goods sector.

A comparative study of the Asian financial system following the Asian crisis concludes that even now: 'All Asian developing countries lack efficient money markets, deep capital markets, an effective governance structure and an effective system for supervising and monitoring financial activities.'[18]

4.2 Monetary (and exchange rate) policy

Under free mobility of capital both fiscal and monetary policies must attempt to minimize volatility of capital flows. Low inflation, balanced budget and an independent central bank are prerequisites for such a policy. Foreign capital inflows may cause additional headaches for the monetary

---

16 Barings crashed in spite of having adhered to these norms.
17 The figures are 5.56 and 2.37 respectively for private and foreign banks.
18 Tsurumi (2001b).

authorities who may first want to sterilize the effects of the flows on money supply to prevent (pro-cyclical) changes in the money stock. This may be done through the usual channels of monetary policy, though for an economy which is financially integrated with the rest of the world, the CRR cannot be too much out of line with the levels abroad. Second, the authorities may conduct an open market operation. This requires some depth in financial markets, which may be missing. Sterilization through this route may have budgetary implications because now the government by engaging in it places in the hands of the public an interest-bearing liability in place of cash. A third alternative is to target a segment of the flows directly. Chile (also Colombia and Thailand) has had some success in transforming the maturity of capital flows through an unremunerated reserve requirement (URR) but whether there was any effect of this on *total* flows is doubtful.[19]

Exchange rate flexibility is also necessary. Much has been written on the impossibility maintaining free mobility of capital, fixed exchange rates and an independent monetary policy — the impossible trinity. A regime of flexible exchange rates has its drawbacks but is clearly preferable to a fixed exchange rate regime in a situation where capital account convertibility is being contemplated. Fixed exchange rates do not allow for inflation differentials, convert returns into foreign currencies one-for-one and are prone to one-way bets against the central bank. In the recent past most developing countries have switched to a floating exchange rate system. Malaysia is still on a fixed exchange rate regime — it had also imposed temporary capital controls — while Argentina was on a currency board till recently. Chile, Colombia, Israel and Mexico have an exchange rate band, which involves intervention by the authorities whenever the band is approached.[20] [21]

There is an even bigger argument against a fixed exchange rate regime in developing economies, especially with implicit guarantees: it causes inflows with the borrowing denominated in the foreign currency, which may then be lent to the non-traded goods sector. If it looks as if an exchange rate crisis could occur, market participants move out of the domestic currency (a one-way bet causes is a run on the foreign exchange reserves of the central bank). This either causes the fixed exchange rate regime to collapse. The collapse makes the domestic banks vulnerable to a

---

[19] Edwards (1999) casts doubt on whether even the composition of the capital flows was altered.

[20] Of course, the market could anticipate such an intervention and take corrective action so that no intervention is actually necessary.

[21] Indonesia also maintained an exchange rate regime where bands were allowed to widen over time. In practice, however, the exchange rate always stayed at the lower (i.e., stronger) limit of the band. It went up from there only when the Asian crisis broke — see Nasution (2001).

crisis because their balance sheets deteriorate in terms of the foreign currency (domestic currency loans especially those to the non-traded goods sector fall in value). This is what happened in Thailand and Indonesia. The central bank may try to protect the peg by raising interest rates. This may cause fragile businesses to go under and thus worsen the banks' balance sheets further (Mishkin 1999).[22]

One justification for some form of a pegged rate is that capital flows are prone to reversals. In this case then with some nominal wage-price inertia it may be optimal not to have a floating exchange rate regime since this would precipitate an immediate real appreciation and a current account deficit with substantial o utput and employment costs. With a pegged exchange rate, on the other hand, the overvaluation occurs gradually over time. It is very difficult for the authorities, given the few episodes of international capital flows, to decide whether the shock (that is, the inflow of capital) is permanent or temporary and therefore deciding what the appropriate policy response should be.

Hard pegs have become less fashionable in light of the Argentine experience. Its fall from grace is due to Argentina tying its fortunes to the US dollar. Having tied its own hand it, suffered the consequences of a strong dollar and an inflexible labour market.[23] To see why compare the recent experience of Brazil, which has a floating rate and Argentina, which had a currency board (this is equally true of Hong Kong versus the rest of east Asia). Some form of nominal exchange rate fixing — with the currency board as an extreme form — pays rich dividends in bringing down inflation in countries prone to high (or hyper-) inflation. It is a good idea, however, to move to a floating regime once this has been achieved. But what is the correct time to dismount the tiger of 'credibility'?

4.3 Fiscal policy

The government's fiscal stance is also important for a successful liberalization of the capital account. If there is a large budget deficit (or more correctly debt) the real interest rate will tend to be high, attracting inflows and lead to a real appreciation, which with a floating rate could be achieved through a nominal appreciation. In the presence of fixed exchange rates this inflow could cause an increase in the nominal money supply and generate inflationary pressures. To sterilize the money supply the central bank could conduct an open market operation, which, as noted above, requires some depth in these markets. But even a sterilization operation is a

[22] Kaminsky and Reinhart (1999) find that the banking crisis occurs before the exchange rate crisis.

[23] Frankel (1999) points out that the dollar for Argentina does not constitute an optimal currency area in terms of the usual criteria.

temporary fix only because, as mentioned earlier, this increases the government debt held by residents and hence adds to the interest cost.[24] In any case the tradeables sector, which was being squeezed before capital mobility was allowed, is hurt even more. This could make the current account deficit unsustainable.[25] In anticipation of such an eventuality, a reversal of capital flows could take place. Brazil was able to attract substantial foreign portfolio capital in the early 1990s. But the government's (both federal and provincial) deficits were sizeable. In 1998, when one of the states, Minas Gerais, ran into financial trouble there was a crisis with foreign capital departing the country.

However prudent fiscal behaviour by itself is not enough to keep a crisis at bay. After all, most of the south-east Asian countries had 'reasonable' deficits and contagion tends not to discriminate between those who are well behaved and those who are not. But the experience of Argentina, Chile and Uganda shows that with the government deficit under control the financial system can handle inflows better, and as mentioned, in Brazil fiscal profligacy did lead to a crisis.

5. The Indian Experience

The Indian capital account remains mostly closed. Those clamouring for opening it up are on the defensive both because the Asian crisis has made the analytical case weaker and because a profligate government and a financial system in the doldrums are not exactly the ideal budgetary and financial launching pads for such an exercise.

Reddy (2001) summarizes the current regime in India's capital account 'First, there is a differentiation between current (convertible) and capital account (subject to some controls) transactions. Secondly, outflows associated with inflows (free) and other outflows (more restricted). Thirdly, residents are treated differently from non-residents (less restrictively). Non-residents Indians have (an) intermediate status. Fourthly, there are also differences in treatment of individuals (highly restrictive), corporate entities (restrictive) and financial intermediaries such as institutional investors (less restrictive) and banks (more restrictive).'

The Tarapore Committee on Capital Account Convertibility in 1997 recommended the fiscal Deficit/GDP ratio be between 4.5 to 3.5 per cent (in 1999–2000) inflation be an average of 3 to 5 per cent. Average CRR was to fall to 3 per cent from 9.3 per cent between 1997–2000. NPAs as a

---

[24] This imposes a quasi-fiscal cost.

[25] China embarked on its liberalization process in 1979 in possession of large foreign exchange reserves without allowing (non-FDI) capital mobility. The reserves provided the necessary cushion against a possible real appreciation.

percentage of total advances from 13.7 per cent in 1996–97 to 5 per cent in 1999–2000. It is difficult to comprehend how the committee could both set targets to be achieved *and* a time frame for achieving them — the latter surely affects agencies other than the RBI. It is clear that we are still far away from meeting the fiscal target. The combined fiscal deficit of the states and the Centre (as seen in Table 6.2) is expected to be in excess of (or close to) ten per cent of GDP. At the time of writing the CRR has been driven to 5.5 per cent due to a lack of demand for credit. The NPAs of banks is well under control but the issue of recapitalisation and privatization still hangs fire. We still have some distance to go before we can be sure that Indian financial institutions are ready to face up to the task of handling capital inflows on a large scale.

6. Conclusions

Monetary policy since liberalization has been successful in tackling the problems of the external sector in India. It handed the capital flows by preventing a real appreciation, keeping the current account deficit under control and sterilizing the effect of capital flows. In this it has been aided by restrictions on capital flows.

There are gains from trade in goods and there are gains from trade in assets. To realize the latter a strong financial sector is required. Even trade in goods requires some sectors to contract and others to expand. The collapse of a few financial institutions could lead to a collapse of the financial system. This in turn will make the domestic (modern) sectors collapse. Even at the international level, Mishkin (1999) among others, has argued persuasively for the International Monetary Fund to play a lender of last resort role. Therefore both the international and domestic 'architecture' need strengthening and possibly remodeling before a developing economy can be sure of avoiding crises associated with mobile international capital.

There is, of course, a moral hazard problem in saying that capital account convertibility must await financial reforms, while acknowledging that by themselves the old habits in the financial system will not go away. I have at least tried to draw attention to the risks — and these are potentially sizeable — of opening up without reforms.[26]

---

[26] It is reminiscent of protection for the infant industry case where the infant never grows up. However it is often the case even recognizing the moral hazard that a policy induces, it is still worthwhile to implement the policy, for example, in deposit insurance.

References

Asian Development Bank, *Asian Development Outlook* (New York: Oxford University Press, 1997).

Bosworth, B., and Collins, S.M., 'Capital Flows to Developing Countries: Implications for Saving and Investment', *Brookings Paper on Economic Activity* (1999).

Caballero, R. 'Macroeconomic Volatility in Latin America: A View and Three Case Studie', *National Bureau of Economic Research (NBER) Working Paper No. 77782* (2000).

Chakrabarti, R. 'FII flows to India: Nature and Causes', *ICRA Bulletin, Money and Finance* 2 (2001), 61–81.

Edwards, S., 'How Effective Are Capital Controls?', *NBER Working Paper No. 7413* (1999).

Frankel, J.A., 'No Single Currency Regime is Right for All Countries or At All Times', *NBER Working Paper No. 7338* (1999).

Feldstein, M., Aspects of Global Economic Integration: Outlook for the Future, *NBER Working Paper No. 7899* (2000).

Gilbert, C.L., Irwin, G. and Vines, D., 'Capital Account Convertibility, Poor Developing Countries, and International Financial Architecture', *Development Policy Review* 19 (2001), 121–41.

Gokarn, S., 'The East Asian Crisis of 1997: Some Implications for India', in Parikh (1999), 256–65.

Johnston, R.B., and Sundarajan, V., *Sequencing Financial Sector Reforms: Country Experience and Issues* (Washington DC: International Monetary Fund, 1999).

Joshi, V. and Little, I.M.D., *India: Macroeconomics and Political Economy* (New Delhi: Oxford, 1994).

Kaminsky, G., Lizondo, S., and Reinhart, C., 'Leading Indicators of Currency Crises', *International Monetary Fund Staff Papers* (1998)

Kaminsky G., and Reinhart, C., 'The Twin Crises: the Causes of Banking and Balance of Payments Problems', *American Economic Review* (1999).

Kletzer, K., 'Capital Inflows and Developing Country Financial Crises: Implications of Competing Explanations for Policy Interventions', *Indian Council for Research in International Economic Relations Working Paper No. 53* (1999).

Mishkin F.S., 'Lessons from the Asian Crisis', *NBER Working Paper No. 7102* (1999).

Nasution, A., 'Financial Policy and Financial Sector Development in Indonesia', in M. Tsurumi (2001a), 190–224.

Parikh, K. (ed.), *India Development Report 1999* (New Delhi: Oxford, 1999).

Reddy, Y.V. 'Operationalising Capital Account Liberalisation: The Indian Experience', *Development Policy Review* 19 (2001), 83–99.

Reserve Bank of India, *Handbook of Statistics on the Indian Economy* (Mumbai, India: RBI, 2001).

Schneider, B., 'Issues in Capital Account Convertibility in Developing Countries', *Development Policy Review* 19 (2001), 31–82.

Sen, P., 'India's Financial Sector Reforms: Progress and Macroeconomic Constraints', in M. Tsurumi (ed.) (2001a), 291–310.

Srinivasan, T.N., *Eight Lectures on the India's Economic Reforms* (New Delhi: Oxford, 2000).

Tsurumi, M. (ed.), *Financial Big Bang in Asia*, (Aldershot, UK: Ashgate, 2001a).

Tsurumi, M., 'Introduction: Financial Crisis and System Reform in Asia' (2001b), in M. Tsurumi (2001a), 1–36.

Williamson, J., 'Issues Regarding the Composition of Capital Flows' *Development Policy Review* 19 (2001), 11–29.

7

Macroeconomics of Credit: An Indian Perspective

Deba Prasad Rath and Dhritidyuti Bose

1. Introduction

The recent literature has been marked by rejuvenated interest in studying macroeconomics of credit. In the context of the Indian economy, this interest is attributable to certain transformations that have taken place in the credit market. First, the credit market has undergone a metamorphosis from essentially a credit-rationing regime to one where market-determined interest rates equilibrate the credit market, the latter facilitated by the introduction of the structural adjustment programme in the 1990s (Rakshit 1994). Second, the co-behaviour of bank credit growth and economic growth in recent years has been a matter of debate. While cycles in output and credit have generally exhibited some co-movement, there have been some episodes of counter movements. Furthermore, even when the two are co-moving like the current deceleration in bank credit growth and economic downturn, the authorities seem helpless in finding ways to reverse the slowdown by pushing up the credit off-take even in the face of strong accretion in deposits. Policy implications of the changing dynamics of the credit process for the targeting procedure of monetary policy are well-recognised — they emanate from the fact that bank lending can impart an endogenous influence to the money supply process. It has been argued that, in a financially deregulated and liberalised regime, money loses the properties of an intermediate targeting variable and credit may provide a better choice. The multiple indicator approach, adopted in India in recent years, includes credit, along with money and a host of real as well as financial variables in the vector of intermediate target variables. Against this backdrop, the present chapter analyzes certain facets of Indian credit process and its relevance for monetary policy formulation.

2. The Theoretical Debate and Cross-Country Experience

The microeconomic foundation of the credit view lies in the credit market promoting allocative efficiency through inter-temporal exchange of resources and modifying a *given* stream of consumption and investment into a *preferred* stream either by borrowing (deficit units) or by saving and lending (surplus units) (Fisher 1930). Thus, 'money to spend' rather than 'money to hold' determines real effective demand. The possibility of asymmetry of information between lender and borrower also exposed the limitation of interest rate as the sole rationing instrument (Stiglitz and Weiss 1981).

The macroeconomic foundation of credit view lay in differentiating loans from bonds and other assets of the banks with their respective rates of interest leading the credit market frictions also to affect equilibrium at the goods market (Bernanke & Blinder 1988). Under information asymmetry, non-price factors also play key role in clearance of credit markets. Finally, the possibility of monetary shocks affecting the net worth of firms and the latter, in turn, feeding back to the credit market and affecting the lending activity of financial institutions (Bernanke, Gertler & Gilchrist 1999) also brought forth a perspective of credit view. It strengthened the case for the credit supplementing the interest rate channel in explaining the fluctuations in real economic activity remaining more prolonged than anticipated by the interest rate channel.

For example, the brisk economic growth and exchange rate stability in most Asian and Latin American economies in the early 1990s was associated with a boom in bank credit and narrowing of intermediation spreads. The subsequent prolonged recession was attributed to the banking crisis due to deposit erosion as also credit squeeze prompted by large non-performing loans (Catao & Rodriguez 2000). Some evidence of credit view was also found in Finland where severe recession in the early 1990s was marked by widespread banking crisis and extensive government intervention.

3. The Indian Experience

Table 7.1 shows that while broad money growth has maintained its momentum in the 1990s with its annual average growth remaining unchanged at 17.2 per cent as recorded for the 1980s, non-food bank credit decelerated to 15.4 per cent from 17.8 per cent. The average industrial production growth rate moved down to 6.3 per cent from 7.5 per cent over the period.

Over a longer horizon, the Indian economy has experienced marked cycles in credit markets (RBI 1999). Economic growth in the pre-reforms period was subjected to marked fluctuations in the agricultural growth mainly emanating from the supply shocks resulting from the behaviour of monsoons. In the post-reform period, while the distribution of monsoons has generally been normal, the economic growth nevertheless is still subject to cycles. This has essentially reflected the cyclicity of industrial production and credit off-take (RBI 2001). The growth cycles of non-food credit and industrial production have generally moved in tandem except towards the end of the 1980s and early 1990s as well as during January 1997 to October 1998 and first three quarters of 2000–01 when the synchronous movements broke. During the 1990s quite often credit and output downswings co-existed despite abundant liquidity (RBI 1999; 2001).

Table 7.1: Select Macroeconomic Indicators for India

Item	1980–81 to 1989–90	1990–91 to 1999–2000
Broad Money	17.2	17.2
Bank Credit	16.8	15.9
Non-Food Credit	17.8	15.4
Investment in Government Securities	19.4	20.9
WPI Inflation	8.0	8.1
Real GDP Growth	5.8	5.8
IIP Growth	7.5	6.3

The comprehensive financial reform programme introduced in the early 1990s marked a fundamental departure in policy from those in the pre-liberalisation phase of the 1970s and 1980s. The economic reforms progressively freed the credit market from the quantitative and interest rate restrictions. Progressive reduction in the statutory cash reserve ratio (CRR) and the statutory liquidity ratio (SLR) to be maintained by the banks and expansion in the coverage for priority sector lending facilitated such a process with market determined lending rates while imparting operational flexibility of banks in managing their credit portfolio. Besides the banks were allowed to raise resources through new financial instruments other than deposits (like certificates of deposits since 1989) that banks resorted to during occasions of liquidity tightness. The cash credit component of bank lending was increasingly substituted by the loan component thereby freeing the banks from the onus of cash management. The central bank support to the banks was also made increasingly market-based. Banks were advised to follow prudential asset-liability management guidelines.

The extant literature reveals a few stylised facts about the credit market behaviour. First, the credit channel hypothesis is found to be working with bank credit influencing inventory accumulations, the size of external finance premium depending on the financial conditions of firms and bank dependent small industries suffering most during the period of quantitative credit control (Mukhopadhyaya 1998). Second, the lending rate, while becoming free, has still exhibited stickiness even amidst free movement in the rest of the financial prices (RBI 2002b). Thirdly, the credit market seemed to switch from credit rationed to a demand constrained loan market with banks parking surplus liquidity even in excess of SLR in government securities as early as 1993–94 (Rakshit 1994). Finally, the supply constraints in the credit market reflect risk-averse approach of banks under prudential guidelines (RBI 1999).

4. A Credit Model for India in the Post-Reform Period

The credit model developed by the Reserve Bank (RBI 2001) adapted the Bernanke and Blinder (1988) framework for India during the post-reform period. It showed that the demand for non-food bank credit was predominantly and positively influenced by the industrial production and, inversely, to a lesser extent, by the lending rate. The supply for non-food bank credit was positively driven by the lending rate, free reserves of the banking system and equity prices.

Taking this RBI study as guidepost, our investigation of the credit market concentrates on the post-reform period (May 1993 to December 2001) through a system of credit demand, credit supply and industrial production equations. As regards the choice of the credit aggregate for analysis, we prefer to study the voluntary behaviour of commercial banks in extending credit to the non-government domestic sector falling outside the ambit of statutory obligations. The credit aggregate selected for our empirical investigation is the non-food credit extended by the scheduled commercial banks including their non-SLR investments in instruments like PSU bonds, equities, debentures *etc* (represented as *NFCADJ* and credit henceforth).

4.1 The Credit Supply Function

The commercial banking system in India serves as the primary source of supply in the credit market. The quantity of loans provided by the banking system is a function of both its willingness and ability to undertake credit creation. In our specification of the credit supply function, a portfolio management approach is followed whereby given the rates of return of various assets, the banks take into account the available resources in deciding the extent of credit to be supplied.

Following Bernanke and Blinder (1988), we approximate the available resources by 'free reserves' (*FR*) left after the statutory CRR and secondary SLR pre-emptions from the aggregate deposits (*Dep*) of the banking system. Thus, available resources are represented as:

$$FR = Dep(1\text{-}crr\text{-}slr) \qquad (1)$$

Credit supply is further posited to depend on a host of financial prices. It is expected that the credit supply would tend to be positively affected by the lending rate of the banks (*LENDRT*), represented here as average prime-lending rate (PLR) of five major public banks and State Bank of India's advance rate till 1996–97. Secondly, the discount rate of 91-day Treasury Bills (*TB91*) being the return of a risk-free asset is considered in this investigation as the proxy of the government bond rate. The supply of credit would be inversely related to the interest rate of an alternate asset, that is, the discount rate of the 91-day Treasury bills. Thirdly, the equity price index, as proxied by the Bombay Stock Exchange Sensitive Index (Base: 1979–80=100) (*SENSEX*) is hypothesised as a determinant so as to capture the balance sheets effects on the credit supply function. Overall economic environment is represented by two proxies. Inflation rate is predicted to have a negative effect on banks' credit supply as high inflation leads to greater uncertainty and banks become more cautious in lending. Industrial output, the second proxy, is expected to have a positive sign.

To sum up, our formulation is:

$$NFCADJ^s = f_1(LENDRT, TB91, SENSEX, FR, IIP, WPI) \quad (2)$$

4.2 Credit Demand Function

Demand for credit by the private sector arises because production costs are normally incurred by the firm at regular intervals and are to be paid even before any sales revenue is received. In an uncertain environment, the firm may not always be able to foresee accurately the working capital requirement because of unexpected changes in structure of its cost as well as revenue. In general, the firm tries to smoothen the twin impact of these cost and revenue shocks through borrowing. The ability of a firm to acquire credit thus determines its current period productive activity. Accordingly, in the specification of the credit demand ($NFCADJ^d$) the scale variable is proxied by the index of industrial production (*IIP*) given its higher frequency data availability than GDP. There is direct dependence of credit demand on the output reflecting the transactions/precautionary demand for credit by the firms on account of working capital or liquidity considerations. It is expected that the demand for credit depends inversely on the lending rate of banks reflecting the tendency of the firms to postpone production plans when the lending rate increases on account of higher cost of working capital, as well as *vice versa*. As higher level of inflation would erode the value of nominal debt, demand for credit depends positively on the expected inflation rate. Industrial output is expected to have a positive effect on demand for credit. Thus,

$$NFCADJ^d = f_2(LENDRT, IIP, WPI) \quad (3)$$

4.3 Estimation Results

Our results are as follows. First, we found that all the relevant variables are I(1) as per the ADF test results. Long- run and short-run relationships are then analysed for both credit demand and supply with co-integrating VAR and ECM, respectively. Then certain causality tests are also run.

Credit Supply: From panels A, B and C of the Table 7.2, reporting the three tests of co-integration, namely Maximal Eigenvalue and Trace of the Stochastic Matrix as well as the using the SBC Model Selection Criteria, we find that there is at least one co-integrating vector among the variables. The F-value being significant in the ECM equation in panel D of the table shows that none of the endogenous variables in the co-integrating VAR is weakly exogenous.

Table 7.2: Co-integrating VAR and ECM Results: Co-integration with unrestricted intercepts and restricted trends in VAR

104 observations from 1993M5 to 2001M12. Order of VAR = 1.
List of variables included in the co-integrating vector:
LNFCADJ, LENDRT, LFR, LSENSEX, TB91, LIIP, LWPI and Trend
List of eigen values in descending order:
.51491 .25073 .20681 .15326 .12959 .099518 .051346

Panel A: Co-integration LR Test Based on Maximal Eigen value of the Stochastic Matrix

Null	*Alternative*	*Statistic*	*95% Critical Value*	*90% Critical Value*
r = 0	r = 1	75.2354	49.3200	46.5400
r<= 1	r = 2	30.0209	43.6100	40.7600

Panel B: Co-integration LR Test Based on Trace of the Stochastic Matrix

Null	*Alternative*	*Statistic*	*95% Critical Value*	*90% Critical Value*
r = 0	r >= 1	177.4714	147.2700	141.8200
r<= 1	r >= 2	102.2359	115.8500	110.6000

Panel C: Choice of the Number of Co-integrating Relations Using Model Selection Criteria

Rank	*Maximised LL*	*AIC*	*SBC*	*HQC*
r = 0	1081.8	1074.8	1065.6	1071.1
r = 1	1119.5	1098.5	1070.7	1087.2
r = 2	1134.5	1101.5	1057.8	1083.8

Panel D: ECM for variable LNFCADJ estimated by OLS based on co-integrating VAR (1)

Regressor	*Coefficient*	*Standard Error*	*T-Ratio [Prob]*
ecm1 (-1)	-.22675	-.046395	4.8873 [.000]

ecm1 = 1.00*LNFCADJ -.0080630*LENDRT -.12441*LFR + -.93628*LIIP 0042392*LSENSEX + .0012025*TB91 + .42102*LWPI — .010145*Trend
R-Bar-Squared = 0.18180
F(1, 102) = 23.8858 [.000]
DW-statistic : 2.3339

We normalise the co-integrating vector and impose successively over-identifying restrictions on the variables under examination. Table 7.3 (Panel B) reports the likelihood ratio test statistics for the null hypotheses of individual variables being not causally linked in the co-integrating VAR.

Table 7.3: Estimated Normalised Co-integrated Vectors in Johansen Estimation (SEs in brackets)

104 observations from 1993M5 to 2001M12
Order of VAR = 1, chosen r =1.
List of variables included in the co-integrating vector:
LNFCADJ, LENDRT, LFR, LSENSEX, TB91, LIIP, LWPI and Trend
List of imposed restriction(s) on co-integrating vectors:
a1=1

Panel A: Co-integrating Vector –Vector 1

LNFCADJ	1.0000 (*NONE*)
LENDRT	-.0080630 (.0073852)
LFR	-.12441 (.15851)
LSENSEX	.0042392 (.026624)
TB91	.0012025 (.0030144)
LIIP	-.93628 (.13814)
LWPI	.42102 (.28799)
Trend	-.010145 (.0026182)

LL subject to exactly identifying restrictions 1119.5

Panel B: LR Test of Restrictions

a1=1; a2=0	CHSQ (1) = 1.1161 [.291]
a1=1; a3=0	CHSQ (1) =.57604 [.448]
a1=1; a4=0	CHSQ (1) = .025289 [.874]
a1=1; a5=0	CHSQ (1) = .15991 [.689]
a1=1; a6=0	CHSQ (1) = 49.5094 [.000]
a1=1; a7=0	CHSQ (1)= 45.6581 [.000]

This test is significant only for *LIIP* and *LWPI* and shows that the null hypotheses of non-causality of these variables in credit supply are rejected. Thus, industrial output as well as prices 'Granger cause' the credit supply by banks. This seems to indicate that the ongoing industrial downturn seems to make the banks less inclined to offer credit to industry. The estimated credit supply function also shows that credit supply by banks is positively related to free reserves, as expected. It is positively driven by the lending rate of banks but negatively influenced by the alternate risk-free rate of return on gilts. Equity prices are found to have a negative relationship with credit supply.

Credit Demand: The results are reported in Tables 7.4 and 7.5. Table 7.4 shows that at least one co-integrating vector exists between the variables and credit demand. The ECM term being negative and significant shows that the short-term deviation from the long-term equilibrium relationships tend to come back to equilibrium with stability. The F-value being significant shows that none of the endogenous variables in the co-integrating VAR is weakly exogenous.

Table 7.4: Co-integrating VAR and ECM Results: Co-integration with unrestricted intercepts and restricted trends in VAR

104 observations from 1993M5 to 2001M12. Order of VAR = 1.
List of variables included in the co-integrating vector:
LNFCADJ, LENDRT, LIIP, LWPI and Trend
List of eigen values in descending order:
.46177 .17920 .14947 .056001 0.00

Panel A: Co-integration LR Test Based on Maximal Eigen value of the Stochastic Matrix

Null	Alternative	Statistic	95% Critical Value	90% Critical Value
r = 0	r = 1	64.4251	31.7900	29.1300
r<= 1	r = 2	20.5380	25.4200	23.1000

Panel B: Co-integration LR Test Based on Trace of the Stochastic Matrix

Null	Alternative	Statistic	95% Critical Value	90% Critical Value
r = 0	r >= 1	107.7939	63.0000	59.1600
r<= 1	r >= 2	43.3688	42.3400	39.3400

Panel C: Choice of the Number of Co-integrating Relations Using Model Selection Criteria

Rank	Maximised LL	AIC	SBC	HQC
r = 0	753.2962	749.2962	744.0074	747.1536
r = 1	785.5087	773.5087	757.6424	767.0808
R = 2	795.7777	777.7777	753.9782	768.1359

Panel D: ECM for variable LNFCADJ estimated by OLS based on co-integrating VAR (1)

Regressor	Coefficient	Standard Error	T-Ratio [Prob]
ecm1 = 1.0000*LNFCADJ -.0051487*LENDRT -.97249*LIIP + .39710*LWPI -.011754*Trend R-Bar-Squared = .18773 F (1,102) = 24.8055 [.000] DW-statistic : 2.3380			
Ecm1 (-1)	-.22339	-.044853	4.9805 [.000]

Table 7.5 Estimated Normalised Co-integrated Vectors in Johansen Estimation (SEs in brackets)

104 observations from 1993M5 to 2001M12
Order of VAR = 1, chosen r =1.
List of variables included in the co-integrating vector:
LNFCADJ, LENDRT, LIIP, LWPI and Trend

List of imposed restriction(s) on co-integrating vectors:
a1=1

Panel A: Co-integrating Vector 1

LNFCADJ	1.0000 (*NONE*)
LENDRT	-.0051487 (.0064394)
LIIP	-.97249 (.14693
LWPI	.39710 (.24642)
Trend	-.011754 (.8609E-3)

LL subject to exactly identifying restrictions : 785.51

Panel B: LR Test Results of Restrictions

a1=1; a2=0	CHSQ (1) = .60763 [.436]
a1=1; a3=0	CHSQ (1) = 46.0095 [.000]
a1=1; a4=0	CHSQ (1) = 51.8144 [.000]

The null hypothesis of non-association of *LIIP* and *LWPI* are rejected given the significant chi-square values whereas the lending rate does not appear to cause credit demand. Credit demand is found to be predominantly and positively influenced by industrial activity. Although credit demand is positively related to the lending rate of banks it is not significant. This reflects the dominant influence of the current slowdown on credit demand.

5. The Relevance of 'Mixed Portfolio-Loan Demand Model' for India

The 'Mixed Portfolio–Loan Demand Approach' (Palley 1994) envisages a structuralist view of endogenous money. Thus, pressures within financial markets are the basic determinants both of money supply growth and of credit availability. Banks actively manage their assets and liabilities position. This brings to the fore a distinct channel for loan accommodation. Howells and Hussein (1998) found endogeneity in broad money in the G7 countries (*viz.*, US, Canada, Italy and Japan (1957.1 to 1992.4), Germany (1969.1 to 1992.4), UK (1975.1 to 1993.4), France (1977.4 to 1992.4)) where loans 'Granger-caused' deposits. There are results for Australia to show that interest rate deregulation in Australia since the 1970s induced banks to switch from asset management to liability management and money stock became demand-determined and coincident rather than a leading indicator of economic activity (Battellino & McMillan 1989).

After the initiation of reforms banks in India were given considerable operational freedom in fixing interest rates on loans and deposits, issue of new money market instruments (like CDs for wholesale deposit mobilisation). The resources raised through CDs were quite substantial when the liquidity situation was tight (Table 7.6). The differential reserve requirements across liability categories raised by banks have also entailed liability management for banks by inducing a shift between different liability categories within the overall liabilities, eventually facilitating deployment of funds by banks. The various concessions from the statutory reserve maintenance prevalent for external deposits till the October 2001 Credit Policy also prompted the banks to draw external deposits. Inter-bank liabilities, still exempted from reserve maintenance, have also emerged as an important source of funds for commercial banks. The banks also take recourse to the RBI in the form of normal or liquidity adjustment facility for undertaking liability management.

Table 7.6: Resources Raised by Scheduled Commercial Banks (Amount in Rs.crore)

Outstanding as on March	*CDs*	*Inter bank Liabilities*	*Borrowing from RBI*	*NRI Deposits*
1990–91	-	6,486	3,468	27,400
1991–92	5,682	7,033	577	40,304
1992–93	9,803	11,148	1,619	46,992
1993–94	5,571	11,283	1,813	50,916
1994–95	8,017	15,327	7,415	54,066
1995–96	16,316	17,648	4,847	59,927
1996–97	12,134	21,193	560	73,204
1997–98	14,296	32,287	395	80,460
1998–99	3,717	45,204	2,894	86,909
1999–00	1,227	53,838	6,491	94,544
2000–01	771	77,088	3,896	1,07,680

We test Palley's 1994 hypothesis on Indian data through a co-integrating VAR approach and examine the causality issues among the variables.

The results reported in Table 7.7 indicate the presence of one co-integrating vector (r = 1) on the basis of the three tests of co-integration *viz.*, maximal eigenvalue of the stochastic matrix, trace of the stochastic matrix and model selection criteria in terms of SBC values.

Table 7.7: Co-integrating VAR Results

237 observations from 1980M7 to 2000M3. Order of VAR = 4.
List of variables included in the co-integrating vector: LM_0, LNFC and Z_3
List of eigen values in descending order: 0.11140 0.066132 0.0012229

Panel A: Co-integration LR Test Based on Maximal Eigen value of the Stochastic Matrix

Null	Alternative	Statistic	95% Critical Value	90% Critical Value
r = 0	r = 1	27.9905	24.3500	22.2600
r<= 1	r = 2	16.2156	18.3300	16.2800
r<= 2	r = 3	3.29001	11.5400	9.7500

Panel B: Co-integration LR Test Based on Trace of the Stochastic Matrix

Null	Alternative	Statistic	95% Critical Value	90% Critical Value
r = 0	r >= 1	44.4961	39.3300	36.2800
r<= 1	r >= 2	16.5056	23.8300	21.2300
r<= 2	r = 3	0.29001	11.5400	9.7500

Panel C: Choice of the Number of Co-integrating Relations Using Model Selection Criteria

Rank	Maximised LL	AIC	SBC	HQC
r = 0	1701.0	1668.0	1610.8	1645.0
r = 1	1715.0	1677.0	1611.1	1650.5
r = 2	1723.1	1682.1	1611.0	1653.5
r = 3	1723.3	1681.3	1608.4	1651.9

The unconstrained equation is given in panel A of Table 7.8 under Johansen's just-identifying restrictions. Panel B gives ML estimates subject to exactly identifying restriction(s) for the normalised values along with their respective standard errors.

We restricted the co-integrating vector by successively taking the coefficients as equal to zero. The resulting CHSQ statistics in all the three cases (reported in panel C of Table 7.8) are above the critical value for the null of the coefficient being equal to zero, thus we reject the null of the coefficient being zero.

We refer to the error correction terms for each of the variables as *dLM0*, *dLNFC* and *dZ3* in panels A, B and C of Table 10. As can be seen, F-values are significant in all three error correction equations so that none of the endogenous variables in the co-integrating VAR is weakly exogenous. We have negative signs for the two error correction terms dLM_0 and *dLNFC*. While dZ_3 has a positive (but insignificant) coefficient for the error correction term, they are both negative and significant for both *dLNFC* and dLM_0, thus displaying stability in their short-run movements.

Table 7.8: Estimated Co-integrated Vectors in Johansen Estimation

237 observations from 1980M7 to 2000M3. Order of VAR = 4, chosen r =1.
List of variables included in the co-integrating vector: LM_0, LNFC and Z_3

Panel A: Co-integrating Vectors using Johansen's Just-identifying Restrictions (Normalised in Brackets)

Variable	Vector 1
LM_0	4.2915 (-1.0000)
LNFC	0.89592 (-0.20877)
Z_3	1.2421 (-0.28944)

Panel B: ML estimates subject to exactly identifying restriction(s): Estimates of Restricted Co-integrating Relations (SE's in Brackets) Converged after 2 iterations

Variable	Vector 1
LM_3	1.0000 (None)
LNFC	0.20877 (0.14006)
Z_3	0.28944 (0.015546)

Panel C: LR Tests of over-identifying restriction(s): Estimates of Restricted Co-integrating Relations (SE's in Brackets)

Restriction	LR Test of Restrictions
A1 = 0	CHSQ (1) = 8.6577 [0.003]
A2 = 0	CHSQ (1) = 2.979 [0.084]
A3 = 0	CHSQ (1) = 8.7533 [.003]

Table 7.9: ECM for variable LM_0 estimated by OLS based on co-integrating VAR(4)

237 observations used for estimation from 1980M7 to 2000M3			
Panel A: Dependent variable is dLM_0			
Regressor	**Coefficient**	**Standard Error**	**T-Ratio [Prob]**
Intercept	4.4833	1.5570	2.8795 [.004]
dLM01	-0.15384	0.24814	-0.61999 [.536]
DLNFC1	0.14555	0.13732	1.0599 [.290]
dZ31	.097722	0.081423	1.2002 [.231]
dLM02	-.73541	0.24630	-2.9859 [.003]
DLNFC2	0.43732	0.13164	3.3222 [.001]
dZ32	-0.17256	0.080577	-2.1416 [.033]
dLM03	-0.12480	0.25285	-0.49359 [.622]
DLNFC3	0.57888	0.13049	4.4362 [.000]
dZ33	-0.024465	0.079735	-0.30683 [.759]
ecm1(-1)	-0.35866	0.12504	-2.8683 [.005]
$ecm1 = 1.0*LM_0 + 0.19440*LNFC + 0.28943*Z_3 — 0.015781*Trend$			
R-Bar-Squared = 0.26235; F (10, 226) = 9.3935 [.000] ; DW-statistic = 2.0015			
Panel B: Dependent variable is dLNFC			
Regressor	**Coefficient**	**Standard Error**	**T-Ratio [Prob]**
Intercept	3.0126	0.85633	3.5180 [.001]
DDLM01	-0.39797	0.13647	-2.9161[.004]
DLNFC1	-0.054601	0.075528	-0.7229 [.470]
dZ31	-0.11664	0.044782	-2.6046 [.010]
dLM02	-0.54192	0.13546	-4.0005 [.000]
DLNFC2	0.16040	0.072398	2.2155 [.028]
dZ32	-0.15764	0.044317	-3.5571[.000]
dLM03	-0.55460	0.13907	-3.9880[.000]
DLNFC3	0.43565	0.071768	6.0703 [.000]
dZ33	-0.16920	0.043854	-3.858 [.000]
ecm1(-1)	-0.23945	0.068773	-3.482 [.001]
$ecm1 = 1.0*LM_0 + 0.19440*LNFC + 0.28943*Z_3 — 0.015781*Trend$			
R-Bar-Squared = 0.26396; F (10, 226) = 9.4635 [.000] ; DW-statistic = 1.9677			
Panel C: Dependent variable is dZ_3			
Regressor	**Coefficient**	**Standard Error**	**T-Ratio [Prob]**
Intercept	-6.2689	4.6831	-1.3386 [.182]
dLM01	0.13944	0.74634	0.18683 [.852]
DLNFC1	-0.44038	0.41304	-1.0662 [.287]
dZ31	-0.49489	0.24490	-2.0208 [.044]
dLM02	1.7831	0.74082	2.4070 [.017]
DLNFC2	-1.1120	0.39593	-2.8086 [.005]
dZ32	0.29694	0.24236	1.2252 [.222]
dLM03	-0.52509	0.76053	-0.69043 [.491]
DLNFC3	-1.2567	0.39248	-3.2018 [.002]
dZ33	-0.25335	0.23983	-1.0564 [.292]
ecm1(-1)	0.50466	0.37610	1.3418 [.181]
$ecm1 = 1.0*LM_0 + 0.19440*LNFC + 0.28943*Z_3 — 0.015781*Trend$			
R-Bar-Squared = 0.27922; F (10, 226) = 10.1422 [.000] ; DW-statistic = 2.04			

6. Credit *Versus* Money as an Intermediate Target

6.1 Monetary Targeting in India with Feedback

Pursuant to the recommendations of the Committee to Review the Working of the Monetary System (Chairman Sukhamoy Chakravarty), monetary targeting approach was adopted in India since mid-1980s with the ultimate target of price stability. Broad money was the intermediate target. This was due to a perception of a stable money demand function which enabled reasonably accurate medium-term price predictions, especially since interest rates were administered and capital flows were discouraged. Further, broad money as an intermediate target was perceived to give an unambiguous signal to the public. M_3 indicative targets were set in line with expected growth in output and tolerable level of prices. The operating procedure was defined in terms of reserve money with bank reserves (CRR) being the principal operating instrument. Although monetary targeting was adopted in the mid-1980s, no specific targets were set during 1985–90 except for fixing a ceiling linked to the average growth of broad money in the previous year(s). However, with the onset of economic reforms and liberalisation, the monetary targeting approach for monetary policy formulation was replaced by a multiple indicator approach in 1998–99.

6.2 Credit as Target

One comes across frequent revisit to credit as an intermediate target for monetary policy. This is partly on account of breakdown of money-income-price relationship in a financially liberalised economy, impact of financial innovations and absence of perfect substitutability of bank loans and other methods of financing expenditure. Credit scores over money in view of stability of credit/GDP ratio in face of significant variability of M_3/GDP ratio. While financial innovations spawn various cash holding close substitutes serving as medium of exchange, no ready substitutes are available for bank loans used for financing expenditures.

Some authors have argued in favour of using credit as an intermediate target (Filc 1993; Rath 2001). For this to be viable, the relationship between credit and *GDP* should be as close as the relationship between M_3 and *GDP* but less volatile. Second, the causal relationship should run from credit to *GDP* and not the other way round.

Table 7.10 presents some descriptive statistics of the *Credit-GDP* and M_3-*GDP* ratios. As can be seen, the coefficient of variation of *Credit-GDP* ratio is higher than that of M_3-*GDP* ratio. Both are I (1) processes.

An empirical exercise was conducted to find out the direction of causation between credit and output with the help of a bivariate VAR. The results are presented in Table 7.11. Panels A, B and C of the table present the co-integration results and panel D the results of the causality test. On the basis of the unrestricted bivariate VAR exercise (with intercept and trend), it is found that IIP and non-food credit are co-integrated (both being I(1) at the appropriate lag chosen by information criteria), suggesting that in the long run both these variables move in equilibrium. The co-integration result between these two variables for the sample period April 1980 to March 2001, suggest that one per cent increase in *IIP* leads to 0.45 per cent increase in non-food credit.

Table 7.10: Descriptive Statistics for M_3 and Credit as Ratios of GDP at factor cost

Item	*Credit-GDP* Ratio	M_3-*GDP* Ratio
Maximum	0.24335	0.58155
Minimum	0.052849	0.21611
Mean	0.14352	0.37686
Std. Deviation	0.062909	0.13186
Skewness	0.16986	0.33748
Kurtosis – 3	-1.5421	-1.5722
Coeff of Variation	0.43834	0.34989
ADF (1)	-1.2141 (-3.5088)	-1.7973 (-3.5112)

Note: Critical values are in parentheses.

The Granger causality of both the variables, however, indicates a bi-directional causation between *IIP* and non-food credit. The null hypothesis of the non-causality of *IIP* in the VAR is rejected with a significant chi-square value of 55.0 (*p* value of 0.0). Similarly, the null hypothesis of non-causality of non-food credit is also rejected with a significant CHSQ value of 54.3 (*p* value of 0.0).

Hence these results support the presence of bi-directional association between these two. As such, the usefulness of credit as an intermediate target seems to be rather limited.

The demand for credit is influenced by the industrial performance, which exerts an independent impact on the credit off-take from the banking system. The supply of credit should rise commensurately if this demand has to be satiated by the banking system to support industrial growth.

Table 7.11: Co-integration and Causality Tests Between NFC and IIP

Panel A: Co-integration LR Test based on Eigen Value of Stochastic Matrix				
Null	**Alternative**	**Statistic**	**95% Critical Value**	**90% Critical Value**
r = 0	r = 1	55.2933	14.8800	12.9800
r<= 1	r = 2	.28826	8.0700	6.5000
Panel B: Co-integration LR Test Based on Trace of the Stochastic Matrix				
r = 0	r >= 1	55.5816	17.8600	15.7500
r<= 1	r = 2	.28826	8.0700	6.5000
Panel C: Choice of the Number of Co-integrating Relations Using Model Selection Criteria				
Rank	**Maximized LL**	**AIC**	**SBC**	**HQC**
r = 0	894.9348	888.9348	878.6732	884.7937
r = 1	922.5815	913.5815	898.1891	907.3697
r = 2	922.7256	912.7256	895.6229	905.8237
Panel D: Estimated coefficients in a co-integrating VAR with Johansen ML Method (SE's in Brackets)				
LIIP	-2.2066 (0.03695)	LIIP		1.0000
LNFC	1.0000	LNFC		-0.45318 (0.00759)
LR Test of Restrictions: a2 =1 and a1 = 0; CHSQ (1) = 54.9993 [0.000]		LR Test of Restrictions a1=1; a2 = 0; CHSQ (1) = 54.2964 [0.000]		

7. Concluding Observations

Given the changes in the monetary policy framework as well as India's experience with credit trends in the post-reform period, this chapter has attempted to understand the possibility of using credit as an intermediate target of monetary policy. The credit-output relationship is shown to be bi-directional. The simplified model pertaining to the post-reform period shows that during the post-reform period, the industrial output continues to exert predominant influence on credit demand and supply.

Given the role of credit in endogenising the money supply process in the context of real sector impulses and innovative liability management practices by banks, the possibility of using credit as an intermediate target variable has been tested in the paper. From the policy angle, credit turns out to be as weak a variable as money.

References

Battellino, R. and N. McMillan (1989), 'Changes in the Behaviour of Banks and Their Implications for Financial Aggregates', in I. Macfarlane and G. Stevens (eds), *Studies in Money and Credit* (Reserve Bank of Australia, Research Department, October 1989).

Bernanke, B. and A. Blinder, 'Credit, Money and Aggregate Demand', *American Economic Review (AEA Papers and Proceedings)*, 78 (1988).

Bernanke, B., M. Gertler and S. Gilchrist, 'The Financial Accelerator in a Quantitative Business Cycle Framework', in J.B. Taylor and M. Woodford (eds), *Handbook of Macroeconomics* (Amsterdam, North Holland, 1999).

Catao, L. and S. Rodriguez, 'Banks and Monetary Shocks in Emerging Markets: How Far can we Go with the Credit View?', *IMF Working Paper* WP/00/68 (2000).

Filc, W., 'Credit as an Intermediate Target of Monetary Policy', in S.F. Frowen (ed.), *Monetary Theory and Monetary Policy — New Tracks for the 1990s* (St. Martin's Press, 1993).

Fisher, I., *The Theory of Interest* (New York: Macmillan, 1930).

Howells, P. and K. Hussein, 'The Endogeneity of Money: Evidence from the G 7', *Scottish Journal of Political Economy* (1998).

Mukhopadhyaya, H. (1998), 'Monetary Transmission Mechanism: The Credit Channel Hypothesis Revisited', paper presented at the 1st Conference on Money and Finance (Mumbai: Indira Gandhi Institute of Development Research, 1998).

Palley T.I., 'Competing Views on the Money Supply Process: Theory and Evidence', *Metronomica*, 54(1) (February 1994).

Rakshit, M., 'Money and Public Finance under Structural Adjustment: The Indian Experience', *Economic and Political Weekly* (16–23 April 1994).

Rath, D., *Endogeneity Issues in the Money Supply Process of India*, Ph.D Thesis (Mumbai: Indira Gandhi Institute of Development Research, September 2001).

Reserve Bank of India, *Report on Currency and Finance*, 1998–99 (1999).

——, Annual *Report*, 2000–01 (2001).

——, *Report on Currency and Finance*, 2000–01 (2002).

——, *Monetary Policy Statement, April* (2002b)

Stiglitz, J. and A. Weiss, 'Credit Rationing in Markets with Imperfect Information', *American Economic Review*, 71(3) (June 1981).

8
The Fiscal Constraint on India's Economic Growth

Raghbendra Jha, Satish Chand, Anurag Sharma

1. Introduction

The role of the state in harnessing resources for provision of public services, a minimal set of which is necessary to induce productive activity, has been well and long recognized. The new institutional economics literature has brought to the fore the necessity of a stable regulatory environment to induce exchange across space and over time; no doubt the trading hubs that were developed over centuries had much of these but their presence was confined to the trading enclaves only. Current thinking on the role of the state in development has undergone rapid transformation and one adequately reflected by India where there has been a steady shift away from an activist state to one focussed on creating and maintaining an enabling environment for growth of private enterprise. This transition is ongoing but perhaps not at the desired pace for many external commentators.

Given weak institutions and a limited capacity of the private sector to supply goods and services that have considerable economies of scale, a developing country state is often compelled to supply goods such as aviaion services and utilities. The resource implications of these obligations are severe and particularly so when the capacity to raise revenues via taxes and user charges are limited by the growing strength of lobbies that inevitably form around public handouts. The ensuing deficits leading to rising public sector debt limit the ability of the state to sustain the provisions over the long run. Moreover, the funding of such deficits impinges on the rest of the economy via its impact on interest rates and inflation.[1]

[1] For an example for the case of India see Ansari and Athabasca (1996).

India provides an interesting case study on the role and ramifications of an activist state in development. Since independence, the Indian government has been active in the provision of several goods and services, many of which may not be considered as being public in nature. For example, the state has been engaged in steel milling, electricity generation, fertilizer production, provision of all forms of public transportation, etc. These interventions were based on the best of intentions, though the outcome has often not been consistent with the aspirations of the architects of the activist policies. Thinking on the role of the state in development has also undergone rapid transformation over the last half century. The thinking following the post World War II period within developing countries was of the state having a lead role in development; this has changed to one where the state acts as a facilitator of commerce some fifty years later. Fiscal policy in India has followed this change in development thinking, but with a considerable lag due to the inertia in the system that inevitably develops around public handouts.

There appear to be three crucial facts about the deficit/debt situation in India. First, total public expenditure has routinely outpaced revenues leading to rising public sector debt. Second, rising debt servicing commitments are crowding out capital investments and provision of public services. Third, given the political factors underscoring the deficit bias, there is little hope for a resolution of the deficit bias in the short to medium term.

2. Three Stylized Facts on Deficits and Debt in India

2.1 The growth in the fiscal deficit shows no immediate sign of waning

Some economists have argued that sustainability tests based on intertemporal government budget constraints reveal that the prevailing deficit and debt levels of the state are not sustainable (for a review see Jha 2001). Jha and Sharma (2003), however, extend this analysis to allow for regime shifts in public expenditure and revenue and conclude that the public debt is not unsustainable. However, given the pressing burden of debt servicing on current resources, there is an urgent necessity to reduce the public debt.

The burden of the debt is illustrated in Table 8.1. Never have primary deficits been negative, indeed they have been growing recently. Hence current budgetary operations are actually leading to a net accumulation of debt. The revenue and fiscal deficits are both high and growing of late. The reduction in the fiscal deficit of the central government in the immediate aftermath of the reforms was partially compensated for by a rise in state government deficits. As a consequence state government debt has been rising steadily and is now above the constitutionally mandated limit of 20 per cent of SDP for a number of states.

Table 8.1: Measures of Deficits of Central and State Governments (% of GDP)

Year	Central Government			State Governments			Central + State Governments		
	Net Fiscal Deficit	*Net Primary Deficit*	*Net Revenue Deficit*	*Net Fiscal Deficit*	*Net Primary Deficit*	*Net Revenue Deficit*	*Net Fiscal Deficit*	*Net Primary Deficit*	*Net Revenue Deficit*
1990–91	5.4	3.15	3.26	2.6	1.5	0.9	8.0	4.65	4.16
1991–92	3.77	1.37	2.49	2.4	1.5	0.9	5.17	3.86	3.39
1992–93	4.04	1.56	2.48	2.1	0.9	0.7	6.14	2.46	3.18
1993–94	5.35	2.83	3.81	1.9	0.6	0.4	7.25	3.43	4.25
1994–95	3.98	1.19	3.06	2.3	0.9	0.6	6.23	2.09	3.66
1995–96	3.57	0.91	2.50	2.2	0.9	0.7	5.77	1.81	3.27
1996–97	3.39	0.66	2.39	2.4	1.2	1.2	5.79	1.86	3.59
1997–98	4.14	1.49	3.05	2.6	1.1	1.1	6.74	2.59	4.15
1998–99	4.59	1.85	3.85	3.8	2.2	2.5	8.39	4.05	6.35
1999–2000	4.66	1.74	3.5	4.1	2.3	2.8	8.76	4.07	6.3
2000–01	5.16	1.96	4.08	3.9	2.0	2.5	9.06	3.96	6.58
2001–02 (RE)	5.27	2.25	3.99	4.2	1.8	2.6	9.47	4.05	6.59
2002–03 (BE)	4.85	1.89	3.73	3.4	1.0	1.8	8.25	2.89	5.53

RE= revised estimate
BE = budget estimate

Source: Computed from Reserve Bank of India Annual Report 2001–02

Table 8.2 reports on the time path of total central and state government debt. As a response to the reforms the public debt (net liabilities of central and state governments) dropped marginally as the government was obliged to lower fiscal deficits. However debt picked up again and then fell in the aftermath of the rapid growth in tax revenues following the high economic growth of mid to late 1990s. Since the fiscal deficit problem was not tackled and economic growth slowed down since the late 1990s public debt picked up again (Table 8.2).

Table 8.2: Public Debt in India (exclusive of Contingent Liabilities)

Year	Total Public Debt as % of GDP
1990–91	61.68
1991–92	60.86
1992–93	60.36
1993–94	62.39
1994–95	59.89
1995–96	57.82
1996–97	56.29
1997–98	58.25
1999–00	58.58
2000–01	62.59

Source: Computed from *Indian Public Finance Statistics, 2001–02* and Reserve Bank of India*Handbook of Statistics on the Indian Economy, 2001.*

During 2002–03 the stock of public debt appears to have gone up to almost 70 per cent of GDP. This computation, however does not take account of contingent liabilities, mainly in the form of guarantees, which are currently close to 14 per cent of GDP.[2] Furthermore these contingent liabilities do not include the much larger obligations of pensions and recapitalization requirements of weak public sector banks and the Unit Trust of India. It is a result of such budgetary pressures that Standard and Poor's credit rating of government bonds has come down substantially. This credit rating is now at par with Colombia and Morocco and behind Tunisia, Thailand and South Africa. Although the debt-GDP ratios of some developed countries have often far exceeded Indian levels, what causes concern is the low tax/GDP ratio of the Indian economy. This ratio has been below 17 per cent

[2] In a press release on 16 October 2002 the Reserve Bank of India deplored the high level of state government guarantees which had gone up from 8 per cent of GDP in March 2000 to 8.1 per cent of GDP in March 2001.

(compared with almost 30 per cent for most OECD economies) and has tended to stagnate of late. In fact economic reforms seem to have little impact on the tax/GDP ratio (Table 8.3).

2.3 Deficits and debt are not likely to be resolved in the short to medium terms.

Although official publications and informed commentators have long called for reductions in fiscal deficits, achieving a primary surplus — an important requirement for inducing a net decrease in the public debt — seems hard to attain. Several reasons can be cited and the following is only a partial list. Beginning at the level of the states the sudden spurt in state level debt in the immediate aftermath of the reforms is to be ascribed to the reduction in federal transfers. Problems got compounded through ever growing burden of the debts of State Electricity Boards (primarily as a result of inefficiency and poor pricing policies), the adoption of the norms of the Fifth Pay Commission in respect of state government employees and deteriorating tax effort. So far as the central government is concerned it has been encumbered by the problems of debt servicing. In addition cutting of major subsidies, for example, on food, fertilizers, higher education and the like — has proved difficult. The efficiency and targeting of these subsidies has been difficult to improve in the short run and many of them are perceived to be needed to shield the most vulnerable sections of the population from the effects of structural reforms (see Chapter 21 in this volume). Furthermore there is a political economy aspect to this. A strong government is needed to take the hard decisions on fiscal deficits and their relation with economic reforms. There is considerable theoretical as well as empirical support to the proposition that multi-party governments with different ideological motivations have a tendency to run budget deficits; this being true even when all the parties in the coalition prefer balanced budgets (see Alesina and Perotti 1995 and Balassone and Giordano 2001). Weak coalition governments have overwhelmed the Indian political scene for much of the past decade; hence the will to take decisive action and at the risk of losing support from some of the vested interests has been absent. The chances of fiscal consolidation within the short to medium term so as to meet sustainability criterion that is necessary to lower interest rates are minimal if any. Thus, lowering service commitments on debt; reduction of subsidies, elimination of cross subsidization and budgetary support to loss-making enterprises; and, inducing greater competition in the financial sector so as to lower interest rate spread on long-term bonds will remain as desirable actions for the foreseeable future. The containment of public expenditure as a mechanism to reduce deficits will be difficult, if not impossible, in the short to medium term.

Table 8.3: Tax–GDP Ratios (percentages): 1950–51 to 2001–02

Year	Total tax revenue (Centre plus states) (A+C)			Central taxes (gross) (A)			States' share in central taxes (B)		
	Direct	Indirect	Total	Direct	Indirect	Total	Direct	Indirect	Total
1	2	3	4	5	6	7	8	9	10
1950–51	2.33	3.99	6.31	1.77	2.31	4.08	0.48	0.00	0.48
1951–52	2.31	4.68	6.99	1.80	3.05	4.85	0.50	0.00	0.50
1952–53	2.43	4.11	6.54	1.79	2.50	4.29	0.54	0.16	0.70
1953–54	2.15	3.81	5.96	1.47	2.25	3.72	0.51	0.13	0.65
1954–55	2.25	4.50	6.74	1.51	2.75	4.26	0.53	0.13	0.66
1955–56	2.38	4.68	7.06	1.57	2.89	4.46	0.52	0.16	0.68
1956–57	2.22	4.65	6.87	1.50	2.90	4.40	0.39	0.21	0.60
1957–58	2.45	5.38	7.83	1.72	3.46	5.18	0.57	0.30	0.87
1958–59	2.31	5.01	7.32	1.60	3.11	4.71	0.50	0.49	1.00
1959–60	2.41	5.35	7.76	1.72	3.35	5.07	0.50	0.47	0.97
1960–61	2.34	5.52	7.86	1.70	3.51	5.21	0.52	0.44	0.96
1961–62	2.47	6.01	8.48	1.85	3.94	5.79	0.54	0.45	0.98
1962–63	2.86	6.67	9.53	2.16	4.41	6.57	0.51	0.64	1.14
1963–64	3.08	7.26	10.34	2.45	4.82	7.27	0.55	0.60	1.16
1964–65	2.83	7.08	9.91	2.29	4.66	6.95	0.50	0.48	0.98
1965–66	2.65	7.91	10.56	2.16	5.29	7.45	0.47	0.53	1.00
1966–67	2.45	7.97	10.42	2.10	5.27	7.37	0.45	0.74	1.19
1967–68	2.13	7.30	9.43	1.79	4.63	6.42	0.49	0.64	1.14
1968–69	2.16	7.52	9.68	1.80	4.67	6.47	0.52	0.75	1.26
1969–70	2.25	7.57	9.82	1.93	4.67	6.60	0.70	0.75	1.45
1970–71	2.21	8.19	10.40	1.90	5.12	7.02	0.80	0.85	1.65
1971–72	2.39	9.00	11.39	2.14	5.78	7.92	0.96	0.97	1.93
1972–73	2.50	9.44	11.93	2.29	6.07	8.35	0.92	1.05	1.97
1973–74	2.37	8.90	11.26	2.10	5.63	7.73	0.82	0.96	1.78

1974–75	2.37	9.54	11.90	2.13	6.03	8.16	0.67	0.91	1.58
1975–76	2.99	10.43	13.43	2.65	6.49	9.14	0.89	1.03	1.92
1976–77	2.88	10.86	13.74	2.59	6.62	9.21	0.74	1.15	1.88
1977–78	2.64	10.39	13.03	2.37	6.35	8.72	0.67	1.10	1.77
1978–79	2.59	11.51	14.10	2.30	7.26	9.56	0.65	1.13	1.78
1979–80	2.56	12.07	14.63	2.33	7.58	9.91	0.72	2.09	2.82
1980–81	2.27	11.53	13.80	2.08	7.08	9.17	0.71	1.93	2.64
1981–82	2.45	11.87	14.32	2.25	7.15	9.40	0.61	1.92	2.53
1982–83	2.39	12.08	14.47	2.20	7.20	9.40	0.61	1.85	2.46
1983–84	2.24	12.13	14.36	2.05	7.39	9.44	0.54	1.85	2.39
1984–85	2.17	12.42	14.59	1.95	7.61	9.56	0.51	1.84	2.35
1985–86	2.25	13.32	15.56	2.02	8.29	10.31	0.67	2.02	2.69
1986–87	2.21	13.71	15.92	2.00	8.55	10.55	0.70	2.03	2.72
1987–88	2.11	13.97	16.08	1.91	8.72	10.63	0.73	1.98	2.71
1988–89	2.31	13.56	15.88	2.09	8.46	10.55	0.65	1.88	2.53
1989–90	2.30	13.68	15.98	2.06	8.56	10.62	0.81	1.91	2.72
1990–91	2.16	13.27	15.43	1.94	8.19	10.12	0.72	1.83	2.56
1991–92	2.55	13.25	15.80	2.35	7.96	10.31	0.78	1.85	2.63
1992–93	2.59	12.66	15.26	2.42	7.55	9.97	0.81	1.93	2.74
1993–94	2.53	11.67	14.19	2.36	6.45	8.82	0.90	1.68	2.59
1994–95	2.85	11.75	14.60	2.66	6.45	9.11	0.85	1.61	2.45
1995–96	3.01	11.74	14.75	2.83	6.54	9.36	0.95	1.52	2.47
1996–97	3.00	11.69	14.69	2.84	6.64	9.48	0.99	1.57	2.56
1997–98	2.82	11.17	13.99	2.67	5.97	8.65	0.89	1.47	2.36
1998–99	2.82	10.56	13.38	2.68	5.58	8.26	0.83	1.42	2.25
1999–2000	3.15	11.59	14.75	3.00	6.42	9.42	0.86	1.40	2.25
2000–01(R.E.)	n.a.	n.a.	15.32	3.57	5.93	9.50	n.a.	n.a.	2.58
2001–02(B.E.)	n.a.	n.a.	16.21	3.72	6.17	9.89	n.a.	n.a.	2 78

Note: 1. The ratios to GDP of the previous years have undergone changes as new series GDP (Base:1993–94)

Source: Indian Public Finance 2001–02, Government of India.

3. Policy Measures to Lower the Pressure of Deficits

Any program to lower the pressure of budgetary deficits must be part of a comprehensive programs of expenditure and tax reform and direct lowering of the public debt through strategic disinvestments in (privatization of) State owned enterprises. Expenditure reform would involve curtailing of inessential subsidies and more effective targeting to eliminate the impact of such reforms on the poor. The first order of business has to be the targeting of public expenditure. From food subsidies to public production of intermediate and capital goods, there is considerable evidence of mistargeting of expenditures. Several authors, e.g. Jha et al. (1999b) have commented on the mistargeting of major subsidy items such as food subsidies. The mistargeting of public expenditures in the design of anti poverty programs has been documented by Gaiha (2000) and others. The deleterious effects of several industrial subsidies have been documented by Jha and Sahni (1993). Thus there is no gainsaying that public expenditures in India whether these be at the central or state levels, on consumer or capital goods or public services need to be better targeted. In addition major reform in pubic expenditures as discussed in Jha (2002b) need to be effected.

Garnering substantial additional public revenues would depend crucially upon tax reforms, particularly those that raise the rate of savings and hence growth. Since the prime determinant of the saving rate appears to be the level and rate of growth of per capita income (Loayza, Schmidt–Hebbel & Serven 2000), all tax-induced distortions that create inefficiencies and lower the potential rate of economic growth should be eliminated. The basic tenets of tax reform are well known and far too elaborate for a complete analysis to be attempted here. (For a recent account see Jha 2002b). These are mentioned here and the performance of the Indian economy with respect to these is briefly assessed.

An important canon of tax reform is that as an economy develops reliance on indirect taxation, as a source of revenue should decline. This is because indirect taxes typically have an excess burden (or deadweight losses) associated with them. Furthermore efficient indirect taxation (one that minimizes excess burden to the representative consumer, for example) can be quite regressive[3]. One can make indirect taxes more progressive by sacrificing some amount of efficiency but the extent of the redistribution possible through such means is quite limited (Sah 1983).

---

[3] Efficient indirect taxation often calls for tax rates to vary inversely with the compensated elasticity of demand. This would make them 'regressive'.

This principle applies to indirect taxes that are differentiated and distortionary. If, however, indirect taxes can be levied on final consumption alone it would be possible to avoid the tax-induced changes in relative prices that characterize production taxes such as excise duties. Then, if consumer utility functions are weakly separable between consumption and leisure, a uniform tax on final consumption goods (say a VAT or, in the case of India, a properly harmonized state and central VAT) would approximate a lump-sum tax.[4] This would be a superior solution to distortionary commodity taxation. It is implicitly understood that a harmonized VAT would replace the existing excise duties of the centre and the sales taxes at the level of states. Since services are now the largest contributor to national product, the amalgamation of services in the VAT tax base is essential.

A related principle of tax reform is that the share of direct taxation in overall tax revenue should rise. Within direct taxation, reliance has to be shifted from corporate to income taxes. Since corporate profits are taxed at the level of personal income anyway, the rationale for separate corporate taxes is rather weak. There are only two arguments in favor of corporate taxes: i) as a tax on foreigners' incomes and ii) as a tax on noncompetitive profits.[5] Within the sphere of income taxation, the rate and exemptions structures need to be rationalized. Tax reform theory advocates taxation of 'full income' the Haig–Simons definition of which is 'all increases in human and physical capital during a period of time'. One cannot pick and choose the types of income one would like to tax. This principle has, of course, been grossly violated in the Indian case with several categories of income exempt from income taxation. The number of income tax brackets should be small, the degree of progression mild and the top marginal tax rate low. In India traditionally agricultural income has been tax exempt as are some sources of investment income. In addition, the ongoing process of globalization, which the economy is going through, creates its own avenues for tax exemptions.

Globalization has followed liberalization. Now firms and individuals are freer to adopt global strategies. However, national governments must, perforce, think in terms of domestic allocation of resources, the national account books, increasing the domestic rate of growth, protecting the domestic poor and so on. In this sense, the scope of activities of governments and those of the best and most dynamic firms and individuals are tending to divert from each other more than at any other time in the

---

4 Separability of the utility function between goods and leisure would indicate that taxation of goods would have no implications for the labor-leisure choice.

5 In developing countries such as India, corporate tax rates are high essentially as a revenue raising measure. It is much harder to evade corporate as compared to income taxes.

past. The future has much more of this in store. Thus increased liberalization of financial markets has improved the international allocation of savings and reduced the cost of capital. But it has also widened the opportunities for tax evasion and avoidance. Tax policy needs to address these issues.

Judicious disinvestments of state owned enterprises area direct method of lowering the public debt. Whereas the central government has made considerable progress in such disinvestments progress at the level of states is still minimal. As part of its recommendations to improve state government finances, the Reserve Bank of India has suggested disinvestment in state government undertakings as well as a higher share of service tax from the Centre. It has further said that states would also need to implement reforms in public sector undertakings in order to make them viable, efficient and profitable. In this regard, power sector reforms are very crucial in view of their fiscal implications.

In addition much work needs to be done to improve the structure of federal transfers to lower level governments. More clarity in respect of tax bases, rates and their cascadation and sharing of proceeds of tax revenues need to be established. There must be efforts to reduce the incidence of moral hazard (Jha et al. 1999a) in transfers to lower level governments.

4. Conclusions

The accumulation of large public debt has the potential of leading to a crisis as exchange rate and country risk premia rise. This, in turn, would increase the margin between domestic and foreign interest rates in an environment of an open capital account. There is little doubt that India will gradually open its capital account. Such a move, in the presence of such large debt, will put increasing pressure on the Rupee to fall in value. The large foreign exchange reserves accumulated to defend the economy against such an eventuality may prove insufficient should the fundamentals remain to be rectified. Moreover, ensuring central bank independence including the independence of monetary from fiscal policy is made increasingly difficult when debt piles up inexorably, primary deficits are high and tax and expenditure reforms are delayed. The comprehensive reform of the fiscal deficit structure of the Indian economy has emerged as one of the most important tasks facing the reforms. Indeed success or failure in this area may well dictate the prospects for success of the reforms themselves.

References

Alesina, A. and R. Perotti, 'The political economy of budget deficits', *IMF Staff Papers* 42 (1995), 1–31.

Ansari, M.I and U Athabasca, 'Monetary vs. Fiscal Policy: Some Evidence from Vector Autoregression for India', *Journal-of-Asian-Economics* 7(4) (1996), 677–98.

Balassone, F. and R. Giordano, 'Budget deficits and coalition governments', *Public Choice* 106 (2001), 327–49.

Gaiha, R., Do Anti-Poverty Programmes Reach the Rural Poor in India? *Oxford Development Studies*, 28 (2000), 71–95.

Goyal, A., 'The political economy of the revenue deficit', in Parikh (ed.), *India Development Report 1999–2000* (New Delhi: Oxford, 2001).

Jha, R., 'Macroeconomics of fiscal policy in developing countries', Working Paper No. 2001/05, Working papers in Trade and Development, The Australian National University (2001).

Jha, R., 'The downward rigidity of Indian interest rates', *Economic and Political Weekly*, 37(2) (2002a).

Jha, R., 'Some Challenges for Fiscal Policy in the New Economy of India' in *Economic Institutions in India,* P. Banerjee and K. Richter (eds), (Hampshire, UK and New Delhi, India: Palgrave Macmillan, 2002b)

Jha, R. and A. Sharma, 'Structural breaks and unit roots: a further test of the sustainability of the Indian fiscal deficit', mimeo, ASARC, RSPAS, (forthcoming) *Public Finance Review*, (2003).

Jha, R., M. Mohanty, S. Chatterjee and P. Chitkara, Tax Efficiency in Selected Indian States, *Empirical Economics*, 24 (1999a), 641–54.

Jha, R., Murthy, K., Nagarajan, H. and A. Seth, Real Consumption Levels and the Public Distribution System in India, *Economic and Political Weekly*, 34 (1999b), 919–27.

Jha, R. and B. Sahni, 1993, *Industrial Efficiency: An Indian Perspective* (New Delhi: Wiley Eastern, 1993).

Lopez, H., K. Schmidt–Hebbel, and L. Serven, How Effective is Fiscal Policy in Raising National Saving, *The Review of Economics and Statistics*, 82 (2000), 226–38.

Sah, R., How much Redistribution is Possible through Commodity Taxes?, *Journal of Public Economics*, 20 (1983), 89–101.

PART III

THE INDUSTRIAL SECTOR

9
Technology, Productivity and Export Growth of Engineering Industry in India

Anita Kumari

1. Introduction

Major economic reforms were initiated in India in July 1991 with the objective of increasing productivity and competitiveness. These policies have liberalized many government controls on production capacity, import of capital goods, intermediate inputs and technology and foreign investment. Imported inputs became cheaper and firms were exposed to domestic and international competition. It is important to analyze how these reforms affected the export growth of companies.

1.1 Factors Affecting Export Growth

In the Heckscher–Ohlin theory technological characteristics of production (as indicated by the capital intensities, assuming identical production functions between countries) determine trade flows. The neo technology theories,[1] particularly the evolutionary approach,[2] focus on firm specific technological capability in their export performance (Rosenberg 1982). Various surrogates for technology have been used: capital intensity, skill intensity, R&D intensity, technology imports in terms of royalty payments, import of capital goods, import of raw materials and technology transfer through foreign participation.

Hence, export growth of firms depends on technology which may take the form of license of designs, import of capital goods, import of raw materials, innovations and adaptations from R&D activities, technology transfer through foreign participation and productivity growth and on size and age of company, advertisement expenditure, capital intensity,

---

[1] See Kravis (1956), Posner (1961), Hafbauer (1966), Vernon (1966), Hirsch (1967), Krugman (1979, 1981), Brander and Spencer (1983).

[2] See Nelson and Winter (1982) and Dosi et al (1988).

skill intensity, vertical integration and lagged export intensity. We now discuss these factors.

1.2 Technology Acquisition Variables

There are many forms/facets of technology: disembodied form of technology (technical know-how and designs) obtained as arms length purchase of technology; and embodied technology (in imported capital and intermediate goods). Technology is also transferred through foreign participation. Further firms may develop innovations and adapt acquired technology to local conditions. The evidence on the links between technology and exports is mixed. Harrison (1996) found import of technology to be positively related to exports in some industries. Gruber et al (1967), Keesing (1967), Caves, et al (1980), Pavitt et al (1980), Hirsch and Bijaoui (1985), Hirsch et al (1988), Wakelin (1997) found a positive relationship between R&D and export performance. However, Willmore (1992) and Wignaraja (1998) found no such relation. Wignaraja (1998) found technological effort such as raw material testing and quality control significant in explaining export performance. Cohen (1975), Haddad et al (1996), Willmore (1976, 1992) found a positive relationship between foreign investment and export performance. Wignaraja (1998) found share of foreign equity to have no influence on export behaviour. Harrison (1996) found that relationship between foreign participation and exports varies from industry to industry.

1.3 Productivity and Size

The reforms of 1991 were supposed to enhance productivity thus lowering cost of production and increasing competitiveness of firms and enhancing their export growth. Size of the company enables it to cope with risk and competition in the world market. It may enhance companies' competitiveness in the domestic market as well and hence may diminish the need to explore the world market. The literature on the size-export relationship is vast. Dosi et al (1990), Abd-el-Rahman (1991), Willmore (1992) and Haddad et al (1996) found a positive relationship between size and exports. Glejsar et al. (1980) found a negative relationship between size and exports. Soete (1987) found the relationship between size and exports to be mixed. Auquier (1980), Hirsch and Bijaoui (1985), Hughes (1986) and Wignaraja (1998) found insignificant effect of size on exports.

1.4 Age

Older companies may be more efficient and may also have a wider trade network. Hence export growth of older companies may be higher than that of new companies. New companies may be more dynamic and thus have higher exports.

1.5 Advertisement Intensity

To capture the sales promotion efforts of companies, advertisement intensity is used. Companies with greater sales promotion efforts are likely to do better in world markets as their products are better known. Thus sales promotion efforts should lead to higher export growth. Hirsch et al. (1988) and Willmore (1992) found a positive association between advertisement expenditure and export performance.

1.6 Capital intensity

Companies with higher capital intensity use better machinery and are thus more competitive. They may also have better product quality than companies with lower capital intensity. Wakelin (1997) found capital intensity as significant determinant of export performance while Willmore (1992) and Wignaraja (1998) found capital intensity to have no influence on export performance.

1.7 Skill Intensity

Skill enhances efficiency in production and competitiveness. Companies employing higher skilled persons will attain larger export growth. Wignaraja (1998) found a positive relationship between skill intensity and export performance. But Willmore (1992) found a negative relationship.

1.8 Vertical Integration

To ensure quality and timely supplies of inputs and intermediate products, companies may often produce their intermediate products in-house rather than procuring from outside. Vertical integration will then have a positive relationship with exports. But procurement of intermediate products through subcontracting or ancilliarisation gives benefits of economies of scale. Hence vertical integration is likely to have an ambiguous relationship with export growth.

1.9 Lagged Export Intensity

Companies, which have low export intensity in the previous year, are likely to make larger efforts to increase their exports in the current year. Export intensity in the previous year may be inversely related to export growth.

2. Review of the Literature

Lall and Mohammad (1983) analyzed the influence of foreign ownership on the export performance of 24 industries in the large corporate sector in India. This study revealed that foreign ownership had a positive effect on export performance. But export incentives had an insignificant effect;

intensity of highly paid employees and capital intensity had a negative effect on export performance.

Lall (1986) considered technological development and export performance in leading engineering and chemical firms in India for the period 1978–80. Results were different for the two industries. Firm size was significant and positive for the engineering firms but insignificant for the chemical firms. Export subsidies and marketing effort had positive effects on export performance in both industries. Age was found to have no significant effect on exports in both industries. Among the technology variables, royalty and licensing fees paid abroad had no effect in both the industries. The number of licensing agreements held by firms had a positive and significant effect for engineering firms but none on chemical firms. Access to foreign technology via foreign direct investment had no impact in the exports of engineering firms but it had a weakly positive and significant impact on the exports of chemical firms. The R&D variable was significant with a negative sign for engineering firms but with a positive sign for chemical firms. Skill intensity was insignificant in both industries.

Patibandla (1988) analyzed export growth in 71 firms over the period 1978–79 to 1983–84. The analysis revealed growth of firm level exports having positive relationship with growth in firm size and interaction term between firm size and growth rate in firm level production inefficiency, but negative relationship with growth in domestic sales and growth in production inefficiency.

Kumar and Siddharthan (1994) analyzed inter firm variation in export behaviour of enterprises in 13 manufacturing industries of India for the period 1987–88 to 1989–90. They examined the role of firm size, in-house innovation, technology imports, skill intensity, advertisement intensity, capital intensity along with profitability, import dependence and dummy for foreign equity and export commitments. Tobit model was used for the analysis. The relationships between exports and various explanatory variables were found to be industry specific. The firm size-export relationship was predominantly U-shaped. R&D expenditure was found to be important determinant of export in medium and low technology industries but not in high technology industries. For electrical machinery, technology imports and capital intensity were found to be significant and positive. For non-electrical machinery, import dependence, technology imports, skill intensity, profitability, dummy for foreign equity and dummy for export commitments were found to be significant with a positive sign.

Agarwal and Goldar (1999) analyzed export performance of Indian engineering firms using technology imports, growth rate of sales, technical efficiency, advertisement intensity, foreign equity participation, firm's size, age of firm and raw material import intensity as explanatory variables. For the pre-reform period foreign equity participation and import of raw materials were significant determinants. But for the post-reform period, technology imports, growth rate of sales and advertisement intensity were significant determinants.

Siddharthan and Nollen (2000) estimated an export performance model for three groups of firms: MNE affiliates, licensees and domestic firms in the information technology sector in India. They found that exports of MNE affiliates were greater for firms which import more explicit technology through purchase of licenses and payments of royalties, and which have larger foreign equity stakes. For other groups of firms, larger firm size, greater capital intensity, and more exposure to foreign market were found to contribute to higher exports. Most of the studies on firm level export behaviour are based on export intensity except a few, which analyzed growth of export.

3. The Empirical Model

The determinants of export performance are modeled as:

GE= f (LS, GP, MT, MMI, CGI, FE, RD, AD, KI, SK, NY, VI, EXIL)

where, GE, LS, GP, MT, MMI, CGI, FE, RD, AD, KI, SK, NY, VI are, respectively growth of exports, size, total factor productivity growth, technology imports intensity, materials input import intensity, capital goods import intensity, foreign equity participation, research and development intensity, advertisement intensity, capital intensity measured alternatively as capital-labour ratio (KL) or capital-output ratio (KO), skill intensity, age of firm, vertical integration and previous year's export intensity. This model is estimated with pooled cross-sectional and time-series data using panel data techniques.

Use of OLS in panel data often lead to heteroskedasticity, which lowers efficiency of the estimates although leaving them consistent. Both the fixed effects (FIE) and random effects (RE) models solve this heteroskedasticity problem, although the random effects model is more efficient. The Lagranges multiplier (LM) test is applied to test for the OLS model against the FIE/ RE model and the Hausman specification (HS) test is applied to test for the RE model against the FIE model. LIMDEP package is used in the estimation.

4. Data and Variables

The database of the Reserve Bank of India (RBI) on finances of medium and large public limited companies are the basic source of data for this study. Different sets of data[3] were obtained from RBI for engineering companies: 1985–86 to 1987–88, 1987–88 to 1989–90, 1988–89 to 1990–91, 1990–91 to 1992–93, and 1992–93 to 1994–95. All these data sets were matched to get a common subset of companies. We cover 44 engineering companies for the years 1985–86 to 1994–95: ten companies in electrical engineering, belonging to the following groups: cables, dry cells, electric lamps and other electrical machinery, apparatus, appliances, etc.; and 34 companies in non-electrical engineering, belonging to machine tools, textile machinery and accessories and miscellaneous machinery not elsewhere classified.

GE is measured as ratio of change of current year export over previous year export to previous year export. Exports are deflated by export unit value index using export unit value index at 1985–86 prices as deflator. The unit value index figures are available only for broad electrical and non-electrical machinery groups. All companies belonging to various industry groups within electrical machinery group are deflated by electrical machinery export unit value index and those in non-electrical machinery group are deflated by non-electrical machinery group unit value index.

LS is taken as the logarithm of sale at constant prices (1985–86). Sales are deflated by product prices (WPI) obtained from monthly index number of wholesale prices of India, Ministry of Industry to get the sales at constant prices.

GP is measured by Translog method (see Annexure 1). MT is measured as the ratio of payments for royalty, technical fees (for know how, of drawings, designs, etc.), professional and consultation fees and others to sales. MMI is computed as the ratio of imports of materials, spares, components, etc. to total materials. CGI is measured as the ratio of import of capital goods to fixed investment. FE is defined as the share of dividends declared in foreign currency to total dividends paid. RD is computed as the ratio of research and development expenditure to sales. AD is defined as the ratio of advertisement expenditure as a ratio of sales. KI is the ratio of real gross fixed assets to measure of labor (KL) and also as ratio of real gross fixed assets to real gross output (KO). SK is measured as the ratio of managerial remuneration to total salaries and wages. NY is the number of years from the date of incorporation till the current year. VI is the ratio of gross value added to value of production. EXIL is measured as previous year's export intensity. Export intensity is computed as the ratio of exports to sales.

---

[3] Each data set is for three years. The coverage of firms differs across the sets.

5. Empirical Results

Some companies had erratic export growth behaviour and were excluded leaving us with 31 exporting companies in the pre-reform period and 35 exporting companies in the post-reform.

Table 9.1 presents basic statistics of the key variables in the pre- and post-reform periods. In the pre-reform period, exports of exporting companies rose at an average annual rate of 283.6 per cent but fell to 157.8 per cent per annum in the post-reform period. Productivity increased in the pre-reform period at an average annual rate of 0.78 per cent and at 1.31 per cent in the post-reform period. Export intensity increased from 7.3 per cent in the pre-reform period to 8.4 in the post-reform period. The average size of these companies was, however, same in the two periods. The average technology import intensity increased from 0.56 per cent in the pre-reform period to 0.82 per cent in the post-reform period. Similarly, the average R&D intensity of the firms increased from 0.09 per cent in the pre-reform period to 0.47 per cent in the post-reform period. The capital goods import intensity declined from 18 per cent in the pre-reform period to 9.48 per cent in the post reform. The average skill intensity has almost doubled in the post-reform period to 1.50 per cent from 0.78 per cent in the pre-reform period. The mean values of other variables did not differ much across the two periods.

Table 9.2 shows the export performance of companies at the aggregate level. The number of non-exporting companies halved in post-reform period from eight (18 per cent) in the pre-reform period to four (9 per cent) in the post-reform period. In the pre-reform period, though a large number of companies recorded growth in exports, two (5 per cent) companies recorded decline in exports. In the post-reform period, however, five (11 per cent) companies recorded decline in exports. There were five (11 per cent) companies showing less than 10 per cent growth in the pre-reform period as compared to four (9 per cent) in the post-reform period. The number of companies showing exports growth of 10 per cent to less than 100 per cent increased to 19 (43 per cent) in the post-reform as compared to 14 (32 per cent) in the pre-reform period. The number of companies showing exports growth of 100 to less than 200 per cent declined remarkably to two (4.6 per cent) in the post-reform period from nine (20 per cent) in the pre-reform period. The number of companies having exports growth of more than 200 per cent increased in the post-reform period to ten (23 per cent) from six (14 per cent) in the pre-reform period. Thus, both companies showing decline in exports and companies showing very high growth rate in exports increased during post-reform period.

Table 9.1: Averages of Variables in the Pre- and Post-Reform Periods

Variable	Pre-Reform	Post-Reform
GE (% p.a.)	283.58[a] (1774)	157.81[a] (596.75)
GP (% p.a.)	0.78 (14.10)	-1.31 (16.14)
LS (%)	15.30 (103.94)	15.37 (105.80)
MT (%)	0.56 (0.71)	0.82 (1.82)
MMI (%)	23.64 (19.32)	21.69 (16.49)
CGI (%)	18.00 (89.69)	9.48 (39.55)
FE (%)	13.39 (16.76)	14.52 (17.53)
RD (%)	0.09 (0.37)	0.47 (0.54)
AD (%)	0.22 (0.42)	0.24 (0.46)
SK (%)	0.78 (0.72)	1.50 (1.76)
KL	9.56 (6.18)	11.45 (5.01)
KO	2.41 (1.48)	2.60 (1.46)
NY	35.90 (14.81)	39.01 (15.50)
VI (%)	40.44 (13.20)	40.91 (11.58)
XI (%)	7.30 (8.46)	8.35 (8.68)
No. of Companies	31	35

Notes: Figures in the parentheses are standard deviations
GE = growth of exports; LS = log of sale;
GP= growth of productivity; MT = technology import intensity,
MMI=materials input import intensity; CGI= capital goods import intensity;
FE = foreign equity participation; RD = research and development intensity;
AD=advertisement Intensity; KL= capital-labour ratio;
KO= capital-output ratio; SK= skill intensity; XI= export intensity.
a) See Table 9.2 for distribution of firms by range of export growth.

Table 9.2: Distribution of Firms According To Export Growth

Export Gr. (%)	*Pre-Reform*	*Post-Reform*
Negative	2 (4.6)	5 (11.4)
Non-Exporting	8 (18.2)	4 (9.1)
0 to <10%	5 (11.4)	4 (9.1)
10% to <100%	14 (31.8)	19 (43.2)
100% to <200%	9 (20.5)	2 (4.6)
Above 200%	6 (13.6)	10 (22.7)
Total No. of Companies	44	44

Table 9.3 presents estimates of the export function. In the pre-reform period, LM statistics is insignificant implying that OLS model to be preferred over FIE/RE models. The OLS model is the preferred specification both periods.

Equations (1) and (4) use capital-output ratio (KO) as a measure of capital intensity and equations (2) and (5) use capital-labour ratio (KL) as a measure of capital intensity along with all other explanatory variables. Equations (3) and (5) are obtained by dropping some explanatory variables. OLS results indicate that size of the company is insignificant, in all equations in the pre-reform period but it is negative and highly significant, in all equations in the post-reform period. This indicates that during pre-reform period all companies sold in the domestic market behind a wall of protection. But in the post-reform period with lowering of import controls foreign markets became more attractive. Small and medium companies, having small value of sales, which were not well established in the domestic market, began making efforts to export to the world market. But large companies, having large sales, which dominated domestic market continued to ignore foreign markets.

Productivity growth is positive but marginally significant in all equations in the pre-reform period. But in the post reform period it is consistently positive and significant at five per cent level. Thus companies with higher productivity growth had higher export growth. Among technology acquisition variables, FE and MMI are significant, with positive sign, in the pre-reform period but insignificant in the post-reform period.

Table 9.3: Determinants of Export Growth Dependent Variable: GE

Explanatory Variables	*Pre-Reform*			*Post-Reform*		
	(1)	*(2)*	*(3)*	*(4)*	*(5)*	*(6)*
Constant	17.045 (0.400)	9.414 (0.222)	4.974 (1.018)	35.899*** (2.691)	36.205*** (2.746)	33.808*** (3.042)
LS	-0.433 (-0.174)	0.145 (0.058)		-1.700** (-2.227)	-1.789** (-2.342)	-1.564*** (-2.553)
GP	13.878 (1.382)	14.059 (1.402)	13.182 (1.361)	6.833** (2.034)	6.895** (2.119)	6.458** (2.149)
MT	-44.245 (-0.199)	-95.949 (-0.440)		-10.817 (-0.348)	-14.070 (-0.492)	
MMI	32.786*** (3.765)	35.234*** (3.918)	32.353*** (3.966)	-2.645 (-0.707)	-2.754 (-0.740)	
CGI	-0.243 (-0.154)	-0.211 (-0.133)		2.067* (1.613)	1.981@ (1.546)	1.943@@ (1.601)
FE	22.824** (2.275)	22.977** (2.340)	26.335*** (3.152)	1.944 (0.558)	1.583 (0.460)	
RD	72.970 (0.192)	97.333 (0.257)		-9.390 (-0.100)	-10.922 (-0.117)	
AD	-189.32 (-0.474)	-267.81 (-0.654)		-25.133 (-0.188)	-14.542 (-0.109)	
KL		-0.304 (-1.189)			0.102 (0.934)	
KO	-1.205 (-1.055)			0.079 (0.174)		
SK	-147.51 (-0.673)	-85.485 (-0.396)		-21.889 (-0.669)	-19.668 (-0.623)	
NY	-0.015 (-0.122)	-0.037 (-0.301)		0.012 (0.317)	0.021 (0.529)	
VI	-23.307 (-1.201)	-26.383 (-1.381)	-23.833** (-1.971)	-16.322** (-2.309)	-16.933** (-2.436)	-16.783*** (-2.978)
EXIL	-58.989** (-2.583)	-56.116** (-2.446)	-57.949*** (-3.120)	-17.608*** (-2.691)	-16.810*** (-2.594)	-16.987*** (-3.205)
LM Test	0.00001[1]	0.043[1]	0.050[1]	1.674[1]	2.057[1]	1.481[1]
HS Test	19.911[13]	18.856[13]	7.159[5]	7.912[13]	2.727[13]	2.025[5]
R-Square	0.16	0.16	0.15	0.16	0.17	0.15
Adjusted R Square	0.08	0.08	0.12	0.07	0.08	0.12
No. of Observation	155	155	155	140	140	140

Notes: Figures in the parentheses () are t ratios, [] are d f

* Significant at 10%; @@ Significant at 11 %

** Significant at 5%; @ Significant at 12 %

*** Significant at 1%

Also companies, which used more imported material had higher export growth. After liberalization, companies with foreign collaboration did not have additional advantage in exports growth. The intensity of imported material did not increase export growth in the post-reform period. This may be because in the post-reform period even domestic material made with imported advanced technology is as good as imported material. Intensity of imported capital goods is insignificant in the pre-reform period but is significant in the post-reform period. Thus during post-reform period, export growth increased with acceleration in intensity of imported capital goods. Import of technology at arms length did not significantly affect export growth in both the periods. Research and development expenditure and advertisement expenditure also did not have significant impact on export growth in both the periods. Skill intensity did not significantly affect export growth in either period. Capital intensity, measured by either capital-labor ratio or capital-output ratio, is insignificant in both the periods. Age of company is insignificant in explaining export growth in both periods. Thus all companies, old as well as new, made efforts to increase their export growth. The impact of lagged export intensity is consistently negative and significant at five per cent or higher in both periods. Thus, companies with smaller share of exports in the previous year made greater efforts to increase their exports in the current year. Impact of vertical integration is found to be negative and significant at five per cent in only one equation in the pre-reform period but at five per cent or higher in the post-reform period. Thus, the companies, which procured, intermediate products on subcontracting or ancilliarisation, took advantage of economies of scale in production and had higher export growth.

6. Conclusions

This chapter has analyzed export growth of companies in Indian engineering industries, electrical and non-electrical machinery, in the pre-reform and post-reform periods. Also the factors affecting inter company variations in export growth in the pre- and post-reforms period have been considered. It was found that the exports increased in both the periods but export growth declined during the post-reform period. Larger numbers of companies showed declines in exports in the post-reform period, but there were fewer non-exporting companies in this period.

An analysis of the factors affecting export growth was carried out by estimating a regression function using panel data techniques. The analysis reveals that productivity growth had a positive impact on export growth in both periods. The impact was more significant in the post-reform period as compared to the pre-reform period where it was marginally significant.

Among the technology acquisition variables, foreign equity participation and imported intermediate inputs had a significant positive relationship with export growth in pre-reform period. In the post-reform period, the export growth of companies having even indigenous intermediate inputs increased. Domestic companies with little or no foreign participation did not have disadvantage in exports during post-reform period. During the post-reform period, export growth of companies with higher intensity of imported capital goods increased. Companies, which procured intermediate products by sub-contracting or ancilliarisation, increased their exports faster than companies with in-house production in both the periods. In the pre-reform period, firm size did not have any systematic relationship with export growth as both small and large companies enjoyed protected domestic markets. Post-reforms, exports of larger companies increased less than the exports of smaller companies. Since after the reforms there was no protected domestic market and control on imported technology was relaxed, small and medium companies were driven to explore world markets but larger companies, which dominated domestic markets, continued to be inward oriented.

Annex 1

Measurement of Productivity Growth

Productivity growth has been measured by translog method. Translog index of productivity growth is based on a translog production function characterized by constant returns to scale. It allows for variable elasticity of substitution and does not require Hicks neutrality. The Translog index is a discrete version of the continuous Divisia index and is obtained as follows:

$$\Delta P(t)/P(t) = \Delta V(t)/V(t) - [S_L(t)(\Delta L(t)/L(t)) + S_K(t)(\Delta K(t)/K(t))]$$

Here $\Delta V(t)/V(t)$, $\Delta L(t)/L(t)$ and $\Delta K(t)/K(t)$ are approximated by corresponding logarithms of ratios of variables over successive years, i.e.,

$$\Delta V(t)/V(t) \sim \ln[V(t)/V(t-1)] = \ln V(t) - \ln V(t-1) = \Delta \ln V(t)$$

$$\Delta L(t)/L(t) \sim \ln[L(t)/L(t-1)] = \ln L(t) - \ln L(t-1) = \Delta \ln L(t)$$

$$\Delta K(t)/K(t) \sim \ln[K(t)/K(t-1)] = \ln K(t) - \ln K(t-1) = \Delta \ln K(t)$$

$$\overline{S_L}(t) = 1/2[S_L(t) + S_L(t-1)]$$

$$\overline{S_K}(t) = 1/2[S_K(t) + S_K(t-1)]$$

Where $S_L(t)$ and $S_K(t)$ are shares of labour and capital in value added. V (t), K (t) and L (t) are real gross value added, real gross fixed assets and labour input respectively. $\Delta P(t)/P(t)$ gives the rate of growth of total factor productivity. Measurement of output, capital and labour are discussed below:

Measurement of Output

Gross value added has been taken as the measure of output. The data tapes give data on value of production, and manufacturing expenses, namely, raw materials and components consumed, stores and spares consumed, power and fuel, and other manufacturing expenses. We subtracted the sum of manufacturing expenses from value of production to get value added. This was then deflated by the Index number of wholesale prices for relevant product groups. Product groups given in the Index Number of Wholesale Prices have not been same as those given in the RBI. Therefore, product-wise indices of wholesale prices have been regrouped to make them comparable to product groups given in the RBI. The groups of WPI used as deflator for different industry groups are given in Annexure-2. Index number of wholesale prices in India for the financial years from 1985–86 to 1994–95 have been taken from Index number of wholesale prices in India, Office of the Economic Advisor, Ministry of Industry, Government of India. This gives the indices at base 1981–82=100. The base of this series has been converted to base 1985–86=100. This method of deflation suffers from the limitation that the same price index has been used for all companies belonging to a product group, which may not be appropriate as their prices may not be same, and also the basket of products produced by various companies belonging to a product group may differ.

Measurement of Capital Input

Gross fixed capital stock at constant (1985–86) prices has been taken as the measure of capital input. RBI tapes give the total gross fixed assets at current prices. It consists of land, buildings, plant and machinery, capital work in progress, furniture, fixtures and office equipments, and others. To estimate real gross fixed capital stock, we have employed the perpetual inventory method. This required bench-year estimates of gross fixed capital stock at 1985–86 prices and real gross investments at 1985–86 prices over successive years for the period under consideration.

Fixed investment for each year has been calculated and then deflated by the capital goods price deflator of that year to get real investment. But where the fixed investment was negative the deflator was taken as the price index for benchmark year because negative fixed investment implies that some of the gross capital in bench year has been discarded (which had been estimated previously at bench year price index). The deflator used for gross fixed assets was the Index number of Wholesale Prices for machinery and machine tools, taken from Chandhok (1990). Chandhok gives two series on index number of machinery and machine tools: (1) a series from 1971–72 to 1988–89 at base 1970–71=100 and (2) a series from 1982–83 to 1988–89 at base 1981–82=100. The wholesale price indices from 1971–72 to 1981–82 (at base 1970–71) have been merged with wholesale price indices of latter series 1982–83 to 1988–89 (at base 1981–82) and then the base of the combined series has been shifted to 1985–86. Once the series with 1985–86=100 was obtained, the deflator for benchmark year i.e., 1985–86 has been obtained as the average of indices from 1971–72 to 1985–86 if the company was incorporated more than 15 years prior to 1985–86. However, if the company was incorporated after 1972–73 (i.e. less than 15 years prior to 1985–86), the average of indices from the year of incorporation to 1985–86 was taken as the deflator for the benchmark year. Deflator for investments from 1986–87 to 1994–95 was the price index of machinery and machine tools at base 1985–86 for the corresponding year. Index number of wholesale price for the years 1989–90 to 1994–95 was taken from Index Number of Wholesale Prices in India, Office of the Economic Advisor, Ministry of Industry, Government of India.

Measurement of Labour Input

The RBI data source does not contain data on the number of workers/employees. But it provides salaries, wages and bonus for all the employees and managerial remuneration. To obtain a measure of labour/employment, we first aggregated salaries, wages and bonus for all the employees and managerial remuneration to get total salaries and wages, and then deflated it by the wage rate (obtained from ASI (Annual Survey of Industries)). From ASI, we get data on total emoluments and total employees for various industry groups belonging to electrical and non-electrical engineering. The industry-wise wage rates (emoluments per employee) have been computed from these data and then used as the deflator for company level salaries and wages to arrive at a measure of labour input.

One difficulty we have faced in making these computations has been that the industrial classification in ASI has not been same as in company finance data of RBI. Thus the industries in the ASI have been re-grouped to match it with the RBI industrial classification. The industry groups combined have been given in Annexure-3.

Annex 2

Output Deflators

Industry Group	**RBI**	**WPI Group**
Cables	445	IIIkb2
Dry Batteries	446	IIIkb3 (414)
Electric Lamps	447	IIIkb4 (417+418)
Other Electrical Machinery, Apparatus, Appliances, etc.	448	IIIkb
Machine Tools	449	IIIka393
Textile Machinery And Accessories	450	IIIka2 (385+386+387)
Miscellaneous Machinery n.e.s	451	IIIka

Annex 3

Wages Deflators

Industry Group	**RBI**	**ASI Group**
Cables	445	361
Dry Batteries	446	362
Electric Lamps	447	363
Other Electrical Machinery, Apparatus, Appliances, etc.	448	36-(361+362+363)
Machine Tools	449	357
Textile Machinery And Accessories	450	353
Miscellaneous Machinery n.e.s.	451	35-(353+357)

References

Abd-el-Raman, Kamal, 'Firms' Competitive and National Comparative Advantages as Joint Determinants of Trade Composition', *Weltwirtschaftliches Archiv*, band 127 (1991), 83–97.

Agarwal, R.N. and B. Goldar, 'Technology Imports, Growth, Efficiency and Export Performance of Indian Engineering Firms in the Pre-and Post-Reform Period', Working Paper No.E/201/99 (Delhi: Institute of Economic Growth, 1999).

Auquier, A., 'Sizes of Firms and Exporting Behaviour and the Structure of French Industry', *The Journal of Industrial Economics*, 24(2), (1980), 203–18.

Baumol, W.J., S.A. Blackman and E.N. Wolff, *Productivity and American Leadership: The Long View* (Cambridge, Mass: MIT Press, 1989).

Brander, J. and B. Spencer, 'International R&D Rivalry and Industrial Strategy', *Review of Economic Studies*, 50(4) (1983), 707–22.

Caves, Richard E. et.al., *Competition in the Open Economy: A Model Applied to Canada* (Cambridge, MA; Harvard University Press, 1989).

Cohen, B.I., *Multinational Firms and Asian Exports* (New Haven, CT.: Yale University Press, 1975).

Dosi, G., C. Freeman, R. Nelson, G. Silverberg, and L. Soete, *Technical Change and Economic Theory* (London: Pinter, 1988).

Dosi, Giovanni; Pavitt, Keith; and Soete, Luc 1990. *The Economics of Technical Change and International Trade* (London: Harvester Wheatsheaf, 1990).

Glejser, H., A. Jacquemin, and J. Petit, 'Exports in an Imperfect Competition Framework: An Analysis of 1,446 Exporters', *Quarterly Journal of Economics*, 94(3) (1980), 507–24.

Gruber, W.H., D. Mehta, and R. Vernon, 'The R&D Factor in International Trade and Investment of U.S. Industries', *Journal of Political Economy*, 75 (1967), 20–37.

Haddad, M., J. deMelo and B. Horton, 'Morocco, 1984–89: Trade Liberalization, Exports, and Industrial Performance', in M.J. Roberts and J.R. Tybout, (eds), *Industrial Evolution in Developing Countries* (Oxford: Oxford University Press, 1996), pp. 285–313.

Hafbauer, G.C., *Synthetic Materials and the Theory of International Trade* (London: Gerald Duckworth, 1966).

Haque, Irfan ul, *Trade, Technology and International Competitiveness*, EDI Development Studies (Washington, D.C.: The World Bank, 1995).

Harrison, Ann, 'Determinants and Effects of Direct Foreign Investment in Cite d'Ivoire, Morocco, and Venezuela', in M.J. Roberts and J.R. Tybout (eds), *Industrial Evolution in Developing Countries* (Oxford University Press, 1996), pp. 163–86.

Hirsch, S., *Location of Industry and International Competitiveness* (Oxford: Clarendon Press, 1967).

Hirsch, S., Kalish, S. and Katznelson, S., 'Effects of Knowledge and Service Intensities on Domestic and Export Performance', *Weltwirtschaftliches Archiv*, 124 (1988), 230–41.

Hirsch, Seev and Bijaoui, Han, 'R&D Intensity and Export Performance: A Micro View', *Weltwirtschaftliches Archiv*, band 121 (1985), 238–51.

Hughes, Kirsty *Exports and Technology* (Cambridge: Cambridge University Press, 1986).

Keesing, D., 'The Impact of Research and Development on United States Trade', *Journal of Political Economy*, 75 (1967), 38–45.

Kravis, I.B., 'Availability and other Influences on the Commodity Composition of Trade', Journal *of Political Economy*, 64(2) (1956), 143–55.

Krugman, P., 'A Model of Innovation, Technology Transfer and the World Distribution of Income', *Journal of Political Economy*, 87 (1979), 253–66.

Krugman, P., 'Intra-industry Specialisation and the Gains from Trade', *Journal of Political Economy*, 89 (1981), 959–73.

Kumar, Nagesh and Siddharthan, N.S., 'Technology, Firm Size and Export Behaviour in Developing Countries: The Case of Indian Enterprise', *Journal of Development Studies*, 31(2) (1994), 289–309.

Lall, S. and Mohammed, S., 'Foreign Ownership and Export Performance in the Large Corporate Sector in India', *Journal of Development Studies*, 20(1) (1983), 56–67.

Lall, Sanjaya, 'Technological Development and Export Performance in LDCs: Leading Engineering and Chemical Firms in India', *Weltwirtschaftliches Archiv*, 122 (1986), 80–91.

Nelson, R.R. and Winter, S.J. 1982. *An Evolutionary Theory of Economic Change* (Cambridge, Mass.: Harvard University Press, 1982).

Patibandla, M. 1988. 'Role of Large and Small Firms in India's Engineering Exports', *Economic and Political Weekly* (28 May 1988), M53–66.

Pavitt, K. and Soete, L., Innovative Activities and Export Share: Some Comparison between Industries and Countries, in K. Pavitt (ed.), *Technical Innovation and British Economic Performance* (London: Macmillan, 1980), pp. 38–66.

Posner, Michael V., 'International Trade and Technical Change', *Oxford Economic Papers*, 13 (1961), 11–37.

Rosenberg, N., *Inside the Black Box* (Cambridge: Cambridge University Press, 1982).

Siddharthan, N.S. and Stanley Nollen, 'Export Perform ance and Strategic Groups of Firms: The Roles of Foreign Collaboration and Knowledge Transfer', paper presented at the Annual Conference of the Academy of International Business (Phoenix, Arizona, US, 17–20 November 2000).

Soete, Luc, 'The Impact of Technological Innovation on International Trade Patterns: The Evidence Reconsidered', *Research Policy*, 16 (1987), 101–30.

Vernon, Raymond, 'International Investment and International Trade in the Product Cycle', *Quarterly Journal of Economics*, 80 (1966), 190–207.

Wakelin, Katharine, *Trade and Innovation: Theory and Evidence* (Cheltenham, UK: Edward Elgar, 1997).

Wignaraja, G., *Trade Liberalization in Sri Lanka: Exports, Technology and Industrial Policy* (London: Macmillan Press Ltd., 1998).

Willmore, L., 'Direct Foreign Investment in Central American Manufacturing', *World Development*, 4(6) (1976), 499–517.

Willmore, Larry, 'Transnationals and Foreign Trade: Evidence from Brazil', *The Journal of Development Studies*, 28 (1992), 314–35.

10

Public and Private Investment Expenditure and its Linkages with FDI: A case study of India

Sadanand Tutakne, Santanu Gupta & Pradeep Apte

1. Introduction

The impact of public expenditure on output and employment occupied an important place in the economic debates of the last century. Mere increase in public expenditure was not enough to drive the economy along a growth path since much of it could be used for non-productive purposes. Hence some policy planners suggested a withdrawal of the state from major economic activities and its confinement only to public administration and defence. Aschauer (1989) pointed out that the slowdown in U.S. productivity growth in the seventies arose not out of low rates of saving but out of a decline in public investment in infrastructure. Several cross-country studies investigating the impact of public investment have been undertaken. During the last decade many developing countries went for a Structural Adjustment Programme as proposed by the World Bank and I.M.F. This included opening up of the economy and deregulation of prices and interest rates. Such measures were expected to boost foreign direct investment (FDI), and this was expected to supplement resources for investment in developing countries.

In this chapter, we formulate a simple overlapping generations model modified to include FDI to investigate the role of public investment on private investment and FDI for India and analyse the role of reforms program. Since national level data may not reveal the impact at a dis-aggregate level, we empirically test the model for three major states: Andhra Pradesh, Gujarat and Maharashtra. To the best of our knowledge, this is the first work trying to link the debate between public and private investment with FDI inflows and examine the impact on public investment at the state level.

In the recent literature on the debate between public and private investment, Khan and Kumar (1997) examined data of 95 developing countries over the period 1970 to 1990. They found a significant difference across income groups, with evidence of higher rates of return to public investment in low-income countries, than high-income countries. Erenburg (1993) investigated the effects of public sector investment using a rational expectations model for the U.S. Their results show a statistically significant positive correlation between increases in public sector investment spending and private sector investment spending. However, Erenburg and Wohar (1995) find absence of uni-directional Granger causality from public to private investment or vice-versa. Our approach uses a Vector Autoregression (VAR) similar to that of Mittnik and Neumann (2001), where with data of six industrial countries they show that public investment induces private investment in three out of six countries. In none of these studies does the crowding out effect dominate. In our study, public investment affects private investment positively in the long run at the national level. The results also seem to hold at the dis-aggregated level for the three states. Neutrality tests do not show any significant impact of public investment on private investment. The impulse response analysis however, does show a general positive trend for private investment in all three states.

FDI flows into developing countries are purported to be influenced by several factors. For Pakistan, Nunnenkamp (1991) finds that restrictions on repatriation of profits act as a detriment on FDI inflows. A country with high outstanding debt is likely to deter FDI, since profits may be expected to be taxed at higher rates to finance debt repayments. Lucas (1993) in a study of seven East and South East Asian countries finds no conclusive evidence to prove that increase in costs in neighbouring and rival countries lead to a rise in FDI in the home country. But political instability in any country leads to lower FDI inflows. Jansen (1995) notes that, in the case of Thailand, increases in FDI led to sharp increase in private investment especially in export intensive industries. We also find a positive and significant impact of net foreign investment on private investment at the national level. At the state level we could not undertake such a study due to lack of consistent annual data on state FDI.

We find that reforms have had a significant and positive impact on net foreign investment into India at the national level. At the state level, reforms have had a positive and significant impact on private investment only in Andhra Pradesh.

2. The Model

We use a simple overlapping generations (OLG) model modified to include foreign direct investment (FDI), where FDI is modelled as capital purchased by domestic firms from abroad that is more productive than domestic capital.

Following the standard OLG model, each consumer lives for two time periods. Consumers maximize the 2-period utility

$$U = \ln c_{1t} + \beta \ln c_{2t+1}, \tag{1}$$

where c_{1t} refers to consumption in period 't' when the consumer is young and c_{2t+1} refers to consumption in period 't+1' when the agent is old. The maximization is subject to the constraints

$$p_t c_{1t} + s_t = w_t - \tau_t \tag{2}$$

and

$$p_{t+1} c_{2t+1} = (1 + r_{t+1}) s_t, \tag{3}$$

where p_t is the price of the consumption good in period 't', s_t refers to the nominal savings of the consumer in period 't', w_t is the money wage rate received by the consumer by supplying one unit of labour inelastically every period, τ_t is the lump-sum tax in money terms imposed on the consumer by the government every period and r_{t+1} is the interest rate on savings made in period 't' received in period 't+1'. For simplicity we are ignoring real world issues like the presence of distortionary income taxes and sales taxes, tariff and non-tariff barriers to movement of goods between countries.

The two constraints can be combined as:

$$p_t c_{1t} + \frac{p_{t+1} c_{2t+1}}{(1 + r_{t+1})} = w_t - \tau_t. \tag{4}$$

The Lagrangian for the consumer's problem is

$$\max_{(c_{1t}, c_{2t+1})} L = \ln c_{1t} + \beta \ln c_{2t+1} + \lambda \left[w_t - \tau_t - p_t c_{1t} - \frac{p_{t+1} c_{2t+1}}{(1 + r_{t+1})} \right]$$

with first order conditions are

$\lambda = \frac{1}{p_t c_{1t}}$, (with respect to c_{1t})

$$\lambda = \frac{\beta(1+r_{t+1})}{p_{t+1}c_{2t+1}}. \text{ (with respect to } c_{2t})$$

(a) and (b) together yield

$$p_{t+1}c_{2t+1} = \beta(1+r_{t+1})p_t c_{1t}. \tag{5}$$

Using (5) in the budget constraint (4), we get

$$p_t c_{1t} = \frac{w_t - \tau_t}{(1+\beta)} \tag{6}$$

and using (6) in (5) gives

$$p_{t+1}c_{2t+1} = \beta(1+r_{t+1})\frac{(w_t - \tau_t)}{(1+\beta)}. \tag{7}$$

Finally, using (7) in (3), we get

$$s_t = \frac{\beta}{(1+\beta)}(w_t - \tau_t). \tag{8}$$

Firms maximize period profits using a Cobb-Douglas type production function, only with foreign capital as one of its inputs. Since public capital stock, especially that in infrastructure will likely affect the productivity of private capital, government capital stock is also introduced as an input into the Cobb-Douglas type production function. The production function of the domestic firm is

$$Y_t = (K_t + \theta K_t^*)^{\alpha} L_t^{\gamma} G_t^{1-\alpha-\gamma}, \tag{9}$$

where Y_t is physical output, K_t is domestically owned capital stock, K_t^* is foreign owned capital stock, θ is an efficiency parameter, greater than unity, denoting the efficiency of foreign investment, L_t is labour input and G_t is government capital stock. For convenience, the production function does not include the total factor productivity (TFP) term Had we included TFP our final equation for capital accumulation would include also an additional explanatory variable. However, since productivity is an unobserved variable, it is probably not wrong to simply leave it as a residual of the capital accumulation equation arising out of the model. One alternative, not explored here, could be to estimate the aggregate production function of the economy and use the Solow residual from that regression as our estimate of TFP. This term could be included as another explanatory variable in our capital accumulation equation.

Interest is paid to foreign capital according to the appropriate market determined rate (r_t^*). Introducing FDI as an input into the domestic firms' production function implies that we conceive of all FDI as entering the economy through collaborations with domestic firms. In return for the collaboration, domestic firms pay foreign capital owners the appropriate market interest. The representative firm's profit maximization problem is

$$\max_{(K_t, L_t, K_t^*)} PROFIT = p_t (K_t + \theta K_t^*)^\alpha L_t^\gamma G_t^{1-\alpha-\gamma} - w_t L_t - r_t K_t - r_t^* K_t^*$$

where the rest of the notation is obvious and conventional.
The first order conditions of the problem are

with respect to L_t: $\gamma y_t = \dfrac{w_t}{p_t}$,

where $y_t \equiv \dfrac{Y_t}{L_t}$;

with respect to K_t: $\dfrac{\alpha y_t}{\bar{k}_t} = \dfrac{r_t}{p_t}$,

where $\bar{k}_t \equiv \dfrac{K_t + \theta K_t^*}{L_t}$; and

with respect to K_t^*: $\dfrac{\alpha \theta y_t}{\bar{k}_t} = \dfrac{r_t^*}{p_t}$.

Now, since foreign capital will not come into the country unless it gets at least the same return as it gets abroad, it must be the case that the foreign currency return (say, dollar return) on investing in the domestic country is the same as the dollar return from investing abroad. In other words, we must have,

$$\frac{r_t^*}{p_t} = \frac{r_t^*}{E_t p_t^*} = \frac{\bar{R}_t}{p_t^*}, \tag{10}$$

where the first equality in (10) follows from the assumption of purchasing power parity (where E_t is the exchange rate in domestic currency units per dollar and p_t^* is the foreign price level) and in the second equality, $\bar{R}_t$ is the dollar rate of return on capital. For convenience, let us define

$$\frac{\bar{R}_t}{p_t^*} = \bar{r}_t . \qquad (11)$$

Further

$$\frac{r_t}{p_t} = \frac{\bar{r}_t}{\theta}, \qquad (12)$$

the first order conditions from the firm's problem now reduce to only two independent equations —

(c') $\gamma y_t = \frac{w_t}{p_t}$, and

(de') $\frac{\alpha y_t}{\bar{k}_t} = \frac{\bar{r}_t}{\theta}$,

where $\frac{\bar{r}_t}{\theta}$ is exogenously given.

Note that while the total capital input $\bar{k}_t$ is determined from (de') given government capital stock and the international real return on capital, the individual components of $\bar{k}_t$, namely k_t and k_t^* , are not yet determined and neither has the equilibrium wage rate been determined yet. The equilibrium is found by using the usual OLG assumption that all domestic savings go into domestic capital formation. This is also a convenient assumption but one we feel might not be a bad approximation for a country like India where there are many restrictions on investing domestic savings abroad and where foreign investment outflows seem to be small relative to domestic capital formation flows. Making this assumption and also assuming full depreciation of fixed capital, the equilibrium of the economy can be represented as the equality between domestic investment and savings, that is,

$$K_{t+1} = \frac{s_t}{p_t} N , \qquad (13)$$

where N is the total population of the economy, assumed to be constant for simplicity. If the effects of population growth (that is, growth in labour force in the model) on capital accumulation are considered to be important, then our final regressions can be run with per-capita variables instead of the aggregate variables.

Using (8), the equilibrium condition can be written as

$$K_{t+1} = \left[\frac{N\beta}{(1+\beta)}\right]\frac{w_t}{p_t} - \left[\frac{N\beta}{(1+\beta)}\right]\frac{\tau_t}{p_t}. \tag{14}$$

Now, using the firm's first order condition (c'), (14) can be written as

$$K_{t+1} = \left[\frac{N\beta\gamma}{(1+\beta)}\right](k_t + \theta k_t^*)^{\alpha} g_t^{1-\alpha-\gamma} - \left[\frac{N\beta}{(1+\beta)}\right]\frac{\tau_t}{p_t}, \tag{14'}$$

where the per-worker private, foreign and government capital stock terms on the right hand side of (14') can easily be converted to aggregate terms by multiplying throughout by the N which is in brackets. This makes no essential difference because we assume a constant population.

Now, since foreign capital can itself be written as a function of government capital stock and the international real return on capital from the first order condition (de'), we could eliminate it from our right hand side variables in (14') if we wanted to. We retain it because the effect of FDI on capital accumulation might, *per se*, be an issue of interest. Thus

$$K_{t+1} = f(K_t, K_t^*, G_t, T_t / p_t), \tag{15}$$

where the last term on the right hand side is the real aggregate tax revenue generated by the government in period t, assumed to be exogenous to the model.

We now specify a government capital stock policy function. It is assumed that the government chooses public capital stock next period by looking at the private and foreign capital stocks in the economy over the past history. Thus, policy could be formulated as

$$G_{t+1} = g(K_{t+1}, K_t, K_t^*, G_t, T_t / p_t), \tag{16}$$

where the presence of K_{t+1} in the policy equation is only an identifying assumption since we are looking forward to estimating a vector autoregression (VAR) with the Choleski decomposition using our data. A formulation like (15)-(16) has the advantage that it captures the two-way effect between private and government capital, found to be significant in several studies of public and private investment.

Finally, we can write foreign capital as from (de')

$$K_{t+1}^* = h(K_{t+1}, G_{t+1}, \bar{r}_{t+1}). \tag{17}$$

We append stochastic error terms to (15)-(17). These errors could be serially correlated but are not heteroskedastic. We use a first order Taylor series approximation of the (15)-(17) to write a VAR as:

$$\begin{bmatrix} a_{11} & 0 & 0 \\ a_{21} & a_{22} & 0 \\ a_{31} & a_{32} & a_{33} \end{bmatrix} \begin{pmatrix} K_{t+1} \\ G_{t+1} \\ K^*_{t+1} \end{pmatrix} = C + A_1 Z_t + \ldots + A_p Z_{t-p} + B_1 \bar{r}_{t+1} + B_2 (T_t / p_t) + U_{t+1}, \quad (18)$$

where $Z_t = \begin{pmatrix} K_t \\ G_t \\ K^*_t \end{pmatrix}$, the international real return to capital and the real aggregate tax revenue are the exogenous variables and the disturbances to this VAR (the U_t's) are white noise disturbances with the identity matrix as the covariance matrix. A more conventional way to linearize is to log-linearize the model, but we did not pursue this route because FDI data at the national level contain negative numbers.

If we are to avoid using capital stock data, the VAR above can be quasi-differenced to generate a VAR where the endogenous variables are private investment, government investment and foreign direct investment, instead of the same variables in stock form. Then we will have one lag each of the two exogenous variables also entering our VAR equations. With this modification, we can run a VAR on our variables with investment data instead of capital stock data. This motivates our VAR run for the all-India data later in the paper.

2.1 The State-Level VAR

We use a version of the model above to motivate a VAR for Indian state level data. We assume that there are two regions, Region I and Region II, and there is perfect mobility of physical capital between these regions. Region I represents the state being analyzed and Region II represents the rest of India. The consumer's problems and firm's problems for each region are exactly the same as above and lead to the same first order conditions. By perfect mobility of capital across the regions, the real return to capital across the regions must be equalized and so we must have,

$$\text{(f)} \quad \frac{\alpha y_t^{I}}{\bar{k}_t^{I}} = \frac{\alpha y_t^{II}}{\bar{k}_t^{II}},$$

which implies that

$$k_t^{II} = j(\bar{k}_t^{I}, g_t^{I}, g_t^{II}, k_t^{*II}). \quad (19)$$

Now, since foreign capital into region II can be written as a function of private capital into region II, government capital in region II and the international real return on capital, we can write (19) as

$$k_t^{II} = j^2(\bar{k}_t^{I}, g_t^{I}, g_t^{II}, \bar{r}_t), \tag{19'}$$

where j^2 is just a function different from j. Similarly, since foreign capital into region I is also just a function of private and government capital of region I and the international real return on capital, we could eliminate it from (19') and write (19') as

$$k_t^{II} = j^3(k_t^{I}, g_t^{I}, g_t^{II}, \bar{r}_t). \tag{19''}$$

Now, since all saving of the economy goes into capital formation either in region I or in region II, the equilibrium condition of the economy becomes

$$\begin{aligned} K_{t+1}^{I} + K_{t+1}^{II} &= N^{I}\frac{s_t^{I}}{p_t} + N^{II}\frac{s_t^{II}}{p_t} \\ &= \left[\frac{N^{I}\beta}{(1+\beta)}\right]\gamma y_t^{I} + \left[\frac{N^{II}\beta}{(1+\beta)}\right]\gamma y_t^{II} - \left[\frac{\beta}{(1+\beta)}\right]\left(\frac{N^{I}\tau^{I} + N^{II}\tau^{II}}{p_t}\right) \end{aligned} \tag{20}$$

The last term on the right hand side of (20) is the aggregate tax revenue in real terms for the entire nation, i.e., for region I and region II taken together. Thus, tax revenues of the individual regions do not enter separately in our regressions.

By arguments (i.e., substitutions) very similar to those made for the all-India model, equation (20) leads to a capital accumulation equation for the individual state of the form

$$K_{t+1}^{I} = f^2(g_{t+1}^{I}, g_{t+1}^{II}, \bar{r}_{t+1}, K_t^{I}, G_t^{I}, G_t^{II}, \bar{r}_t) \tag{21}$$

where foreign capital has now been eliminated because we did not have data on foreign direct investment at the state level. As in the national level analysis, FDI at the state level can be retained as another equation in the model if we so choose to.

Making some required identifying assumptions, equation (21) along with a policy equation each for state government capital stock and rest of India government capital stock, we arrive at a VAR of the following form —

$$\begin{bmatrix} a_{11} & 0 & 0 \\ a_{12} & a_{22} & 0 \\ a_{31} & a_{32} & a_{33} \end{bmatrix}\begin{pmatrix} g_{t+1}^{II} \\ g_{t+1}^{I} \\ K_{t+1}^{I} \end{pmatrix} = C + A_1 Z_{t-1} + \dots + A_p Z_{t-p} + B_1\bar{r}_{t+1} + B_2\bar{r}_t + B_3(T_t/p_t) + U_t \tag{22}$$

where the notation and the assumptions on the VAR follow the VAR for national level data. Finally, let us keep in mind that FDI at the state level can be introduced as a fourth equation into this model if appropriate data is made available to us at a later date.

3. Data and Results

Private gross fixed capital formation (GFCF) for the national level was obtained by adding private sector GFCF and household sector GFCF obtained from the National Accounts Statistics (NAS) of India. All-India public sector GFCF was also obtained from the same source. Since FDI was not available for a long enough time period, we took foreign investment as reported in Handbook of Statistics on the Indian Economy published by the RBI. The data series for GFCF and FDI were available in nominal terms and hence were deflated using the GFCF deflator provided by the NAS. Since data on the real return to capital in the rest of the world is not easy to find, we used the average annual real federal funds rate as a proxy for the same. Data for the federal funds rate and the US Consumer Price Index (with which the series was deflated) were obtained from the FRED database available at the Federal Reserve Bank of St. Louis web site. The nominal tax revenue of the union and state governments of India were added together to obtain the total tax revenue for the country as a whole. This data was obtained from various issues of the RBI Bulletin. Tax revenues were deflated by the GDP deflator, available in NAS. Since the exogenous variables that enter our VAR are the quasi-differenced real federal funds series and real tax revenue series (and not their levels), we used a rough estimate of the depreciation rate for India to arrive at the quasi-differenced series. Taking depreciation data for several years in the 1960s and 1970s, we arrived at an average value of 7.5 per cent for the rate of depreciation for India.[1] The exogenous variables used were constructed as the difference between the series and 0.925 times the lagged value of the series. Finally a dummy representing reforms of 1991 was added to the VAR model outlined above. This would capture the results of a change in the institutional regime after 1991.

3.1 Results at the National Level

Using a maximum possible lag length of eight for our unrestricted levels-VAR, we arrived at a lag length of two as a good choice for the lag order. While the SBC selected an order of three, the likelihood ratio tests

---

[1] The average for India was calculated as the average rate of depreciation for these years for the three states of Andhra Pradesh, Gujarat and Maharashtra.

suggested that the order could further be reduced to two. We chose two lags because the regression residuals at three lags had serial correlation in at least one of the equations. A length of four could have been chosen but, given that our sample size is small, parsimony was certainly an issue. Also, the second best order by the SBC criterion (after three) was two lags and so two seemed to be the natural choice by the SBC criterion as well. At a lag length of two, the VAR residuals displayed no serial correlation or heteroskedasticity by the LM tests for serial correlation and heteroskedasticity.

To test whether public investment has a significant explanatory power for private and foreign direct investment, we used block Granger causality tests, the neutrality test and impulse responses. The block causality test examines whether lagged values of one variable (public investment) enter the equations for the other (two) variables jointly. It turned out that the block non-causality hypothesis was accepted by the data, with a Chi-squared (4) statistic of 8.19. The neutrality test checks the significance of the sign of the sum of the coefficients of the lagged variables by using a Wald test. The results are given in Table 10.1. They show that public investment impact on private investment is not statistically significant at five per cent. The effect of public investment on foreign investment is not significant either. The effect of private investment on foreign investment also seems to be negative and significant (based on the Toda and Yamamoto (1995) method of causality testing). Reassuringly for those in favour of increasing foreign participation in Indian industry, the effect of net foreign investment on private investment is positive and significant.

Table 10.1: Neutrality Test Results

Series	**RPVT**		**RPUB**		**RFI**	
Coefficients of lagged values of	N[a]	CHISQ[b]	N[a]	CHISQ[b]	N[a]	CHISQ[b]
RPVT		n.a.[c]		n.a.	-	10.5416*
RPUB	+	0.26406		n.a.	-	0.55001
RFI	+	23.0113*		n.a.		n.a.

Notes: a This column gives the sign of sum of the coefficients of the lagged values of the independent variables.
b This column gives the Chi-squared statistics of the neutrality test. The d.f. for the statistic are 1.
c not applicable — test not done.
* significant at the 5 per cent significance level.
RPVT: Real private investment expenditure,
RPUB: Real public investment expenditure,
RFI: Real Net foreign inflow.

Thus, the neutrality tests do not give much support for the hypothesis that public investment causes private and foreign investment and the forecast error variance decompositions corroborate this finding. The decompositions show that shocks in public investment explain only up to 13 per cent of the variation in private investment for our horizon of 0–12 years. Rather, it is foreign investment that explains up to 65 percent of the variation in private investment at certain horizons. Public investment also does not explain much of the variation in net foreign investment — indeed the contribution does not exceed 20 per cent at any horizon. Private investment also explains no more than 14 per cent of the variation in foreign investment. Thus the variance in FDI turns out to be largely independent of other endogenous variables.

Nevertheless, impulse response analysis does give us reason to believe that public investment contributes towards growth of private and foreign investment. The impulse responses of private, public and foreign investment to an orthogonalized shock in the equation for public investment from the levels VAR are given next. The responses show that private investment gradually increases and keeps increasing till the end of the horizon of 12 years after such a shock. Foreign investment jumps upon impact, falls somewhat thereafter, but again rises back to above initial levels after a couple of years. Public investment increases and shows a moderate tendency to increase even several years after the shock.

Figure 10.1: Levels VAR: Impulse responses to an orthogonalized shock in public investment

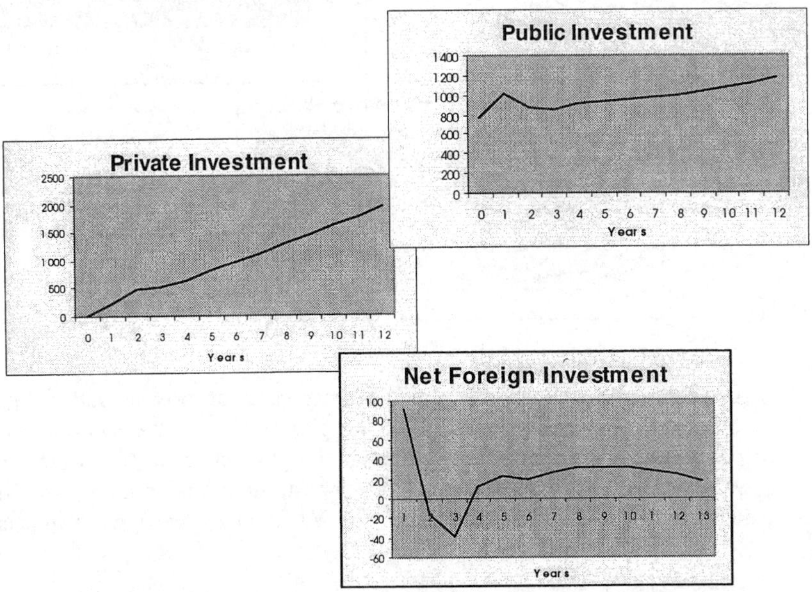

Given the Phillips (1998) argument that for a levels-VAR with some unit roots, the consistency of 'long horizon' impulse responses cannot be relied upon, it would be prudent to look at the same impulse responses from a cointegrated (reduced rank) version of this VAR. As Phillips (1998) has shown, even 'long horizon' impulse responses from a reduced rank regression are consistent and this is the basis for the following exercise. The impulse responses of private, public and foreign investment to an orthogonalized shock in the public investment equation from the cointegrated version of the above levels-VAR follow next. The fact that all three endogenous variables are I(1) was established by using Phillips-Perron unit root tests, results for which are not reported here.

Figure 10.2: Cointegrated VAR: Impulse responses to an orthogonalized shock in public investment

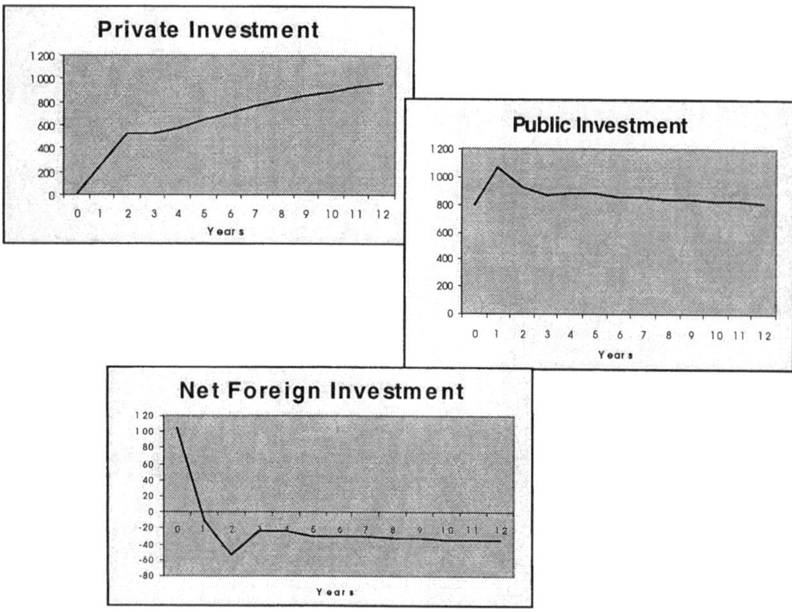

As Figure 10.2 shows, the impulse responses of private and public investment in the cointegrated VAR are almost exactly the same as the responses from the levels-VAR. Foreign investment, however, seems to stay below its initial value after its upward jump upon impact in the cointegrated VAR. Thus, while both the VARs show an upward impact jump in net foreign investment, they tell slightly different stories about the effect of public investment on foreign investment for the later periods in the horizon.

A final word is due regarding the effect of reforms on private, public and foreign investment in the national data. The coefficient of the dummy for reforms beginning in 1991 is clearly negative but statistically insignificant in the equations for both private and public investment. Reforms, seem to have had a positive and significant impact on net foreign investment into India.

3.2 Results at the State level

State level data on private GFCF on all sectors (agriculture, industry and services) taken together is not published. We therefore had to construct and use private *industrial* GFCF for each individual state by subtracting public *industrial* investment (constructed from various issues of the RBI Bulletin) from the total state *industrial* GFCF data (published by the Annual Survey of Industries). The first variable in our state level VAR (rest of India public GFCF) was constructed by subtracting the state level development expenditure (available from various issues of the RBI Bulletin) from all-India public investment (available from NAS). Finally, public investment of the state government was approximated by the development expenditure of the respective state government. Thus we are considering the effect of state level public investment on private *industrial* investment. A reform dummy representing the reforms of 1991 was added to the state level VAR. FDI flows into the state have not been included as a separate equation in our state-level VAR because data on FDI into states was not available for any considerable length of time.

3.3 Andhra Pradesh

Using a maximum lag length of six, we found that the Likelihood Ratio (LR) test led to the acceptance of a much smaller model. The SBC criterion resulted in the choice of five lags, but at least one of the equations had residual serial correlation at this lag length. The next best SBC choice was one lag indicated this was also what we would have chosen based on theory and the LR tests taken together. At one lag, two of the three equations were free of serial correlation and heteroscedasticity by the F version of the LM tests, but one equation contained heteroscedastic disturbances. This problem had to be ignored because other lag lengths resulted in similar problems.

Neutrality tests for the state level were conducted only for the private industrial investment equation. We find that the non-causality of public investment for private investment is accepted at the 5 per cent significance level but not at the 10 per cent significance level. The sign of the coefficient of public investment in this equation was negative.

Forecast error variance decompositions showed that roughly 15 to 34 percent of the variation in private investment was explained by shocks to rest of India public investment and about 8 to 9 percent of the variation in private investment was explained by shocks to state public development expenditure of Andhra Pradesh.

A look at the impulse responses to an orthogonalized shock in state development expenditure leads to the conclusion that while upon impact, private industrial investment falls as a result of the shock, it soon recovers to reach a level above its initial level. It turns out that rest of India public investment also responds clearly positively to the shock especially over the long run. Finally, it is seen that state public investment returns to its initial level after a few years post shock. These impulse responses are given in Figure 10.3 below.

Figure 10.3: Levels VAR: Impulse responses to an orthogonalized shock in state public investment for Andhra Pradesh

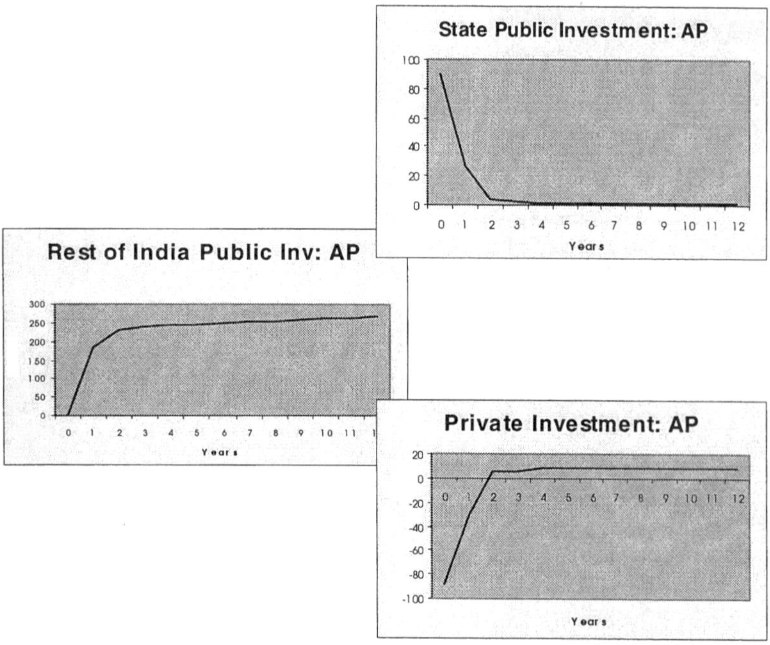

Following the national level study, one could have estimated a cointegrating version of the above VAR for Andhra Pradesh too. However, at least one of the endogenous variables for each of the three states under consideration (Andhra Pradesh, Gujarat and Maharashtra) turned out to be stationary by the Phillips-Perron tests (using p-values and/or critical values of the adjusted t-statistics). We therefore thought it better not to run a cointegrating VAR with the three variable system in question for the state level data.

The coefficient of the dummy representing reforms of 1991 is negative and insignificant in the equations for state and rest of India public investment but can be considered to be positive and significant for private industrial investment in Andhra Pradesh. It seems, therefore, that the reforms have indeed impacted private investment in this state.

3.4 Gujarat

Based on considerations similar to those discussed for the case of Andhra Pradesh, we arrived at a lag length of 1 for the Gujarat VAR. While one equation contained heteroscedasticity with one lag, the problem had to be ignored because of similar problems with higher lags as well.

Neutrality tests for the private investment equation for Gujarat showed that the effect of state development expenditure on state private investment was insignificant at the 5 per cent as well as at the 10 per cent significance level. The sign of the relevant coefficient was, however, positive.

Forecast error variance decompositions showed that only about 8–10 per cent of the variation in state private investment is explained by shocks to state development expenditure. On the other hand, about 10–33 per cent of this variation is explained by shocks to rest of India public investment.

Impulse response analysis showed that while private investment shoots up following a shock to state development expenditure, the positive effect does not last long and the effect in the later years is to reduce private investment below its initial level. Thus, we see a tapering of the effect of state public investment on private investment as opposed to what we saw in the case of Andhra Pradesh. The impulse responses for Gujarat are reported in Figure 10.4.

On the question of reforms, the t-ratios for the coefficient on the dummy representing the reforms of 1991 show that the dummy has a positive but statistically insignificant impact on each of the three dependent variables in the state level VAR. Thus, the reforms seem to have had no essential impact on the investment undertaken in this state, whether public or private.

Figure 10.4: Levels VAR: Impulse responses to an orthogonalized shock in state public investment in Gujarat

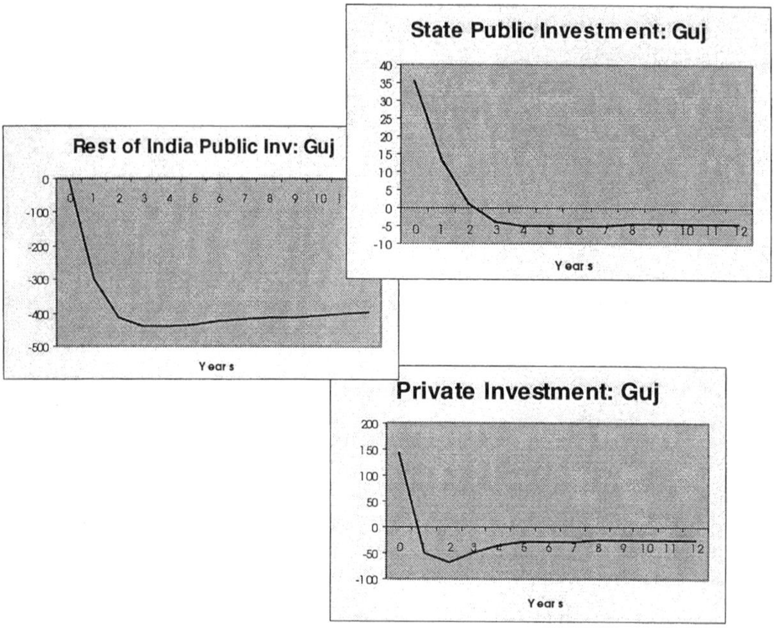

3.5 Results from Maharashtra

The SBC criterion indicated three lags. The VAR residuals turn out to be serially uncorrelated and homoskedastic at this lag length.

The neutrality test of the effect of lagged state investment on state private investment showed that public investment spending is insignificant at 10 per cent, although the sum of the coefficients of lagged state development expenditure in the private investment equation was positive.

Rest of India public investment shocks explain about 15 to 20 per cent of the variation in private investment at shorter impulse horizons and about 40 to 50 per cent of the variation in state private investment at longer impulse horizons. State public investment explains up to 36 per cent of the variation in state private industrial investment for the impulse horizons of 0 to 12 years considered.

Impulse response analysis shows that a shock to state public investment leads to rising trend in the impulse response for private investment although there are discernible fluctuations. After the shock, state public investment quickly comes back to its initial level, stays there for a few years and then shows fluctuations of increasing amplitude. The response of rest of India public investment has an upward trend much like that of Maharashtra private investment and also shows similar fluctuations. These responses are depicted in Figure 10.5.

Figure 10.5: Levels VAR: Impulse responses to an orthogonalized shock in state public investment in Maharashtra

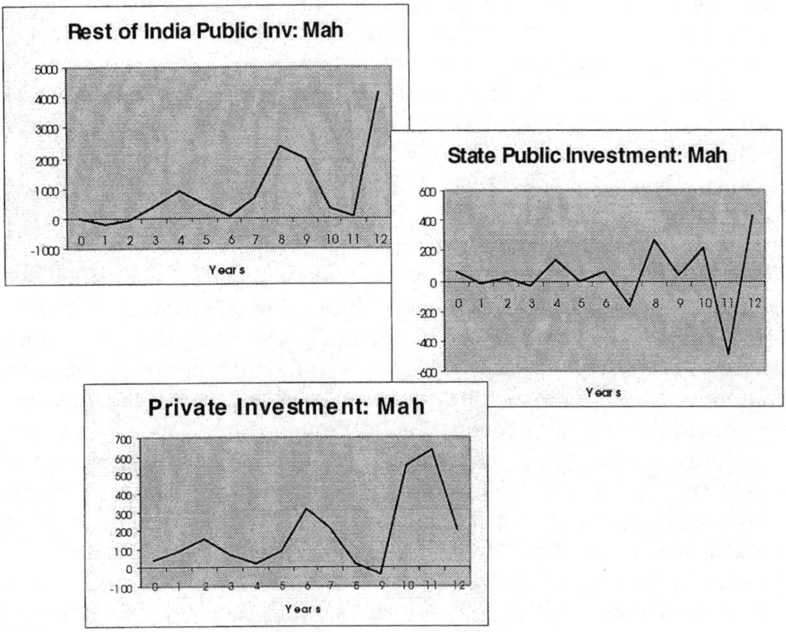

The coefficient of the 1991 reform dummy is negative and significant in the equations for state and rest of India public investment. However, the dummy coefficient in the private investment equation is positive but statistically insignificant, implying that reforms may have reduced public investment but may not have increased private investment significantly.

4. Conclusion

We have analysed the relationship between public investment, private investment and FDI in India, using an overlapping generations model where the representative consumer maximises consumption stream over two periods. Firms maximise profits and import foreign capital since it is more productive than domestic capital. FDI is dependent on the rate of return in the domestic country as well as abroad. A vector autoregressive model is formulated where public investment, private investment and FDI are the endogenous variables and the international real return to capital and the real aggregate tax revenue are the exogenous variables at the national level for which data has been used. In the state level analysis, we consider a two-region model where the state is one of the regions and the rest of India, the other. There exists perfect capital mobility so that the rate of return to capital is equalised across regions. The VAR analysis is also along similar lines as the national level. At the national level, we do find some evidence of public investment having a positive impact on private investment. The results are much stronger however for the case of net foreign investment, which has a significant and positive impact on private investment at the national level. Reforms have definitely had a positive and significant impact on national FDI. At the state level, it is only in the case of Andhra Pradesh that we find reforms having a positive and significant impact on private investment. According to the annual report of the Ministry of Commerce and Industry, the choice of location by a foreign investor in any particular state depends on the market size, availability of skilled manpower, availability and dependability of skilled manpower and other incentives provided by the State governments. Ongoing incentives such as simplification of procedures, de-licensing, setting up of regulatory commissions will further encourage FDI into the country. Despite Andhra Pradesh, Gujarat and Maharashtra cornering a major chunk of the FDI investment approvals, their experience with reforms and well as the interactions between public and private investment seem to be varied. For future work, one can model FDI flows into particular sctors and examine links with public policies at the national and state level. Finally, our approach can easily be extended to estimate the effects of public expenditure on private consumption expenditure too.

References

Aschauer D.A., 'Is Private Capital Productive', *Journal of Monetary Economics*, 23 (1989), 177–200.

Erenburg S.J., 'The Real Effects Of Public Investment on Private Investment', *Applied Economics*, 25 (1993), 831–7.

Erenburg S.J. and M.E. Wohar, 'Public and private investment. Are there causal linkages?', *Journal of Monetary Economics*, 17(1) (1995), 1–30.

Jansen K., 'The Macroeconomic Effects of Direct Foreign Investment: The case of Thailand', *World Development*, 23(2) (1995), 193–210.

Khan Mohsin S. and Manmohan Kumar, 'Public and Private Investment and the Growth Process in Developing Countries', *Oxford Bulletin of Economics and Statistics*, 59(1) (1997), 69–88.

Lucas Rebert E.B., 'On the Determinants of Direct Foreign Investment: Evidence from East and South East Asia', *World Development* 21(3) (1993), 391–406.

Mittnik S. and T. Neumann, 'Dynamic Effects of Public Investment: Vector autoregressive evidence from six industrialized countries'. *Applied Economics* 26 (2001), 429–46.

National Accounts Statistics of India 1950–51 to 1996–97 (Mumbai, India: EPW Research Foundation, 1998).

Nunnenkamp P., 'Developing Countries' Attractiveness for Foreign Direct Investment — Debt overhang and sovereign risk as major impediments?', *Pakistan Development Review*, 30(4) (1991), 1145–58.

Phillips Peter C.B. 'Impulse Response and forecast Error Variance Asymptotics in Non-Stationary VAR's', *Journal of Econometrics*, 81(1–2) (1998), 21–56.

Toda, H.Y and T. Yamamoto, 'Statistical Inference in Vector Autoregressions with Possibly Integrated Processes', *Journal of Econometrics*, 66(1–2) (1995), 225–50.

11

Liberalization and Business Investment in India

Prema-chandra Athukorala and Kunal Sen

1. Introduction

There are several studies on the determinants of private investment in developing countries.[1] These studies, however, suffer from a number of methodological flaws. First, whereas the theory of investment is basically about investment behaviour of *the firm* (business investment), the dependent variable commonly used is *total private investment*. Total private investment is a poor proxy for business investment because there are fundamental differences in terms of the underlying determinants between household residential investment (which is the key component of household investment in most developing countries) and business investment. Second, many of these studies employ *ad hoc* investment functions, not derived from a specific model but formulated largely to suit the nature of readily available data. For instance, none of the studies have appropriately captured the effect of user cost of capital on private capital formation — a key link between financial markets and real economic activity in any industrial-country macroeconomic model. The effect of the level of existing capital stock on investment — another key postulate of the received theory of investment — has also largely been ignored.

Thirdly, given the paucity of data for most developing countries, the overwhelming majority of studies have been conducted using cross-country data.[2] Cross-country regression analysis is based implicitly on the restrictive assumption of 'homogeneity' in the observed relationship across countries. It is common knowledge that there are considerable variations

---

[1] See Rama (1993) and Agenor and Montiel (1996, pp. 84–88) for surveys and references.

[2] Two notable exceptions are the country case-studies in Chibber, Dailami and Shafik (1992) and Fielding (1997).

among developing countries in relating to various structural features and institutional aspects that have a direct bearing upon investment behaviour. Moreover, given vast differences among countries with respect to the nature and quality of data, cross-country comparison is fraught with danger. Not only the statistical procedures for measuring investment, but also the magnitude of errors in data arising from differences in the implementation of these procedures, vary significantly among countries (Srinivasan 1994). Finally, the estimation procedures used in most studies have not appropriately handled simultaneity problems and issues of spurious correlation.

The purpose of this chapter is to develop a model of business investment in developing countries for use in examining investment behaviour in India following the market-oriented structural adjustment policy reforms implemented in 1991. The model is derived from the standard (neoclassical) theory of business investment, with appropriate adoption to reflect structural features specific to investment behaviour in developing countries. It is estimated using an econometric procedure which captures the dynamic lag structure of investment behaviour, while guarding against the problem of spurious correlation and simultaneity bias.

India is chosen as the laboratory to test the model for two reasons. First, the Indian macroeconomic database is relatively rich by developing country standards and meets the data requirement of our exercise. India is perhaps the only developing country for which a separate data series on corporate investment is available for a period of sufficient length for econometric investigation. The availability of disaggregated data on the capital stock and the key variables required for the construction of an index of the relative price of capital allows us to implement an investment function specified in line with the received theory of investment. The second reason stems from the policy focus on investment behaviour in the Indian economic policy debate following the policy reforms initiated in 1991. A large number of studies have consistently reported a significant negative impact of structural adjustment programs (SAPs) on private investment in the immediate post-reform years.[3] In contrast to this stylised fact, there has been a marked increase in private corporate investment in India in the post-reform period. As a policy application of our empirical model, we examine its usefulness in explaining this investment expansion.

---

[3] See the World Bank (1988), Harrigan and Mosley (1988), and Greenaway and Morrissey (1992) and the works cited therein.

2. The Model

The basic premise of the neoclassical investment model is that firms 'maximize utility of a consumption stream subject to a production function relating the flow of output to the flows of labor and capital services' (Jorgenson 1967, p. 136). The firm supplies capital services to itself through the acquisition of investment goods. The demand for capital is therefore a derived demand and is assumed to positively depend on expected output and negatively depend on the expected rental cost of capital. Assuming constant elasticity of substitution (σ) between capital and variable inputs, we observe the following relation between desired capital stock (K^*), the expected level of output (Y) and the expected rental cost of capital (C):

$$K^*_t = \alpha Y_t C_t^{-\sigma} \tag{1}$$

where C_t is,

$$C_t = [PK_t[r_t - \pi^e_t + \delta]/P_t, \tag{2}$$

Here, α is the distribution parameter, *PK* is the price of capital goods, *P* the output price level, *r* the nominal bank lending rate, π^e the expected inflation rate of capital goods and δ the rate of capital depreciation.[4] If there are costs to adjusting the capital stock and gestation lags in the adjustment process, then firms gradually respond to changes in the desired capital stock. Equation (1) highlights the dependence of the desired capital stock on a quantity variable (*Y*) and a set of price variables (*PK* and *r*).

To derive the investment function, we divide total (gross) investment into net and replacement components. Net investment (I^n_t) is determined by a distributed lag on new orders, which equal in a given period the change in the desired capital stock:

$$I^n_t = \sum_{j=0}^{J} \beta_j \Delta K^*_{t-j} \tag{3}$$

Where β represents the delivery lag distribution extending for J+1 periods. Replacement investment (I^r_t) is taken to be proportional to the capital stock available at the beginning of the period and adjusts instantaneously,

$$I^r_t = \delta K_{t-1} \tag{4}$$

Combining (1), (3) and (4) and appending a stochastic error (u_t), we obtain the neoclassical model of investment:

---

4 Investment tax credit, depreciation allowances and corporate income tax are ignored for lack of data.

$$I_t = \delta K_{t-1} + \sum_{j=0}^{J} \alpha\beta j \Delta(Y_{t-j} C_{t-j}^{-\sigma}) + u_t \tag{5}$$

We approximate K* linearly on the assumption that expectations of the output and rental cost terms are based on extrapolations of past values. This gives the following modified model:

$$I_t = \delta K_{t-1} + \sum_{j=0}^{J_1} \theta_{1j} \Delta Y_{t-j} - \sum_{j=0}^{J_2} \theta_{2j} \Delta C_{t-j} + u_t \tag{6}$$

where the distributed lag coefficients are an amalgam of the delivery lag, expectational and production parameters.

For the purpose of this study we augment this basic model by adding the following explanatory variables: credit availability (*BC*), uncertainty in the macroeconomic environment [proxied by the standard deviations of output (*SY*) and cost of capital (*SC*)], a post-reform intercept dummy (*PRD*), and public investment (*IPB*). The rationale behind this augmentation is discussed below.

The basic model is based on the assumption of perfect capital markets, which implies that firms can borrow freely in order to implement their investment plans. The validity of this assumption in the context of developing countries can be questioned on the basis of the neo-liberal literature on financial repression due to McKinnon (1973) and Shaw (1973). These authors have forcefully argued that, in the typical developing country, the availability of loanable funds may influence investment behaviour independent of the cost of capital. This view suggests the inclusion of a credit constraint (proxied by real bank credit to the private sector (*BC*) as an additional explicator in the investment function (Solimano 1992). Policies of financial repression were followed in India since the early 1970s to the early 1990s. The 'priority sector lending requirements' and the use of the banking sector for deficit financing may have led to a 'rationing of credit' from commercial banks to private firms in the manufacturing sector.

The use of *BC* as an explicator of investment can be further supported by drawing upon the recent theoretical literature on the implications of the 'finance constraint' for the firm's investment decisions.[5] According to this literature, external finance, if available at all, may be more costly than internal finance because of transactions costs, contract enforcement (agency cost) problems and asymmetric information. The argument rests on the distinction between 'insiders' (the firm's owners/managers) who have full

[5] For useful surveys of this literature, see Gertler (1988).

information about a particular firm's investment prospects, and 'outsiders' who may correctly perceive the prospects for a population of firms but cannot distinguish the quality of individual firms. An empirical implication of the application of asymmetric information and agency cost issues to financial markets is that that the availability of finance (in particular, bank credit) may constrain the investment decisions of certain firms (especially those which are smaller in size or younger in age).[6] One can reasonably argue that problems of asymmetric information and contract enforcement will be more severe in developing countries such as India where greater heterogeneity among firms exist, capital markets are quite segmented and there is a lack of a well developed system of property rights.

The basic model also assumes that the investment decision is reversible (that is, invested capital can be sold easily to other users) and that each decision is a once and for all opportunity. A 'new view' of investment has, however, stressed that many real-world investment decisions violate these assumptions and that irreversibility and the possibility of delay are important considerations in the investment decision (Pindyck 1991, Dixit and Pindyck 1994). Plant and equipment investment can be considered 'sunk costs' if capital, once installed, is firm- or industry-specific and cannot be put to productive use in a different activity or if secondary markets are not efficient. The decision to undertake an irreversible investment in an uncertain environment can be viewed as involving the exercising of an option — that of waiting for new information that might affect the desirability and timing of the investment. The value of the lost option is a component of the opportunity cost of investment. According to the 'new view', this opportunity cost can be substantial in most circumstances and a higher degree of uncertainty about the future can have a significant negative effect on investment. Here, uncertainty can originate from two independent sources — the macroeconomic environment and policy factors. The second source of uncertainty can be considered to be of more relevance in a reforming economy where entrepreneurs' willingness to invest in certain sectors (say, export-oriented activities) would depend on whether they perceive certain reforms (such as trade liberalisation) to be credible and sustainable (Rodrik 1991; Ibarra 1995).

Empirical studies of the effect of macroeconomic conditions on investment have used a variety of measures of macroeconomic uncertainty (Ferderer 1993, Pindyck and Solimano 1993 and Price 1995). In this study, we use the three-year moving average standard deviations of the change in output (*SY*) and the change in rental cost of capital (*SC*) as measures of the

---

6 Empirical studies that have tested the 'finance constraint' using firm-level panel data include Fazzari, Hubbard and Petersen (1988), Devereux and Schianterelli (1990), and Hoshi, Kashyap and Scharfstein (1991).

degree of uncertainty.[7] Capturing the impact of policy credibility on investment performance poses a more serious problem (Rodrik 1991). The Indian government embarked in 1991 on a structural adjustment program that was comprehensive in its coverage and far-reaching in its nature. In such a context, there are both conceptual and measurement problems in deciding on the relevant policy variable where credibility is the issue. Rather than focusing on a specific policy variable, we include an intercept dummy variable, PRD, which takes the value 1 for the post-reform years and zero otherwise, to test whether the structural adjustment policy reforms *per se* has influenced investment behaviour, over and above its impact operating through other variables explicitly allowed for in the regression specification.

Finally, we chose public sector fixed capital formation (*IPB*) as an explanatory variable for the following reasons. Public investment may affect private investment both *via* supply and demand sides. On the supply side, the private sector relies on public investment for most of the infrastructure, because this is either a natural or a legal monopoly of the government. Thus public investment in infrastructure and private investment should be complementary (Blejer and Khan 1984). On the demand side, in theory, the relationship is ambiguous. If there is some slack in the economy one would expect a change in public investment to push private investment in the same direction. Otherwise, some private investment will probably have to be 'crowded out'. This ambiguity notwithstanding, given the dominant role played by the government in the provision of infrastructure and in key intermediate- and investment-goods producing industries in India, it is generally assumed that 'the stimulation effect of public investment on private investment tends to dominate any possible negative effect through competing for investible funds' (Bardhan 1984, p. 25).

With these additional variables and an intercept term, the investment function can be written as:

$$I_t = c + \delta K_{t-1} + \sum_{j=0}^{J} \theta_{1j} \Delta Y_{t-j} - \sum_{j=0}^{J} \theta_{2j} \Delta C_{t-j} + \theta_3 BC_t \qquad (7)$$

$$+\theta_4 PBI_t - \theta_5 SY_t - \theta_6 SC_t + u_t$$

[7] For a variable x, the 3 year moving average is y(t) = Σx(t-j)/3, where j =1 to 3. The standard deviation of x as time t [sdx(t)], then, is

$$sdx(t) = \sqrt{\frac{\{\Sigma[x(t-j) - y(t)]^2\}}{4}}$$

where j=0,3.

Before turning to the estimation of the model, a methodological issue needs to be addressed — that of the 'Lucas Critique' of reduced-form models (Lucas 1976). As we have already noted, the coefficients of equation (7) are a combination of both expectation and structural (technology) parameters and are, therefore, not invariant to changes in policy regimes. Following the Lucas Critique, one can argue that the preferred route to the modeling of dynamic models is the estimation of stochastic first order conditions for optimal choice by rational, forward-looking representative agents (the 'Euler Equation' approach). The Lucas Critique seems particularly relevant in our case; with the sharp changes in policy that occurred in the Indian economy in 1991, parameter instability of a reduced form model (such as equation (7)) between the pre- and post-reform periods is a distinct possibility. Should this be the case, the use of an empirical model estimated for the pre-reform period to make post-reform inferences is problematic.

Our preferred strategy is to use a data-based approach to guard against the possibility of parameter instability, i.e., to employ a recursive estimation technique to check for possible structural instability of the empirical model. The choice of this approach is based on two considerations. First, the presence of credit constraints on the firm's investment demand implies that at any point in time, there will be some firms which are credit constrained and some which are not. The Euler equation approach invariably precludes this possibility. The preferred modeling strategy from a time-series perspective is, therefore, to include a proxy for the credit constraint as an additional variable in the investment demand function.[8] Second, Oliner, Rudebusch and Sichel (1995 and 1996) have found that traditional reduced-form investment models exhibit only modest amount of parameter non-constancy even in the presence of significant policy shifts, and that the 'empirical Euler equations appear to provide no improvement when judged by the metric of structural stability.' (Oliner, Rudebusch and Sichel 1996, p. 311).

We will estimate investment functions separately for private corporate investment and non-residential business investment. For estimation purposes, equations for private corporate investment can be specified as follows:

[8] The analogue to this in the time-series consumption function literature is the modeling of current consumption as a function of past period's consumption and current income (popularised by Campbell and Mankiw, 1987). Such a formulation is justified on the grounds that the Rational Expectations — Permanent Income Hypothesis may apply to some individuals but not to others (who may, for example, be liquidity constrained).

ICP = f(KCP, DY, DCCP, IPB, BC, SY, SCCP, PRD) (8)

where:

ICP	Real fixed investment, private corporate sector,
KCP	Real capital stock, private corporate sector,
DY	Change in Real GDP,
DCCP	Change in the Cost of capital, private corporate sector,
IPB	Real fixed investment, public sector,
BC	Real bank credit to the private sector,
SY	3 year moving average of the standard deviation of Y,
SCCP	3 year moving average of the standard deviation of CCP,
PRD	Post-reform dummy, value of 1 for years 1991–96, 0 otherwise.

3. Results

Equation (8) is estimated over the sample period 1954 to 1996 using annual data. All variables, except *SY*, *SCCP* and *CCP* (which are measured in proportional form) and of course *PRD*, are measured in natural logarithms. Data sources are listed and methods of data transformation adopted are discussed in the Appendix. A summary of the variables used in the regressions is presented in Table 11.1.

We test the time series properties of the data. The results for the ADF test (presented in Table 11.2) suggests that the variables do not have the same order of integration; *ICP*, *KCP* and *IPB* are found to be I(1) while *DCCP*, *DY*, *BC*, *SY* and *SCCP* are I(0). We opt to use the general to specific modeling procedure. This minimizes the possibility of estimating spurious relations but retains long-run information.

The use of the ordinary least squares (OLS) method to estimate equations (8a) and (8b) can yield biased coefficient estimates because autonomous shocks to the error term (such as a shock to technology or to demand) may be correlated with the change in output *(DY)*, as a profit-maximising firm decides on the combination of capital, other factors of production and output simultaneously. To guard against the potential simultaneity bias, the equation was estimated using two-stage least squares (2SLS). The growth rates of real agricultural output and real government consumption and the lagged dependent variable were used as instruments for *DY*.

Table 11.1: Tests for Unit Roots*

Data series	ADF test of H_0:I(1) versus H_1:I(0)#	Whether I(1) or I(0)?
ICP	-1.70 (0)	I(1)
KCP	-1.72 (1)	I(1)
DY	-6.76 (0)+	I(1)
DCCP	-5.72 (0)+	I(0)
BC	-5.72 (0)+	I(0)
IPB	-2.77 (1)	I(1)

Notes: * Except in the cases of DY and DCCP, all the tests were conducted 'with trend' to allow for the possibility that, for most economic time-series, the usual competing alternative to the presence of a unit root is a deterministic linear trend. The critical value at the 5 per cent level is 3.52.

Figures in parentheses indicate the order of augmentation required to obtain residual whiteness.

+ Rejection of null hypothesis.

Table 11.2: Determinants of Private Corporate Investment in India: Regression results#

$$\Delta ICP_t = -1.28 + 0.13\Delta BC_{t-1} + 2.98DY_t - 3.89DCCP_t + 0.68\Delta IPB_t + 1.06IPB_{t-1}$$
$$(1.62) \quad (1.76)^{*} \quad (2.06)^{**} \quad (2.14)^{**} \quad (1.53) \quad (3.33)^{***}$$

$$-0.50KCP_{t-1} + 0.75PRD - 0.45ICP_{t-1}$$
$$(2.01)^{**} \quad (3.71)^{***} \quad (3.41)^{***}$$

$\bar{R}^2 = 0.30$	$F(8,32) = 3.18^{**}$	S.E. of regression $= 0.24$
$DW = 2.19$	$LM1 - \chi^2(1) = 1.03$	$LM2 - \chi^2(2) = 0.17$
$RESET - \chi^2 = 0.01$	$JBN - \chi^2(2) = 2.60$	$SPEC - \chi^2(2) = 3.46$

Long-run (steady-state) Investment Elasticity:

Income (DY)	6.64**
Cost of Capital (DCCP)	-8.69**
Public investment (IPB)	2.36*
Capital Stock (KCP)	-1.11*

Notes: # t-ratios of regression coefficients are given in brackets. Approximate critical values for the *t*-ratios are as follows: 10 per cent = 1.31 (*), 5 per cent = 1.69 (**) and 1 per cent = 2.44 (***). The test statistics are : *LM* = Lagrange multiplier test of residual serial correlation; *RESET* = Ramsey test for functional form mis-specification; *JBN* = Jarque-Bera test for the normality of residuals; *SPEC* = Sargan's test for the correct specification of instruments.

The final parsimonious estimated equation, together with a set of commonly used diagnostic statistics, are reported in Table 11.3. The equation is statistically significant at the one per cent level (in terms of the standard F test) and it performs well by all diagnostic tests. Apart from these tests, a residual correlogram of up to six years was estimated for each equation, with no evidence of significant serial correlation. To determine whether the parameters of the equation were constant over the post-reform period, the equation was re-estimated using recursive 2SLS. By plotting the recursive estimates of the coefficients of the key explanatory variables in the equation — $DCCP_t$, DY_t, ΔIPB_t , IPB_{t-1} and ΔBC_{t-1} — we found no evidence of structural instability in the parameter estimates.[9] Thus, the coefficient estimates can be used for making inferences about the impact of policy reforms on investment behaviour.

Table 11.3. Summary Data on Variables Used in Econometric Analysis*

Variables	1954–59	1960–69	1970–79	1980–84	1985–90	1991–96
Dependent Variable						
ICP	121	187	191	540	764	2150
Explanatory Variables						
KCP	612	1426	1964	3077	5246	10699
BC	61	122	329	563	687	897
Y	5918	8089	11445	15207	20616	28230
IPB	352	635	879	1442	1913	2204
CCP(%)	8.6	6.4	9.9	13.9	15.7	13.8

Notes: * Value series are in billions of Indian rupees at constant (1981) prices. Figures reported are annual averages for the given sub-period.
Source and methods: Data sources and methods of data compilation are explained in *Appendix*.

The results support the hypothesis that business investment in a given year is negatively affected by the size of the initial capital stock; the coefficient on *KCP* is statistically significant at one per cent and suggests a long-run investment elasticity of -1.11 with respect to *KCP*. The coefficient on change in rental cost of capital (*DCCP*) is statistically significant with the postulated (negative) sign. A one percentage point rise in the rate of increase in real rental cost of capital is associated with a 8.69 per cent

[9] Graphs are not reported due to space constraints. They are available from the authors on request.

decline in corporate investment in the long run.[10] The standard accelerator mechanism is important in explaining corporate investment behaviour; the coefficient on the income variable (*DY*) is positive and statistically significant at the five per cent level. It suggests that one per cent increase in income is associated with a 6.64 per cent increase in business investment in the long run.

There is evidence of a significant positive short run effect of bank credit (*BC*) on private investment. An increase in real bank credit by one per cent is associated with 0.13 per cent increase in annual increase in corporate investment. However, the coefficient on the lagged level term of *BC* turned out to be statistically insignificant with erratic sign changes in various experimental runs (and therefore was omitted in the reported regression). This implies that the availability of bank credit is not important in determining the long-run (steady-state) level of investment.

The results for the public investment variable provide support for the proposition that, in the Indian economy, public investment has a strong complementarity relationship with corporate investment. The impact (short-run) and steady-state elasticities of corporate investment with respect to public investment are 0.68 and 2.36 respectively.

In the experimental runs, the variables representing uncertainty in the macroeconomic environment (*SY* and *SCCP*) consistently had statistically insignificant coefficients with some sign reversal. These variables were, therefore, dropped in the final equation. The absence of a statistically significant impact of *SY* and *SCCP* on investment in the Indian case may perhaps reflects the fact that, unlike most other developing countries, India has had a stable macroeconomic environment for most of the time-period under consideration (Joshi and Little 1994).

The positive and significant coefficient attached to the post-reform dummy (*PRD*) can be interpreted to imply a favourable perception on the part of entrepreneurs on the credibility and sustainability of the reform process, which has led to an increase in corporate investment. We defer further discussion of the post-reform dummy to the next section where we discuss the effect of the SAP on corporate investment in more detail. We next present the results for non-residential business investment.

---

[10] This apparently large elasticity coefficient does not seem unrealistic given the fact that the value of *DCCP* has varied with a narrow margin (between -2.5 to 3.2 per cent) during the study period.

4. The 1991 SAP and its Effect on Private Corporate Investment

An important 'stylised fact' of private investment behaviour in developing countries is the negative impact that a stabilisation *cum* structural adjustment program may have on private investment in the immediate post-reform years (see the World Bank 1988, Harrigan and Mosley 1988, and Greenaway and Morrissey 1992). Following a balance of payments crisis, the Indian government initiated a comprehensive stabilisation *cum* SAP. In contrast to the evidence on the impact of SAPs on private investment from other developing countries, we noted a marked increase in private corporate investment in India in the post-reform period. Annual average corporate investment more than doubled between 1985–90 and 1991–96 as compared to 1985–90 (Table 11.1). This increase is vividly shown by the mean-adjusted investment series plotted in Figure 11.1.

Figure 11.1: Private Corporate Investment (ICP), Mean-Adjusted, 1980 to 1996

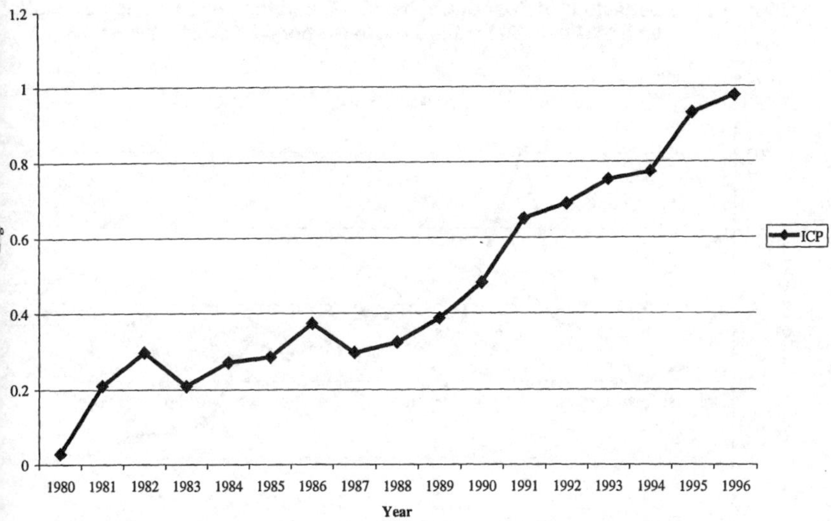

Source: CSO, *National Accounts Statistics*, various issues.

The estimated investment function for private corporate investment, when analysed in the context of data reported in Table 11.1, yield the following inferences.

The slowdown in the growth of real public sector investment (the average annual rate of growth in real public investment decreased from six per cent in 1980–90 to 3.8 per cent in 1991–94) and the decline in real bank credit (from an annual average level of Rupees 687 billion during 1985–90 to 651 billion during 1991 to 1994)[11] during the *immediate* post reform years seem to have had an adverse impact on corporate investment. However, these negative effects were more than offset by the positive effect of a recovery in economic activity (real GDP growth averaged 5 per cent in 1992 to 96 as compared to 0.4 per cent in 1991) and the decline in real rental cost of capital brought about by the policy reforms. The cost of capital index fell by 12 per cent between 1985–90 and 1990–96. An inspection of the composite data series of CCP (Figure 11.2) suggests that the dominant force behind this decline was a decline in the price of investment goods brought about by import liberalisation.[12] Interestingly, the decline in the investment goods price was much larger in magnitude than the combined cost raising effects of currency depreciation and the increase in bank lending rates.

Figure 11.2: Behaviour of Cost of Capital (CCP) and the Relative Price of Capital Goods (PKCP/P) for the Private Corporate Sector, 1980–1996

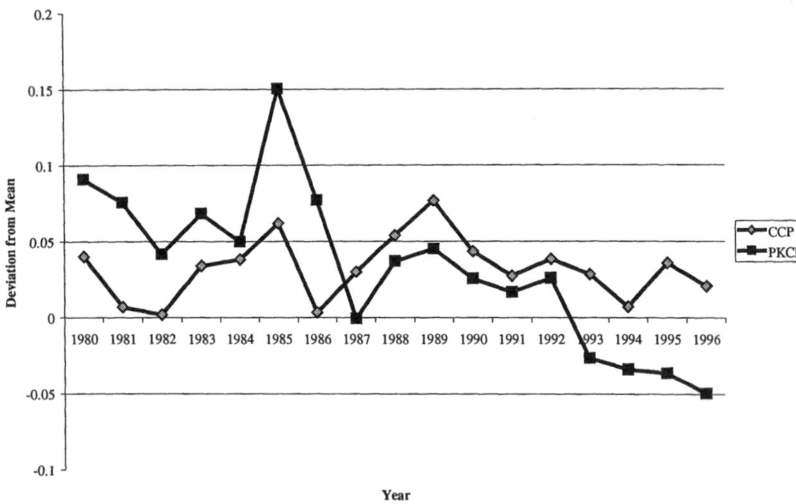

Source: authors' calculations from CSO, *National Accounts Statistics*, various issues.

[11] This was due to tight monetary policy that accompanied the reform package.
[12] The average nominal tariff rate on capital goods declining from 85 per cent in 1991 to 25 per cent in 1994.

Added to these positive effects has been the general investment-enhancing impact of the new investment climate in the post reform era. The statistically significant positive coefficient on the post-reform dummy (*PRD*) in the estimated regression is consistent with the view that the reforms have had a positive impact on investment over and above their impact operating through the explanatory variables. It can be argued that the corporate sector may have considered the reforms to be credible for two reasons; firstly, the reforms measures were 'forceful and explicit', and secondly, the reform process 'moved over a number of areas, in rapid succession' (Bhagwati 1993, pp. 84 & 85).

5. Conclusion

This chapter has attempted to enrich the literature on the determinants of investment in developing countries by developing a fully specified investment function rooted in the received theory of business investment. It analyzes the determinants of business investment in India over the period 1955 to 1995. The results suggest that the level of capital stock and rental cost of capital are important determinants of business investment along with changes in output and public investment.

The estimated investment function proved to be useful in explaining the remarkable increase in increase in business investment in India following the market-oriented structural adjustment reforms initiated in 1991. It is evident that that the net impact of the reforms on corporate investment has been salutary. The decline in the rate of growth of real public sector investment brought about by the reform-related fiscal squeeze seems to have had a significant adverse impact on corporate investment. However, this adverse impact was outweighed by the salutary effects of the decline in real rental cost of capital brought about by the reform process, and favourable changes in investor perception in the aftermath of the reforms.

Appendix

The data series used in this study have been directly obtained or compiled from the following publications: (1) Central Statistical Organisation (CSO), *National Accounts Statistics*, Delhi (various issues) and (2) Reserve Bank of India, *Report on Currency and Banking*, Delhi (various issues). In the selection and compilation of most of the data series, we have simply followed established practice in this field of research. However, the choice of data series for the compilation of the C index and the construction of the real capital stock series (K) need some explanation.

The bank lending rate used in constructing the C series is the one year lending rate of the State Bank of India (the premier commercial bank in India). The measure of the general price level is the GDP deflator (1980 = 1.00). Capital good prices are measured in terms of the implicit deflator for private corporate fixed capital formation (1980 = 1.00). The expected rate of change in capital goods price is measured as the three year moving average of the rate of change of capital goods price (measured by the implicit deflator for private corporate fixed capital formation) with a one-year lag. The adaptive expectation hypothesis that undergirds this variable choice is considered appropriate, for a low-inflation country like India, especially when working with annual data. Data on real capital stock are readily available from Source (1) for the years since 1981. This series was extended back to 1955 applying the formula, $K_{t-1} = K_t + DEP_t - I_t$, where K is real capital stock at the end of year 1981, and DEP and I denote real depreciation and real private corporate fixed investment during each year.

References

Athukorala, Prema-chandra and Kunal Sen, *Saving, Investment and Growth in India* (Delhi and Oxford: Oxford University Press, 2002).

Agenor, P. and P.J. Monteil, *Development Macroeconomics* (Princeton, NJ.: Princeton University Press, 1996).

Agrawal, P., S.V. Gokarn, V. Mishra, K.S. Parikh and K. Sen, *Economic Restructuring in East Asia and India: Perspectives on Policy Reform* (London: Macmillan, 1995).

Banerjee, A., J. Rolado, J.W. Galbraith and D.F. Hendry, *Co-integration, Error-Correction, and the Econometric Analysis of Non-stationary Data* (Oxford: Oxford University Press, 1993).

Bardhan, P., *The Political Economy of Development in India* (Oxford: Basil Blackwell, 1984).

Bhagwati, J.N., *India in Transition: Freeing the Economy* (Oxford: Clarendon Press, 1993).

Blejer, M. and M.S. Khan, 'Government Policy and Private Investment in Developing Countries', *IMF Staff Papers*, 31 (1984), 379–403.

Campbell, J. and N.G. Mankiw, 'Permanent Income, Current Income and Consumption', *NBER Working Paper* No. 2436 (New York: NBER, 1987).

Chibber, A., M. Dailami and N. Shafik, *Reviving Private Investment in Developing Countries: Empirical Studies and Policy Lessons* (Amsterdam: North-Holland, (1992).

Devereux, M. and F. Schianterelli, 'Investment, Financial Factors and Cash Flow: Evidence from U.K. Panel Data', in R.G. Hubbard (ed.), *Asymmetric Information, Corporate Finance and Investment* (Chicago: University of Chicago Press, (1990).

Dixit, A. and R. Pindyck, *Investment under Uncertainty* (Princeton: Princeton University Press, (1994).

Fazzari, S.M, R.G. Hubbard and B.C. Petersen, 'Financing Constraints and Corporate Investment', *Brooking Papers on Economic Activity*, 1 (1988), 141–95.

Fielding, D., 'Aggregate Investment in South Africa: A Model with Implications for Political Reform', *Bulletin*, 59(3) (1997), 349–69.

Ferderer, J.P., 'The Impact of Uncertainty on Aggregate Investment: An Empirical Analysis', *Journal of Money, Credit and Banking*, 25 (1993), 30–48;

Gertler, M., 'Financial Structure and Aggregate Economic Activity: An Overview', *Journal of Money, Credit and Banking*, 20 (1988), 559–88.

Greenaway, D. and O. Morrissey, 'Structural Adjustment and Liberalisation in Developing Countries: What Lessons have We Learned?', *Kyklos*, 46 (1992), 241–61.

Greene, J. and D Villanueva, 'Private Investment in Developing Countries', *IMF Staff Papers*, 38 (1991), 33–58.

Harrigan, J. and P.Mosley, 'Evaluating the Impact of World Bank Structural Adjustment Lending', *Journal of Development Studies*, 27 (1) (1988), 95–134.

Hendry, D.F. (1996), Dynamic Econometrics, Oxford: Oxford University Press.

Hoshi, T., A. Kashyap and D. Scharfstein, 'Corporate Structure, Liquidity and Investment: Evidence from Japanese Industrial Groups', *Quarterly Journal of Economics*, 106(1) (1991), 33–60.

Ibarra, L.A., 'Credibility of trade policy reform and investment: The Mexican experience', *Journal of Development Economics*, 47 (1995), 39–60.

Jorgenson, D.W., 'The Theory of Investment Behaviour', in Robert Ferber (ed.), *Determinants of Investment Behavior,* Universities–National Bureau Conference Series No. 18 (New York: Columbia University Press (1967), 129–55.

Jorgenson, D.W., 'Econometric Studies of Investment Behaviour: A Survey', *Journal of Economic Literature*, 11 (1971), 1111–47.

Joshi, V and I.M.D. Little, *India: Macroeconomics and Political Economy, 1964–1991* (Washington, DC.: World Bank, 1994).

Joshi, V. and I.M.D. Little, India's Economic Reforms 1991–2001 (Oxford: Clarendon Press, (1996).

Kwiatkowski, D., P.C.B. Phillips, P. Schmidt and Y. Shin, 'Testing the Null Hypothesis of Stationarity Against the Alternative of a Unit Root: How Sure are We that Economic Time Series Have a Unit Root?', *Journal of Econometrics*, 54 (1992): 159–79.

Lucas, R.E. Jr., 'Econometric Policy Evaluation: A Critique', *Carnegie–Rochester Conference Series on Public Policy*, 1 (1976), 19–46.

McKinnon, R.I., *Money and Capital in Economic Development* (Washington DC: Brooking Institute, 1973).

Oliner, S., G. Rudebusch and D. Sichel, 'New and Old Models of Business Investment: A Comparison of Forecasting Performance', *Journal of Money, Credit and Banking*, 27 (1995), 809–26.

Oliner, S., G. Rudebusch and D. Sichel, 'The Lucas Critique Revisited: Assessing the Stability of Empirical Euler Equations for Investment', *Journal of Econometrics*, 70 (1996), 291–316.

Pindyck, R.S., 'Irreversibility, Uncertainty and Investment', *Journal of Economic Literature*, 29 (1991), 1110–48.

Pindyck, R.S. and A. Solimano, 'Economic Instability and Aggregate Investment', *NBER Macroeconomics Annual 1993* (Cambridge: MIT Press (1993), 259–303.

Price, S., 'Aggregate Uncertainty, Capacity Utilization and Manufacturing Investment', *Applied Economics*, 27 (1995), 147–54.

Rama, M., 'Empirical Investment Equations in Developing Countries', in L. Serven and A. Solimano (eds), *Striving for Growth after Adjustment* (Washington, D.C.: World Bank, 1993).

Rodrik, D., 'Policy uncertainty and Private Investment in Developing Countries', *Journal of Development Economics*, 36 (1991), 229–43.

Serven, L. and A. Solimano, 'Debt Crisis, Adjustment Policies and Capital Formation in Developing Countries: Where do we stand?', *World Development*, 21 (1993), 127–40.

Shaw, E., *Financial Deepening in Economic Development* (Oxford: Oxford University Press, 1973).

Solimano, A., 'How Private Investment Reacts to Changing Macroeconomic Conditions', in A. Chibber, M. Dailami and N. Shafik, *Reviving Private Investment in Developing Countries: Empirical Studies and Policy Lessons* (Amsterdam: North-Holland, 1992).

Srinivasan, T.N., 'Data Base for development Analysis: An Overview', *Journal of Development Economics*, 44 (1994), 3–27.

World Bank, *Adjustment Lending*, PPR Policy and Research Papers No. 1 (Washington D.C.: World Bank, 1988).

12

The Current State of Corporate Governance in India

Shri Bhagwan Dahiya and Desh Gupta

> Profits earned by hook or crook cannot be the sole criterion for judging the success of a business. The success of liberalization requires the steady development of a new corporate ethic.
>
> Prime Minister Vajpayee in his 15 August 2001 address.

1. Introduction

Corporate governance relates to the internal means by which corporations are operated and controlled. It involves a set of relationships between a company's management, its board, its shareholders and other stakeholders. It also provides the structure through which the objectives of the company are set, and the means of attaining those objectives and monitoring performance are determined. Effective monitors are needed, because of the asymmetry of information between management (the agent having the information and being able to manipulate it to the disadvantage of the principal or shareholders), who are dependent on the management for such information. Generally it is the minority shareholders and other stakeholders, such as employees, creditors and customers, who need protection, from such information asymmetry. Corporate governance then refers to the procedure and rules, explicit and implicit, that provide the incentive framework for companies to attract financial and human capital, perform efficiently and avoid corruption.

There has been a steady shift away from bank financed and bank monitored systems of corporate governance to equity financed and arms-length contracts, where the government acts as a referee. Governments have often responded to corporate scandals and introduced changes to corporate governance rules and to funding and enforcement powers of the regulatory agencies.

There are three key constituents of corporate governance: the Shareholders, the Board of Directors and the Management. The shareholders role in governance is to appoint the directors and the auditors and to satisfy themselves that an appropriate governance structure is in place. The Board of Directors is responsible for the governance of the company. They steward the company, set its strategic aim, the financial policy and oversee the implementation and the financial controls and report the activities and the progress of the company to the shareholders to whom they are accountable. The board's actions are subject to applicable laws, rules and regulations. The responsibilities of the management include ensuring that control systems are in place to achieve the objectives laid down by the board, and to help the board discharge its responsibilities to the shareholders.

Corporate governance extends beyond corporate law. Thus the imperative for corporate governance lies not merely in drafting a code of corporate governance, but in practising it. While governments play a central role in shaping the legal, institutional and regulatory climate within which individual corporate governance systems are developed, the main responsibility lies with the corporate sector.

Corporate governance is affected by the relationships among participants in the governance system. Controlling shareholders, which may be individuals, family holdings, bloc alliances, or other corporations acting through a holding company or cross shareholdings, can significantly influence corporate behaviour. As owners of equity, institutional investors are increaseingly demanding a voice in corporate governance in some markets. Individual shareholders usually do not seek to exercise governance rights but may be highly concerned about obtaining fair treatment from controlling shareholders and management. Creditors play an important role in some governance systems and have the potential to serve as external monitors over corporate performance. Employees and other stakeholders play an important role in contributing to the long-term success and performance of the corporation. The role of each of these participants and their interactions vary widely among countries. These relationships are subject, in part, to law and regulation and, in part, to voluntary adaptation and market forces.

The fundamental objective of good corporate governance is the maximization of long-term shareholder value. Since shareholders are residual claimants, this objective follows from a premise that, in well performing capital and financial markets, whatever maximises shareholder value must necessarily maximise corporate prosperity, and best satisfies the claims of all the stakeholders — creditors, employees, shareholders and the state.

The seeds of modern corporate governance were probably sown by the Watergate scandal in the United States of America. As a result of subsequent investigations, the US regulatory and legislative bodies were able to highlight control failures that had allowed several major corporations to make illegal political contributions and to bribe government officials. This led to the development of the Foreign and Corrupt Practices Act of 1977 in USA that contained specific provisions regarding the establishment, maintenance and review of systems of internal control. This was followed in 1979 by the Securities and Exchange Commission of USA's proposals for mandatory reporting on internal financial controls. The 1985 Treadway Commission and its Report published in 1987 highlighted the need for a proper control environment, independent audit committees and objective internal Audit function in response to a series of high profile scandals. It called for published reports on the effectiveness of internal control and requested the sponsoring organizations to develop an integrated set of internal control criteria to enable companies to improve their controls. Accordingly, COSO (The Committee of Sponsoring Organizations of the Treadway Commission, 1992) was born to stipulate a control framework.

Developments in the USA and a spate of scandals and collapses in UK in the late 1980s and early 1990s led shareholders and banks to worry about their investments. The London Stock Exchange set-up the Cadbury Committee in May 1991 in response. Both the Treadway Report and the COSO report were precedent influences on the Cadbury Report, which investigated accountability of the Board of Directors to shareholders and to society. The Cadbury Committee submitted its report and associated 'Code of Best Practices' in December 1992 wherein it spelt out the methods of governance needed to achieve a balance between the essential powers of the Board of Directors and their proper accountability.

The intellectual lead in the area of corporate governance is given by the OECD through evolving a set of cogent principles of corporate governance released in late 1999. These principles have been accepted as an international benchmark to bring about suitable improvements in their legal, institutional and regulatory framework for facilitating good corporate governance regimes. On the basis of OECD's Principles of Corporate Governance, one can identify the following basic issues in corporate governance:

- How to ensure the protection of shareholders' rights?
- How to ensure the equitable treatment of all shareholders?
- How to ensure that the corporate governance framework recognises the rights of stakeholders as established by law and encourages cooperation between corporations and stakeholders in creating wealth, jobs, and the sustainability of financially sound enterprises?
- How to ensure that timely and accurate disclosure is made on all material matters regarding the corporation, including the financial situation, performance, ownership, and governance of the company?

- How to ensure the strategic guidance of the company, the effective monitoring of management by the board, and the board's accountability to the company and the shareholders?

Despite above discussed reforms, the creative accounting displayed by and increasing implosion of some extremely large US based corporations, such as energy giant Enron, the telecommunications giants WorldCom and Qwest, the pharmaceuticals giants Merck and Bristol–Myers Squibb, have heightened concerns with poor corporate governance practices in a country touted at times as a leader in the field of corporate governance. There is the recognition of the absence of an arm's length relationship between some accounting firms and the corporations they are auditing, as well as of analysts and the investment bankers. It is also becoming clear that these practices emerge and remain hidden during a stock market bubble, but as the market crashes in a downward vicious spiral, they come increasingly to light. There is an incentive for the CEOs and their management teams, paid as they are on the basis of rising recorded profits, to cook the books, often with the help of auditing firms, serving as consultants. Three general lessons have emerged from the US scandals. First, there is a need to rotate the auditors and the auditing and consulting functions create a conflict of interest and should not be performed by the same accounting firms. Second, shareholders should be cautious in awarding stock options to the management team, because it encourages management to massage and manipulate the accounts and mis-inform the public; stock-options should be counted as expense, as economic theory requires, even though accounting standards do not require them currently. Third, the regulatory agencies should be more watchful of firms, especially of merging firms, during a stock market boom, as the capacity to hide information is enhanced and the public is more gullible during this period.

2. Corporate Governance in India

The Indian corporate sector has seen substantial and significant changes in the last decade. Faced with the most serious balance of payments crisis since independence, India adopted in mid-1991 economic reform measures of far reaching consequences. While the short-run objective of these measures was to meet the payments crisis, the long-term objective was to put the economy on a higher growth path on a sustainable basis by enhancing the efficiency and productivity of the system. This initiated the process of liberalisation, privatisation and globalisation of the Indian economy. Corporate governance did not receive much attention in the initial phase of the post-1991 reform period. This may be, because there had been steady improvements in laws relating to rules-based governance, given that India had inherited a rules-based system from Britain at independence. For instance, the quality of financial and non-financial disclosures mandated by law, were stronger in India than most developing countries and a number of developed European countries.

In India 'Corporate Governance' as a phrase came to prominence only in 1993 mainly due to three episodes that occurred during the process of economic liberalisation. The *first* was Harshad Mehta's major securities scam that was uncovered in April 1992. It involved a large number of banks and resulted in the stock market index nose-diving sharply from a peak of 4475 on 22 April 1992 to 2548 on 5 August 1992. This crash ruined a large number of small retail investors and brokers. It questioned the ability of banking and capital market regulators to ensure transparency and safety. The *second* was a sudden growth of cases where multinational companies started consolidating their ownership by issuing preferential equity allotments to their controlling group at steep discounts to their market price. In this way one block of equity holders were treated more equal than others. This process continued until November 1994 when the government put an end to it. The *third* scam involved disappearing companies of 1993–94. During the period from July 1993 to September 1994; the stock index shot up by 120 per cent. During this boom, hundreds of obscure companies made public issues at large share premia, buttressed by sales pitch of obscure investment banks and misleading prospectuses. The management of most of these companies siphoned off funds and a vast number of small investors were saddled with illiquid stocks of dud companies. This shattered investor confidence.

Despite these scandals, major corporate governance initiatives were only launched in late nineties and early part of this decade. The first and third were by Securities and Exchange Board of India (SEBI) and the second was by the Confederation of Indian Industry (CII) which is India's largest industry and business association.

Until February 1997, companies could structure quietly negotiated takeover deals, which left minority shareholders in the lurch. This changed with the SEBI (Substantial Acquisition of Shares and Takeovers) Regulation, 1997, which is popularly known as the *Takeover Code*. The SEBI regulation has had two beneficial effects. First, it has created a transparent market for takeovers. Second, by legislating in favour of open offers, it has ensured that minority shareholders will have the right to obtain a market driven price in any takeover.

2.1 The CII Code

The CII, convinced that good corporate governance was essential for Indian companies to access domestic as well as global capital at competitive rates set up a committee in 1996 to examine corporate governance issues, and recommend a voluntary code of best practices. The first draft of the code was prepared by April 1997, and the final document (*Desirable Corporate Governance: A Code*), was publicly released in April 1998. The code focuses on listed companies. It recognised that as India gets integrated in the world market, Indian as well as international investors will demand greater disclosure, more transparent explanation for major decisions and better shareholder value. It pointed out that:

> the objective of good corporate governance is maximising long-term shareholder value. Since shareholders are residual claimants, ... whatever maximises shareholder value must necessarily maximise corporate prosperity, and best satisfy the claims of creditors, employees, shareholders and the State.

The Committee's key recommendations appropriately focussed on the board of directors, which were expected to meet six times a year. Any listed company with a turnover of Rs. 1 billion and above would need to have professionally competent, independent, non-executive directors, constituting at least 30 per cent of the board if the Chairman of the company was a non-executive director, or at least 50 per cent of the board if the Chairman and Managing Director was the same person. No single person would hold directorships in more than 10 listed companies. Company would pay a commission to the non-executive directors over and above the sitting fees for the use of the professional inputs and consider offering stock options, so as to relate rewards to performance. While re-appointing members of the board, companies would not re-appoint any director who had not attended at least one half of the meetings. Obviously, the success of the board depended on key information being made available by the management and this was made a part of the CII Code.

At the same time, the role of the Audit Committee, was acknowledged. Listed companies with either a turnover of over Rs. 1 billion or a paid-up capital of Rs. 200 million were required to set up Audit Committees within two years. Audit Committees would consist of at least three members, all drawn from a company's non-executive directors, and would need to have adequate knowledge of finance, accounts and basic elements of company law. Audit Committees would ould assist the board in fulfilling its functions relating to corporate accounting and reporting practices, financial and accounting controls, and financial statements and proposals that accompany the public issue of any security and thus provide effective supervision of the financial reporting process. They would periodically interact with the statutory auditors and the internal auditors to ascertain the quality and veracity of the company's accounts as well as the capability of the auditors themselves.

As regards desirable disclosures the Committee recommended that listed companies would be required to give data on high and low monthly averages of share prices in a major stock exchange where the company is listed; major Indian stock exchanges would gradually insist upon a corporate governance compliance certificate; if any company went to more than one credit rating agency, then it would need to divulge in the prospectus and issue document the rating of all the agencies that did such an exercise; companies which were making foreign debt issues could not have separate sets of disclosure norms for foreigners, and Indian investors; and companies that defaulted on fixed deposits would not be permitted to accept further deposits and make inter-corporate loans or investments or declare dividends until the default was made good.

The CII code is voluntary but since 1998, CII has been trying to induce companies to disclose much greater information to their boards and shareholders. Consequently, annual reports of companies that abide by the code provide public information based on that code.

2.2 The SEBI Code

The Committee on Corporate Governance was set up on 7 May 1999 by SEBI under the Chairmanship of Kumar Mangalam Birla (hereafter referred to as KMBC) to promote and raise the standards of corporate governance. KMBC kept in view the fact that any code of Corporate Governance should be dynamic, and should change with changing context and times.

KMBC divided its recommendations into mandatory and non-mandatory categories. The mandatory recommendations were on composition of the Board, constitution of the various sub-committees of the Board of Directors, and the voluntary code formulated by CII.

Apart from specifying the composition and role of the Board of Directors, which was to have at least one-third independent directors and subjected to improved quality and information on other company boards on which they served, the major focus of KMBC was on the composition and role of the audit committee and of the remuneration committee; both of which were to be sub-committees of the board. There was focus on issues dealing with conflicts of interest.

The **audit committee** was expected to act as the bridge between the board, the statutory auditors and internal auditors. Its major functions were the oversight of the company's financial reporting process and the disclosure of financial information to ensure that the financial statement was correct, sufficient and credible and conformed to the requirements of the accounting standards as well as those of SEBI. It was, also, expected to review the company's financial and risk management policies and to look into the reasons for substantial defaults in the payments to the depositors, debenture holders, share holders (in case of non-payment of declared dividends) and creditors.

To avoid conflict of interest, **the remuneration committee**, which was to determine the remuneration packages of the executive directors, should comprise at least three non-executive directors, the chairman of committee being an independent director. In turn, all elements of these packages and the policy on which they were based had to be reported to the annual general meeting of the shareholders.

Since information could be hidden through separate accounts and transactions of and between the subsidiaries, the companies were required to give consolidated accounts in respect of all its subsidiaries in which they hold 51 per cent or more of the share capital.

KMBC highlighted the importance of the Board by requiring it to clearly define the role of the management. Among other things the management was expected to carry out the following functions:

- Assisting the board in its decision making process in respect of the company's strategy, policies, code of conduct and performance targets, by providing necessary inputs.
- Implementing the policies and code of conduct of the board.
- Providing timely, accurate, substantive and material information, including financial matters and exceptions, to the Board of Directors, board-committees and the shareholders.
- Ensuring compliance of all regulations and laws.
- Ensuring timely and efficient service to the shareholders and to protect shareholders' rights and interests.
- Setting up and implementing an effective internal control system, commensurate with the business requirements.
- Implementing and complying with the Code of Ethics as laid down by the board.

In addition, the board would require all members of the management to report all transactions, where there was a potential conflict of interest.

To expedite the process of share transfers the board of the company would delegate the power of share transfer to the registrars and share transfer agents.

For transparency reasons, a separate section on Corporate Governance in the annual reports of companies, with a detailed compliance report on Code of Corporate Governance and reasons for non-compliance were recommended.

KMBC was considered and adopted by SEBI Board in January 2000. The recommendations were to be implemented through the amendment to listing agreement of the stock exchanges. Accordingly, on February 21, 2000, SEBI issued directions to stock exchanges to amend the listing agreement in this regard. The amendments to the listing agreement were to be implemented over a phased period between 2000 and 2003. The first phase completed by March 31, 2001 covered more than 80 per cent of the market capitalization. In February 2000 SEBI issued a letter to all the stock exchanges proposing that 'a new clause, namely clause 49, be incorporated in the listing agreement'. Clause 49, called 'Corporate Governance', contains eight sections and follows recommendations of KMBC dealing with the Board of Directors, Audit Committee, Remuneration of Directors, Board Procedure, Management, Shareholders, Report on Corporate Governance, and Compliance, respectively.

In addition, the Companies (Amendment) Act, was passed in 2000. The act introduces arms-length auditors, provides for improved protection of small investors, improves the transparency of Initial Public Offerings (IPOs) and requires a clear statement on Director's responsibilities in the reports of Boards of companies.

2.3 Changes to Indian Financial Institutions

As the regulatory authority of banks RBI has a special role to play in upgrading quality of corporate governance in all banks. RBI has been laying stress on five major aspects of governance in banks, encapsulated in the acronym CAMEL, meaning Capital adequacy, Asset quality, Management, Earnings, and Liquidity. The Basel Committee on Banking Supervision of the Banks for International Settlements (BIS) has issued a framework of good corporate governance for banks.

There were a number of developments with regard to the financial sector, which led to increased competitiveness and improved corporate behaviour. Entry of private mutual funds and private banks has been allowed. Ten new private banks were licensed in the post-1993 period, while the minimum risk-weighted capital adequacy ratio was lifted for scheduled commercial banks from 8 per cent to 9 per cent from 1 April 2000. For new private banks it was set at 10 per cent from January 2001. The entry of new private banks and foreign institutional investors (FII) has forced the government-owned financial institutions to lift their game or risk losing market share. The enhanced capital adequacy ratio is aimed at reducing systemic risk. Non-performing assets of both private and public sector banks have declined continuously in the post-reform period. FII have with the aid of their analysts and by moving funds to those Indian companies with the highest returns, improved corporate governance in India.

Even today, a decade after the advent of economic reforms and liberalisation, a substantial proportion of the equity of India's private sector companies is held by the development finance institutions, the nationalised insurance companies, and the Unit Trust of India (UTI) a government owned mutual fund. This kind of indirect state ownership of equity fosters poor corporate governance through inefficient monitoring. Given their shareholdings, the institutional shareholders insist on nominating their directors on corporate boards. Most of these nominee directors are incompetent; at worst, they are instructed to support the incumbent management irrespective of performance.

2.4 The Quality of Financial Disclosure in India

The quality of financial disclosure in the annual accounts of incorporated companies in India is determined by three agencies: (i) The Department of Company Affairs, which administers the Companies Act, (ii) SEBI, which mandates special disclosure requirements for listed companies, and (iii) the Institute of Chartered Accountants of India (ICAI) which lays-down the parameters of Indian accounting standards. While these standards are better than what prevails in most of Asia, including Korea and Japan, they are behind the norms laid down by US–GAAP. The most serious lacunae are the absence of consolidation, lack of segment reporting, and low standards of disclosure of related party transactions.

There is only limited oversight of most listed Indian companies. This is because their boards are dominated by management (executive directors) or 'gray outsiders' (defined to include family members of executive directors, attorneys who represent the company, investment or commercial bankers who have close financial relationship with the company, long term consultants, or directors who have substantial business dealings with the company). At the same time, the Companies Act allows one person to hold up to 20 directorships, which is too many, if effective oversight is desired. Even if this is amended, given the fact that insiders are likely to have more information than outsiders, the directors representing minority shareholders are often helpless to protect the latter. There is also the problem of the inadequacies of SEBI. A SEBI list of uncompleted investigations continues to rise, while the maximum penalty of Rs.500,000 is too low to deter market manipulations by insiders. The former reflects the inadequacies of staff at SEBI, the latter the inadequacies of law. The former needs to be strengthened through the addition of more competent and motivated staff, while the latter requires amendments to the law to raise penalties, which would act as deterrence to market manipulators.

Unlike the German lead banks, which have played an effective monitoring role, as major debt and equity holders, Indian banks and financial institutions, owned as they are by the government, have failed to provide such a role.

The government involvement also raises the moral hazard problem with the financial institutions exposing themselves to risky lending and activities, because they know that they will be bailed out by the government, if they run into difficulties, for instance, UTI's Cyberspace investment and the excessive exposure of its US-64 to the info tech stocks.

The most serious concern is with India's bankruptcy and liquidation laws and procedures. These are inadequate, time consuming and contribute to poor governance by management. Bankruptcy reorganization of large industrial organizations is governed by the Sick Industrial Companies (Special Provisions) Act, 1985 and the process is supervised by the Board for Industrial and Financial Reconstruction (BIFR). The latter tends to support the rights of existing management and of old shareholders over fully secured creditors. Liquidation poses even more serious problems. This is because most liquidation cases take between one to two decades to complete, resulting in a system that works against the interests of workers and secured creditors. Since management fears neither attachment nor bankruptcy, it leads to companies funding highly risky investments, which has several adverse consequences. It raises the cost of credit, it debases the disciplining role of debt and it increasingly risks the health of the financial sector. Under planned legislation BIFR will be replaced by National Company Law Tribunal, which will oversee revival, amalgamation and winding up of sick companies. The new legislation will also end the open-ended nature of BIFR proceedings by requiring winding up operations to be completed within 24 months. The legislation also requires the criterion for defining sickness to be made tighter, thus making it more likely for the failing company to be revived. The proposed legislation has run into opposition, because it requires the payment of a levy of 0.005 per cent rising to 1 per cent on companies' turnover. Given that it will provide a revolving fund for failing companies and it is in the interest of the corporate sector to have a healthy corporate sector, it should not be seen as an attempt to fleece the healthy to support the poorly managed.

It is apparent from the above that though new laws will help, especially if they facilitate speedier resolutions and protect workers and secured creditors. The major problems relate to delays in enforcing existing laws and securing outcomes, as in the case of SEBI and BIFR, within a reasonable time frame.

3. Conclusion

A major business innovation of the 1990s involved the rapid spread of codes of corporate governance worldwide, following the publication in 1992 of the report of the Cadbury Committee in the UK. The new feature of Cadbury was a model where market-based regulation, institutional investors, and codes of best practice would work in synergy to produce greater transparency and accountability in business, boosting investor confidence and contributing significantly to the liquidity of the market. The market was seen as the general medium of accountability. The intellectual lead in the area of corporate governance is given by the OECD through evolving a set of cogent principles of corporate governance released in late 1999.

India was slow in moving towards changes in corporate governance in the early part of the post-reform period, despite a number of scandals. But starting from 1997, with the introduction of the SEBI's Takeover Code, there have been reforms introduced firstly through CII's voluntary Code and then through implementations of the recommendations of the KMBC committee. These have set in place a Code of Corporate Governance and have moved India's corporate governance regime away from one dominated and monitored by insiders and towards the Anglo–Saxon one, seeking an arm's length relationship. Conflicts of interest are clearly highlighted and an attempt is made to resolve them. But problems of corporate governance remain, not only in India, but, also, in more developed jurisdictions, such as the USA.

The major problems arise either because of non-compliance with the spirit and letter of the law, as in the case of the 2001–02 corporate scandals in the USA or because of inadequacies of the regulatory agencies and legal infrastructure, as in the case of India. In the former case, the incentive structure has to be altered. In the latter case, granting additional resources to the appropriate agencies, on the basis of a specific timeframe for clearing the backlog of cases may help. India, also, faces other problems. Gray insiders still continue to dominate the boards and government-owned financial institutions' appointed board members play the role of a doormat for the company management. Its bankruptcy and exit policies, do not allow for the emergence of best practices. It has still a long way to go in adopting best practice accounting standards. Nevertheless, it is slowly, but steadily, improving its corporate governance and accounting standards. Its disclosures standards for companies are reasonably satisfactory.

One of the most important reforms in the area of corporate governance in India should be the restructuring of the boards of directors. This should be brought about through suitable amendments to the Companies Act. It should be made mandatory that majority of the board members are really independent and with sufficient time directors, who are not obliged either to the executive director or the promoters of the company.

As regards the composition of India's corporate sector, the number of closely held companies vastly outnumber the publicly held ones, and constitute the bulk of small scale enterprises. However, the public limited companies account for almost two-thirds of the book-value of equity. As regards the size of the government corporate sector, while it accounts for a mere 0.24 per cent of the number of companies, it has about 39 per cent of corporate India's paid-up capital.

In 1991, 20 out of the top 50 companies were controlled by family groups that held their sway during the licence — control regime. By February 2000, the roles were reversed: 35 were professionally managed, of which 14 were first generation businesses; only 4 out of the 50 were run by older business families. This change augurs well for corporate governance.

The subject of corporate governance is of enormous practical importance. Even in advanced market economies, there is a great deal of disagreement on how good or bad the existing governing mechanisms are. Most of the studies on corporate governance are on the United States' corporate sector. More recently, there has been a great surge of work on Japan, and to a lesser extent on Germany, Italy and Sweden. Unfortunately, except for these countries, there has been extremely little research done on corporate governance around the world. Therefore, the subject of corporate governance constitutes a very rich field for research.

References

Banaji, J. and G. Mody, 'Corporate Governance and the Indian Private Sector', *Working Paper Series 73* (Queen Elizabeth House, University of Oxford, May 2001).

Cadbury Committee, *Report of the Committee on the Financial Aspects of Corporate Governance* (London: Gee & Co., 1992).

Carati, G. and A.R. Rad, 'Convergence of Corporate Governance Systems', *Managerial Finance* 26(10) (2000), 66–83.

Caves, R.E., 'Corporate Strategy and Structure', *Journal of Economic Literature* 18 (1980), 64–92.

Charkham, J., *Keep Good Company: A Study of Corporate Governance in Five Countries* (Oxford: Oxford University Press, 1994).

CII (Confederation of Indian Industry), *Desirable Corporate Governance: A Code* (1998).

Dimsdale, N. and M. Prevezer (eds), *Capital Markets and Corporate Governance* (Oxford: Oxford University Press, 1994).

Fama, E., 'Agency Problems and the Theory of the Firm', *Journal of Political Economy* 88 (1980), 288–307.

The Federal Reserve Board, (2002), Testimony of Chairman Alan Greenspan, semi-annual monetary policy report to the Congress: Before the Committee on Banking, Housing and Urban Affairs, US Senate (16 July 2002).

Government of India (2001), *Economic Survey 2000–2001* (New Delhi: Ministry of Finance, 2001).

Grossman, S. and O. Hart, 'The Costs and Benefits of Ownership: a theory of vertical and lateral integration', *Journal of Political Economy* 94 (1986), 691–719.

Hart, O., *Firms, Contracts, and Financial Structure* (Oxford University Press, 1995).

Hart, O. and B. Holmstrom, 'The Theory of Contracts', in *Advances in Economic Theory*, T. Bewley (ed.), Fifth World Congress (Cambridge: Cambridge University Press, 1987).

Hart, O. and J. Moore, (1990), 'Property Rights and the Nature of the Firm', *Journal of Political Economy* 98 (1990), 1119–58.

Hart, Oliver, 'Corporate Governance: Some Theory and Implications', *The Economic Journal* 105 (May 1995a), 678–89.

Ikenberry, D. and J. Lakonishok, 'Corporate Governance Through the Proxy Contest: evidence and implications', *Journal of Business* 66 (1993), 405–35.

Jensen, M., 'Agency Costs of Free Cash Flow, Corporate Finance and Takeovers', *American Economic Review* 76 (1986), 323–29.

Khanna, Tarun and K. Palepu, 'Emerging Market Business Groups, Foreign Investors, and Corporate Governance', *Working Paper No. 6955*, National Bureau of Economic Research Inc. (1999).

Lehmann, Jean-Pierre, 'Corporate Governance in East Asia and Western Europe: Competition, Confrontation and Cooperation', in Oman *et al.* (1997).

Milgrom, P. and J. Roberts, *Economics, Organization, and Management* (Englewood Cliffs, NJ: Prentice Hall, 1992).

OECD, *Principles of Corporate Governance* (Paris: OECD, 1999).

Oman, C.P., D.H. Brooks and C. Foy (eds), *Investing in Asia* (Paris: Development Centre of the OECD, 1997).

Oman, CP., 'Corporate Governance and National Development', *Technical Papers No. 180* (Paris: OECD Development Centre, 2001).

Reserve Bank of India, *Report of the Advisory Group on Banking Supervision* (Mumbai, 2000).

Reserve Bank of India, *Report of the Advisory Group on Corporate Governance* (Mumbai, 2001).
Sarkar, J. and S. Sarkar, *Large Shareholders Activism in Corporate Governance in Emerging Economies: Evidence from India* (Mumbai: Indira Gandhi Institute of Development Research, 1999).
Securities and Exchange Board of India, SEBI (2000), *Report of Committee on Corporate Governance* (Kumar Mangalam Birla Committee).
Shleifer, A. and R.W. Vishny, 'A Survey of Corporate Governance', *Journal of Finance* LII(2) (June 1997), 737–83.
Sikka, P. and A. Mitchell, 'Accountability of the Accountancy Bodies: The Peculiarities of the British', *Working Paper No. 02/01* (University of Essex, Department of Accounting and Finance, 2002).
The Hindu, 'End of the BIFR era' (22 August 2001).
Thompson, S. and M. Wright, 'Corporate Governance: The Role of Restructuring Transactions', *The Economic Journal* 105 (1995), 690–703.
Vaghul, Narayanan, 'Indian Specificities', in Oman *et al.* (1997).
Vinten, G., 'Corporate Governance: an International State of the Art', *Managerial Auditing Journal* 13(7) (1998), 419–31.
World Bank, *Corporate Governance: A Framework for Implementation* (Washington, DC: September 1999).
World Bank, *India: Policies to Reduce Poverty and Accelerate Sustainable Development* (Washington, DC: 2000).

PART IV

INDIA'S EXPOSURE TO THE GLOBAL ECONOMY

13
The Impact of a Decade of India's Trade Reforms

Kaliappa Kalirajan

1. Introduction

The objective of this chapter is to review the impact of a decade of trade policy reforms on the Indian economy. Our analysis is restricted to examining the trade policy reforms that have been implemented in India since 1991 and their impact on export promotion and import liberalisation. Empirical evidence from a number of studies points to a strong and significant effect of openness to trade on growth performance (Srinivasan 1998, 202–8). An important empirical question that is investigated in this context is: How open has India's trade been after a decade of economic reforms?

Literature shows that dramatic policy changes in some countries have not always lead to significant improvements in actual performance. The end results in terms of the actual performance of the economy provide a measure not only to show how effectively the policy reforms were carried out, but also to gauge the appropriateness of such reform in terms of stated objectives. Under the assumption that India has been effectively implementing appropriate reform measures, it is rational to expect significant growth in GDP and trade consistently.

Figure 13.1 shows India's total exports, total imports and GDP at current market prices in US dollars. Consistently, the ratio of imports to GDP has been higher than the ratio of exports to GDP in the 1990s and the gap has been widening. Figure 13.2 shows India's merchandise exports, merchandise imports, and GDP at current market prices in US dollars. The ratio of merchandise exports to GDP steadily increased from 4 per cent in 1970–71 to 11 per cent in 2000–01, which indicates the rising importance of exports to the Indian economy. During 2000–01 exceeding the target of 18 per cent, the merchandise exports at US$44 billion have grown by 19.8 per cent over 1999–00 (RBI, 2001).

Figure 13.1: Total Exports as percentage of GDP (US$ million at factor cost and current prices)

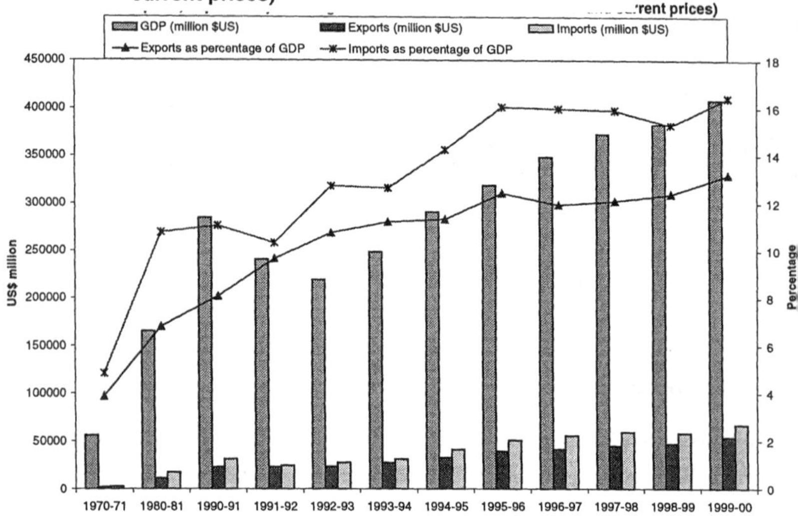

Source: RBI (2001)

Figure 13.2: Merchandise Exports, Imports and GDP (in US$ million)

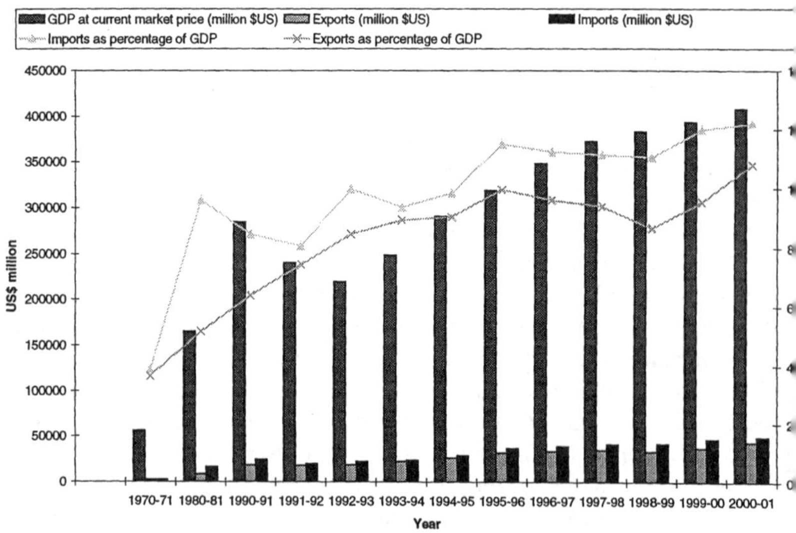

Source: RBI (2001)

India has always enjoyed trade surplus with respect to services trade. But this used to be less than a billion US dollar until recently. After the reforms only in 1995–96, India had negative balance in services trade (due to global recession). However from 1996–97, surplus in services trade has been surging steadily. Export of services touched the level of US$15 billion during 1999–00 from US$13 billion in 1998–99, which translates to a growth rate of 15 per cent. This success is mainly attributable to 'miscellaneous services' component, mainly software services, which touched US$9 billion in 2000–01 from US$6.5 billion in 1999–00 registering a growth rate of about 35 per cent (RBI 2001).[1] Thus, services trade has recently been helping the economy to narrow the current account deficit.

2. India's Trade Liberalisation

Within a broader perspective, the reforms implemented in India were similar to those undertaken by many developing countries. An important difference lies in the speed of implementation. As in China, India's reforms were implemented in a gradual manner. Being the largest democracy with a pluralist society has made it necessary for India to obtain reasonable consensus across different interest groups before policy changes could be implemented. This has slowed implementation. How open is India's trade today after a decade of trade policy reforms?

2.1 Export Promotion Measures

EXIM Policy 1992–97

Several schemes were introduced or modified to eliminate regulatory measures and discretionary controls. These are now discussed.

The Export promotion capital goods (EPCG), a scheme to liberalise capital goods imports, was introduced to boost exports. The EPCG scheme allows exporters to import machinery both new and second-hand duty free or at concessional duty if the importer agrees to achieve a fixed export target within a specified period of time. Under the scheme, the duty on import of capital goods was reduced from 25 per cent to 15 per cent subject to an export obligation of 3 times the c.i.f. value of imports and the period of achievement was increased from 4 years to 5 years. Currently under the EPCG scheme, import of capital goods carry 10 per cent customs duty

---

1 Software exports in physical form are captured under the item 'merchandise exports' in the data on India's Balance of Payment (BoP), while software exports through on-site and off-site routes are recorded under computer services in 'miscellaneous receipts' which form part of 'non-factor services' under invisibles.

though duty free imports are permitted, subject to a minimum import volume. Exemptions are available for certain sectors like agriculture and garments even if the minimum floor limit is not met. If a computer system is imported under this scheme, supporting manufacturers and service providers are also eligible to import capital goods. Industry uses this scheme for modernisation and upgradation (CMIE 2000).

Consequently capital goods imports increased by 23 per cent between 1992–93 and 1993–94 and facilitated an export growth of 30 per cent in 1993–94 over the previous year. Manufacturing exports increased by 29 per cent, which is 5 percentage points more than the previous year's growth. Trade deficit declined drastically to US$1billion in 1993–94 from US$3 billion in 1992–93. These data clearly indicate that schemes such as the EPCG have paid off. This situation is analogous to the Chinese reform process. When the Chinese reform started in 1978 with the introduction of the household responsibility system replacing the commune system, economic growth surged in the following years.

The other major schemes are as follows: Duty Exemption Scheme (DES), Scheme for Gems and Jewellery, and policies enlarging the scope of instruments of export promotion such as export oriented units (EOU)[2] and export processing zones (EPZ), joint ventures and different types of trading houses.[3]

Duty Exemption Scheme: Under this scheme, import of raw materials, intermediates, components, consumables, parts, accessories, packing materials and computer software required for direct use in the export product is permitted duty free for processing and export by the competent authority under the categories of advance licences, advanced intermediate licence, special imprest licence, licences under export production programme, advance customs clearance permit and advance release orders.[4]

Scheme for Gems and Jewellery: Exporters of gems and jewellery are allowed to import inputs by obtaining Replenishment Licences and Diamond/DTC Imprest Licences (DTCIL). The replenishment licences are

---

[2] EOUs can be started anywhere in the country and mostly they are located in places where there are easy access to raw materials and other inputs such as power and transportation. It can be private, government owned or joint ventures. Government does not fund the EOUs, though they provide some concessions such as duty free imports (Ministry of Commerce).

[3] Details on different types of trading houses are given in Appendix I.

[4] Advance licences are issued under the Duty Exemption Scheme (DES) for duty free import of inputs and are subject to fulfilment of a time-bound export obligation as well as specified rate of value addition. These licences may be either value based or quantity based and are regulated in freely convertible currency, their FOB value or exports and CIF value of imports to be specified accordingly. It is allowed to dispose of raw materials imported against advance licences without prior permission of the concerned authorities (Ministry of Finance).

transferable. Exports effected in fulfilment of export obligation against DTCILs do not quality for this benefit. The latter licence can be issued in advance for import of rough diamonds and for export of cut and polished diamonds. Though DTCILs are not transferable, imported goods may be transferred but the responsibility to fulfil the export obligation vests in the licencee. These licences carry an export obligation fixed in the inverse ratio of 65 per cent of replenishment. That is, if the licence is issued for a CIF value of $65, the FOB value of export obligation will be $100.

The export oriented unit (EOU) and export promotion zone (EPZ) schemes were liberalised. 100 per cent foreign equity participation in EOU/EPZ units was allowed (Ministry of Commerce).

The EXIM Policy 1992–97 was modified in March 1993 giving added thrust to exports of agricultural and allied sectors, and services. Ironically, minimum export price was introduced to discourage the export of non-*basmati* and low-grade rice, which would affect the domestic market. This was a step backward and also not in the interest of the farmers because the border price for rice was lower than the international price during the early nineties. Exports of high value durum wheat and non-fair average quality of *jowar* were subject to a ceiling. These measures, which were discouraging rather than encouraging exports of cereals, were introduced to build buffer stocks with grains for the use of the public distribution system.

The EXIM Policy was modified in 1995 to boost agricultural exports. The highlights were: (a) in the category of agricultural and food exports only beef and tallow were in the negative list during 1995–96; (b) horticulture and floriculture exports were encouraged by providing various supports to farmers such as airfreight subsidy; and (c) quantitative ceiling and minimum export price in respect of rice was abolished; exports of wheat up to 2.5 million tonnes in case of non-durum wheat and 0.5 million tonnes in case of durum wheat was permitted; and in the case of coffee, free sale quota was raised to 70 per cent for large producers and 100 per cent for small producers. As a consequence to these policy changes, fruits, vegetables and flowers emerged as export products. EOUs in floriculture facilitated export of the perishable products. Airfreight subsidy provided a boost to export items.

EXIM Policy 1997–2002

Some of the major policy changes include (a) the threshold limit for EPCG zero duty scheme was brought down to Rs. 10 million (for agricultural and allied sectors from Rs.50 million and for electricals, textiles, leather, gems and jewellery, sport goods and food processing from Rs.200 million) and to Rs. 1 million in case of the software sector; (b) DEPB scheme was modified to neutralise not only the basic customs duty but also the special customs duty which was introduced as a temporary measure in 1998; and (c) exports of oilseeds for consumption purpose and vegetables were made free without any quantitative and licensing requirements (Ministry of Commerce).

Several modifications to the earlier schemes were done mainly to boost services trade, particularly IT exports. Thus the export promotion capital goods (EPCG) scheme for services sector was introduced. This allows capital goods to be imported for rendering services for which payments are received in a freely convertible currency. The scheme is applicable to professionals and other providers of services such as architects, consultants, economists, charted accountants, engineers and tour operators. Exemption was given to exports under all export promotion schemes from the applicability of the special additional duty of 4 per cent introduced in the 1998–99 budget. Promotional measures and procedural changes that were made in 1998 include facilities such as extension of holiday for EOU/EPZ to 10 years, sub-contracting facility for Domestic Tariff Area and permission to set up private software technology parks.

India unilaterally removed all QRs on imports of 2300 items from SAARC countries with effect from 1 August 1998. On 28 December 1998, a free trade agreement was concluded between India and Sri Lanka which would result in zero import tariff for most commodities on both sides by 2007. Following the third round of negotiations held under SAARC Preferential Tariff Agreement (SAPTA), the Revenue Department notified in August 1999 concessional customs duties — ranging from 25 per cent to 60 per cent for least developed countries (Bangladesh, Maldives, Nepal and Bhutan) and 10 per cent to 50 per cent for the other three countries — covering items in 1800 tariff lines which account for 60 per cent of imports (Ministry of Finance).

On 31 March 1999 the setting up of Special Economic Zones (SEZs) was announced to provide internationally competitive and hassle free environment for exports. Together with the Foreign Direct Investment policy initiatives for SEZs, it is expected that these zones will have the potential to act as 'magnets' for investments for export production. As a first step, four existing Export Processing Zones (EPZs) — at Kandla, Santa Cruz, Cochin and Surat — were converted into SEZs with effect from 1 November 2000. Setting up of new SEZs in Positra (Gujarat), Nangunery (Tamil Nadu), Kakinada–Vizag (Andhra Pradesh), Paradip (Orissa), Kulpi (West Bengal) and Bhadohi (Uttar Pradesh) has been progressing steadily. Their success will depend on how effectively domestic regulations and infrastructure bottlenecks are eliminated in these zones. In order to encourage infrastructure development deemed export benefits have been extended to infrastructure projects with a minimum investment of Rs. 100 crore.[5]

With a view to making exports a national effort by involving all the State Governments, a Scheme has been evolved for granting assistance to the States on the basis of their export performance for development of export related infrastructure. This amount will be distributed on the basis of absolute and incremental export performance. An allocation of Rs. 2.5 billion was proposed for 2001–02 to be increased in subsequent years. The amount would be utilised by the states for complementary export related infrastructure, such as roads connecting the production centres with ports, research and development of state specific ethnic products, development of cold chains for agro exports, development of minor ports, creation of new export promotion industrial parks, human resource development and for the purpose of developing marketing infrastructure. The units may be allowed to dispose of obsolete or unusable capital goods, spares and other goods in the domestic tariff area (DTA) on payment of applicable customs duty. Such disposal shall, however, be subject to the Import Policy in force.

Under the SEZ scheme, the goods cleared from the Zone will be treated as imported goods. Therefore, in case of DTA clearances, though the duty

---

[5] Deemed Exports refer to those transactions in which the goods supplied do not leave the country. The following categories of supply of goods by the main/sub-contractors shall be regarded as Deemed Exports under the Export and Import Policy, provided the goods are manufactured in India:

(a) Supply of goods against Advance Licence/ under the Duty Exemption/Remission Scheme (DERS);
(b) Supply of goods to Export Oriented Units (EOUs) or units located in Export Processing Zones (EPZs) or Special Economic Zones (SEZs) or Software Technology Parks (STPs) or to Electronic Hardware Technology Parks (EHTPs);
(c) Supply of capital goods to holders of licences under the Export Promotion Capital Goods (EPCG) scheme;
(d) Supply of goods to projects financed by multilateral or bilateral agencies/funds as notified by the Department of Economic Affairs, Ministry of Finance under International Competitive Bidding in accordance with the procedures of those agencies/funds, where the legal agreements provide for tender evaluation without including the customs duty;
(e) Supply of capital goods, including in unassembled / disassembled condition as well as plants, machinery, accessories, tools, dies and such goods which are used for installation purposes till the stage of commercial production and spares to the extent of 10 per cent of the FOR value to fertiliser plants;
(f) Supply of goods to any project or purpose in respect of which the Ministry of Finance, by a notification, permits the import of such goods at zero customs duty;
(g) Supply of goods to the power and refineries not covered in (f) above;
(h) Supply of marine freight containers by 100 per cent EOU (Domestic freight containers–manufacturers) provided the said containers are exported out of India within 6 months or such further period as permitted by the Customs; and (i) Supply to projects funded by UN agencies.

charged will be central excise duty, this duty will be equal to the aggregate of all duties of customs (WTO). Thus SEZ units will have to pay full customs duty on their DTA clearances. SEZs will be subjected only to laws related to labour and banking.

A SEZ unit shall maintain proper account financial year-wise, of all foreign exchange inflow by way of exports and other receipts, all foreign exchange outflows on account of imports, payment of dividend, royalty, fees etc, consumption and utilisation of the materials in the DTA. RBI will permit banks to open branches in the SEZ and permit transactions to be operated in dollars for all units.

Most of the units within SEZ employ fewer than 1000 workers. With the recent change in the labour laws announced in the Union Budget 2001–02 that a firm employing less than 1000 employees is not required to get the approval from the Government to layoff any employee or to close down the unit, labour laws may not be a constraint. Further, the new law allows outsourcing and employing contract labour, which facilitates reducing employer-employee frictions in work places.

Since agriculture is the responsibility of state governments, the central government has insisted through the revised EXIM policy of 1997–2002 that the state governments should identify and develop product-specific agricultural export zones (AEZ). It is expected that the states will identify product-specific AEZ for end-to-end development from a geographically contiguous area. They will also have to evolve a comprehensive package of services provided by all state government agencies, agricultural universities, and some Central institutions and agencies for 'intensive delivery' in these zones. The AEZ would have access to the Centre's proposed market access initiative, which will provide market research, warehousing and retail marketing infrastructure in select countries, and direct market promotion activities. Two AEZ exist, one in Tamilnadu and another in Gujarat.

2.2 Imports Liberalisation

India categorized import of items under five heads — the prohibited list, the special import licence (SIL) list, the restricted list, the canalised list and the free list. Of these, the restricted list has been freed and SIL abandoned and freed. The canalised list is being retained, but under a new nomenclature (the special list) and a new set of products. The number of import lists has come down to three — the prohibited list, the special list and the free list. The prohibited list contains only a few products prohibited on grounds of religious and cultural sensitivity and the list includes tallow, fat and oils of animal origin, animal rennet and wild animals including their parts and products and ivory. Bulk agricultural commodities that include grains excluding feed grade maize, edible oils, oilseeds, sugar, and non-agricultural products such as urea, petroleum products are in the special list that was earlier called canalised list.

Apart from the special list of consumer products, gold will continue to be imported through designated banks. Import of all primary products of plant and animal origin will also be subject to import permits to be issued by the ministry of agriculture after an import risk analysis based on sanitary and phyto-sanitary measures and provisions. In addition, conditions have been prescribed for the import of new and second hand cars. Import of foreign liquor, processed food products and tea wastes has to be made subject to already existing domestic regulations concerning health and hygiene. Rest of the commodities are in the free list. Imports of these freed items attract high tariffs with bound rates.

EXIM Policy 1992–97

In 1990 India's peak tariff[6] was 300 per cent. During 1992–93, the peak rate was reduced to 150 per cent (WTO 1998). The Government introduced a system of value-based advanced licences to export houses, trading houses and star trading houses which permitted duty free imports of necessary raw materials as components up to a stipulated ratio of the value of anticipated exports. Special Import Licences (SIL), which could be traded in the market, were issued to certain categories of exports like exports to Asian clearing union countries, deemed export, trading houses and manufacturers who have acquired the ISO 9000 or other international certificating quality. Before the Uruguay Round Agreement (URA), only 5 per cent of India's tariff lines were bound. After the URA came into force, about 68 per cent of India's tariff lines were to be bound. As of 1 December 1995 more than 3000 tariff lines covering raw materials, intermediates and capital goods were freed from import licensing requirements. However, replacing licences with high tariffs, indicates that India's promotion of free trade is not without restraint.

In 1995–96, India had bound tariffs at 40 per cent on industrial raw materials, components and capital goods, (where they were above 40 per cent in 1993–94) and at 25 per cent in other cases. Countervailing duties at the rate of 30 per cent to 40 per cent were imposed as additional tariff above 25 per cent for goods other than raw materials, components and capital goods. QRs were present as the rest of the goods were classified into either negative list or special licence list during that period. India indicated ceiling bindings of 100 per cent on primary products, 150 per cent on

---

6 Peak tariff rate is the general guide for setting the tariff rates. Higher tariff rates are exceptions. However, higher tariffs should be equal to or lower than the WTO approved bound rates.

processed products and 300 per cent on edible oils. With an improvement in India's balance of payments, the country was under pressure to eliminate the QRs. India had entered into bilateral agreement with the EU, New Zealand and Australia, to remove QRs on 1,429 items from 1 April 2003. Such an understanding was not reached with the USA.

EXIM Policy 1997–02

During 1997–98, the peak rate of import duty was reduced to 40 per cent *ad valorem* except for passenger luggage, alcoholic beverages, dried grapes and a few other products. The peak rates for imports of raw materials and capital goods for projects were reduced to 30 per cent and 20 per cent respectively. However, the special additional customs duty was raised from 2 per cent to 5 per cent on all imported goods except petroleum products and certain project imports.[7] A surcharge of 10 per cent on basic duty was introduced in 1998–99 mainly to control imports of consumer goods.

From 1 April 2001, removal of QRs became necessary since India lost a case against the USA. QRs were replaced with high tariffs. WTO permits tariff setting, so far as the applied rates do not surpass bound rates. India's applied rates are mostly lower than bound tariffs. The recently announced peak tariff rate is 35 per cent plus a 3.5 per cent surcharge on tariffs and a 4 per cent special duty on items from which QRs have been removed. In addition, countervailing duties ranging from 16 per cent to 32 per cent are imposed on certain goods. Basic tariffs have been increased on vegetable oils from 25 per cent to 45 per cent, on tea, coffee, copra and coconut from 35 per cent to 70 per cent. Uniform rates of 75 per cent and 85 per cent are imposed on crude edible oils and refined oils respectively. Maximum tariffs on imports of rice are 80 per cent. Without doubts, these tariffs substantially raise the import prices of several agricultural products. The duty on used cars has been put at 105 per cent, which translates into 180 per cent including countervailing and special additional duties.

Customs duties during 2001–02 were 35 per cent, 25 per cent, 15 per cent and 5 per cent. The Special Additional Duty imposed in 1998–99 (for all products except petroleum products) is still applicable. However, the surcharge of 10 per cent on basic duty that was introduced in 1998–99 was removed. At present, most consumer goods, which have been in the free list of imports effective 1 April 2000, are being placed at the peak rate 35 per cent plus the surcharge. A number of agricultural and horticultural products placed on the free list of import in earlier years are being brought to the peak rate to ensure adequate protection to Indian farmers (Table 13.1).

[7] The argument for imposing the additional duty was to provide some relief to domestic producers from internal sales tax.

For sensitive agricultural products such as wheat, rice, sugar and edible oils in which the Indian experience with supply management has underlined the importance of occasional tariff adjustments, the Finance Minister would make suitable enabling provisions to fix the statutory tariff rates at approximately high levels.

Table 13.1: Items on which Import Duties were Raised in April 2001

Items	*Previous Tariff*	*Revised Tarif*
Skimmed Milk Powder	0 per cent	60 per cent
Wheat	0 per cent	50 per cent
Rice in the husk(paddy or rough)	0 per cent	80 per cent
Husked (brown) rice	0 per cent	80 per cent
Semi-milled or wholly milled rice,	0 per cent	70 per cent
Broken rice	0 per cent	80 per cent
Maize (corn) seeds	0 per cent	50 per cent
Grain sorghum	0 per cent	50 per cent
Millet (Jowar)	0 per cent	50 per cent
Arecanut	35 per cent	100 per cent
Apples	35 per cent	50 per cent
Tea	15 per cent	35 per cent
Coffee	15 per cent	35 per cent
Sugar	40 per cent	60 per cent
(+a countervailing duty of Rs. 850 per tonne).		

Source: Ministry of Commerce.

What is this experience, and why does it result in upward tariff adjustments? Government policy has tried to regulate international trade in a manner to ensure adequate availability of essential food items to consumers at reasonable prices and to protect farmers from foreign competition. The objective is to maximise agricultural exports in order to earn foreign exchange and provide remunerative prices to farmers. Policy aims to regulate agricultural imports, keeping in view the domestic demand and supply situation, the interests of the farmers, and consideration of outflow of foreign exchange.

Whenever supply appears to meet demand, import of that commodity is restricted through high tariffs or canalisation, even when the international price is lower than the domestic price. When supply exceeds demand, export is encouraged only after building up buffer stock for the public distribution system. Imposing minimum export price and/or ceilings has regulated exports of rice and wheat.

In the case where there is excess demand, particularly when international price is lower, the Government has encouraged imports by lowering tariffs. An example is edible oils imports in view of increase in edible oil consumption, stagnating oil seeds production and falling international prices. Differential duty structure in favour of refined oil led to an upsurge in edible oil imports. When in 1992–93 the golden revolution to achieve self-sufficiency in oil production was launched, many oil solvent extractors set up extraction units as they saw huge potential in the market. But with oil seeds production not catching up with the demand plus lower per hectare yield of just 850 Kgs compared to the world average of 1600 Kgs of oil seeds imports became necessary.

At present, India has more than 15,000 oilseeds crushing units more than 600 solvent extractors, more than 400 vegetable oil refiners and more than 190 Vanaspati oil units — all working at below 40 per cent capacity. Thus the solvent extraction industry is in doldrums with many units already shut down. The Government is keen to protect the domestic oilseeds industry. In Budget 2002, it increased the basic duty on RBD (Refined, Bleached and Deodorized) Palmolein to 85 per cent from 65 per cent and maintained the special additional duty at 4 per cent. It even increased the basic duty on Crude Palm imports to 75 per cent. For refined Soybean however the government maintained the status quo with 45 per cent basic customs duty.

An implication of the agricultural tariff policy is that there may be misuse of bound rates. Bound tariff rates are the highest tariff rates that a country agrees, under the WTO regime, to apply to a particular import or class of imports. The general peak tariff rate is 35 per cent — too high in relation to almost any other country.

The policy of keeping applied rates close to bound rates is counterproductive. Bound rates are meaningful at times of crisis. Applied rates should not be set close to 'crisis rates'. The question to ask is does India want to revert to its severely protectionist past or to lower its tariffs.

Import of agricultural products like wheat, rice, maize, other coarse cereals, copra and coconut oil has been placed in the category of State Trading though on commercial lines. This is a kind of non-tariff barrier to free trade.

Is it necessary? 'License Raj'— heavy government interventions, were a major feature of the Indian economy in the pre-reform period. This generated institutional complementarity in an Indian context in the pre-reform period. It appears that this characteristic of the Indian economy has not changed completely yet. The procedure of State Trading in agricultural products in the post-reform period has the potential to slow down liberalization. Though wheat, rice, maize, coarse cereals, copra, coconut oil and urea are no longer on the QRs list, the government has kept an eye on the rural vote bank by restricting their trade by putting them in the special list. Import of all these products remain canalised through state trading enterprises.

This is in conjunction with high bound rates under WTO for wheat, rice, and maize; sanitary and phyto-sanitary restrictions; safeguard measures to prevent dumping; a 'war cell' to monitor imports of 300 sensitive items; besides a new enabling law to impose temporary QRs. There is no valid reason to have a special list at all which constraints free trade. Domestic supply conditions should be tackled by appropriate domestic policies aimed at improving productive efficiency.

3. Conclusions

India has taken major steps towards trade liberalisation since 1991, partly on its own initiative and partly from its commitments to WTO. During the WTO Second Trade Policy Review of India, the members complimented India for reduction in the tariffs (WTO 1998). However, some members raised questions about the complex structure of the tariff system, particularly high tariff rates on the import of consumer goods. The average tariff on consumer goods in 1997–98 was reduced to 25 per cent as against 153 per cent in 1990–91. The 2000–2001 budget reduced the peak rate to 38.5 per cent. However, the additional special duty and countervailing duties add up and increase the tariff. Thus, simply comparing the peak rates will not give a true picture of trade restrictions. Though the peak rate is used as a guide for imposing tariff, applied tariff can be much higher but below the bound rates. India's applied rates on several items are still very high compared to ASEAN countries (East Asia Analytical Unit 2001). Though policymakers have mentioned on several occasions inside and outside the Parliament that India's tariff will be similar to ASEAN very soon.

India has bound 68 per cent of its tariff lines compared to 6 per cent prior to the UR. All agricultural tariff lines and 62 per cent of the tariff lines of industrial goods are bound. Though at present, the applied rates are below the bound levels, producer lobby may put pressure at any time on the Government to impose tariff very close to the bound rate. If that happens, this would be equivalent to the 'licence raj' system.

What would be the impact of removal of QRs on Indian industries? One reason for the continuation of QRs was that the Indian producers could not compete with the best in the world. The industries that have been reaping the benefits of QRs now want the government to provide a level playing field. There are also pressures to provide them protection through high tariff walls (Mehta 2000). It is also contented that Indian exporters still face many obstacles which affect their export prospects, for example, reservation of items for the small scale sector, labour laws which restrict flexibility in hiring and firing, and complicated port procedures. It is time that the Government takes necessary steps in a time bound manner to remove the obstacles facing the exporters. While India borrows the Chinese model of SEZs, it still applies the existing labour laws to units in the SEZs. Similarly reservation for small scale sector constrains India's export prospects. The government must also look at trade policy issues from the interests of consumers and the economy as a whole.

India appears to be using the conventional 'domestic failure argument' against free trade. India's negotiations for upward revision of tariff bindings under Article XXVIII of GATT 1994 in respect of certain agricultural products which were bound during the previous rounds of GATT negotiations at zero or low levels of tariffs warrant attention (WTO, 1998). Upward revision on these tariff bindings for such agro products under Article XXVIII was done with a view to giving the necessary protection to domestic agriculture and agro-industry. This will affect the Indian economy in various ways as long as institutional complementarity is re-established. The existing productive inefficiency in agriculture, public sector industry and small-scale industries are the consequences of heavy protection so far given to the industrial sector. Such domestic failures should be corrected through a proper domestic policy measures such as the removal of all subsidies to farmers and industries; and effective removal of internal and international restrictions on agricultural products, particularly cereals. This implies that India's trade liberalizing reforms are forced to slow down or could be counter-productive if highly regulated spheres of other markets remain untouched. The ratio of trade to GNP in India increased from 14.1 per cent in 1980 to 20 per cent in 1999, indicating increased openness. However, in China the ratio of total trade to GNP increased from 12.6 per cent in 1980 to 37 per cent in 1999. Thus India needs to open up much more.

References

CMIE (Centre for Monitoring the Indian Economy), *Trade*, July (Mumbai: CMIE, 2000).

East Asia Analytical Unit, *India: New Economy, Old Economy* (Canberra: Department of Foreign Affairs and Trade, 2001).

Hayami, Y., 'Toward an East Asian Model of Economic Development', in Y. Hayami and M. Aoki (eds), *The Institutional Foundations of East Asian Economic Development* (London: Macmillan, 1998), pp. 3–35.

Joshi, V. and I.M.D. Little, *India's Economic Reforms: 1991–2001* (Delhi: Oxford University Press, 1996).

Mehta, R., (2000), 'QR Removal and India's Import', *Research and Information System for the Non-Aligned and Other Developing Countries* (New Delhi, Monograph, 2000).

Ministry of Commerce, *Export-Import Policy Statements* (New Delhi: Government of India, various years).

Ministry of Finance, *Economic Survey, Economic Division* (New Delhi: Government of India, various years).

Ministry of Finance, *Budget Speech of the Finance Minister* (New Delhi: Government of India, various years).

Ministry of Finance, *Tax Reforms Committee Reports*, 3 parts (New Delhi: Government of India, 1991, 1992, 1993).

RBI (Reserve Bank of India), *Handbook of Statistics on Indian Economy 2000* (Mumbai: RBI, 2001).

Srinivasan, T.N., 'India's Economic Performance: A comparative Analysis', in I.J. Ahluwalia and I.M.D. Little (eds), *India's Economic Reforms and Development: Essays in honour of Manmohan Singh* (New Delhi: Oxford University Press, 1998).

WTO (World Trade Organization), *Annual Report* (Geneva: WTO, various years).

——, *Trade Policy Review: India 1998*, WTO, Geneva, 1999).

14
Do Productivity Spillovers from Japanese and US FDI Differ?

Rashmi Banga

1. Introduction

Spillovers from foreign direct investment (FDI) have been studied widely. Caves (1974) Globerman (1979), Nadiri (1991) Blomstrom and Wolf (1994) and Djankov and Hoekman (2000) found positive spillovers from foreign firms on productivity of domestic firms, while Kokko (1994); Aitken, Hansen and Harrison (1997), and Haddad and Harrison (1993) suggest that foreign firms have negative effects on the productivity performance of domestically owned firms. A probable reason for the lack of consensus is that spillovers are FDI-industry-firm-host economy specific. The magnitude and direction of the spillovers will depend on factors like the type of technology brought in by the FDI, the mode of transfer of the technology, the technological levels prevailing in the industry, the learning capabilities of the domestic firms, the absorptive capacity of the host economy which determines the rate of technical diffusion of the technology, etc.

While the industry, firm and host economy specific factors have been taken into account hardly any of the studies on spillovers of FDI have tried to disaggregate the spillovers from different sources. It is generally believed that Japanese firms behave differently from other firms, either because of their protected domestic base or because they have different cultural and institutional structures (Graham and Krugman 1995). Japanese FDI also differs in its industrial pattern from US FDI. US FDI in manufacturing is usually undertaken in most technologically sophisticated industries with not yet standardised products that are more capital-intensive in nature, while Japanese FDI generally enters industries that are less capital-intensive, producing standardised products that are less technology-intensive. Further, the transfer of technology from Japanese firms is termed as orderly transfer of standardised production and differs from the American 'reverse-order' transfer of technology (Kojima 1978).

In Indian manufacturing US FDI concentrates on pharmaceuticals, electronics, chemicals-organic, personal care, dry cells and electric equipment; which is technologically advanced sectors as compared to Japanese FDI which are prominently present in industries such as auto-ancillary, automobiles–LCVs/HCVs, glass-sheet/float and rubber-retreading. Given the differences in their industrial patterns and the belief that Japanese FDI differ from US FDI in terms of their levels of technology and modes of technology transfer it is expected that the spillover effects of Japanese and US FDI on Indian firms should differ. This chapter attempts to identify the spillover effects of Japanese FDI and US FDI on total factor productivity growth of domestic firms in Indian manufacturing using panel data of seven years: 1993–94 to 1999–2000. This period is of significance for the Indian economy since it marks the post-liberalisation period.

2. The Extant Empirical Evidence

The empirical evidence on spillovers from FDI is mixed. The positive effects on productivity of domestic firms, emphasised by studies are via competitive pressures; learning by doing and diffusion of knowledge through demonstration effects, labour turnover or reverse engineering (Caves 1974; Globerman 1979; Nadiri 1991; Blomstrom and Wolf 1994; Djankov and Hoekman 2000). However, other authors (Blomstrom and Kokko 1997; Aitken, Hansen and Harrison 1997; Haddad and Harrison 1993) find that foreign firms have negative effects on the productivity performance of domestically owned firms.

These studies together establish the fact that productivity spillovers are industry-firm-host economy specific. For the Indian economy Kathuria (2000) and Basant and Fikkert (1996) have studied the spillover effects.

However, these studies have failed to take into account the heterogeneity of FDI and the differences in their nature and behavior across sources. Hardly any of the studies on spillovers of FDI have tried to disaggregate the spillovers of FDI from different sources and compare them. This chapter attempts to bring out the inter-source differences in the productivity spillovers from FDI to Indian firms

3. The Analytical Framework and the Hypotheses

The debate about whether significant differences exist between Japanese and US FDI has a long if not altogether distinguished history. Many of the arguments made by early commentators, such as Kojima's (1978; 1986)

distinguish between the trade-enhancing nature of Japanese FDI and the trade-undermining characteristic of US FDI. Ozawa (1979) emphasised the importance of relative factor endowments in driving Japanese FDI. However, these studies have not withstood the test of time and empirical examination (for criticisms see Hill 1988; Hill 1990; Ramstetter 1987).

Further, the presence of Japanese FDI in export-oriented manufacturing in different parts of Asia in the last decade appears to be little different from US FDI in its motivations. Along with this the importance of global trends to which all firms must respond regardless of home base, inspires caution in any attempt to make *a priori* comparisons between Japanese FDI and US FDI. However, the characteristics of Japanese corporations displayed in their domestic operations that are regarded as unique (Aoki 1988; Womack, Jones and Roos 1991) and which, if they are changing at all, are doing so only slowly (Yamamura 1990; 1994) suggests that it is likely that the operations of Japanese FDI will continue to differ from those of US FDI. Some of the unique dimensions of Japanese corporations are inter-corporate relations, and the relations between corporations and the home government. Some of the unique production techniques like just-in-time sourcing, total quality management, FMEI, quality control circles, ringi system etc. if replicated in overseas affiliates, may benefit the host economy. Others, such as the *keiretsu* relations that link assemblers and suppliers and maximising market-share rather than short-term profitability may not lead to any potential benefits, in fact may lead to negative influences in the host economy.

Based on the literature on the characteristics of Japanese FDI we advance some hypotheses regarding the spillover effects of Japanese and US FDI.

3.1 Hypotheses

HYPOTHESIS 1: Japanese FDI are expected to have larger positive spillover effects on total factor productivity growth (TFPG) of domestic firms as compared to US FDI.

This hypothesis is derived on the basis of certain unique characteristics of Japanese FDI: type of technology transfer, mode of technology transfer, and its industrial pattern. The unique characteristics of Japan's transfer of technology is that it is an orderly transfer of technology of standardised production which begins in those industries where the technical gap between the providing and receiving countries is the lowest. This should make transfer of technology easier and spread its effects further. On the other hand, US FDI in manufacturing is seen to be undertaken in the most technologically sophisticated industries, with not yet standardised products that are more capital intensive and rank on the top of the comparative advantage of the home economy. Kojima calls this 'reverse-order' transfer of technology. This implies a large gap between the existing technology of the host developing country and that transferred through the US FDI, which makes spillovers of the transfer of technology to the domestic firms difficult.

In the specific case of India, the industrial pattern of Japanese and US FDI also differs. US FDI is concentrated in chemicals and pharmaceuticals industries, which involve process technology. This makes their technology less susceptible to the reverse engineering or imitation, unlike the technologies in industries like auto-ancillary and electricals where Japanese firms dominate. These differential characteristics of the two FDI sources make Japanese FDI more susceptible to leakages or spillovers as compared to their overseas competitors. Japanese firms are therefore expected to have larger positive spillover effects as compared to the US firms.

HYPOTHESIS 2: The market share of foreign firms is expected to be negatively associated with the total factor productivity growth (TFPG) of domestic firms.

The earlier studies have tested the hypothesis that productivity spillovers are strictly proportional to foreign presence but Kokko (1996) argues that this is not always the case. Spillovers from competition, in particular, are not determined by foreign presence alone but rather by the simultaneous interaction between foreign and local firms. Hence, it is possible that the spillovers are larger in cases where a few foreign firms stir up a previously protected market than in a situation where foreign affiliates hold large market shares, but refrain from competing hard with local firms. In fact, sometimes a large foreign presence may even be a sign of a weak local industry, where local firms have not been able to absorb any productivity spillovers at all and have therefore been forced to yield market shares to foreign MNCs. Harrison (1994) also suggests that in imperfectly competitive markets entry by foreign investors implies that domestic incumbents lose market share, impeding their ability to attain scale economies. Based on these studies we derive our second hypothesis that market-share of foreign firms is negatively associated with the ability of domestic firms to raise their productivity growth rates, since they are unable to reap economies of scale.

HYPOTHESIS 3: The initial productivity gap between domestic firms and Japanese firms will be positively related to the TFPG of domestic firms and therefore support the 'catch-up' theory. However the initial productivity gap between domestic firms and US firms may not be related positively.

There are conflicting views on the relationship between the rate of diffusion and the gap between the level of technology in MNC's home country and the country hosting FDI. In Findlay (1978) and Wang and

Blomstrom (1992) the rate at which new technology is diffused is an increasing function of the gap. The larger the gap, the greater the potential for 'catch-up'. On the other hand, some studies argue that spillovers are negatively related to the technology gap between the relatively 'backward' host country and the 'advanced' home country, due to the fact that the superior technology may not be appropriate for the backward country.

Taking an evolutionary approach, Perez (1983) argued that the ability of indigenous firms to 'catch-up' depends on their level of technical competence. This competence is characterised by 'path-dependency', i.e., the absorptive capacity of indigenous firms depends on their past accumulation of technology. The influence of these multiple factors suggests a non-linear relationship between spillovers and the size of the technology gap. Spillovers increase as the technology gap widens up to a certain critical level. Beyond this level spillovers begin to fall because technical competence by indigenous firms will be too low to exploit fully the technical opportunities arising from foreign presence and at still higher level spillovers may become negligible or even negative.

It is observed that US FDI in manufacturing is usually undertaken in most technologically sophisticated industries. We therefore expect the technological gap between US and Indian firms may fall beyond the critical levels. However, Japanese FDI generally enters industries that are less capital-intensive, producing standardised products that are less technology-intensive. The technological gap between Japanese and Indian firms is therefore expected to be within the critical level. The 'catch-up' theory can be expected to hold for the Indian firms *vis-à-vis* Japanese firms but not *vis-à-vis* US firms.

4. The Model: the Variables and the Sample

4.1 The Model

The basis of our analysis here is a firm, and we start with a four input production function with output Y and inputs as material inputs M, labour L, Fuel and Power E (Energy) and capital K. The production function can be written as

$$Y_{it} = F(Lit, K_{it}, M_{it}, E_{it})$$

Typically the model to be estimated is the Cobb-Douglas representation of technology relating factor inputs and output, i.e.,

$$\text{Ln } y_{it} = \alpha + X'_{it}\beta + v_{it} - u_{it} \qquad (1)$$

where *i* indexes firm and *t* indexes time periods. v_{it} is a normally distributed statistical noise with zero mean and standard error (σ_v) accounting for random disturbances, measurement error and factors beyond the control of firms. u_{it} represents a time-varying productive inefficiency of the firm. u_{it} implies that the output of the firm must lie on or below the frontier $\alpha + X'_{it} \beta + v_{it.}$ From the firms' point of view, it may observe u_{it} and take the level of u_{it} into account while choosing its inputs. This violates the assumption of linear model of uncorrelated regressors with the error term and renders the estimation inconsistent. However, if u_{it} is included as regressor (that is, fixed effects model), it would remove any biases that would have resulted from correlation between u_{it} and the regressor. If we assume that technical efficiency is time-invariant the model becomes

$$\text{Ln } y_{it} = \alpha + X'_{it}\beta + v_{it} - u_i$$

where $u_{it} = u_i$ for all t

However, with the presence of foreign firms and their spillover effects due to increased knowledge, awareness of better technology and accumulated learning experience and increased competitive pressures, it becomes important to look at the changes in efficiency overtime. Using standard panel data estimation techniques Cornwell Sickles and Schmidt (1990) have outlined the procedure for estimating equation (1) without making any distributional assumptions regarding the firm-specific error terms.

Equation (1) can be rewritten as

$$\text{Ln } y_{it} = \alpha - u_{it} + X'_{it}\beta + v_{it}$$

$$\text{Ln } y_{it} = \alpha_{it} + X'_{it}\beta + v_{it} \qquad (2)$$

Where α_{it} is the time variant productivity level of a firm and is modeled as

$$\alpha_{it} = \theta_{i1} + \theta_{i2} + \theta_{i3} t^2$$

Equation (2) can be written as

$$\text{Ln } y_{it} = x'_{it}\beta + \omega'_{it}\,\delta_{i1} + v_{it}$$

Where $\omega'_{it} = [\,1\ t\ t^2]$

And $\delta'_i = [\theta_{i1}\ \theta_{i2}\ \theta_{i3}]$

This specification allows efficiency levels to vary both over time and across firms.

The estimation procedure for the present model is to estimate δ_i by regressing the residuals (yit - x'_{it} b) for firm i on unity, time, and time squared.

The predicted values from this regression provides an estimate of α_{it} that is consistent for all i and t as $t \rightarrow \infty$. Thus the change in productivity level (or productivity growth) of the firm can be estimated as

$$\Delta\hat{\alpha}_{it} = \hat{\alpha}_{it} - \hat{\alpha}_{it-1}$$

To test the hypotheses that TFPG of domestic firms is affected by the productivity spillover effects a cross-section model is applied taking seven year averages for the firm-specific and industry-specific variables and three-year averages for the spill variables, since data is available only for three years for these variables. The model applied is as follows:

$TFPG_i$= f (spill variables; firm-specific variables; and industry-specific variables) + error term

where *i* denotes domestic firms. The final model is linear in form.

4.2 Variables

The spillover effects of FDI on the domestic firms in the host country are generally considered to be positive by most studies. However, some studies have shown that spillover effects of FDI can also be negative. The proxies used for the presence of foreign firms have generally been either the foreign equity in the industry or the market share of the foreign firms. To take into account both positive as well as negative spillover effects we have used the ratio of Japanese and US equity invested in the industry to total equity invested in the industry along with the market share of Japanese and US firms in the industry as spill variables. The type of technology imported by Japanese and US firms may also have a differential impact on the productivity growth of the domestic firms. To take this into account interaction terms are considered, that is, technology imported by the Japanese firms* proportion of Japanese equity in the industry and technology imported by the US firms* proportion of US equity in the industry. The spill variables are defined as follows:

4.3 Spill-Variables

a) Foreign equity as a ratio of total equity invested in the industry (FOREQ)

b) Japanese Equity as a proportion of total equity invested in the industry (JE)

c) US Equity as a proportion of total equity invested in the industry (USE)

d) Market Share of Japanese firms,i.e., sales by Japanese firms/total sales in the industry (MKTSHJ)

e) Market Share of US firms, i.e., sales by US firms/total sales in the industry (MKTSHUS)

f) Technology imports by Japanese firms*Japanese equity in the industry (TECHM*J)

g) Technology imports by US firms*US equity in the industry (TECHM*US)

The productivity growth of firms is also dependent on firm-specific variables like size of firms, age of firms and R&D intensity of firms. To control for firm-specific variables the following variables are considered:

4.4 Firm-Specific Variables

a) Size of the firm, i.e., log of sales of the firms ($SIZE_i$)
b) Age of the firm (Age_i)
c) R&D Intensity of the firm, that is, R&D expenditure/sales ($R\&D_i$)
d) Export Intensity of the firms (XI_i)
e) Import Intensity of the firm (MI_i)
f) Capital-Intensity of the firm (KI_i)
g) Gap between initial productivity levels of domestic firms and
h) average productivity levels of foreign firms (GAP)
i) Gap between initial productivity levels of domestic firms and average productivity levels of Japanese firms (GAPJ)
j) Gap between initial productivity levels of domestic firms and average productivity
k) levels of US firms (GAPUS)

The fact that Japanese and US FDI may have a different industrial pattern necessitates modelling of industry specific effects. The following industry-specific variables are considered:

4.5 Industry-Specific Variables

a) Capital imports by the industry (IMPCAP)
b) R&D intensity of the industry (R&D)
c) Export Intensity of the industry (XI)
d) Import intensity of the industry (IMPI)
e) Effective Rate of Protection in the industry (ERP)
f) Advertisement Intensity of the industry (ADVT)
g) Capital-Labour Ratio in the industry (KL)

4.6 The Sample

In order to estimate the production frontier and the final models at the firm level, we have collected data from Capitaline package, various issues of *Annual of Survey of Industries* (ASI), various issues of *National Accounts Statistics* and some publications of the Ministry of Industry. A balanced panel is used for 153 firms for the years 1993–94 to 1999–2000 across 25 three-digit level industries. Only those industries where at least 15 per cent of the total equity invested in the industry is from Japan and/or US are selected. Not much spillover effect is expected in the industries where this is less than 15 per cent. A matching of industries from Capitaline package to ASI is done so as to construct data on variables that are not provided by the Capitaline package, e.g., data on number of employees.

All the variables used in the panel data estimation are measured at 1993–94 prices. We have used the actual prices of the major outputs and inputs of the firms to arrive at the indices for deflating output and input series of the firms. The variables constructed are as follows:

OUTPUT: The Capitaline package provides data on total sales and finished goods inventory of the firms. Total value of output of the firms is the sum of the two. In most of the earlier studies on Indian manufacturing the wholesale price indices are used as deflators for output. However, Capitaline package provides data on major outputs of the firms along with their prices. A weighted output price index series is constructed using the prices of two major outputs of the firms. The value (price*quantity) of the output is used as the weights in the series.

INPUTS: Capitaline package also provides data on the major inputs used by firms along with their prices. The total raw-materials consumed by the firms is deflated by the weighted input price index series, which is constructed using the total cost of inputs as weights.

LABOUR: The series on labour is constructed using data from ASI. The data on total employee cost of the firms is collected from the Capitaline package and the series on number of employees is constructed using the wage-rate in corresponding industries estimated from ASI (Total Emoluments/ number of employees).

CAPITAL: I use the methodology of Srivastava (1996). However, the deflators used for deflating different series of capital are more disaggregated. Capital stock is taken to consist of Plants and Machinery, Land & Building and other Fixed Assets. Two separate series of capital are constructed: i.e., one for Plants and Machinery along with other fixed assets and the other for Land & Building. These are deflated separately to arrive at estimates of capital stock in the base year (1993–94) for each firm. Data on gross capital formation in plants and machinery and construction at current and constant prices are collected from NAS and an implicit deflator is arrived at. Applying this implicit deflator, capital stock in the year 1993–94 is estimated. However, since in the base year the firm's asset mix is valued at historic cost, the value of capital at replacement cost for the current year is arrived at by revaluating the base year of capital. Implicit deflators are constructed for last 15 years in case of plants and machinery of the firms and for last 25 years for construction in the firms or the date of incorporation of the firm, if it is after these years.

A revaluation factor (as used by Srivastava) is then applied to each series to obtain capital stock at replacement costs at current prices. Deflating these values we arrive at capital stock in real terms for the base year. Subsequent years investment is then added, that is, gross fixed assets $_{t}$ - gross fixed assets $_{t-1}$ to the capital stock existing at every time period using the perpetual inventory method. The capital stock series is hence arrived at for the firms.

FUEL AND POWER: Capitaline package provides data on expenditure on fuel and power. A weighted price index is constructed to deflate the expenditure on fuel and power. This is done by using wholesale price indices for electricity for industrial purposes and furnace oil from CMIE publications. Weights used are the firms' expenditure on oil and power. Data for the firm-specific, industry-specific and spill variables are collected from the Capitaline package.

5. Empirical Results

Table 14.1 presents some descriptive statistics. Table 14.2 presents the results of firm level analysis of productivity spillovers in four different equations, taking account of firm-specific as well industry-specific variables that may affect the TFPG of domestic firms. Though a number of variables have been used, the equations with the best fit are presented.

Table 14.1: Descriptive Statistics

1. Number of industries	25
2. Number of firms	153
3. Number of domestic firms	78
4. Number of Japanese firms	32
5. Number of U.S. firms	35
6. Number of other foreign firms	8

Table 14.2: Productivity Spillovers from Japanese and US FDI: Dependent Variable: TFPF of domestic firms

VARIABLES	(1)	(2)	(3)	(4)
CONSTANT	0.007 (-0.449)	-0.011 (-0.693)	-0.003 (-0.208)	0.003 (0.241)
FOREQ	0.001 (0.313)	–	–	–
JE	–	0.012*** (1.67)	–	–
USE	–	-0.009 (-0.244)	–	–
SIZE	0.003 (1.21)	0.003 (1.12)	0.002 (1.07)	0.002 (0.744)
XI	-0.133 (-1.28)	-0.126 (-1.22)	-0.134 (-1.29)	-0.09 (-0.878)
KI_i	0.001* (2.62)	0.001* (2.72)	0.001* (2.85)	0.001* (2.76)
MKTSHFF	-0.028 (-1.25)	-0.052** (-1.98)	–	–
IMPI	2.47 (1.45)	3.04*** (1.79)	3.9* (2.08)	–
MKTSHJ	–	–	-0.058* (-2.159)	-0.062* (-2.25)
MKTSHUS	–	–	-0.304 (-1.271)	-0.130 (-0.72)
TECHM*US	–	–	–	-0.009 (0.015)
TECHM*J	–	–	–	0.006* (2.74)
ADJ R^2	0.115	0.140	0.141	0.116
N	78	78	78	78

Notes: Seven year averages are taken (1993–94 to 1999–2000)

* indicates significant at 1%

** indicates significant at 5%

*** indicates significant at 10%

Equation (2) of Table 14.2 presents the results of the effect of market share of foreign firms on the TFPG of the domestic firms. We find that the average market share of foreign firms is negatively associated with TFPG of domestic firms supporting the hypothesis that foreign firms may capture a larger market share as a result of which the domestic firms may not be able to attain scale economies. This is in line with the findings of Harrison (1996). However, market share of Japanese firms has a significantly larger negative impact as compared to the US FDI (Equation (3), Table 14.2). A probable reason for this could be that Japanese FDI has entered smaller industries as compared to US FDI as a result of which it has been easier for the Japanese firms to have large market shares. Also, their marketing strategy of emphasising market share rather than short-term profits may have helped.

Spillover effects of Japanese FDI on the TFPG of domestic firms are therefore positive however larger market share of Japanese firms may have a negative influence on their productivity growth. Spillover effects of US FDI are not significant. A reason for this could be the nature of technology brought in by the Japanese and US firms. To test this an interaction term (the import of technology (both embodied and disembodied) is considered by Japanese and US firms with the amount of Japanese and US equity invested in the industry respectively). Equation (4) of Table 14.2 shows that the impact of the technology imported by Japanese firms and US firms on TFPG of domestic firms varies. Technology import by Japanese firms has a significant positive impact on TFPG of domestic firms while that of US has a negative though insignificant impact. From this it can be said that domestic firms are learning from the technology brought in by Japanese firms.

Equation (1) of Table 14.2 presents the results with foreign equity (FOREQ) as one of the spill variables. We find that FOREQ, as an aggregate has no significant impact on the TFPG of the domestic firms. Equation (2) presents results by disaggregating FOREQ into Japanese equity and US equity invested in the industry. We find that JE has a significant positive spillover effect on the TFPG of the domestic firms, after controlling for the firm and industry specific effects. US equity has no significant effect on the TFPG of the domestic firms. This shows that FDI from different sources may have differential spillover effects. Therefore aggregating FDI to estimate the spillover effects, as has been done by most of the studies on spillover, may not reflect the true picture.

Taking the initial gap in the productivity levels of the domestic firms and the average productivity levels of foreign firms in the industry, we find that the gap has no significant effect on the TFPG of the domestic firms (Equation (1), Table 14.3). However, when we consider the initial gap between the productivity levels of domestic firms and Japanese and US firms separately, we find that the gap with Japanese firms has a significant positive impact on the TFPG of the domestic firms, thus supporting the 'catch-up', theory while the gap with US firms does not have any significant effect. Since the ability of indigenous firms to 'catch-up' depends to a large extent on their level of technical competence and Japanese firms have entered low technology industries where this gap is lower as compared to industries where US firms have entered, this result seems justified and is in line with Blomstrom and Wolff (1994) and Kokko et al. (1996).

Table 14.3: Productivity Spillovers with Initial Productivity Gap from Japanese and US Firms Dependent Variable: TFPG of domestic firms

VARIABLES	EQUATION 1	EQUATION 2
CONSTANT	-0.002 (-0.193	-0.13 (-0.934)
R&D	0.02 (1.02)	0.03 (1.40)
XI	-0.142 (1.41)	-0.089 (-0.91
KI_i	0.001* (3.01)	0.001* (2.88)
GAP	0.016 (1.22)	–
GAPJ	–	0.004* (2.22)
GAPUS	–	-0.008 (-0.006)
MKTSHJ	-0.04** (-1.73)	–
MKTSHUS	-0.285 (-1.35)	–
IMPI	397.5* (2.11)	434.3* (2.22)
PRESENCEJ	–	0.016* (2.45)
ERP	–	-0.051* (-3.29)
ADJ R2	0.12	0.14
N	78	78

Notes: Seven year averages are taken (1993–94 to 1999–2000)
* indicates significant at 1%
** indicates significant at 5%
*** indicates significant at 10%

Overall it can be said that Japanese FDI in the Indian manufacturing has positively contributed to the TFPG of the domestic firms though the same cannot be said for the US FDI. The reasons for this may be the differences in the type of industries that Japanese FDI and US FDI have entered and within the same industry the type of technology brought in by them, the modes of transferring the technologies and also the technological capabilities of the domestic firms in the industries they have entered.

6. Conclusion

The chapter contributes to the literature on productivity spillovers from FDI by differentiating productivity spillovers from FDI from different sources. An attempt is made to compare the productivity spillovers from Japanese and US FDI to domestic firms in Indian manufacturing using the panel data for the period 1993–94 to 1999–2000 to estimate the average annual total factor productivity growth rate. An attempt is made to control for firm-specific and industry-specific effects.

The results show that foreign capital, as an aggregate, may not have any significant productivity spillovers. However when disaggregated into Japanese equity and US equity invested in the industry we find diverse results. Japanese equity has a significant positive impact on the total factor productivity growth of the domestic firms but US equity has no significant effect. The spillovers effects of FDI may also be negative. Negative spillovers occur due to a large market share of the foreign firms, which may not allow the domestic firms to attain scale economies. It was found that the market share of Japanese firms is negatively associated with the TFPG of domestic firms. However, the net spillover effect of Japanese FDI seems to be positive. The productivity spillovers from US firms appear to be negative though the result is not significant.

The study suggests that a number of factors contribute to raise the absorptive capacity of the host country. Amongst them are local competence, the types of technology brought in by the foreign firms and the competitive environment created by the foreign firms. The study also suggests a possible role for economic policy in host countries. Policies supporting a more competitive environment should be followed in those industries where the local firms have higher competence levels and there are fewer chances for the foreign firms to capture the market share. A more protective environment would lead to higher TFPG of domestic firms in industries where local firms do not have the competitive ability. The study also highlights the need to formulate policies that enable domestic firms to upgrade their technology levels in high-tech industries so as to encourage larger spillovers from the US firms. Thus, a policy mix is required for maximising the productivity benefits from FDI.

References

Aitken, B., and Harrison A., 'Do Domestic Firms Benefit from FDI? Evidence from Venezuela', *American Economic Review*, 89(3) (1999), 605–18.

Aoki, M., *Information, Incentives and Bargaining in the Japanese Economy* (Cambridge: Cambridge University Press, 1988).

Basant, R., and Fikkert, B., 'The Effects of R&D, Foreign Technology Purchase and Technology Spillovers on Productivity in Indian Firms', *The Review of Economics and Statistics,* 78(2) (1996), 187–99.

Blomstrom, M., and Wolf, E., 'Multinational Corporations and Productivity Convergence in Mexico', in W. Bahmol, R. Nelson and E. Wolff (eds), *Convergence of Productivity: Cross National Studies and Historical Evidence* (New York: Oxford University Press, 1994), pp. 243–59.

Caves, R.E., 'The Distinctive Nature of the Multinational Enterprise', in J.H. Dunning (ed.), *Economic Analysis and the Multinational Enterprise* (London: Allen & Unwin, 1974), pp. 13–30.

Cornwell, C., Schmidt, P., Sickles, R.C., 'Production Frontier with Cross-Section and Time-Series Variation in Efficiency Level', *Journal of Econometrics*,, 46(1–2) (1990) 317–32.

Djankov, S., and Hoekman, B., 'Foreign Investment and Productivity Growth in Czech Enterprises', *The World Bank Economic Review*, 14(1) (2000). 49–64.

Findlay, R., 'Related Backwardness, Direst Foreign Investment and the Transfer of Technology: A simple dynamic mode', *Quarterly Journal of Economics*, 92 (1978) 1–6.

Gagelmann, K.Z., 'Productivity Spillovers from Foreign Direct Investment in Poland', *Economic Systems*, 24(3) (2000) 223–56.

Globerman, S., 'Foreign Direct Investment and Spillover Efficiency Benefits in Canadian Manufacturing Industries', *Canadian Journal of Economics*, 12 (1979), 42–56.

Graham, E.M., and. Krugman P.R., 'Foreign Direct Investment in the United States' (Washington, DC, 1995). ,

Grether, J.M., 'Determinants of Technological Diffusion in Mexican Manufacturing: A Plant-Level Analysis', *World Development*, 27 (1999), 1287–98.

Haddad, M., and Harrison, A., 'Are there Positive Spillovers From Foreign Direct Investment? Evidence from Panel Data for Morocco', *Journal of Development Economics*, 42(1) (October 1993), 51–74.

Harrison, A., 'Productivity, Imperfect Competition and Trade Reform: Theory and Evidence', *Journal of International Economics*, 36 (1994), 53–73.

Hill, H., *Foreign Investment and Industrialization in Indonesia* (Singapore: Oxford University Press, 1988).

Hill, H., 'Foreign Investment and East Asian Economic Development', *Asian-Pacific Economic Literature*, 4(2) (September 1990), 21–58.

Kathuria, V., 'Productivity Spillovers from Technology Transfer to Indian Manufacturing Firms', *Journal of International Development* 12(3) (2000), 343–69.

Kojima, K., *Direct Foreign Investment: A Japanese Model of Multinational Business Operations* (London: Croom Helm, 1978).

Kojima, K., 'Japanese-Style Direct Foreign Investment', *Japanese Economic Studies*, 14(3 (Spring 1986), 52–82.

Kokko, A., Tansini, R., and Zejan, M.C., 'Local Technological Capability and Productivity Spillovers from FDI in the Uruguayan Manufacturing Sector', *Journal of Developmen Studies*, 32 (4) (April 1996), 60–11.

Kokko, A., 'Technology, Market Characteristics and Spillovers', *Journal of Development Economics*, 43 (1994), 279–93.

Ozawa, T., *Multinationalism: Japanese Style* (Princeton, N.J.: Princeton University Press, 1979).

Perez, C., 'Structural Change and the Assimilation of New Technologies in the Economic and Social Systems', *Futures*, 15(4) (1983).

Ramstetter, E.D., 'The Impact of Direct Foreign Investment on Host Country Trade and Output: A Study of Japanese and US Direct Foreign Investment in Korea, Taiwan and Thailand', in S. Naya, et al. (eds), *Direct Foreign Investment and Export Promotion: Policies and Experience in Asia* (Honolulu: East–West Resource Systems Institute, 1987), pp. 223–57.

Srivastava, V., *Liberalisation, Productivity and Competition: A Panel Study of Indian Manufacturing* (Delhi, Oxford University Press, 1996).

Tsou, M.W., and Liu, J.T., 'The Spillover Effect from FDI: Empirical Evidence from Taiwan Manufacturing Industries', *Taiwan Economic Review* (June 1998) 155–81.

Wang and Blomstrom, M., 'Foreign Investment and Technology Transfer: A Simple Model', *European Economic Review*, 36 (1992), 137–55.

Womack, J.P., Daniel T.J., and Ross. D., *The Machine that Changed the World: The Story of Lean Production — How Japan's Secret Weapon in the Global Auto Wars will Revolutionize Western Industry* (New York: Harper Collins, 1991).

Yamamura, K., 'Will Japan's Economic Structure Change?', in K. Yamamura (ed.), *Confessions of a Former Optimist. Japan's Economic Structure: Should It Change?* (Seattle: Society for Japanese Studies, 1990), pp. 13–64.

Yamamura, K., 'Comment. Does Ownership Matter?' in M. Mason and D. Encarnation (eds), *Japanese Multinationals in Europe* (Oxford: Clarendon Press, 1994), pp. 87–90.

PART V

SECTORAL AND REGIONAL ISSUES

15

Growth in India's State Economies Before and With Reforms: shares and determinants

Shashanka Bhide and Ric Shand

1. Introduction

The overall growth performance of the Indian economy has been characterized by substantial regional variation in growth over the decades. This is despite the focus in successive Five-Year Plan policies and programs on reducing the incidence of poverty and of achieving balanced regional development. Shares of the All India Gross Domestic Product (GDP) among the 14 major states[1] varied in 1998–99 from 13.1 per cent for Maharashtra to 2.2 per cent for Orissa (Table 15.1). The regional distribution of population also varied widely, ranging from 168.6 million for Uttar Pradesh (17.9 per cent of the total) to Haryana's 19.7 million (2.1 per cent). These distributions did not coincide, leading to a wide dispersion of average income per capita among states. In 1998–99, the range was from US$657 down to $159.

Maintaining a balanced regional development has always been a policy objective for India's planners. From 1951, a range of policies for balanced development was introduced, including industrial licensing, area specific development programs, fiscal incentives for industries to locate in 'backward areas', and equated pricing policies for a key industrial

1 India today has 28 states and Union Territories. The latter have fewer powers of fiscal management and administration as compared to the states. The 14 states (taking the states of Uttar Pradesh, Madhya Pradesh and Bihar before their subdivision in 2000) that are considered in this study, due to limitations of data on the other states, account for about 92 per cent of India's total population as per the Census of 2001.

input such as steel. Development of educational, health and physical infrastructure at the state level was also a goal of the planning process on an equitable basis.

Table 15.1: Regional Variation in the Size, Population and GSDP Per Capita of India and its Major States, 1998–99

State	*GSDP Rs billion*	*% Share of All India*	*Population million*	*% Share of All India*	*GSDP/Capita in 1998–99*		*Ranking*
					Rs	*US$*	
Maharashtra	1718	13.1	90.7	9.6	27,650	657	1
Uttar Pradesh	1100	12.3	168.6	17.9	10,189	242	12
Tamil Nadu	813	7.5	61.6	6.5	19,014	452	6
Andhra Pradesh	755	7.0	75.1	8.0	15,198	361	8
Gujarat	749	6.9	48.0	5.1	21,312	507	4
West Bengal	734	6.8	78.6	8.3	14,001	333	9
Madhya Pradesh	655	6.1	79.2	8.4	11,462	272	11
Karnataka	636	5.9	51.8	5.5	17,433	414	7
Bihar	493	4.6	99.2	10.5	6,680	159	14
Rajasthan	460	4.3	53.2	5.6	11,800	280	10
Punjab	385	3.6	23.4	2.5	23,460	558	2
Kerala	351	3.2	32.2	3.4	19,576	465	5
Haryana	290	2.7	19.7	2.1	22,151	527	3
Orissa	234	2.2	35.7	3.8	10,031	238	13
14 States	9372	86.6	917.0	97.2	14981	356	
All India	10818	100.0	943.0	100.0	16,532	393	

Sources: Central Statistical Organisation, Government of India, New Delhi, available at the India States' Reform Forum 2000: Fiscal and Governance Reforms for Poverty Reduction, November 23–25, 2000, Taj Palace Hotel, NewDelhi (www.statesforum.org)

Note: Gross State Domestic Product (GSDP) at state level and Gross Domestic Product (GDP) at the national level are in constant 1993–94 market prices

Rules for allocation of resources from the Central government to the states have been established for the same purpose both through the Planning Commission with the 'Gadgil formula' and through the Finance Commission.[2]

Divergence of state economies prevails not only in terms of overall incomes but also with respect to sources of income. Substantial structural change has also taken place. This has altered the relative importance of sectors in the economy, from an agrarian emphasis to one of growing prominence of the industrial and service sectors at the national level. This, too, has varied regionally owing to differences in state level sector growth rates. At the national level, the share of agriculture and allied activities has come down from 54.7 per cent in GDP in 1960–61 to half that level in 2000–01.

A close understanding of the regional patterns of growth within India is desirable for several reasons. First, central importance in policy continues to be the objective of achieving and sustaining a higher overall growth rate in the Indian economy. Policy makers need insights on past performance at state level in order to formulate future policy directions more effectively. Second, high levels of foreign and domestic investment are needed to reach the growth target. Foreign and domestic investors need information on state level performance and prospects to guide their choice of location between states. Third, there are fiscal problems in the states, which are exacerbating those at the Centre, and the issue of fiscal stability now requires these problems at state level to be addressed. Finally, with greater decentralization of the policy making process consequent to the economic reforms in the 1990s, information on the states' performance is important for the policy makers at the state level also. Policies will be based on such assessments in each state.

---

[2] The transfer of resources from the Central government to the states is needed under the federal structure of Indian government given the wide vertical fiscal imbalances. Transfers are achieved mainly through two mechanisms. One, through the recommendations of a Finance Commission, constituted every five years, deals with the imbalances in the revenue account of the states. These transfers include tax revenue sharing and grants on revenue account. The transfers are increasingly based on a variety of indicators including fiscal performance of the states. The second mechanism is the Planning Commission transfers as assistance to states for their plan expenditures. The original formulation used for the Fourth Five Year Plan (1969–74) was termed the 'Gadgil formula', named after the Deputy Chairman of the Planning Commission at the time, included criteria for devolution such as population, per capita income and ongoing projects of irrigation and power. The formula has since been revised in subsequent Plans and now includes criteria such as tax effort, fiscal management and national policies towards literacy, female welfare programs and land reforms.

Under the federal system of government in India, the States play a key role. They have exclusive jurisdiction over public health, roads and bridges (other than national highways), agriculture, power, water supply and irrigation, urban services, and play a major role in education. In a sense, for any business enterprise, it is the government services and regulations at the state level that determine the policy environment at ground level.

The economic reforms in the 1990s at the national level have also led to a greater focus on the activities of the States. The dominance of central planning and the grip of economic controls have waned with the change in focus to market-driven and private sector-fuelled development and by growing globalisation. There is a shift towards decentralization of government, with local urban and rural government strengthened by the Constitutional amendments of 1992. It is recognized too that the priority areas in government expenditure for development are in physical infrastructure (roads, waterworks, power), and in social infrastructure (schools, hospitals, family planning), where mainly State governments determine public funding and provision.

While there is evidence of changes in perception of the role of the states among the policy makers in the various policy statements, actual implementation of the new policies is less impressive. Lahiri and Fardoust (2000) have commented,

> As a direct consequence of … economic and political developments of the past decade, appropriate policy responses, expenditure allocations and revenue efforts of the Indian State governments have become very important for growth and welfare. Perhaps, most States have lagged behind the central government in introducing economic reforms in the post 1991 period. This relative lack of progress is evident in the areas of tax reforms, disinvestment and liberalization of rules and procedures. A large majority of the States has followed shortsighted, populist policies that have harmed their economic and social development. The composition of expenditures as well as the stock of infrastructure assets has deteriorated with the neglect of cost recovery mechanism for maintaining public assets. Reform at the State level is critical for the country.

Clearly a large part of the onus for stimulating economic development and attracting the necessary investment resources lies with the States. Their capacity to rise to this challenge is central to the theme of this paper. States 'will be competing more intensely than before, in market place for resources in future and, States may find it somewhat difficult to place a significant responsibility on the Centre for their relative performance' (Reddy 2000).

A number of studies have examined the issue of regional disparities in India's economic performance.[3] This chapter profiles India's states, with particular reference to recent growth, development and investment outcomes. It examines output growth rates, and output shares at the state level and their determinants. Due to limitations of length, the paper does not include analysis at sectoral level by states, nor does it attempt a more rigorous explanation of the pattern of growth of state economies in an econometric framework.

2. Recent Performance of State Economies

2.1 Growth Rates of Gross State Domestic Product (GSDP)

The reform period is generally regarded as having commenced in 1993–94. The economic crisis occurred in 1990–91 with its major impact in 1991–92. The economy recovered from the crisis in 1992–93, so both the years 1991–92 and 1992–93 show the impact of the crisis and the subsequent recovery and do not reflect the impact of reforms on overall growth performance. So we consider the reform period to have commenced in 1993–94 and examine the growth performance from 1993 to 1999 (that is, FY1993–94 to FY1998–99) in terms of average annual growth rates and growth shares of GSDP compared with the pre-reform period of 1980–90. We first highlight the features and contrasts in the growth performance of states during the decade of the 1980s and the reform period 1993–99. We then proceed with an analysis of variables that are likely to have influenced the growth rate performance and thus have policy implications.

A key result of comparison of output growth rates between the two periods is the acceleration of growth in the 'reform period' from the levels of 'pre-reform period'. The All India average growth rate (GDP) for 1993–99 was 6.6 per cent per annum, a significant increase on the average of 5.7 per cent for 1980–90, as were the average for the 14 major states at 6.1 per cent and 5.4 per cent respectively (Table 15.2).

For convenience in analysis the 14 major states have been grouped into high, medium and low performing economies (HPSE, MPSE and LPSE) according to their average growth rates of GSDP in the 1993–99 reform period (Table 15.2). The four states with the most improvement in growth rates over the 1980s are Karnataka, Maharashtra, Tamil Nadu and Gujarat. As a group, they averaged a growth rate of 7.4 per cent per annum in real GSDP during the period 1993–99, well above the 5.9 per cent per year average for 1980–90. All four showed a marked acceleration in growth,

---

3 Ahluwalia (2000), Shand and Bhide (2000) and Bajpai, Jian and Sachs (1997) are some of the recent contributions.

particularly Karnataka (5.7 per cent to 8.1 per cent) and Tamil Nadu (5.6 per cent to 7.4 per cent). West Bengal also showed a substantial increase, but on the basis of a number of other indicators discussed below, it was not included in the HPSE group.

Table 15.2: High, Medium and Low Performance State Economies in India

State	*% Average Annual Growth Rates of GSDP (real)*	
	1980–90	*1993–99*
High Growth		
Karnataka	5.7	8.1
Maharashtra	6.3	7.7
Tamil Nadu	5.6	7.4
Gujarat	6.4	6.8
Medium Growth		
West Bengal	4.3	6.9
Andhra Pradesh	6.7	6.3
Kerala	3.3	6.3
Haryana	6.3	5.6
Madhya Pradesh	4.3	5.4
Rajasthan	7.2	5.3
Low Growth		
Orissa	5.4	5.1
Punjab	5.7	5.0
Uttar Pradesh	5	4.3
Bihar	4.4	4.0
14 States	5.4	6.1
HPSEs	5.9	7.4
MPSEs	5.2	5.9
LPSEs	4.9	4.4
All India	5.7	6.6

Note: see footnote on Table 15.1 for data source.

A second group of six states recorded average growth rates around the 14-state average of 6.1 per cent per annum in 1993–99 and were grouped as medium performing state economies (MPSEs). These comprised West Bengal, Andhra Pradesh, Kerala, Haryana, Madhya Pradesh and Rajasthan. In this group, there was no consistent improvement in growth rates over the 1980s. While there were significant increases for West Bengal, Kerala and Madhya Pradesh, there were decreases for Andhra Pradesh, Haryana and Rajasthan.

The remaining four states were grouped as low performing state economies (LPSE). Their reform period growth rates were well below the All India and 14 state averages, in the range of 5.1 per cent down to 4 per cent. The group, which comprised Orissa, Punjab, Uttar Pradesh and Bihar, all recorded average growth rates in the 1990s well below those in the 1980s, as did the LPSE group (4.9 per cent down to 4.4 per cent).

2.2 Growth in Per Capita Incomes

- Growth rates of average per capita incomes for the three performance groups in 1980–90 and 1993–99 (Table 15.3) show substantial increases for the HPSE (from 3.9 per cent to 5.9 per cent) and MPSE (from 2.9 per cent to 4.1 per cent), while in the LPSE group, there was a reduction in the growth rate from 2.7 per cent to 2.5 per cent.
- In 1980–90, the range in growth rates of per capita incomes over the three groups of 1.2 percentage points was quite narrow. In 1993–94 to 1998–99, it had increased substantially to 3.4 percentage points, which indicates widening disparities between the three groups and reflects the relatively rapid increase in average per capita income in the HPSEs and the lack of improvement in the LPSEs.
- Within the HPSEs, increases in per capita growth rates occurred for all four states but particularly for Karnataka, Maharashtra and Tamil Nadu. In the MPSE group, increases in growth rates were most notable for West Bengal and Kerala and less so for Andhra Pradesh and Madhya Pradesh, while Haryana and Rajasthan showed reductions. In the LPSEs, Orissa and Bihar showed slight increases, but Punjab and Uttar Pradesh experienced reductions in per capita growth rates.

2.3 Levels of Per Capita Income

Per capita incomes in 1998–99 show a wide gap between averages for HPSEs (US$529) and LPSEs (US$239) (Table 15.4). As argued above, this gap has widened from the 1980s due to the higher growth rates in per capita incomes of the HPSEs relative to the LPSEs. The rankings of some states on average per capita incomes do not reflect their location in the state growth performance groups. This is because past growth rates of these states differed from those in the reform period of the nineties. For example in the HPSE group, Karnataka and Tamil Nadu had slower growth rates in the past and showed lower per capita rankings. In contrast, Haryana and Punjab had higher growth rates in the past, which gave high per capita rankings, but left them in lower performance groups in the 1990s.

Table 15.3: Average Growth Rates (%) of Per Capita Incomes in Major States, 1980–90 and 1993–94 to 1998–99: 1993–94 Prices

State	*Average Growth Rate*	
	1980–90	*1993–99*
High Growth		
Karnataka	3.7	6.5
Maharashtra	3.9	6.0
Tamil Nadu	4	6.2
Gujarat	4.4	5.1
Medium Growth		
West Bengal	2	5.2
Andhra Pradesh	4.4	4.9
Kerala	2	5.1
Haryana	3.8	3.6
Madhya Pradesh	1.8	3.3
Rajasthan	4.6	2.5
Low Growth		
Orissa	3.5	3.8
Punjab	3.8	3.3
Uttar Pradesh	2.6	2.1
Bihar	2.2	2.3
All India	3.5	4.7
HPSEs	3.9	5.9
MPSEs	2.9	4.1
LPSEs	2.7	2.5
14 States	3.2	4.3

Note: See footnote on Table 15.1 for data source.

2.4 State Growth Shares

We have calculated the shares of individual states and state groups in the growth of GSDP during the pre-reform decade and the 'reform period' (Table 15.5). The estimates further distinguish the 'better performing states' from the rest. The growth shares are estimated first by calculating the change in GSDP during a specified period at the state or state-group level and then calculating the share of a state or state-group in the total. The main patterns that emerge are:

- The HPSE, led by Maharashtra, contributed 39.3 per cent of growth in the reform period, which was 8 per cent more than in the 1980s.

Gujarat, Tamil Nadu and Karnataka all showed increases in shares over the pre-reform period, particularly Karnataka (2.7 per cent).

- In the MPSE group, West Bengal recorded the highest growth share of 6.8 per cent in the reform period, which was 1.9 per cent higher than in the 1980s. Andhra Pradesh, Madhya Pradesh and Rajasthan all had significant growth shares in the reform period but lower than in the 1980s, particularly Andhra Pradesh with a 2 per cent reduction. Kerala and Haryana had modest growth shares but improved on the 1980s. The MPSE group as a whole contributed a substantial 26.6 per cent share with reforms, but this was marginally less (0.1 per cent) than in the 1980s.

Table 15.4: Average GSDP Per Capita by States, 1998–99

State	*GSDP per capita*		*Rank*
	Rs	*US$*	
High Growth			
Karnataka	17,433	414	7
Maharashtra	27,650	657	1
Tamil Nadu	19,014	452	6
Gujarat	21,312	507	4
Medium Growth			
West Bengal	14,001	333	9
Andhra Pradesh	15,198	361	8
Kerala	19,576	465	5
Haryana	22,151	527	3
Madhya Pradesh	11,462	272	11
Rajasthan	11,800	280	10
Low Growth			
Orissa	10,031	238	13
Punjab	23,460	558	2
Uttar Pradesh	10,189	242	12
Bihar	6,680	159	14
14 States	14981	356	
HPSEs	22234	529	
MPSEs	14333	341	
LPSEs	10058	239	
All India	16532	393	

Note: See footnote on Table 15.1 for data source.

Table 15.5: Average Shares (%) of States and Groups in All India Real GSDP Growth Before and With Reforms

State	*Growth Share*		*Change % points*	*Population share %*
	1980–1990	*1993–1999*		
High Growth				
Maharashtra	14.4	16.3	1.9	9.6
Gujarat	6.1	8.3	2.2	5.1
Tamil Nadu	6.5	7.8	1.3	6.5
Karnataka	4.2	6.9	2.7	5.5
Medium Growth				
West Bengal	4.9	6.8	1.9	8.3
Andhra Pradesh	7.8	5.8	-2	8
Madhya Pradesh	4.8	4.2	-0.6	8.4
Rajasthan	4.6	4	-0.6	5.6
Kerala	2	2.9	0.9	3.4
Haryana	2.8	2.9	0.1	2.1
Low Growth				
Uttar Pradesh	10.3	7.3	-3	17.9
Bihar	4.5	2.9	-1.6	10.5
Punjab	3.8	2.7	-1.1	2.5
Orissa	2.5	1.6	-0.9	3.8
14 States	79.2	81.2	3	97.2
HPSE	31.3	39.3	8	26.7
MPSE	26.9	26.6	-0.3	35.8
LPSE	21.1	15.2	-5.9	34.7
All India	100	100		

Note: See footnote on Table 15.1 for data source.

- In the LPSE group, Uttar Pradesh recorded a relatively high growth share of 7.3 per cent with reforms but this represented a 3 per cent share reduction from the 1980s. Bihar, Punjab and Orissa had low growth shares with reforms and lower than in the 1980s, particularly Bihar (-1.6 per cent) and Punjab (-1.1 per cent). The LPSE group contributed 15.2 per cent of growth with reforms, which was 5.9 per cent, less than in the 1980s.
- Thus 7 of the 14 major states achieved increases in GSDP growth shares with reforms. The pattern also indicates a highly concentrated and skewed distribution of growth across the country. The growth share of the 14 major states in the reform period was 81.2 per cent, an increase of 2 per cent over the 1980s.

3. Determinants of GSDP Growth and Shares

At a conceptual level, several factors can be proposed as having significant impact on a state's development or economic growth. We have selected a few and compared their variation with the variation in economic performance. The factors examined here relate to investment, infrastructure (economic and social) and public finance. They are summarised in Table 15.6.

Table 15.6: Some Determinants of State Level Economic Performance

Sl. No.	*Item*	*HPSE*	*MPSE*	*LPSE*	*14 States*	*All India*
1	Financial Disbursements by All India Financial Institutions: 1993–99					
1a	Average annual growth rate (real) %	18.9	12.4	12.2	16.0	16.3
1b	Average share % in total disbursements	59.8	21.1	12.9	93.7	100.0
2	Average share % in proposed Industrial Investment (IEM + LOI)	54.6	22.3	16.8	93.7	100.0
3	Average share % in FDI approvals (Aug 1991 to Jan 2000)	33.3	15.4	6.9	55.6	100.0
4	Share % in Capital Outlays by State Governments: 1993–99	34.1	34.9	18.4	83.0	100.0
5	Share % in total investment proposals					
5a.	In 1999	42.1	26.5	18.5	87.0	100.0
5b.	In 2000	41.8	26.0	18.3	86.1	100.0
6	Infrastructure Index: mid 1990s					
6a.	Economic	113.9	90.0	92.4	100.0	--
6b.	Social (based on outcome Indicators)	116.2	97.5	78.6	100.0	--
7	State Fiscal Deficit as % of GSDP	3.1	4.4	5.0	3.8	--
8	State government debt as % of GSDP					
8a.	In 1993–94	15.1	20.8	29.8	21.5	--
8b.	In 1999–00	16.7	25.3	35.3	24.3	--

Note: The data for various indicators presented here are compiled from a number of sources.

3.1 Investment

Growth of investment is a key determinant of GSDP growth rates as it affects short-term growth performance through its impact on aggregate demand as well as long-term performance through its impact on the creation of productive capacity in the economy. The key components of investment are private and public sector investment. Private investment comprises domestic and foreign direct investments. Public investment comprises capital outlays in the budget and resources mobilised by public sector units (PSUs) outside the budget, such as borrowings.

No single time series covers all these types of investment for India at the state level, so it is necessary to choose proxies that best represent the components. Those selected here for private domestic investment[4] are the state-level growth rates and shares of disbursements of credit from the All India Financial Institutions (AIFI), and total proposed industrial investment by the companies/agencies listed in the stock exchanges in the country. The proxy used for foreign direct investment is total approvals for foreign direct investment, as there is no series available for actual foreign direct investment at state level. The proxy used for public sector investment is total state capital outlay.

Private Investment — Domestic

Disbursements by All India Financial Institutions are a proxy for domestic private investment activity and thus for domestic private capital formation. Although not all disbursements by the financial institutions result in fixed capital formation, as they are also used for corporate restructuring, they are still a good proxy variable for investment activity in the private corporate sector. The pattern of shares and growth of disbursements by All India financial institutions in real terms is presented in Table 15.6. Data for the 1993–99 reform period show:

[4] The sources on private sector investment in India comprise the following:

a) Data on sanctions and disbursement of assistance/ credit provided by the All India Financial Institutions;
b) Data on Foreign Direct Investment provided by the Secretariat for Industrial Approvals, Government of India;
c) CMIE data on total investment: is a good proxy but reflects only book value of investment, not in real terms;
d) CMIE data on investment under implementation: is also a good proxy for actual investment, but again the values are nominal;
e) Annual Survey of Industries data on Gross Fixed Capital Formation: are useful, but in this study, these are used for only three years.

- The HPSE group was by far the most dominant. The average annual rate of growth of real disbursement (18.9 per cent) was higher than those of the other two groups.[5]
- The overall share of the HPSE group was dominant at 60 per cent of the total over the period.
- The average rate of increase for the MPSE group of 12.4 per cent was well below that of the HPSE but higher than that of the LPSE group.
- The MPSE group's share of disbursements (21 per cent) was substantial.
- The average rate of growth of disbursement of the LPSE group (12.2 per cent) was the least among the three performance groups as also was its share of total disbursements (13 per cent).
- Although we have not presented the state level data due to limitations of space, it is important to note that the rankings of disbursement growth rates of individual states within the HPSE group were high. Not all were in the top four, but they were the top four states in terms of disbursement shares over the period.
- In the LPSE, the exception to the general pattern was Uttar Pradesh, which had a low rate of growth of disbursement of 13.3 per cent in keeping with its classification in the LPSE group, but because of its size, it was ranked fifth in terms of disbursement share over the period (7.4 per cent).

A second measure of private investment discussed here is proposed industrial investment. This combines investment through Industrial Entrepreneurs' Memoranda (IEM) and Letters of Intent (LOI) for the period from August 1991 to November 2000 (Table 15.6). The emerging pattern is summarised below:

- The HPSEs dominated with a 54.6 per cent share. This group itself was dominated by two states — Maharashtra and Gujarat. Their investment proposal shares were disproportionately high in relation to their population shares.
- The MPSE group attracted a 22.3 per cent share of proposed investment, with Andhra Pradesh and Madhya Pradesh as the two largest state recipients. Shares of investment proposals for West Bengal and Kerala were low, and well below their population shares.

---

[5] Disbursements are calculated in real terms by deflating the nominal values by the wholesale price index for manufactured products.

- The LPSE group attracted only 16.8 per cent of total proposed investment, and achieved this share only because of Uttar Pradesh and Punjab. UP and Bihar's shares were disproportionately low in relation to their population shares.

Private Investment — Foreign Direct Investment Approvals

In the absence of actual foreign direct investment data, FDI approvals provide a good proxy for changes in the investment climate. However, it is not a satisfactory proxy for actual FDI as the latter is a varying fraction of approvals. A recent calculation showed investment 'actuals' as only 37 per cent of approvals from January 1991 to August 2000 (Nabhi 2001, p. 31). Highlights of statewise data on FDI approvals for the period August 1991 to January 2000 (Table 15.6) are:

- The HPSE group dominated, attracting 33.3 per cent of total approved investment
- MPSEs (15.4 per cent) accounted for less than half that amount and LPSEs less than half that of the MPSE group (6.9 per cent)
- Within the HPSE group, Maharashtra alone received 13.7 per cent of approvals, while Karnataka (7.6 per cent) and Tamil Nadu (6.7 per cent) and Gujarat (5.3 per cent) were also very significant. In the MPSE group, Madhya Pradesh (4.5 per cent), Andhra Pradesh (4.2 per cent) and West Bengal (3.7 per cent) attracted significant proportions of approvals. In the LPSE group, only Orissa (3.8 per cent) attracted a significant proportion of approvals. Uttar Pradesh and Bihar were virtually ignored.

Public Investment

Public sector investment was measured for each state over the 1993–99 period with the proportions of total state capital outlays for development to the All India total over the period (Table 15.6). Capital outlays are drawn from the state budgets only and do not include resources mobilised by public sector undertakings outside of the budget, such as by borrowing. It is a reasonable proxy for infrastructure investment by state governments. The highlights are the high growth (HPSE) group of four states accounted for 34.1 per cent of total state government capital outlay during the 1993 to 1999 period. This was on a par with the 34.9 per cent outlay of the MPSE group of six states and considerably greater than the 18.4 per cent allocated by the LPSE group. The group pattern is consistent with a positive association between public capital outlays and GSDP growth rates of states.

3.2 Total Investment

A third indirect measure of fixed capital formation available at the state level is the 'total investment' proposed mainly in the 'organised sector' of the economy. The Center for Monitoring Indian Economy compiles information on proposed investment available through various published sources. We have provided a summary of such investment information under 'total investment' in Table 15.6. For total investment in the two years for which we were able to compile the information, 1999 and 2000, there was a steep reduction in shares from HPSE to LPSE groups — from 42 per cent to 18 per cent. Thus, the HPSEs have a clear advantage in attracting new capital over the slower growth states.

3.3 Infrastructure

The role of adequate infrastructure facilities for setting up industrial or other production capacities needs no elaboration. Infrastructure is not merely physical assets: roads, electricity supply or communication facilities but also the social overheads such as the type of human resources available. We have attempted to construct two indices reflecting economic (or physical) and social infrastructure facilities available in the states.

Economic infrastructure

A composite index of economic infrastructure was calculated for the mid-1990s for each state comprising a range of variables:

- ➢ percentages of villages electrified,
- ➢ number of irrigation pumps energised per geographical area,
- ➢ electricity generation capacity per population,
- ➢ road length per geographical area,
- ➢ railway length per geographical area,
- ➢ telephone lines per population, and
- ➢ post offices per population

In each case, the state's index was scaled relative to the value of the variable at the national level by taking the latter as 100. The overall index is a simple average of all the sub-indices. The resulting indices aggregated to the three performance groups of the states are provided in Table 15.6.

- The indices for the three state performance groups show a positive association with growth performance between the HPSEs and the other two groups, with an index value of 113.9 for the HPSE, 90.0 for the MPSE and 92.4 for the LPSE. There is no clear distinction between the two lower performance groups.

- At a more disaggregated level, the positive link between high economic infrastructure index values and high GSDP growth rates is more apparent when we consider Tamil Nadu, Maharashtra and Gujarat with relatively high index values, and Orissa and Bihar in the LPSE group, which had the lowest index values. This association does not hold consistently for all individual states. Punjab had the highest index value but was in the LPSE. Kerala with the next highest index was in the MPSE group. On the other hand, Karnataka with average infrastructure was in the HPSE group and Madhya Pradesh and Rajasthan had low index values but were in the MPSE group.
- This suggests that relatively favourable economic infrastructure does not guarantee high growth performance, nor does relatively poor infrastructure necessarily prevent high growth rates. Clearly, there are other factors that influence economic growth.

Social infrastructure

A composite index of social indicators was also constructed from variables including number of hospital beds, female literacy and infant mortality rate (IMR). The values for their performance groupings (Table 15.6) indicate:

- The three state performance groups showed a positive association between growth rates and this index, with average index values ranging from 116.2 for the HPSE group, to 97.5 for the MPSE and to 78.6 for the LPSE. This strongly suggests that high GSDP growth rates are associated with better social infrastructure.
- Individual states' infrastructure rankings generally matched their grouping in growth performance, but there were exceptions. Kerala enjoyed the highest state index value, but was placed in the MPSE group. Also, third ranked Punjab was in the lowest growth group.
- As for economic infrastructure, these findings suggest that high index values and rankings for social infrastructure alone do not ensure high growth performance.

3.4 Fiscal imbalances

An important element of reform programs envisaged for the Centre and the States is the elimination of revenue deficits and reduction of fiscal deficits as key measures for the conduct of prudent and accountable fiscal policy and to facilitate greater macro-economic stability. Fiscal deficits have an impact on growth performance through the influence of fiscal stability or instability and through restrictions on funds available for developmental purposes.

Fiscal deficits

Comparison of average fiscal deficits from 1994 to 1998 for the three state performance groups (Table 15.6) show:

- a negative association of growth rates and size of fiscal deficits. Deficits increase from 3.1 per cent for the HPSE group to 5.1 per cent for the LPSEs and suggest that greater fiscal responsibility has been exercised by the faster growing states.
- This pattern was also fairly consistent among states within each growth performance group.

State level public debt

Public debt is another aspect of fiscal responsibility of the states. A comparison of debt as a percentage of GSDP with growth performance at state level in 1993–94 and 1999–2000 (Table 15.6) shows:

- a negative association between size of debt and growth rates. In 1993–94, debt rose from 15.6 per cent of GSDP for HPSEs to 21.3 per cent for MPSEs and to 31.4 per cent for LPSEs.
- In 1999–2000, debt had grown for all three performance groups, rising to 16.7 per cent for HPSEs, 25.3 per cent for MPSEs and 35.3 per cent for LPSEs.
- Debt had grown faster for the two slower performing state groups. Average annual debt growth was only 1.6 per cent for HPSEs, but was 3 per cent for LPSEs and 4.5 per cent per annum for MPSEs.
- Rising interest and repayment bills are hampering the lower growth states much more than the high performers.

4. Concluding Remarks

The ordering of the 14 major states into three performance groups based on their rates of growth of GSDP in the reform period of 1993–99 has been fruitful in a number of ways. First, the ordering suggests some important geographical differentiation. The four HPSEs are maritime states and the three states with the most potential to become HPSEs (West Bengal, Andhra Pradesh and Kerala) are also maritime. Only one coastal state, Orissa, is excluded from this pattern. By contrast, states in the LPSE group, together with the relatively low performers in the MPSE group, are all northern hinterland states.

Second, the ordering revealed a consistent pattern with a range of variables that may be considered as determinants of growth rates. All of these variables behaved in the expected fashion in their association with GSDP growth rates. These associations are suggestive of several messages:

- A central message is given by the strong positive association between GSDP growth rates and investment levels in the reform period of the 1990s in the government and private sectors. This held for public and private sectors, and for the latter, for domestic and foreign direct investment with few state level exceptions. It also held for total investment most recently, with few state exceptions.
- A second message is the importance of adequate economic and social infrastructure. This was manifest most strongly at the low end of the GSDP growth rates. States that rated low on these indexes were low growth states. This appears to be consistent with investment flows also.
- This gives rise to a third message for state governments in the light of the strong inverse associations between fiscal deficits and debt levels and GSDP growth rates. State governments with high fiscal deficits and growing debt levels choke off the flow of government outlays on fixed capital formation. Moreover they fail to provide the necessary investment environment for private investors.
- A fourth message is the need for state governments to develop effective policy packages to accelerate growth in all three sectors simultaneously. The record of the 1990s reveals disappointing performances for most major states in industrial and agricultural sectors in the new era of economic reform. States have to be able to identify and promote investment opportunities on a sectoral basis that will be competitive enough to attract investment flows.
- At this point in time, the most prospective states for elevation to the HPSE group are those showing the best signals on key development variables of infrastructure, investment and policy environments. West Bengal already has a GSDP growth rate to qualify in the HPSE group. But the question is whether this can be sustained. Many of the other indicators put this in question. A first concern is its low ranking for industrial growth and its relatively narrow industrial base. A second is its low ranking for economic infrastructure. A third is its low ranking for a number of investment indicators, including low shares in proposed industrial investment in the 1990s and in FDI approvals. Fourth, the state has a weak record on fiscal responsibility and debt control.
- Andhra Pradesh is a second candidate for promotion. In many respects, this state closely parallels its neighbour Karnataka, but without the latter's high growth performance. In the 1990s, it was ranked fourth in

agricultural sector growth and ranked for industrial growth. Its weakness was in services, as Karnataka's was in agriculture. It is endeavouring to rectify this, particularly with the promotion of its expanding IT sector for which the state has a number of considerable advantages. It was ranked not far below Karnataka in economic and social infrastructure and was lower ranked in a majority of key investment indicators including FDI approvals and average growth rate and shares of private investment. It has an ambitious and visionary government policy on agricultural, industrial and service industry development, including measures to attract new foreign investment. It is making a strong competitive pitch for its IT sector. It needs firmer fiscal control, but overall, it has the potential to lift performance progressively to achieve HPSE status.

- Other states currently are more seriously disadvantaged by weaknesses in investment performance (Kerala, Haryana and Punjab) or weak infrastructure (Madhya Pradesh and Uttar Pradesh) or both (Orissa, Rajasthan, and Bihar) and are unlikely candidates for promotion in the short to medium term. Some of the reasons for the widening disparities, and the ways they can be narrowed have been identified in the above analysis, and can be a source of guidance for policy makers.

References

Ahluwalia, M.S., 'Economic Performance of States in Post-Reforms Period', *Economic and Political Weekly*, 35 (2000) 1637–48.

Bajpai, N., Jian, T. and J. Sachs, 'Economic Reforms in China and India: Selected Issues in Industrial Policy', *Development Discussion Paper No. 580* (Harvard Institute for International Development, 1997).

Lahiri, Ashok K. and Shahrokh Fardoust 'Indian States: The Road to Reform', paper presented to the *Indian States Reform Forum*, 23–25 November (2000), New Delhi (mimeo).

Nabhi, *Manual for Foreign Collaboration and Investment in India*. 9th edn (New Delhi: Nabhi Publications, 2001)

Reddy, Y.V.,'Fiscal Reforms at State-Level: Review and Prospects', paper presented to the *Indian States Reform Forum*, 23–25 November (2000), New Delhi (mimeo).

Secretariat for Industrial Assistance, *Compendium on Industrial Policy and Procedures* (New Delhi: Department of Industrial Policy and Promotion, Ministry of Commerce and Industry, Government of India, August, 2000).

Shand, Ric and S. Bhide, 'Sources of Economic Growth: Regional Dimensions of Reforms', *Economic and Political Weekly*, 35 (2000), 3747–57.

16

Testing Market Integration in Indian Agriculture

Edgar J. Wilson

1. Introduction

The analysis and measurement of agricultural market integration is important because integrated markets will be able to more efficiently allocate commodities through the price system. India's recent liberalisation of agricultural food crop marketing in the early 1990s has renewed interest in testing for market integration.

However much of the research on market integration has relied on correlation and single equation Engle–Granger cointegration analyses. Correlation analysis is faulty since high correlations between agricultural prices might only reflect spurious relationships caused by common temporal trends. The single equation cointegration analysis, whilst taking non-stationarity into account, restricts itself to pairwise relationships. This is inconsistent with a complete analysis of market integration.

This chapter develops a simultaneous vector autoregressive model of non-stationary prices, which is estimated using Johansen's full information likelihood estimation techniques to derive efficient and consistent parameter estimates. This procedure provides a number of measures of market integration, although the most important is the estimates of long run equilibrium cross-price elasticities. These elasticities measure the sensitivity of each market price to proportionate changes in other market prices of the same commodity. We also quantify a short run equilibrating price elasticity, which indicates the ability of individual markets to return to equilibrium when faced with short-term commodity price shocks. The elasticities are estimated and tested for their significance using end-of-month wholesale price data for selected Indian markets for wheat, *jowar*, paddy rice, groundnut, rapeseed and mustard seed. The periods prior to and after Indian agricultural marketing liberalisation (beginning early 1990s) are compared.

2. Characteristics of the price data

End of month wholesale market price data are available for the Indian commodities wheat, *jowar*, paddy rice, groundnut and rapeseed/mustard seed. The data cover the formal Indian markets for food crops two periods in the 1980s and the 1990s. The periods for which wheat prices are available are January 1982 to June 1988 and January 1992 to June 1998. Price data were able to be collected for the other commodities for the common periods October 1981 to February 1988 and October 1991 to February 1998. The earlier periods predate the significant agricultural marketing reforms, which started to occur in the early 1990s, and will be called the pre-liberalisation period for the purpose of this chapter. The periods in the 1990s, whilst including the effects of ongoing agricultural reforms, will be referred to as the post-liberalisation period.

The markets for which the end of month wholesale prices are available cover a wide range of geographical regions and are shown in Table 16.1. It was possible to collect price data for ten of the major markets for wheat in both periods. However, there were larger variations in the availability of price data for the other markets. *Jowar* had data available for seven markets in the first period and eleven markets in the second period. Although only consistent paddy price data were available for five markets in the 1980s we were able to collect data for fifteen paddy markets in the post-liberalisation period. The groundnut price data cover five and seven markets respectively whilst the rapeseed and mustard seed price data were available for seven markets in both periods.

The data showed wide variation, consistent with agricultural price data. There were also variable temporal trends so the time series were tested for stationarity using the augmented Dickey–Fuller (ADF) test on the log of prices.[1] The markets for which the price variables were identified as $I(1)$ are listed in Table 16.2. Only two wheat markets, Karnal and Hapur in the first period and Mehasana in the second period were found to be stationary, $I(0)$. Interestingly, the Karnal and Hapur markets became non-stationary in the second period. Kolhapur, Bahraich and Gauhati were the only stationary markets for *jowar*, paddy and rapeseed/mustard seed respectively in the pre-liberalisation period. Again the Kolhapur and Bahraich markets

[1] If the absolute values of the test statistics were greater than the critical values then the null hypothesis of non-stationarity was rejected. The optimum order of the distributed lag was selected according to the Schwarz Bayesian criterion (SBC). The tests for stationarity were sometimes sensitive to the inclusion of a trend in the ADF regressions. If the test was ambiguous the price series was assumed to be $I(1)$ and included in the non-stationary category.

became non-stationary in the second period. All prices were non-stationary for *jowar* and rapeseed/mustard seed in the second period and for groundnut in both periods. In contrast only five of the fifteen paddy markets (Nizamabad, Purnea, Darbhanga, Palakkad, Simoga, Durg, Amritsar, Thanjavur, Kanpur and Attara) were non-stationary in the post-liberalisation period.

Table 16.1: Markets where End-of- Month Wholesale Price Data are Available

	Pre-liberalisation	*Post-liberalisation*
Wheat	Patna Rajkot Indore Kanpur Bahraich Delhi Amritsar Karnal Hapur Mehasana	Patna Rajkot Indore Kanpur Bahraich Delhi Amritsar Karnal Hapur Mehasana
Jowar	Nandyal Patan Gulbarga Indore Nagpur Madurai Kolhapur	Nandyal Patan Gulbarga Indore Nagpur Kolhapur Hyderabad Coimbatore Salem Kanpur Bahraich
Paddy Rice	Raipur Kolhapur Jatni Amritsar Bahraich	Raipur Kolhapur Tadepaligudam Bahraich Manipuri Nizamabad Purnea Darbhanga Palakkad Simoga Durg Amritsar Thanjavur Kanpur Attara
Groundnut	Nandyal Rajkot Bombay Chennai Kanpur	Nandyal Rajkot Bombay Chennai Kanpur Vizianagaram Kapadvanj
Rapeseed and Mustard Seed	Nowgong Purnea Kanpur Hapur Calcutta Delhi Gauhati	Nowgong Purnea Kanpur Hapur Calcutta Delhi Mehasana

Notes: [1] The pre-liberalisation period for wheat is 1/1982 – 6/1988, whilst the pre-liberalisation period for *jowar*, paddy, groundnut and rapeseed/mustard seed is 10/1981 – 2/1988.

[2] The post-liberalisation periods are 1/1992 – 6/1998 for wheat and 10/1991 – 2/1998 for *jowar*, paddy, groundnut and rapeseed/mustard seed.

Table 16.2 shows the non-stationary markets which are common to both periods in bold. There are only two common non-stationary paddy markets, Raipur and Kolhapur. However wheat has seven common markets, rapeseed/mustard seed has six, with *jowar* and groundnut having five each. These numbers should be sufficient to compare changes in these agricultural markets before and after liberalisation.

Table16.2: Markets With Non-Stationary End-of-Month Wholesale Prices (Pre- and Post-Liberalisation Periods) [1 2]

Wheat		*Jowar*		*Paddy Rice*		*Groundnut*		*Rapeseed and Mustard Seed*	
1/1982–6/88	*1/1992-6/98*	*10/1981-2/88*	*10/1991-2/98*	*10/1981-2/88*	*10/1991-2/98*	*10/1981-2/88*	*10/1991-2/98*	*10/1981-2/88*	*10/1991-2/98*
Patna	**Patna**	**Nandyal**	**Nandyal**	**Raipur**	**Raipur**	**Nandyal**	**Nandyal**	**Nowgong**	**Nowgong**
Rajkot	**Rajkot**	**Patan**	**Patan**	**Kolhapur**	**Kolhapur**	**Rajkot**	**Rajkot**	**Purnea**	**Purnea**
Indore	**Indore**	**Gulbarga**	**Gulbarga**	Jatni	Tadepaligudam	**Bombay**	**Bombay**	**Kanpur**	**Kanpur**
Kanpur	**Kanpur**	**Indore**	**Indore**	Amritsar	Bahraich	**Chennai**	**Chennai**	**Hapur**	**Hapur**
Bahraich	**Bahraich**	**Nagpur**	**Nagpur**		Manipuri	**Kanpur**	**Kanpur**	**Calcutta**	**Calcutta**
Delhi	**Delhi**	Madurai	Kolhapur				Vizianagaram	**Delhi**	**Delhi**
Amritsar	**Amritsar**		Hyderabad				Kapadvanj		Mehasana
Mehasana	Karnal		Coimbatore						
	Hapur		Salem						
			Kanpur						
			Bahraich						

Notes: [1] The markets common to both periods are marked in bold. Only those markets which were non-stationary according to the ADF test were included.

[2] The periods for wheat are pre-liberalisation: 1/1982 – 6/1988 and post-liberalisation: 1/1992 – 6/1998. The periods for *jowar*, paddy, groundnut and rapeseed and mustard seed are pre-liberalisation: 10/1981 – 2/1988 and post-liberalisation: 10/1991 – 2/1998.

Table 16.3: Estimated Coefficients of Determination for Each Market Price (Pre- and Post-Liberalisation Periods) [1]

Wheat			*Jowar*			*Paddy Rice*			*Groundnut*			*Rapeseed and Mustard Seed*		
Period [2]	*Pre*	*Post*	*Period* [3]	*Pre*	*Post*	*Period* [3]	*Pre*	*Post*	*Period* [3]	*Pre*	*Post*	*Period* [3]	*Pre*	*Post*
Patna	0.74	0.91	Nandyal	0.45	0.86	Raipur	0.64	0.69	Nandyal	0.90	0.82	Nowgong	0.81	0.46
Rajkot	0.81	0.87	Patan	0.43	0.52	Kolhapur	0.49	0.54	Rajkot	0.82	0.80	Purnea	0.83	0.68
Indore	0.74	0.87	Gulbarga	0.34	0.80	Jatni	0.19		Bombay	0.88	0.86	Kanpur	0.97	0.90
Kanpur	0.89	0.97	Indore	0.49	0.61	Amritsar	0.64		Chennai	0.90	0.83	Hapur	0.96	0.87
Bahraich	0.89	0.96	Nagpur	0.32	0.76	Tadepaligudam		0.68	Kanpur	0.75	0.76	Calcutta	0.94	0.90
Delhi	0.87	0.98	Madurai	0.22[4]		Bahraich		0.71	Vizianagaram		0.68	Delhi	0.96	0.92
Amritsar	0.50	0.96	Kolhapur		0.86	Manipuri		0.76	Kapadvanj		0.70	Mehasana		0.92
Mehasana	0.76		Hyderabad		0.88									
Karnal		0.97	Coimbatore		0.92									
Hapur		0.96	Salem		0.82									
			Kanpur		0.73									
			Bahraich		0.80									
Average	0.78	0.94	Average	0.38	0.78	Average	0.43	0.68	Average	0.85	0.78	Average	0.91	0.81

Notes: [1] The adjusted coefficient of determination, $\overline{R}^2$, was calculated by regressing each market price on all other market prices for each commodity.
[2] The periods for wheat are pre-liberalisation: 1/1982 – 6/1988 and post-liberalisation: 1/1992 – 6/1998.
[3] The periods for *jowar*, paddy, groundnut and rapeseed and mustard seed are pre-liberalisation: 10/1981 – 2/1988 and post-liberalisation: 10/1991 – 2/1998.
[4] The adjusted coefficient of determination (calculated using a constant in each regression) was negative for Madurai, so the coefficient of determination was used.

Table 16.3 reports the estimated adjusted coefficients of determination, $\bar{R}^2$, calculated from the regression of each price against all other prices for each commodity group (listed in Table 16.2) and time period.[2] The average adjusted coefficient of determination increases marginally from 0.78 to 0.94 for wheat and decreases from 0.85 to 0.78 for groundnut and from 0.91 to 0.81 for rapeseed/mustard seed. Despite these changes, the measures indicate considerable interdependence between prices within these commodity groups, for both periods. In comparison, *jowar* and paddy have lower average measures of 0.38 and 0.43 respectively for the first period. Note however, that the average correlation has increased significantly from 0.38 to 0.78 for *jowar* and 0.43 to 0.68 for paddy in the post-liberalisation period. The *jowar* markets with the largest increases in their correlations over the two periods are Nandyal (from 0.45 to 0.86), Gulbarga (from 0.34 to 0.80) and Nagpur (from 0.32 to 0.76). The explanation for the increase in the average $\bar{R}^2$, for paddy rice is different to that for *jowar*. There are only marginal increases in correlation for paddy prices for the Raipur (from 0.64 to 0.69) and Kolhapur (from 0.49 to 0.54) markets. The difference is due to the presence of different paddy markets for the pre and post-liberalisation periods, with the new markets in the second period having larger measures and Jatni having a measure of only 0.19 in the first period.

Analysis of the individual market measures show that some market prices appear less correlated than indicated by the average of the adjusted coefficients of determination. For example the Amritsar market for wheat has an $\bar{R}^2$, of 0.50 (compared to the average of 0.78) for the first period, increasing to 0.96 in the second period. Conversely the measure for the Nowgong market for rapeseed and mustard seed falls from 0.81 to 0.46, which is well below the average of 0.81 for the post-liberalisation period.

In summary we note that, with only a few exceptions, the end-of-month wholesale market prices for wheat, groundnut and rapeseed/mustard seed are highly correlated for the pre and post-liberalisation periods. The markets for *jowar* and paddy demonstrate much lower correlations in the first period, which increase to relatively high correlations in the second period.

3. Formal estimation of the market price relationships

We now want to examine more closely the tentative conclusion from the preceding section, that important Indian agricultural markets are becoming

---

[2] This measure was preferred to the pairwise correlation coefficient because it summarises the relationships between the relatively large number of prices variables for each commodity and time period.

increasingly integrated. It is certainly possible that the observed high correlations (in the form of large adjusted coefficients of determination) may be spurious due to the presence of common time trends in the price data series. It was reported in the preceding section that all of the market prices included in the correlation analysis were found to be non-stationarity, $I(1)$, according to the augmented Dickey–Fuller test. So there is the possibility that the correlations reflect temporal trends rather than close behavioural relations between the prices. Moreover the presence of non-stationarity introduces problems of statistical inference for the ordinary least squares estimator of the variance of the parameters. The variance and associated t-statistic are undefined so that the normal tests of statistical significance of the parameters cannot be conducted.

It is therefore necessary to estimate the price relationships with cointegration techniques in a non-stationary framework. The Engle-Granger framework restricts itself to pairwise analysis and ignores the simultaneous interdependencies of prices across markets (see the adjusted coefficient of determination reported in Table 16.3). To address this issue we examine the simultaneous vector autoregressive process (VAR) for the $n \times 1$ vector of market prices, $\underline{p}_t$:

$$\underline{p}_t = \Theta + \sum_{s=1}^{k} \Phi_s \underline{p}_{t-s} + \sum_{\tau=0}^{l} \Psi_\tau \underline{x}_{t-\tau}, \quad \forall t = 1, 2, \ldots, T \tag{1}$$

The VAR has general error correction mechanism

$$\text{(ECM)}: \Delta \underline{p}_t = \Theta + \sum_{s=1}^{k-1} \Gamma_s \Delta \underline{p}_{t-s} + \Pi \underline{p}_{t-k} + \sum_{\tau=0}^{l} \Psi_\tau \underline{x}_{t-\tau},$$

$$\forall t = 1, 2, \ldots, T \tag{2}$$

with $\Pi \underline{p}_{t-k}$ matrix:

$$\Pi \underline{p}_{t-k} = \begin{bmatrix} \pi_{10} & \pi_{11} & . & . & \pi_{1n} \\ \pi_{20} & \pi_{21} & . & . & \pi_{2n} \\ . & . & & & . \\ . & . & & & . \\ \pi_{n0} & \pi_{n1} & . & . & \pi_{nn} \end{bmatrix} \begin{bmatrix} 1 \\ p_{1,t-k} \\ . \\ . \\ p_{n,t-k} \end{bmatrix} \tag{3}$$

The VAR and ECMs can be estimated using Johansen's full information maximum likelihood (FIML) estimation.[3] Johansen's model selection

[3] See Johansen (1991, 1995), Johansen and Juselius (1992) and Pesaran and Pesaran (1997).

criteria can be used to test for the length of the lag, *k* and the rank, *r* of the Π matrix.[4] The Johansen method decomposes the $n\times(n+1)$ coefficient matrix, Π, into two conjoint vectors, given by $\Pi=\underline{\alpha}\underline{\beta}$. The $\underline{\beta}$ vector includes the parameters for the long run cointegrating vectors and the $\underline{\alpha}$ vector determines the error correction process. The rank, $1\leq r\leq n$ of Π will indicate the minimum number of market prices necessary to describe the price system for each agricultural commodity. If the rank of the Π matrix is unity $(r=1)$, then only one market price is required to explain all other market prices for the commodity. This means that the markets are fully integrated with the law of one price applying. On the other hand if Π has full rank $(r=n)$ then all of the market prices are required to fully explain the behaviour of the commodity prices, which means that markets are not integrated at all.[5] For other values, $1<r<n$, the rank will indicate the degree of the interdependencies between market prices, with a lower value indicating a higher degree of market integration.[6]

The rank, *r* establishes the number of $r\times 1$ long run cointegrating vectors of prices, $\underline{\beta}\underline{p}_t$, with the reduced rank, $\underline{\beta}\subset\Pi$ having dimension $r\times(n+1)$. The cointegrating vectors given by:

$$\underline{\beta}\underline{p}=\begin{bmatrix}\beta_{10} & \beta_{11} & . & . & \beta_{1n}\\ \beta_{20} & \beta_{21} & . & . & \beta_{2n}\\ . & . & & & .\\ . & . & & & .\\ \beta_{r0} & \beta_{r1} & . & . & \beta_{rn}\end{bmatrix}\begin{bmatrix}1\\ p_1\\ .\\ .\\ p_n\end{bmatrix} \tag{5}$$

are stationary, $\underline{\beta}\underline{p}_t \sim I(0)$. The mth cointegrating vector for $1\leq m\leq r$ is therefore:

$$\left\{\beta_{m0}+\beta_{m1}p_1+\beta_{m2}p_2+\ldots+\beta_{mi}p_i+\ldots+\beta_{mj}p_j+\ldots+\beta_{mn}p_n\right\} \tag{6}$$

and normalising for p_i gives:

---

4 The model selection measures include the Schwarz Bayesian (SBC), Hann–Quinn (HQC) and Akaike Information (AIC) criteria, as well as the likelihood ratio (LR) rank and maximal eigenvalue tests.

5 Full rank also means the system of prices is stationary, *I*(0).

6 A value of $r=0$ indicates there is no cointegrating relationship. This means that no long run relationship exists between the market prices.

$$p_i = -\frac{\beta_{m0}}{\beta_{mi}} - \frac{\beta_{m1}}{\beta_{mi}} p_1 - \frac{\beta_{m2}}{\beta_{mi}} p_2 - \ldots - \frac{\beta_{mj}}{\beta_{mi}} p_j - \ldots - \frac{\beta_{mn}}{\beta_{mi}} p_n . \tag{7}$$

Given that $p_i = \ln P_i$, $\forall i = 1, 2, \ldots, n$, the ratio of coefficients for each price defines an elasticity:

$$\varepsilon_{ij}^m = \frac{\partial p_i}{\partial p_j} = -\frac{\beta_{mj}}{\beta_{mi}}, \quad \forall\, 1 \le i, j \le n,\ i \ne j \tag{8}$$

This 'cross-price' elasticity measures the proportionate change in the market price *i* in response to a proportionate change in the market price *j*. Whilst it is a pairwise measure, it is derived from the mth cointegrating vector (6) which specifies the linear combination of all the prices in long run equilibrium.

Johansen's full information maximum likelihood (FIML) method can be used to provide efficient and consistent estimates of the $\hat{\beta}_{ij}$ coefficients and their standard errors. However this requires each of the *r* cointegrating vectors to be exactly identified by *r* restrictions on the price variables in each cointegrating vector. Whilst the normalisation of (6) to give (7) provides one restriction, another $r-1$ zero restrictions are necessary. The procedure adopted here was to omit the $r-1$ prices with the smallest coefficients from the cointegrating vector.[7] The number of significant cross-price elasticities found in the cointegrating relationships will importantly indicate the degree of market integration in long run equilibrium.

The effects of changes in the constant term on each of the *n* market prices can also be calculated from normalised m^{th} cointegrating vector:

$$\varepsilon_{i0}^m = -\frac{\beta_{m0}}{\beta_{mi}}, \quad \forall i = 1, 2, \ldots, n \tag{9}$$

This elasticity measures the proportionate 'non-price' effects on long run equilibrium prices.[8]

The other component of the decomposition of $\Pi = \underline{\alpha}\underline{\beta}$ is the $n \times r$ matrix $\underline{\alpha}$, which describes the error correction (ECM) responses of the *n*

---

[7] If the restrictions coincided across the cointegrating coefficients, the next smallest coefficient was restricted to zero.

[8] These effects are additional to those which become incorporated into the equilibrium market prices over time.

market prices to short run deviations from the long run equilibrium price relationships, $\underline{\beta}\underline{p}$, i.e.:

$$\begin{bmatrix} \Delta p_1 \\ \Delta p_2 \\ \cdot \\ \cdot \\ \cdot \\ \Delta p_n \end{bmatrix} = \begin{bmatrix} \alpha_{11} & \alpha_{12} & \cdot & \cdot & \alpha_{1r} \\ \alpha_{21} & \alpha_{22} & \cdot & \cdot & \alpha_{2r} \\ \cdot & \cdot & \cdot & \cdot & \cdot \\ \cdot & \cdot & \cdot & \cdot & \cdot \\ \cdot & \cdot & \cdot & \cdot & \cdot \\ \alpha_{n1} & \alpha_{n2} & \cdot & \cdot & \alpha_{nr} \end{bmatrix} \underline{\beta}\underline{p} \tag{10}$$

For market price *i* with the mth cointegrating vector, $1 \le m \le r$:

$$\Delta p_i^m = \alpha_{im}\underline{\beta}_m\underline{p}, \quad \forall i = 1, 2, \ldots, n \tag{11}$$

where $\underline{\beta}_m$ represents the mth row of the $\underline{\beta}$ matrix. The expected sign of α_{im} is negative, indicating a short run deviation of the price in the ith market from the long run cointegrating vector of prices, will cause the price to return towards the equilibrium. Since α_{im} determines the proportionate responsiveness of prices to disequilibrium we call this measure the 'equilibrating price' elasticity.

4. Estimation results

Given the assumption that agricultural commodity prices are fully revealing the $\underline{x}$ matrix in the VAR model (1) and ECM extension (2) was restricted to include only non-stochastic dummy variables. These variables comprised eleven seasonal dummy variables for the months of January to November for each commodity.[9] Structural dummy variables were also included for the periods listed in Table 16.4. Whilst *jowar* appeared unaffected in the pre-liberalisation period there was apparent structural changes for paddy in 1982–83, rapeseed/mustard seed in 1983–85, wheat in 1984–85 and groundnut in 1986–88. The post- liberalisation period appeared to be more consistent with a common period of structural changes in 1991/2–93 for wheat, *jowar* and rapeseed/mustard seed. The observed change for groundnut occurred later in 1993–95, whilst paddy experienced structural

[9] The constant term π_{i0} for $1 \le r \le n$ was included in the ECM and β_{m0} was included in each of the $1 \le m \le r$ cointegrating vectors.

change over the combined period 1991–95. There were other periods of structural change (especially towards the end of the second period for wheat) although it was decided to limit their use, consistent with our wish to evaluate how effective prices equilibrate across agricultural markets.

The first step in the Johansen estimation procedure is to determine the optimum lag length, *k*, of the VAR and ECM model represented by (1) and (2) above. Both the Schwarz Bayesian criterion (SBC) and the adjusted likelihood ratio (LR) test indicate a uniform lag of order 1. This indicates that these commodity markets equilibrate relatively quickly over one to two months.

The second step is to determine the ranks of the price system for each commodity and time period. The estimated eigenvalues of the first order cointegrating VAR, with restricted intercept and no trend, are listed in Table 16.5, for each commodity and period. Selecting the rank of the system was not straightforward because of the frequent disagreement between the model selection criteria including the SBC, Akaike Information (AIC) and Hann–Quinn (HQC) criteria as well as the likelihood ratio trace and maximum eigenvalue tests. Since the SBC is consistent for large samples when the 'true' model is known, then under the assumption of efficient markets with prices revealing the true unknown model, the SBC measure will be the most consistent. So the SBC measure was used to select generally lower values of the rank and only when the other measures collectively indicated a higher rank, this value was chosen.

Table 16.4: Selected Periods for Structural Dummy Variables

	Sample Period	*Dummy Variable Period*
Wheat	1/1982 – 6/1988	3/1984 – 7/1985
	1/1992 – 6/1998	1/1992 – 3/1993
Jowar	10/1981 – 2/1988	-
	10/1991 – 2/1998	10/1991 – 3/1993
Paddy Rice	10/1981 – 2/1988	7/1982 – 10/1983
	10/1991 – 2/1998	10/1991 – 1/1995
Groundnut	10/1981 – 2/1988	3/1986 – 2/1988
	10/1991 – 2/1998	10/1993 – 8/1995
Rapeseed and Mustard Seed	10/1981 – 2/1988	12/1983 – 8/1985
	10/1991 – 2/1998	10/1991 – 3/1993

Note: [1] **The structural dummy variable took the value one for the designated period (inclusive) and zero elsewhere.**

The eigenvalues are shown in bold in Table 16.5. The commodities which have a rank of three are wheat and rapeseed/mustard seed for both periods, groundnut for the first period and paddy for the second period. *Jowar* and paddy appear to have a rank of one for the pre-liberalisation period, implying perfect market integration. However the ranks for paddy and *jowar* increase to three and four respectively in the second period.[10] The rank for groundnut also increases to four in the post-liberalisation period.

Table 16.6 summarises the Johansen FIML results. The proportion of all possible cross-price elasticities, which are significant at the 10 per cent level, are shown in column four. Wheat and paddy have the highest proportions. Interestingly, these proportions increased from 45 per cent to 58 per cent over the two periods for wheat whilst the proportions for paddy increased from 33 per cent to 55 per cent. The markets for rapeseed and mustard seed started from a much lower proportion of 7 per cent in the first period but increased to 21 per cent in the post-liberalisation period. This evidence suggests that these markets are becoming increasingly integrated with agricultural market liberalisation. Note the contrasting results for the *jowar* and (to a lesser extent) groundnut markets which have experienced large reductions in the proportion of significant cross-price elasticities in the post-liberalisation period. The proportions for *jowar* have fallen from a relatively high value of 40 per cent in the first period to a very low 5 per cent in the second period. There has also been a significant fall in the proportions for groundnut from 45 per cent to 19 per cent over the two periods.

The calculated averages of these significant cross-price elasticities are shown in column five of Table 16.6. These elasticities measure the proportional change in a market price relative to a proportional change in another market price, conditional on all equilibrium prices in the long run cointegrating vector (8). Column five of Table 16.6 shows the averages for *jowar* and rapeseed and mustard seed are lower than for wheat. There has been a significant increase in the average cross-price elasticity for paddy from 1.77 to 2.87 whilst the groundnut elasticity has fallen dramatically from a high of 3.58 to 1.25. These results tell a very different story to the analysis presented earlier in this chapter using the adjusted coefficients of determination. Our new results show that paddy is experiencing increasing market integration since liberalisation, they also clearly indicate the markets for *jowar* and groundnut have experienced significantly lower levels of market integration in the post-liberalisation period.

---

[10] Because of the difficulty in determining the ranks it was decided to not conclude that the markets for *jowar* and paddy were perfectly integrated in the first period. The elasticities will be examined to determine this.

Table 16.5: Estimated Eigenvalues in Descending Order (Pre- and Post-Liberalisation Periods) [1]

Wheat		*Jowar*		*Paddy Rice*		*Groundnut*		*Rapeseed and Mustard Seed*	
1/1982–6/88	*1/1992-6/98*	*10/1981-2/88*	*10/1991-2/98*	*10/1981-2/88*	*10/1991-2/98*	*10/1981-2/88*	*10/1991-2/98*	*10/1981-2/88*	*10/1991-2/98*
0.55	***0.74***	***0.53***	***0.69***	***0.35***	***0.42***	***0.51***	***0.48***	***0.53***	***0.61***
0.51	***0.63***	0.36	***0.67***	0.25	***0.33***	***0.41***	***0.42***	***0.44***	***0.51***
0.43	***0.59***	0.17	***0.64***	0.18	***0.24***	***0.30***	***0.39***	***0.34***	***0.38***
0.31	0.47	0.14	***0.51***	0.05	0.13	0.17	***0.34***	0.28	0.31
0.30	0.34	0.10	0.45		0.04	0.01	0.26	0.20	0.23
0.18	0.29	0.06	0.38				0.21	0.02	0.16
0.07	0.24		0.34				0.01		0.10
0.03	0.17		0.28						
	0.14		0.19						
			0.10						
			0.03						

Note: [1] **The eigenvalues selected to determine the rank *r* of the Π matrix are marked in bold italics. The eigenvalues were selected according to the Schwarz Bayesian (SBC), Hann-Quinn (HQC) and Akaike Information (AIC) criteria, and the likelihood ratio (LR) rank and maximal eigenvalue tests.**

Table 16.6: Johansen FIML estimate results using end-of-month wholesale prices

Commodity Pre-liberalisation Post-liberalisation	*Number of Non-Stationary Markets (n)*	*Estimated Rank* $(\hat{r})$	*Percent of Significant Cross-Price Elasticities* [1] $(\frac{\tilde{n}}{n(n-1)}\times 100)$	*Average Cross-Price Elasticity* [2] $(-\frac{1}{\tilde{n}^2}\sum_{i,j=1, i\neq j}^{\tilde{n}}\frac{\hat{\beta}_{mj}}{\hat{\beta}_{mi}})$	*Average Non-Price Elasticity* [3] $(-\frac{1}{\bar{n}}\sum_{i=1}^{\bar{n}}\frac{\hat{\beta}_{m0}}{\hat{\beta}_{mi}})$	*Average Equilibrating Price Elasticity* [4] $(\frac{1}{\underset{\sim}{n}}\sum_{i=1}^{\underset{\sim}{n}}\hat{\alpha}_{im})$
Wheat						
1/1982–6/1988	8	3	45	1.55	1.93	-0.11
1/1992–6/1990	9	4	58	1.70	1.05	-0.14
Jowar						
10/1981–2/1988	6	1	40	0.78	-0.49	-0.16
10/1991–2/1998	11	4	5	0.85	-	-0.24
Paddy Rice						
10/1981–2/1988	4	1	33	1.77	-	-0.16
10/1991–2/1998	5	3	55	2.87	-1.84	-0.82
Groundnut						
10/1981–2/1988	5	3	45	3.58	0.51	0.01
10/199–2/1998	7	4	19	1.25	-0.28	0.13
Rapeseed/Mustard Seed						
10/1981–2/1988	6	3	7	0.65	-	0.18
10/1991–2/1998	7	3	21	-0.24	-	-0.08

Notes: [1] Measured as the number of significant cross-price elasticities (at the 10 per cent level), $\tilde{n}$, as the percentage of all possible cross-price elasticities, $n(n-1)$.

[2] Only those $\tilde{n}$ coefficients, which are significant at the 10 per cent level, are included in the calculation of the average.

[3] Only those $\bar{n}$ coefficients, which are significant at the 10 per cent level, are included in the calculation of the average.

[4] Only the most significant coefficient (which is greater than the 5 per cent level) is included for each market. The average is calculated from the sum of these $\underset{\sim}{n}$ coefficients. A negative error correction sign shows the price reverts to the long run equilibrium value.

Columns six and seven of Table 16.6 provide some additional information on the behaviour of market prices. The average of the significant non-price elasticity measures indicates that not all effects are incorporated in the prices for wheat and to some extent groundnut. The last column shows the averages of the ECMs which are significant at the 5 per cent level. These indicate the proportionate short run responsiveness of prices to return to equilibrium when shocked from equilibrium. The markets for wheat, *jowar* and especially paddy show the increasing abilities of these markets to equilibrate in the short run. The increasing average elasticity for *jowar* (from -0.16 to -0.24) is consistent with individual *jowar* markets relying on their own equilibrating mechanisms, whilst experienceing less integration with other *jowar* markets. However the average elasticity of 0.13 for the groundnut markets in the second period implies that prices will on average overshoot the equilibrium. This instability, along with the changing non-price elasticity effects and the diminishing degree of market integration of groundnut give reason for concern.

Whilst these comparisons of average elasticities over the pre and post-liberalisation periods give a valuable general impression of the degree of market integration, we need to be careful because we are comparing different markets for some commodities over the two time periods. This is particularly true for *jowar* and paddy markets listed in Table 16.2. Tables 16.7 to 16.10 detail the individual cross-price elasticities for the markets which appear in both the pre and post-liberalisation periods. The bold entries in Table 16.2 show wheat has seven markets which are common to both periods, *jowar* and groundnut have five markets each, with rapeseed and mustard seed having six. Paddy has only two markets common to both periods because price data were only available for five paddy markets in the first period and only five of the fifteen paddy markets were non-stationary in the second period. These markets, Raipur and Kolhapur, did not have any significant cross-price elasticities and so no tabulated results are included in Tables 16.7 to 16.10.

The significant (10 per cent) cross-price elasticities for wheat are shown in Table 16.7. Where there were more than one significant cross-price elasticity for the r cointegrating vectors the elasticity with the highest t-statistic was reported. The bold elasticities on top in each cell apply to the second period whilst the italic figures below refer to the first period. Each elasticity represents the percent change in the equilibrium price for the market listed in the left hand column of each row, which is associated with a one percent change in the equilibrium price for the market listed at the head of the relevant column. For example, in the post-liberalisation period a one per cent increase in the equilibrium price for wheat in the Rajkot market will cause an elastic 2.2 per cent increase in the Indore equilibrium price. Compare this with the inelastic response of 0.7 per cent for the Kanpur price. The elasticities for the second period show that Patna and Indore are very sensitive to changes in the equilibrium prices of the other wheat markets, but not to each other. Overall, the proportion of all possible elasticities which are significant, has increased from 40 per cent to 69 per cent over the two periods.

For *jowar* only 30 per cent of the elasticities being significant in the earlier period and no significant elasticities for the post-liberalisation period (Table 16.8). Nandyal and Nagpur markets are not related to any of the other *jowar* markets for both periods. Contrast this with results from Table 16.3. The increase in the $\bar{R}^2$ for the Gulbarga market was 0.34 to 0.80 yet unlike these other markets, Table 16.8 shows there were two significant cross-price elasticities in the first period with the Patan and Indore markets. The simultaneity and temporal effects appear complicated and very important.

The estimated elasticities for groundnut (Table 16.9) show the proportion of significant elasticities have fallen from 45 per cent to 25 per cent. Nandyal had three significant highly elastic measures in the first period and none in the second. Table 16.10 shows the proportions of significant elasticities increased from 7 per cent to 17 per cent for rapeseed and mustard seed. The main links in the post-liberalisation period appear between the Kanpur and Hapur markets and the Calcutta and Delhi markets.

5. Conclusion

This chapter considers the extent of market integration for important Indian food crop markets prior to and after the agricultural food crop marketing liberalisation reforms in the early 1990s. The degree of market integration was considered in terms of the finding of significant interdependencies between end-of-month wholesale commodity prices for wheat, *jowar*, paddy rice, groundnut, rapeseed and mustard seed. The chapter critiques the approaches taken in other studies which rely on correlation analysis and single equation Engle-Granger cointegration techniques. Both approaches are restricted to pairwise analyses of market price data which contradicts the idea of testing for market integration. Attempts to consider the simultaneity effects were incorporated into preliminary analysis of this chapter using the adjusted coefficient of determination, derived from regressing each market price against all other market prices for the commodity and time period. These initial findings strongly imply that the degree of market integration for *jowar* and paddy has increased significantly from a low level to around the higher levels for wheat, groundnut and rapeseed/mustard seed.

Table 16.7: Estimated Equilibrium Cross-Price Elasticities: Wheat [1,2]

	Patna	Rajkot	Indore	Kanpur	Bahraich	Delhi	Amritsar
Patna		5.5 -	- *-1.5*	-6.2 *-1.9*	5.2 *2.1*	- *3.6*	8.9 -
Rajkot	0.2 -		- -	1.1 -	-1.0 -	3.5 -	-1.6 *0.8*
Indore	- -	2.2 -		-2.7 *-0.7*	-1.9 -	- *2.8*	-2.3 -
Kanpur	- *-0.5*	0.7 *-0.3*	- -1.4		1.4 *1.1*	-1.1 3.7	0.8 -
Bahraich	- *0.5*	-0.5 *0.3*	-0.6 -	0.7 *0.9*		0.8 -	-1.1 -
Delhi	- -	0.7 -	- *0.4*	-0.9 -	1.2 -		- -
Amritsar	- -	-0.9 *1.2*	-0.3 -	1.3 -	-0.9 -	- -	

Notes: [1]**Only the most significant elasticities (at 10 per cent or better) are include in this table. Insignificant estimates are indicated with '-'.**

[2] **The bold figures on top represent the elasticities for the second period January, 1992 to June, 1998 whilst the italicised figures below represent the elasticities for the first period January 1982 to June 1988.**

Table 16.8: Estimated Equilibrium Cross-Price Elasticities: Jowar [1 2]

	Nandyal	*Patan*	*Gulbarga*	*Indore*	*Nagpur*
Nandyal		- -	- -	- -	- -
Patan	- -		- *1.4*	- *2.0*	- -
Gulbarga	- -	- *0.7*		- *-1.5*	- -
Indore	- -	- *0.5*	- *-0.7*		- -
Nagpur	- -	- -	- -	- -	

Notes: [1] Only the most significant elasticities (at 10 per cent or better) are include in this table. Insignificant estimates are indicated with '-' .

[2] The bold figures on top represent the elasticities for the second period October, 1991 to February, 1998 whilst the italicised figures below represent the elasticities for the first period October 1981 to February 1988.

Table 16.9: Estimated Equilibrium Cross-Price Elasticities: Groundnut [1 2]

	Nandyal	Rajkot	Bombay	Chennai	Kanpur
Nandyal		- *6.3*	- *0.6*	- -	- -
Rajkot	- *3.6*		0.6 -	- -	- *0.7*
Bombay	- *1.7*	1.6 -		- *0.7*	- -
Chennai	- -	1.1 -	- *0.7*		0.5 -
Kanpur	- *4.9*	- *1.4*	- -	1.9 -	

Notes: [1] Only the most significant elasticities (at 10 per cent or better) are include in this table. Insignificant estimates are indicated with '-' .

[2] The bold figures on top represent the elasticities for the second period October, 1991 to February, 1998 whilst the italicised figures below represent the elasticities for the first period October 1981 to February 1988.

Table 16.10: Estimated Equilibrium Cross-Price Elasticities: Rapeseed and Mustard Seed[1 2]

	Nowgong	Purnea	Kanpur	Hapur	Calcutta	Delhi
Nowgong		- -	-3.4 -	- *3.6*	- -	- -
Purnea	- -		- -	- -	- -	- -
Kanpur	- -	- -		0.9 -	- -	- -
Hapur	- *0.3*	- -	1.1 -		- -	- -
Calcutta	- -	- -	- -	- -		0.7 -
Delhi	- -	- -	- -	- -	1.4 -	

Notes: [1] Only the most significant elasticities (at 10 per cent or better) are include in this table. Insignificant estimates are indicated with '-' .

[2] The bold figures on top represent the elasticities for the second period October, 1991 to February, 1998 whilst the italicised figures below represent the elasticities for the first period October 1981 to February 1988.

The Johansen full information maximum likelihood method allowed the efficient and consistent estimation of long run equilibrium cross-price elasticities. These results show that the markets for *jowar* and groundnut, whilst originally at a relatively high level of integration, were becoming significantly less integrated after agricultural liberalisation. These findings are in direct contrast to the preliminary correlation analysis using adjusted coefficients of determination, which implied significantly increasing degrees of market integration. In contrast, the preferred Johansen method found that the markets for wheat and paddy, which were originally at high levels of integration, further increased in the 1990s. The markets for rapeseed and mustard seed were found to start at lower levels of integration prior to liberalisation, which increased significantly after liberalisation, but were still behind the degrees of market integration for wheat and paddy.

The responses to disequilibrating shocks to commodity prices indicate that wheat, paddy and *jowar* markets are effective in returning to equilibrium in the short run. However the markets for groundnut demonstrate short run overshooting of market prices to equilibrium in the post-liberalisation period. This instability is problematic for policy makers given the findings of significantly lower levels of market integration for groundnut after agricultural market liberalisation.

References

Engle, R. and C. Granger, 'Co-integration and Error Correction: Representation and Testing', *Econometrica*, 55 (1987) 251–76.

Johansen, D., 'Food Security and World Trade Prospects: Invited Address to the American Agricultural Economics Association', *American Journal of Agricultural Economics: Proceedings*, 80 (1998) 941–7.

Johansen, S., 'Estimation and Hypothesis Testing of Cointegrating Vectors in Gaussian Vector Autoregressive Models ', *Econometrica*, 59 (1991) 1551–80.

Johansen, S., *Likelihood Based Inference on Cointegration in the Vector Autoregressive Model* (Melbourne: Oxford University Press, 1995).

Johansen, S. and K. Juselius, 'Testing Structural Hypotheses in a Multivariate Cointegration Analysis of the PPP and UIP for UK', *Journal of Econometrics*, 53 (1992) 211–44.

Palaskas, T. and B. Harriss-White, 'Testing Market Integration: New Approaches with Case Material from West Bengal Food Economy', *Journal of Development Studies*, 30 (1993) 1–57.

Pesaran, M. and B. Pesaran, *Working With Microfit 4.0 Interactive Econometric Analysis* (Melbourne: Oxford University Press, 1997).

Wilson E.J., 'Testing Integration of Agricultural Produce Markets In India: Conceptual and Empirical Considerations Using Wholesale Prices', in S.S. Acharya and D.P. Chaudhri (eds) *Indian Agricultural Policy at the Crossroads: Priorities and Agenda* (Jaipur: Rawat Publications, 2001) pp. 213–46.

17

Indian Software Industry: Growth Patterns, Constraints And Government Initiatives

Chandana Chakraborty and Dilip Dutta

1. Introduction

Measured by age, the computer or information technology (IT) software industry in India is still in its infancy. Yet, its growth has caught the attention of the world market, so much so that India now is identified as the major powerhouse for incremental development of computer software. This attention is not due as much to the size of the industry but its rapid growth rate during the 1990s and its projected growth rate in the first decade of the new century. According to the National Association of Software and Services Companies (NASSCOM), India's quasi-governmental software industry promotion organization, the software industry in India was worth Rs.243.5 billion or US$5.7 billion in 1999–2000, whereas ten years back its worth was not more than Rs.3 billion or US$150 million.[1]

Although India's domestic software market is burgeoning fast, exports have been more important.[2] In rupee terms the compound annual growth rate (CAGR) for India's software export revenues over the past five years has, according to NASSCOM, been as high as 62.3 per cent — compared to 46.8 per cent of CAGR for its domestic market revenue during the same period. With a modest beginning in 1984–85, software exports have moved up from Rs.25.2 billion or US$734 million in 1995–96, to

1 Statistics are obtained from www.nasscom.org/template/itinindia.htm.

2 Heeks (1996) and Wheatley (1997) provide time series on India's software export earnings for the earlier period of 1980–1996. Recent figures on export earnings are obtained from the National Association of Software and Services Companies (NASSCOM) web-site (*www.nasscom.org*), which are 61 per cent in 1994–95, 64 per cent in 1995–96, 55 per cent in 1996–97, 67 per cent in 1997–98, 68 per cent in 1998–99 and 57 per cent in 1999–2000.

Rs.171.5 billion or US$4 billion in 1999–2000.[3] NASSCOM's survey in 2000 indicates that more than 185 of Fortune 500 companies, i.e., almost two out of every five global giants, outsourced their software requirements to India during 1999–2000.

The set of factors fueling the demand for Indian software services in the world market includes the following. Cost is an obvious, although diminishing, factor. As reported in *Business Week* (26 February 2001), with a booming domestic and export market, the gap between Indian software professionals and their counterparts in the developed countries has started to narrow. Furthermore, worldwide interest in business process reengineering; the economic imperatives in developed countries of outsourcing; cost-efficient maintenance of existing mainframe systems, and continuous development of new software for personal computers (PCs), have all played significant roles. Finally, India's comparative advantage in the software industry is grounded in its relative abundance of qualified software engineers, coupled with the government's timely national action plan for rapidly improving communications infrastructure. As is evidenced by the rapid growth in demand, Indian software engineers have made themselves known in the world market for providing an unconquerable combination of quality software at a relatively low cost; Vijayan (1996) observes that Indian software developers offer a cost advantage of 40 per cent to 60 per cent over their American counterparts.

This chapter attempts to provide an analytical framework to examine the organization and the size of the software industry in India as well as the role of government in this sector's rapid growth. Organizational structure and size are key determinants of the strength of an industry. Both factors receive close attention in this chapter. Organization is discussed in terms of the industry's legal structure and degree of concentration. The size of the industry is analyzed by examining the relative significance of its domestic and export markets. In addition, we examine the industry's strength in generating employment and its impact on national economy.

Analysis regarding the industry's structure and organization is based on the reports of a preliminary survey conducted among a wide group of software related companies in India.[4] Because of our particular interest in patterns of growth, we decided to include a variety of software companies engaged in activities ranging from software development to custom designing and programming. For balance, we decided to survey relatively newer companies in addition to the leading software groups. More than 200

---

[3] Recent estimate, Merchant (2001), suggests that export sales of software services will grow to $6.3 billion for the current year.

[4] The first author conducted the survey while spending her sabbatical in IIM, Bangalore, India in 1999.

questionnaires were sent to selected companies in the major cities of India, including Bangalore, Chennai, Hyderabad, Pune, Mumbai and Calcutta. 35 per cent of the questionnaires were returned with completed responses. The respondent firms include leading software groups as well as those with future potential, and represent a range of activities related to software development and servicing. Information offered by the respondent firms has been processed to generate data for the present study.

2. Organization and Structure of the Industry

The computer software industry is by no means easily defined. Hence, there is scope for disagreement regarding which groups of firms should be included in the industry or how to describe the structure of the industry. In assessing the size and growth of the Indian software industry, we have followed the definition provided by the standard industrial classification codes (SIC) of the US government, specifically the 1987 revised codes, which includes nine industries in this category. We view the following three groups of firms as defining the 'core' software industry in India: custom computer programming services; custom designing services; and prepackaged software services.[5] In India, software developers, in general, choose to have their sources of revenue linked to a variety of activities and not to a specialized line of services; the definition of programming services therefore needs to be broadened to accommodate commonly performed activities, such as data processing, body shopping and manpower training. The category of custom computer designing services needs to be modified to include custom software designing as well as designing of integrated systems. With these criteria the organizational structure of the sample companies surveyed is shown in Table 17.1.

The organizational structure of the computer software industry in India is dominated by private limited companies 37 out of 68. The significance of the privately organized companies is visible across the industry groups listed. The majority of the companies in each of the three groups listed are private limited companies. This might be indicative of the influence of liberalization policies of the Indian government. Despite the popular belief regarding the contribution of the major microelectronics corporations

[5] As per the 1987 revision of SIC codes, the basic computer software industry is defined to be composed of the following nine product and service groups: i) Custom Computer Programming Services (SIC 7371); ii) Pre-Packaged Software (SIC 7372); iii) Computer Integrated Systems Design (SIC 7373); iv) Data Processing and Preparation (SIC 7374); v) Information Retrieval Services (SIC 7375); vi) Computer Facilities Management (SIC 7376); vii) Computer Rental and Leasing (7377); viii) Computer Maintenance and Repair (SIC 7378); and, ix) Computer Related Services NES (SIC 7379).

of the West in creating production facilities in India, subsidiary organizations, as per our sample, define only a small proportion of the software industry groups. Only 12 of the 68 respondents reported having a parent organization outside India, (in the UK or the US).

Table 17.1: Industry Organization: Computer Software

Structure	Custom Programming	Prepackaged Software	Custom Designing	Total
Private Limited	15	16	6	37
Public Limited	8	7	4	19
Subsidiary	8	3	1	12
Total	31	26	11	68

Source: Authors' compilation of survey results

Given the relative youth of the Indian software industry, time series data on growth of establishments are difficult to obtain. Most of the companies in our sample report their date of establishment to be between 1992–1995, a period of rapid growth. The vast majority of the firms in the software industry are small, with only 11 claiming an asset size larger than Rs.300 million. This resembles the structure of the software industry in Western Europe described in Mowery (1996). Table 17.2 describes the concentration of firms in the industry. Companies engaged in packaged software services and custom computer programming services account for the major share of industry assets. Custom designing services account for only 19 per cent of the total assets.

The small asset share of the group of custom designing firms explains their negligible contribution to total business revenue. All the custom designing companies together define only 17 per cent of the business revenue; a meagre Rs.2596 million out of a total of approximately Rs.14 billion. Although the average size of the companies providing programming services is relatively small, they are the largest source of revenue for the aggregate industry; together, these companies earn 45 per cent of total business revenue.[6] As individual entities, however, only 15 claim revenues in excess of Rs.500 million.

6 As explained by Kopetz (1993) contract programming usually appears to be an interesting activity for developing countries. It requires little capital investment, other than state-of-the art training facilities and access to an international electronic network.

Table 17. 2. Industry Concentration: Computer Software

Industry Group	*No. of Firms*	*Total Assets (millions of rupees)*	*Firms with asset size more than Rs.300 mil*	*Total Revenue (millions of rupees)*	*Firms with more than Rs.500 mil in revenue*	*Industry revenue concentration of 4 largest firms*
Custom Programming	31	3224	2	6240.3	5	32.1%
Prepackaged Software	26	3228	6	5070.0	7	39.6%
Custom Designing	11	1562	3	2596.0	3	72.3%
Core Industry	68	8114	11	13906.3	15	53.4%

Source: Authors' compilation of survey results

The industry groups of programming and prepackaged software services do not appear to have a significant share. The four largest firms in programming services account for only 32.1 per cent of total business revenue in that group. For prepackaged software services, the four largest firms claim slightly over 39 per cent of the group revenues. Interestingly, companies related to custom designing services appear to be highly concentrated; the four largest firms in this group earn 72.3 per cent of the total revenue.

3. Employment Potential

The significance and strength of the computer software industry can be estimated by its contribution to employment growth. In the absence of time series data, the growth rate of employment could not be computed directly. We examined the employment impact of the industry taking note of the actual levels of employment in the three different groups described above, together with their share in total industry employment and national employment. Results are presented in Table 17.3.

Because of their relatively large numbers, companies providing custom computer programming services constitute the major source of employment in the Indian software industry, accounting for more than 47 per cent of total industry employment. The companies grouped under packaged software services play an almost equally significant role (45.96 per cent of total industry employment). Companies engaged in custom designing services have a relatively insignificant presence (6.8 per cent of total industry employment).

Table 17.3: Employment in Core Software Industry of India (1000s of employees)

	Custom Computer Programming	Prepackaged Software	Custom Designing	Total
No. of Employees (thousands)	18.63	18.12	2.68	39.43
Share of industry Employment	47.24%	45.96%	6.8%	100%
Share of National Employment	0.005%	0.005%	0.0006%	0.01%

Source: Authors' compilation of survey results

According to NASSCOM Report 2000, the number of software professionals employed in India's IT software and services industry was 410,000 on 31 December 2000. From the national standpoint, this is only one hundredth of one percentage of national employment. At first blush, this may appear to be an underwhelming achievement for the core computer software industries. The Indian government, however, lists hundreds of industries in the private sector, and relatively few industries or industry groups are larger than the computer software industries as sources of employment

4. Markets for Software Products and Services

As mentioned at the outset, the shortcomings of the domestic market have forced the Indian software companies to seek growth by moving towards the export market. This is in sharp contrast with the pattern of growth described in Mowery (1996) for the leading software industries in Western Europe, Japan and the United States. For these countries, growth in the software industry was aided significantly by growth in domestic demand; the latter growth, in turn, was caused by rapid diffusion of low cost microcomputer technology and wider scope of its application across different economic sectors. The relative significance of the domestic market for software industries in India, Western Europe, Japan and the U.S can be seen in Table 17.4, which breaks down domestic market share of revenue for each of these countries by product category.

Western European software industries tend to sell their products and services mainly within European markets. For the U.S. software industries, about three fourth of the revenues are generated in the domestic market. Though not as significant as in Europe and the United States, the domestic market in Japan accounts for more than half of its total software revenues. The domestic market for Indian software industries, with a meagre share of 17.5 per cent, appears of comparatively negligible importance.

Table 17.4: Domestic Share of Software Revenue for India, Western Europe, Japan and the US

Product Group	*United States*	*Western Europe*	*Japan*	*India*
Custom Programming services	52%	41%	21%	19.4%
Software Packages	42%	36%	21%	23%
Custom Designing	18%	8.2%	14%	----
Core Industry	75%	90%	56%	17.5%

Source: Mowery (1996), Authors' compilation of survey results

Growth in Indian software industries has been spurred mainly by growth in export market demand. Our survey indicates that the export market is mostly concentrated in the US and Europe. To capture the differences in market specific demand and their significance in industry revenue, Table 17.5 provides a breakdown of the sources of industry revenue by category.

Table 17.5: India's Computer Software Industry: Sources of Revenue (in percentages)

Industry Groups	Sources of Revenue			
	Domestic	United States	Europe	Asia and others
Custom computer Programming	19.4%	60%	13.2%	7.4%
Prepackaged Software	23%	58%	7%	12%
Custom Designing	---	74%	20%	6%
Core Industry	17.5%	61.5%	12.1%	8.9%

Source: Authors' compilation of survey results

Thus almost two thirds of the software revenue for the Indian companies examined in this chapter comes from servicing the US market. The US is the largest source of income for all three groups in our list. Europe's contribution to industry revenue is smaller than that of the Indian domestic market and explains only 12.1 per cent of the aggregate revenue reported with the domestic market at 17.5 per cent. Interestingly, the highly developed East Asian market seems to be of little consequence for the firms in the Indian software industry, at least up until the late 1990s.

The two factors that are key to the significance of the US market for Indian software exports are size and India's own interest in developing linkages with the American market. There has been a substantial increase in the number of software related collaborations with US firms since the early 1990s. These collaborations offer a way to circumvent barriers to open market competition.

5. Qualitative Aspects of Software Exports

We now highlight some problems with Indian software exports, arguing that though they are impressive in terms of annual percentage of growth, these have been poorly diversified with respect to product category, type of contracts, and level of skills.

Though the US market is the major source of export earnings for Indian firms, the majority of the sales reflect demand for software services that include custom software work and programming services. Sales of software packages are negligible. Similarly, although most of the major software exporters have sold compilers and financial program packages overseas, total sales figures have remained insignificant. The only exception is Wipro Systems Limited (WSL). With sales figuring in tens of thousands, they have been identified as the major seller in the 1990s.

Major reliance on software service exports places India at a disadvantage in the global market where competitors rely much less on export of software services and more on export of software packages. An estimated breakdown of export type for Indian software companies in relation to competitors is shown in Table 17.6.

India's export profile is skewed compared to that of its close competitors, which have been somewhat more successful in diversifying their exports. Lack of diversification, makes India vulnerable in the future. This is compounded by the fact that much of India's 'export' of software services actually is carried out at the client's overseas site in India; i.e., 'onsite services', rather than offshore. Approximately 70 per cent of export services in our survey consisted of onsite work. This was even true for software companies located in technology parks constructed to be the bases for offshore work.

Table 17.6: Software Export Profiles of India and its Competitors in the mid-1990s

	Proportion of Exports in Each Category (%)		
Country	*Software Services (excldng data entry)*	*Software Packages*	*Data Entry*
India	90	5	5
Ireland	65	21	14
Mexico	53	32	15
Philippines	39	20	41
Singapore	25	58	17
China	17	56	27
Israel	19	76	5

Source: Heeks (1996): India's Software Industry: State Policy, Liberalization and Industrial Development

The persistence of onsite work can be explained by several factors. First, clients' perception of worker productivity in India appears biased: clients demonstrate a lack of trust in the credibility of Indian firms' and perceive a higher degree of risk in sending work offshore. Thus they prefer to retain most of the control over production themselves; only the relatively risk-free tasks like coding and testing are, contracted out. Second, as suggested by Info Tech Consulting (1992), the factors determining onsite work are: costs, credentials, efficiency and quality. The growing number of Indian firms working onsite suggests that they rank quite high in all these areas. By contrast, for offshore, more popularly known as 'turnkey projects', cost becomes much less of a consideration with managerial skills, quality control and access to technology ranked higher. The existing perception among clients abroad is that Indian firms tend to rank lower in these areas.

Project size is also an important factor guiding foreign firms in their decisions about onsite and offshore work. In general, a minimum project size of US$100,000 defines the threshold for foreign firms to consider sending their work offshore. As is apparent from our survey, the majority of the contracts received by Indian firms fall below this minimum threshold.

Finally, software company managers in India have always been apprehensive about the direction of Government policy changes, at least until recently. Frequent changes in government and in political ideologies have encouraged Indian firms to undertake business activities free of bureaucratic control at home and focus on short term, low risk opportunities abroad.

The software development process can be broken into two stages. The earlier stage of analysis and design can be defined as one where the idea of the software is conceived and the specific requirements are analyzed and designed. The subsequent stage of coding and testing involves actual writing of the program and testing of its effectiveness in applications. The first stage is understood to require mature and sophisticated level of skills and experience. The stage is composed of basically non-creative segments of the production process and has low skill requirements. With a major share of software contracts listed in the category of coding and testing, Indian software personnel have most often been employed by their foreign clients as programmers rather than as system engineers or designers.

6. Future Opportunities and Challenges

Indian software exporters are focusing on custom computer programming, manpower training, consulting and developing customized software products with little attention on development of standardized indigenous software packages. Systematic analyses of factors that explain such specific pattern of growth are rare so this section focuses on a neglected segment of the software industry — software packages — and makes a modest attempt to identify the opportunities and constraints for this sector.

The breakdown of industry revenue by products (Table 17.5) reveals that prepackaged software accounts for less than 30 per cent of total export revenue. Yet, the latter product, by its very nature, is the most profitable segment of the industry. Because they can be copied at no extra cost, standardized software packages allow for increasing returns to scale. Hence, this product group offers a significant advantage over all other product groups in the software industry.

Info Tech (1992) has concluded that India could be rated above all of its competitors as a software development location. India ranked above most competitors on availability of skilled labor force widespread use of the English language and competitive labor costs. The score was above average on areas of technical competence, education and training, and telecommunication infrastructure. India falls behind its competitors only in regard to government incentives and the size of the domestic market. Given India's potential, the question that naturally arises is: why doesn't India diversify into production and sale of software packages?

With a constant flow of new entrants in the global software industry, profits from the sale of traditional services for the Indian software industry are likely to fall in the future; revenue growth would depend only on growth in the number of software workers. In order to survive the increased level of competition in the world market, Indian companies would have to develop new products at the high end of the value chain. *Business Week* (February 26, 2000) notes that while India's largest software services companies, Wipro and Infosys, reported significant increase in profit in the year 2000, they experienced increasing competition from a number of low-cost Asian nations.

Demand estimates suggest that diversification into development and sales of software packages would open up a very large potential market, worth as much as US$150 billion in 2001. However, there are some major barriers to entry into this market. To understand the factors that hinder Indian firms from shifting the thrust of their production to standardized software packages, we asked the companies in our sample to identify the difficulties encountered within four broad groups of constraint factors: infrastructural constraints; regulatory constraints; risk elements; and marketing and distribution related constraints. Summary results appear in Table 17.7.

Thus a number of issues related to infrastructure development, regulation, estimated risks, and marketing and distribution networks are responsible for keeping Indian software developers from venturing into the packaged software market. Lack of internationally compatible hardware capabilities (India has just 1 million PCs), inadequate telecommunication services, and limited Research and Development (R&D) facilities define the major set of constraints faced by the Indian software producers. Further the rate of attrition is high.

The infrastructure of specific interest to the software industry is the provision of a telecommunications network. Software companies in India encountered a number of telecommunications problems, including shortages of telecommunication links; time lag in accessing such links, poor transmission, and high cost of installation and use.

Two other elements in software infrastructure are human resources and power. While the growth of software services export has increased opportunities for employment generation in the export sector, this growth masks a major problem of worker turnover, especially the loss of workers to overseas markets, facilitated by increased number of onsite contracts. Figures from our survey suggest that software companies were losing 10–15 per cent of their employees each year; in some companies, the losses have been as high as 30 per cent in a single year. Such a high turnover has translated into slower growth, poor transfer of skills, reduced incentives for training investments and reinforced dependence on programming services.

Table 17.7: Constraints Encountered by Indian Software Industries

Constraint Factors	Agree	Disagree	Not Sure
Infrastructure			
Limited R&D Facilities	41	24	3
Lack of Hardware Capabilities	46	22	2
Poor Quality Control	35	33	2
Inadequate Telecom. Services	43	23	4
High Attrition Rate	48	16	4
Regulation			
Inability to Protect Copyright	51	15	2
Non-Conducive Tech. Policies	23	40	5
Risk			
Long designing--marketing Lag	53	13	2
Limited Funds for Investment. in Continuous Innovation	42	26	---
Mktng & Distribution			
Limited Domestic Market	54	13	1
Poor Intnl. Distrbn. Network	49	18	1
Absence of After-sale-services	50	16	2

Source: Authors' Compilation of survey results

Research and Development (R&D) investment is a major constraint on the growth of software industries. Software developers have experienced poor levels of R&D investments within the industry. Such low levels of R&D have resulted in missed opportunities for development of indigenous technologies and, hence, of new software products.

Further, more than 75 per cent of the producers sampled consider poor enforcement of copyright protection laws, both at home and abroad, to be of significance. Most producers agree that piracy of software in India is standard practice. The legal issues surrounding piracy are overlooked at best and ignored at worst. With pirated versions of sophisticated software frequently costing less than Rs. 500 (approximately US$11) domestic producers see shrinkage in their market share and falling prices for their products. The two effects reduce revenues for domestic producers.

Apparently, the perceived long lag in the production of packaged software products (the time required to conceive, design, develop and market these products), together with changes in technology and demand in this market, raise the risks to Indian producers. In order to reduce this risk, survive the competition, and stay ahead of other producers in the market, Indian producers would need to invest significantly in continuous product and process innovation. Further, since rapid diffusion of innovation prevents full appropriation of returns on investments, individual producers are unwilling to commit themselves to significant investment in these directions. The only way out, therefore, is to have a complementary investment program supported by the government.

Lack of a sizable domestic market has long been a major problem for Indian software developers. Though the market grew by over 50 per cent during 1990–95, its size is still small. Further, capturing a major share of the international market requires success in the development of a global distribution network to respond effectively to clients' needs and standards, and setting up after-sale-service shops to provide support, maintenance and upgrades for the product line. India lags on both these fronts.

7. Government Policy Initiatives during the 1990s

Acknowledging the constraints outlined above, the government of India has recently designed a series of major policy initiatives to enhance competitiveness in the software industry and strengthen the information technology sector in general. As part of this a *National Task Force on Information Technology and Software Development* was set up in May 1998. The Task Force had a mandate to formulate the draft of a long term National IT Policy and to recommend immediate steps the Government needed to take to remove bottlenecks and provide a boost to the IT industry in general, and the software industry in particular. The Task Force submitted three key reports[7] to the government during July 1998–April 1999.

The major recommendations[8] included opening of Internet Gateway access; encouragement for private sector Software Technology Parks (STPs), zero customs and excise duty on IT software, income tax exemptions for software and services exports, encouragement to set up venture capital funds, 1–3 per cent of the Budget of every Ministry/Department for IT applications, networking of all Universities and research institutions, allowing US dollar linked stock options to employees

[7] The three reports are *Information Technology Action Plan- Part I* (4 July 1998), *Information Technology Action Plan- Part II* (October 26, 1998), and *Information Technology Action Plan- Part III* (16 April 1999). While the first two reports are on software and hardware industries respectively, the third one is on long-term national IT policy.

[8] *Economic Survey: 1998–99*, Government of India, p. 109.

of Indian software companies, new schemes for students, including attractive package for buying computers, and as range of other measures. The Government has accepted almost all the recommendations and has directed all concerned departments to implement them. A new Ministry of Information Technology was set up in October 1999, as the nodal agency for facilitating all initiatives in the Central Government, the State Governments, academia, the private sector and among successful Indian IT professionals abroad.[9]

- The Task Force's third report has focused on the long-term (strategic) national IT policy. It highlighted the urgent necessity of raising both productivity and quality of the Indian software industry.
- In order to promote quality movement in India's software industry, various initiatives have been taken by the Government, NASSCOM, and other organizations.

It is noteworthy[10] that India's software industry has achieved distinction for providing quality services. As of December 1999, 170 Indian software companies have acquired international quality certification.

Recently, the Government of India has approved setting up of an IT venture capital fund of Rs.1 billion[11] for software companies and suggested measures to develop a road map for e-commerce development.[12] These include information and communication technology infrastructure; legal and regulatory framework; technology for electronic commerce (e-commerce) including test-beds; issues related to international domain names; and related areas. More recently, the Government has enacted the *Information Technology (IT) Act, 2000* not only to provide a legal framework for e-commerce and prevention of computer crimes, but also to accelerate induction of IT in critical sectors of the Indian economy. The Act aims to recognize electronic contracts, electronic filing/documentation, digital signatures, and the like. Rules under the Act have been notified, and the Act came into force on 17 October 2000. The Controller of Certifying Authority has been appointed.

Evans (1992) chronicled the evolution of state involvement in the Indian informatics industry during the 1960s, 1970s and 1980s. While the state combined restrictive regulation with attempts to substitute state-owned for private production during the 1960s and 1970s, conscious attempts have since been made by the central government regulatory agencies and state-owned enterprises in the high technology industry to increase state actions

---

[9] *Economic Survey: 1999–2000*, Government of India, p. 125.

[10] Quoted from *Economic Survey: 2000–2001*, Government of India, p. 143.

[11] This is approximately equal to US$21.5 million.

[12] *Economic Survey: 1999–2000*, Government of India, p. 125 and *Economic Survey: 2000–2001*, Government of India, p. 143.

aimed at complementing and promoting private entrepreneurship during the 1980s. This change has been reinforced more strongly since the adoption of a liberalized economic policy in July 1991. Moreover, announcement of IT policies by many state governments has further strengthened India's position in the software-driven IT sector.[13]

8. Conclusions

This chapter has critically examined the organization, size and export performance of the Indian software industry. Our analysis has revealed that foreign participation in terms of joint-venture corporation or subsidiary organization still remains limited in the Indian software industry. The industry is represented mainly by private domestic limited companies. A majority of these firms are engaged in contractual programming and designing activities. Though large in number, most of the programming and designing related firms are small in terms of both their assets and level of earnings. Only a handful have an asset size larger than Rs. 300 million. Similarly, very few earn revenue in excess of Rs. 500 million. Within the group of prepackaged software, however, more than 25 per cent of the firms claim to have annual earnings in excess of Rs. 500 million.

Firms engaged in programming services account for the major share of employment in the industry. However, each of the three groups of firms examined in this paper fared poorly when seen in terms of their contributions towards national employment. Altogether, they define only 0.01 per cent of national employment.

The domestic market explains only 17.5 per cent of the total software revenue and contrasts strikingly with that in the developed countries of United States, Western Europe and Japan. A breakdown of sources of revenue by product groups confirms a significant dependence on export market. What compounds this dependence is the evidence of excessive reliance on one principal market, viz. the United States. More than 60 per cent of revenue for this industry is generated in the U.S. market.

A close scrutiny of the export profile reveals that while being concentrated in the U.S. market, India's software exports are skewed towards custom software work and programming services. Development and sale of prepackaged software define a negligible share of software exports. This is in sharp contrast with the export pattern exhibited by India's close competitors in Asia and South America which have demonstrated varying degree of success in diversifying their exports to sale

---

[13] According to NASSCOM report in 2000, 19 state governments have announced their IT policies, while many more are in the offing.

of software packages. Further, the majority of India's software exports are produced abroad at client's site rather than at offshore locations. Such predominance of onsite work has added to India's vulnerability by characterizing its exports as low-skill, low-technology, low-investment and low-return options.

Both the domestic and the international market for its products and services are growing at a rapid rate. To take advantage of the opportunities generated by these expanded markets, both the industry and Government of India currently are taking some bold and purposeful steps. These include path-breaking measures by the government to further liberalize the economy, simplification of procedures, deployment of additional resources for technical manpower development, new marketing channels, enhancing global brand equity, and providing state-of-the-art infrastructure for software development. E-commerce solutions, software development, interactive integration services, Application Service Providers and IT-enabled services are leading the way.[14]

[14] Quoted from NASSCOM Report 2001.

References

Bhargava, Sunita Wadekar, 'Software from India? Yes, It's for Real,' *Business Week*, 18 January (1993), 77.

Chandrasekaran, V., 'Business Quality- The Cutting Edge,' *Management Review*, January–March (1996), 12–20.

Economic Survey: 1998–99 (New Delhi: Government of India, 1999).

Economic Survey: 1999–2000 (New Delhi: Government of India, 2000).

Economic Survey: 2000–2001 (New Delhi: Government of India, 2001).

Einhorn, Bruce, Manjit Kripalani and Pete Engardio, 'India 3.0: Its Software Outfits Take on the World', *Business Week*, 26 February (2001), 44–6.

Evans, Peter, 'Indian Informatics in the 1980s: The Changing Character of State Involvement,' *World Development*, 20(1) (1992), 1–18.

Heeks, Richard, *India's Software Industry: State Policy, Liberalization and Industrial Development* (New Delhi: Sage Publications, 1996).

Info Tech Consulting Inc., *India's Software & Services Export Potential & Strategies* (New Jersey: Parsippany, 1992)

Information Technology Action Plan-I (New Delhi: Government of India, July 1998).

Information Technology Action Plan-II (New Delhi: Government of India, October 1998).

Information Technology Action Plan-III (New Delhi: Government of India, April 1999).

Kopetz, Hermann, 'The Software Market: Emerging Trends,' in *Software Industry: Current Trends and Implications for Developing Countries* (Vienna: United Nations Industrial Development Organization, 1993).

Merchant, Khozem, 'India: IT and Communications', *Financial Times*, 21 February (2001).

Mowery, David C. (ed.), *The International Computer Software Industry: A Comparative Study of Industry Evolution and Structure* (New York: Oxford University Press, 1996).

Premchander, 'Indian Software Industry: A Diagnostic Analysis,' *Management Review*, January–March (1997), 11–19.

Siwek, Stephen E. and Harold W. Furchtgott–Roth, *International Trade in Computer Software* (Westport: Quorum Books, 1993).

Vijayan, Jaikumar, 'In Depth: Look Out, Here Comes India,' *Computerworld*, 26 February (1996), 101–4.

Wheatley, Malcolm, 'IT's Passage to India', *Management Today*, April (1997), 56–8.

Zielenziger, Michael, 'By Design: India's Software Houses Lure Foreign Money', *Far Eastern Economic Review*, 10 August (1995), 64–5.

18
Infrastructure and Electricity Sector Reforms in India

Raghbendra Jha and Prem Jung Thapa

1. Introduction

India's economic reform, begun in 1991, has played a key role in improving the living conditions of a vast majority of its people. But the reform process has also highlighted and exacerbated existing regional inequalities within India (Bhide and Shand 2003). The growing inequality in part is determined by varying levels of regional infrastructure and pace of economic reforms adopted by the states. It is widely recognized that post-1991 the high performing states in India have better infrastructure services on average (Ahluwalia 2000; DFAT 2001). Political antipathy to increasing regional inequality has led to some resistance to further economic reforms. This creates a dilemma: how to make the fruits of economic reforms more equitably distributed and lay the groundwork for an expanded reform agenda in the future. In the process of consolidating the reforms and setting an expanded reform agenda for the future, this chapter presents a brief overview of the reforms directed towards the infrastructural sectors, and assesses the role and appropriate approach to future reforms.

Infrastructure is a vital productive input in promoting economic growth, but India's record in providing high quality, reliable and reasonably priced infrastructural services to its households and businesses has been inadequate. In fact, The World Economic Forum's 1998 *Global Competitiveness Report* ranked India last among 53 countries on the quality of overall infrastructure services.[1] Indian households and businesses still receive infrastructure services largely through the public sector — often

[1] This ranking is cited in World Bank (2000).

through government departmental undertakings. To many observers there is an obvious link between the inadequacy and poor quality of Indian infrastructural services and the mode of public provision (World Bank 2000). But it is also clear that even though the potential of the private sector to meet India's pressing infrastructure needs is largely untapped, and hence can be expanded considerably, there will continue to be a major role for the public sector in providing infrastructural services, particularly in the less developed regions/states of India.

The mere scale of the required infrastructural investments — one estimate puts this at US$215 billion in the 2001 to 2006 period[2] — and the political economic compulsions which mean that the infrastructure poor states can't be left to fend for themselves in an increasingly private market for infrastructure services, indicate that both the Central and State level governments will continue to play a major role in providing the bulk of infrastructure services in India for the foreseeable future. Herein lies one of the principal challenges for the consolidation of the ongoing economic reform process in India. It is now imperative to develop a strategy for a more active role for the government — both as provider of infrastructural services and as a facilitator in building an effective public and private partnership — in order to have a more rapid and widespread increase in regional infrastructural services. The initial phase of India's reforms has focussed on de-regulation and liberalization and a reduced economic role for the government. But from the perspective of most infrastructural services, there is a clear rationale for an expanded role of the government which must adopt innovative approaches to expanding infrastructural services equitably in India (Das 2002). Given the key linkages between rural infrastructure and agricultural productivity (Binswanger and Khandker 1993) and social opportunities for rural residents (Dreze and Sen 1995), expanding rural infrastructure services becomes the key vehicle through with to take the fruits of India's economic liberalization program to its rural areas. The main items on this agenda will be harnessing more resources for new infrastructural investments — public and private, including FDI; increasing the efficiency of public sector providers of infrastructure; adopting appropriate public sector pricing and cost recovery schemes; designing effective regulatory institutions and mechanism which increase private sector participation; and instilling a general culture of market discipline and good governance for the necessary private — public partnership.

---

[2] Estimates by the Expert Group on the Commercialization of Infrastructure Projects reported in NCAER (1996).

2. Overview of India's Economic Reforms in Infrastructural Sectors

The core economic infrastructure sectors in India, as recognized in its official national accounting and industrial classification scheme are: power generation, other energy (coal and petroleum), transport (road, railways and ports) and communications.[3]

As indicated in Table 18.1, even from the perspective of aggregate availability of these key infrastructural services, the record in the post-reform period has been unremarkable. Except for telecommunications, the growth in the main infrastructural industries has barely improved in the post-reform era. In fact, in one key sector — electricity generation — growth performance has deteriorated in the post-reform era.

Table 18.1: Performance of Key Infrastructural Industries, 1980–91 and 1992–99 (average annual growth rates - per cent)

	1980–1991	*1992–1999*
1. Electricity Generation	8.8	6.7
2. Railways		
a. Revenue earning goods traffic	4.8	3.9
b. Passenger kilometers	3.9	4.1
3. Ports: cargo handled at major ports	6.1	7.1
4. Roads		
a. Length of Roads	3.6	0.7
b. Length of National Highway	0.5	0.6
5. Telecommunications (new telephone connections provided)	19.0	27.1

Source: GOI, Economic Survey 2000–2001, pp. 171, Box 9.1.

Another indicator of the deterioration of the infrastructural sector in the post-reform era is that investment in infrastructure as a per cent of GDP has declined. As indicated in Table 18.2, public sector investment in infrastructure as a ratio of GDP has steadily fallen since the early 1990s, and the private sector has not made up for this slackening, in spite of the strong encouragement given to the private sector, including FDI.

3 Cement production is often added to this list of infrastructure industries (see GOI, *Economic Survey 2001-2002*, Chapter 9); but this sector will be ignored in our chapter.

Table 18.2: Investment in Infrastructure as percentage of GDP

	1991–92	*1992–93*	*1995–96*	*1996–97*	*1997–98*
Total	5.4	5.3	4.2	4.4	4.6
Public	4.0	3.7	3.2	2.9	3.0
Private	1.4	1.6	1.0	1.5	1.6

Source: World Bank (2000), pp. 4 (Table 4).

The government's initiatives for infrastructural development have been grouped under six headings (Economic Survey, Government of India, 2001–02, pp. 209). **Fiscal incentives** include ten-year tax holiday for the core sector of infrastructure, i.e., roads, highways, waterways, water supply, solid waste management systems to be taken during the first twenty years. For airports, ports, inland ports, industrial parks and generation and distribution of power this tax holiday was to be taken in the first fifteen years. A five-year tax holiday and 30 per cent deduction for the subsequent five years has been announced for the telecommunications sector. Tax incentives have also been announced for investors providing long-term finance for infrastuctural activity with all income from such investment fully tax exempt. For the **Power Sector** a new Electricity Bill was introduced in Parliament. A government committee to examine revamping the State Electricity Boards (SEBs) was set up under the chairmanship of Montek Ahluwalia. The committee's proposals have not yet been implemented. An Energy Conservation Act was passed by Parliament in 2001 and investment in the Accelerated Power Development Program was increased to Rs.15 billion from Rs.10 billion a year earlier. Commercialization of distribution has begun, and a commitment to introduce 100 per cent metering has been introduced. In the **Telecom Sector** public policy has tended to act as facilitator of competition. A Communication Convergence bill was introduced in Parliament. The total outlay for the **Roads Sector** has been enhanced. A Quadrilateral National Highway Program linking four major cities (Mumbai, New Delhi, Calcutta and Chennai) is underway, with the first phase due to be completed by December 2003. States have been given additional funds to improve roads. To improve **Rural Infrastructure** the Pradhan Mantri Gram Sadak Yojana (PMGSY) (Prime Minister's Village Roads Scheme) has been set up with an initial capital of Rs. 25 billion. The PMGSY was subsequently expanded to include rural electrification. In the important area of **Railways** investment has been stepped up. Plans have been drawn up for the commercial utilization of land and airspace of the railways. Some decentralization of authority in decision-making has occurred with additional railway zones being created. However, there is serious paucity of funds for much-needed capital equipment as well as track improvement. There are important issues affecting the promotion of FDI, such as regulatory structures, price reform, procedural difficulties as well as caps on FDI, which need to be sorted out before FDI can be attracted into the infrastructure sector in a substantial way.

3. Regional Variation in Infrastructure Development and its Consequences

The infrastructure stock — both in the public and private sector — varies immensely between the States and Territories of India. This is a reflection of the considerable inequalities one finds in the socioeconomic condition within India. For instance, infant mortality in Orissa is seven times higher than in Kerala partly because (in 1991) rural Kerala had seventeen times as many hospital beds per head as Orissa.[4] A rural household would be almost fourteen times more likely to have electricity connection if located in Punjab instead of Bihar (in 1991).[5]

Table 18.3 presents some measures of alternative indicators of the levels of various infrastructural services for India's major states in the 1990s. The first indicator is per capita energy consumption in 1996–97. The highest energy consumption is in Punjab, which has a level of energy use (790 kWh) that is more than seven times that of the lowest energy use level for Assam (108 kWh). Per capita energy consumption is a measure of both demand and supply factors and hence is not a pure infrastructural service availability measure. Nevertheless, it is a useful indicator of the remarkable variability in the energy resource base across the major states of India.

---

4 The discussion and examples of regional contrasts in this paragraph follows that in A. Banerjee (2002), where the references to the original data or source are provided.

5 India National Human Development Report 2001, Table 3.11.

Table 18.3: Regional Variation in Infrastructure Development

State	*Consumption of power per capita (kWh) in 1996–97*	*Registered Vehicles per 1,000 persons (31/3/1997)*	*Telecom Lines per 100 persons (March 1999)*	*Percentage Irrigated Area in Gross Cropped Area (1994–95)*	*CMIE Relative Infrastructure Development Index*
	(1)	(2)	(3)	(4)	(5)
Andhra Pradesh	332	42.1	2.36	39.6	96.1
Gujarat	686	91.5	3.75	28.9	122.4
Haryana	508	64.6	3.18	77.2	141.3
Karnataka	338	56.5	3.25	23.9	96.9
Kerala	236	46.5	4.66	13.6	157.1
Maharastra	557	57.2	4.93	15.3	107.0
Punjab	790	103.2	5.34	94.8	191.4
Tamilnadu	469	56.9	3.84	49.5	144.0
Assam	108	19.9	0.95	15.0	78.9
Bihar	145	16.4	0.58	43.2	81.1
Madhya Pradesh	368	38.8	1.38	22.3	75.3
Orissa	447	22.9	1.05	25.8	97.0
Rajasthan	295	45.1	2.11	29.1	83.0
Uttar Pradesh	194	22.7	1.21	62.6	103.3
West Bengal	197	19.8	1.86	28.7	94.2
All-India	338	44.0	2.55	36.5	100

Source: *Ninth Five-Year Plan (1997–2002), Profiles of States*, March 1997, as quoted in Kurian (2000).

Transport services, proxied by the number of registered vehicles per 1,000 persons, and an indicator of communications services measured as the number of telecommunication lines per 100 persons are also presented. On both of these indicators, again, Punjab is the most advanced and Bihar the least. The share of irrigated area in gross cropped area (Indicator 4) is an important measure of infrastructural services available to the agricultural sector. Farm productivity depends in a critical way on assured irrigation facilities. On this indicator, again Punjab, which has almost 95 per cent of its cropped area under irrigation, is by far the most advantaged state. At the other end, the two least advantaged states — Bihar and Maharastra — have only about 15 per cent of their cropped area under irrigation.[6] The last column in Table 18.3 presents a composite index of infrastructural development, which has been prepared by the Center for Monitoring of the Indian Economy (CMIE). The index includes the following components (with relative shares indicated in brackets): transport facilities (26 per cent), energy consumption (24 per cent), irrigation facilities (20 per cent), banking facilities (12 per cent), communications (6 per cent), educational institutions (6 per cent) and health facilities (6 per cent).[7] The value of this index is normalized to 100 for an all-India average. The data for the individual components relate to varying years in the 1990s. On this index, Madhya Pradesh (with a score of 75.3) has the lowest level of infrastructural development among India's major states, and Punjab (with a score of 191.4) has the highest level of infrastructural development.[8]

These variations in the regional level of basic social and economic infrastructural services not only lead to differences in the quality of life in these regions, but also to enduring concerns about how unevenly distributed will be the benefits of India's liberalizing economic reforms. There is now increasing evidence about the widening of regional disparities within India that has picked up even more pace in the post-reform era (Ahluwalia 2000). Several studies examining regional growth convergence within India, using the Barro and Sala-I-Martin (1995) framework, find a distinct trend of divergence in inter-state growth both during the post and pre-reform eras (Sachs, Bajpai and Ramiah 2002). Sachs *et al.* (2002) in particular find that (within a sample of India's 14 major states) there is a significant positive relationship between initial per capita income in 1990 and the growth in state level per capita income in the 1990s.

While the variations in regional economic growth in India depend on many factors, including geographic and climatic variables that are beyond anyone's control, there is a clear indication that relative growth performance is correlated with the level of infrastructural development. In Table 18.4 we show how the per capita growth rates for the 14 states that feature in the Sachs *et al.* (2002) study can be linked to the level of

---

[6] However, since Maharashtra has a much larger manufacturing base than Bihar, it enjoys far higher per capita income.

[7] The sub-components of the CMIE infrastructural development index are not shown in Table 3. In particular, the CMIE index does not reflect a weighted sum of the other indicators of infrastructure services shown in the previous columns of Table 18.3.

[8] It should be noted that the CMIE composite is sensitive to the weights used for the specific components. Kurian (2000) in particular has noted that the relatively large weight given to irrigation in this index gives a large boost to Uttar Pradesh's composite score because the irrigation potential within UP is high due to its river systems. A smaller weight to irrigation would make the composite score for UP less than the all India average score of 100, since on most other components UP lags considerably behind other states.

infrastructure development. Using the CMIE composite index of infrastructural development by states, we categorize these 14 states into two groups. Group I consists of 7 states for each of which the infrastructure development index is below the all India average score (set to 100). Group II consists of another 7 states where the infrastructure development index is above the all India average. While we are unable to document a clear statistical relationship between the level of infrastructural development and per capita growth at the level of the individual states,[9] at the Group level there is a clear indication that Group I states on average have a lower level of growth in per capita income, and this divergence between Group I and Group II states has increased in the post-reform era. As indicated in Table 18.4, in the period 1980 to 1990 the average growth rate in Group I states was 2.84 per cent per annum compared to 3.22 per cent in Group II, which is a difference of -0.38 per cent. In the 1992 to 98 period, per capita growth in the infrastructure-rich states accelerated more than in the infrastructure-poor states, leading to a much larger gap of -1.05 per cent in the relative growth rate of the Group I states. In terms of growth in per capita GSDP, the relative disadvantage of the infrastructure-poor states almost tripled in the post-reform period.

A similar picture on the importance of the regional stock of infrastructural facilities emerges when one compares the relative performance of India's major states in reducing poverty in the 1990s. Tables 18.5 and 18.6 present data on the state-level incidence of aggregate poverty and rural poverty for 1993–94 and 1999–2000. The Group I and Group II categorization of states, based on the level of the CMIE composite index of infrastructural development, is the same as in Table 18.4. Tables 18.5 and 18.6 show that there have been significant drops in the head count index of poverty incidence in India between 1993–94 and 1999–00. The all India incidence of aggregate poverty (that is, for both urban and rural areas) is estimated to have declined from 36 per cent in 1993–94 to 26.1 per cent in 1999–00. Again, there is no clear correlation at the level of individual states between the decline in poverty and the level of the infrastructural development index (since several of the infrastructure-poor states have also recorded impressive falls in poverty in this period, for example, Bihar and Karnataka). Nevertheless, aggregate poverty has fallen more sharply in infrastructurally advantaged Group II states (-10.96 percentage points) than in the Group I states (-8.78 percentage points). The larger relative decline

[9] The level of infrastructure is only one of many determinants of aggregate and per capita growth in state level economic output, which in India's national accounting framework is measured as Gross State Domestic Production (GSDP). Hence it is not unusual that the CMIE infrastructural index alone would not be a significant determinant of per capita GSDP growth in a simple regression format that excluded all other determinants of growth.

in poverty in the Group II states is even more pronounced with respect to rural poverty (Table 18.6). Rural poverty in the Group II states declined by almost 12 per cent percentage points during the 1993–94 to 1999–00 period, compared to only a 8.7 per cent point decline in the Group I states.

Table 18.4: Regional Infrastructure and Growth in Per Capita State Output

State	*Infrastructure Development Index*	*Per capita GSDP growth% 1980–90*	*Per capita GSDP growth % 1992–98*
Group I			
Madhya Pradesh	75.3	2.08	3.87
Bihar	81.1	2.45	1.12
Rajasthan	83.0	3.96	3.96
West Bengal	94.2	2.39	5.04
Andhra Pradesh	96.1	3.34	3.45
Karnataka	96.9	3.28	3.45
Orissa	97.0	2.38	1.64
Group II			
Uttar Pradesh	103.3	2.60	1.24
Maharastra	107.0	3.58	6.13
Gujarat	122.4	3.08	7.57
Haryana	141.3	3.86	2.66
Tamil Nadu	144.0	3.87	4.95
Kerala	157.1	2.19	4.52
Punjab	191.4	3.33	2.8
All India average *	100	3.03	4.02
Average growth rate %			
Group I (below average infrastructure) states		2.84	3.22
Group II (above average infrastructure) states		3.22	4.27
Gap in average growth rates %		-0.38	-1.05
(Group I – Group II)			

Notes: Group I states have an Infrastructure Development Index score of less than 100 (the All India average); while Group II states have an index higher than 100.

* The All India average Infrastructure index score of 100 includes values for other States not indicated in the above Table.

* The All India average growth in per capita Gross State Domestic Production (GSDP is the combined average growth of the 14 States indicated above.

The CMIE Infrastructure Development Index is derived from Kurian (2000) Table 8, and the per capita growth rates in GSDP is from Ahluwalia (2000), Table 2, which estimates period-wise growth rates by fitting a log linear trend to real per capita GSDP at 1980–81 prices.

Table 18.5: Regional Infrastructure and Poverty Incidence

State	*Infrastructure Development Index*	*Poverty Incidence*	*Poverty Incidence*	*Percentage Point Fall in Poverty*
		1993–94	*1999–00*	*93–94 to 99–00*
Group I				
Madhya Pradesh	75.3	42.52	37.43	5.09
Bihar	81.1	54.96	42.6	12.36
Rajasthan	83	27.41	15.28	12.13
West Bengal	94.2	35.66	27.02	8.64
Andhra Pradesh	96.1	22.19	15.77	6.42
Karnataka	96.9	33.16	20.04	13.12
Orissa	97	48.56	47.15	1.41
Group II				
Uttar Pradesh	103.3	40.85	31.15	9.7
Maharastra	107	36.86	25.02	11.84
Gujarat	122.4	24.21	14.07	10.14
Haryana	141.3	25.05	8.74	16.31
Tamil Nadu	144	35.03	21.12	13.91
Kerala	157.1	25.43	12.72	12.71
Punjab	191.4	11.77	6.16	5.61
All India average *	100	35.97	26.1	9.87
Group Level Poverty Incidence per cent (population weighted)				
Group I (below average infrastructure) states		38.47	29.69	8.78
Group II (above average infrastructure) states		33.99	23.03	10.96

Notes: Poverty Incidence for 1999–2000 period is based on the NSS estimates from the 30-day recall period.

The All India average Infrastructure Development index score of 100 and the poverty incidence per cent also includes values for other States not indicated in the above Table.

See also the Notes to Table 18.4.

Table 18.6: Regional Infrastructure and Rural Poverty Incidence

State	*Infrastructure Development Index*	*Rural Poverty Incidence*	*Rural Poverty Incidence*	*Percentage Point Fall in Poverty*
		1993–94	*1999–00*	*1993–94 to 1999–00*
Group I				
Madhya Pradesh	75.3	40.64	37.06	3.58
Bihar	81.1	58.21	44.3	13.91
Rajasthan	83	26.46	13.74	12.72
West Bengal	94.2	40.8	31.85	8.95
Andhra Pradesh	96.1	15.92	11.05	4.87
Karnataka	96.9	29.88	17.38	12.5
Orissa	97	49.72	48.01	1.71
Group II				
Uttar Pradesh	103.3	42.28	31.22	11.06
Maharastra	107	37.93	23.72	14.21
Gujarat	122.4	22.18	13.17	9.01
Haryana	141.3	28.02	8.27	19.75
Tamil Nadu	144	32.48	20.55	11.93
Kerala	157.1	25.76	9.38	16.38
Punjab	191.4	11.95	6.35	5.6
All India average *	100	37.27	27.9	9.37
Group Level Poverty Incidence per cent (population weighted)				
Group I (below average infrastructure) states		39.24	30.53	8.71
Group II (above average infrastructure) states		34.70	22.82	11.88

Note: See Notes to Table 18.5 above.

4. Electricity Sector Perspectives

The argument in this chapter has essentially been twofold. First it has established the necessity of augmenting resource flow into the infrastructure sector. Secondly it has demonstrated that variations in infrastructural development help explain regional variations in growth and poverty. We now examine some specific problems and reform agenda for two key infrastructural sectors: electricity and oil and gas.

A problem with the power sector reforms is that the central issue of the financial non-viability of the SEBs has not been confronted. This has thwarted the growth of independent power projects and reduced the flow of funds into this critical sector. With financially insolvent SEBs, independent power projects have had to look for temporary solutions such as escrow arrangements and central government guarantees which simply do not address the central issue. A way out to reduce the huge transmission and distribution losses is to privatize power distribution, but this must also await the financial restructuring of SEBs. Apart from inefficiency in generation and transmission of electricity, another factor leading to insolvent SEBs is the poor pricing policies followed.

Pricing of electricity in India is influenced by several political and economic compulsions at the central and state levels. There appears to be a hangover of the old policy that the cost of supply of a critical input such as electricity should be kept low (since this industry is highly capital intensive) in order to facilitate rapid economic growth. Although electricity is the most significant sector facing this problem, the practice of underpricing of inputs is quite ubiquitous in India and covers agricultural fertilizers, petroleum products and several other sectors. Several consumers find ways of circumventing these policies and mechanism, which results in some of them not paying for the services they use, or adulteration of one product with another (adulteration of petrol and/or diesel by kerosene).

SEBs are in precarious financial health. They have accumulated losses to such an extent they are neither able to invest in building the capacity required for meeting ambitious economic growth targets, nor are able to pay for inputs to maintain their present level of production. In the face of their rapidly deteriorating fiscal deficits, state governments are unable to meet the deficits of SEBs. Electricity tariffs in India are structured in a relatively simple manner. While the domestic and commercial customers do not pay any demand charges in most states (West Bengal, Orissa, Karnataka and Kerala being a few exceptions), the industrial customers do pay demand charges depending on their connected load. The price per kWh varies significantly across states as well as customer segments within a state. Tariffs are not structured to consider the time of usage and voltage level of supply. In addition to the base tariffs, some SEBs have additional recovery from customers in form of fuel surcharges and electricity duties. Table 18.7 lists average tariffs across customer segments in different states.

Table 18.7: Average Electricity Tariff in India by Category (paise per kWh)

State Electricity Board	Domestic	Commercial	Agriculture	Industrial	Railway	Outside State	Average
Andhra Pradesh	167.0	367.8	16.1	330.3	374.3	80.0	188.1
Assam	146.0	297.0	156.6	233.0			216.8
Bihar	109.3	211.0	14.0	275.9	313.0	177.6	210.8
Delhi Vidyut Board	258.7	237.0	116.0	299.4			270.7
Gujrat	254.0	424.0	20.0	396.5	421.0		325.0
Haryana	241.0	341.0	55.0	341.0	341.0	138.0	180.5
Himachal Pradesh	70.0	230.0	60.0	194.0		190.0	172.7
Jammu & Kashmir	40.8	74.0	15.8	59.0			50.0
Karnataka	144.0	545.0	86.0	325.0	330.0		188.7
Kerala	83.4	295.7	55.1	165.9			173.2
Madya Pradesh	74.5	337.5	9.1	385.1	529.4	101.3	168.5
Maharashtra	156.3	365.3	25.4	351.2	363.2	175.8	214.1
Meghalaya	93.3	181.2	50.0	184.7		173.7	156.9
Orissa	141.0	281.0	72.0	277.5	421.0		240.0
Punjab	150.2	278.5		243.2		190.0	146.7
Rajasthan	144.0	308.0	38.0	311.8	320.0	219.5	198.5
Tamil Nadu	166.7	459.4		365.9	380.3	211.3	224.7
Uttar Pradesh	108.9	360.0	46.6	341.6	390.4	7.3	171.9
West Bengal	108.5	246.1	34.1	283.7	328.5	318.3	218.0
Average	**131.1**	**345.3**	**29.7**	**297.5**	**398.9**	**156.7**	**197.9**

Source: Planning Commission, 1999 Annual Report on the Working of State Electricity Boards and Electricity Departments, New Delhi, Power and Energy Division, Government of India

However, average tariffs are below the average cost of supply for most SEBs and the situation has deteriorated over the years (Tables 18.7 and 18.8). As for the tariff adjustment mechanism, even when some of the states have regulatory commissions for tariff review, the decisions to effect changes are still political, and there is no automatic adjustment mechanism which can ensure recovery of costs for the electricity boards.

Studies on efficiency of power generation, transmission and distribution have found high levels of inefficiency (Chitkara 1998, 1999, Jha et al. 1992). In addition there are large transmission and distribution losses — to the extent of over 20 per cent of plant availability in fiscal 1999. These losses are far in excess of international average. Some unofficial estimates put these losses at about 40 per cent.

Financial losses of the electricity sector are estimated to amount to over Rs.300 billion or US$7 billion. Major reasons for losses include non-metering, pilferage and theft of power and also that part of power shown against used for agriculture.

Table 18.8: Electricity Sales Realisation as a Ratio of Cost in India (per cent)

State Electricity Board	1992/93	1993/94	1994/95	1995/96	1996/97	1997/98	1998/99
Andhra Pradesh	94.2	90.5	72.1	62.2	73.1	86.2	80.6
Assam	47.4	49.7	53.9	57.1	53.4	51.2	63.3
Bihar	63.7	73.5	66.4	70.6	63	71.4	78.4
Delhi Vidyut Board	81.7	0	0	72.9	72	72.6	71.1
Gujrat	68.4	76.6	74.6	63.6	81.8	81.9	85.9
Haryana	54	50.4	61.5	98.8	67.4	73.2	64.1
Himachal Pradesh	88.5	74.5	91.9	13.2	101.5	92.7	90.2
Jammu & Kashmir	21.3	16.7	10.3	74.9	10.9	12.2	16.2
Karnataka	96.5	95.3	86.8	69	72.4	86.8	89.9
Kerala	84.7	83.5	79.6	79.5	56.3	63.9	75.1
Madya Pradesh	84	80.7	77.3	91.2	84.9	80.3	72.3
Maharashtra	98.5	88.8	99.4	72.7	96.2	97.9	90.5
Meghalaya	81.3	93.6	71.2	77.1	80.2	77.3	38.7
Orissa	78.1	71.2	80.7	69.7	75.2	80.1	85.5
Punjab	57.6	61.8	66.7	67.8	73.2	61.6	60.9
Rajasthan	76	70.4	67.8	67.8	69.6	75.1	74.5
Tamil Nadu	86	88.7	98.8	97.1	93.4	90.8	92
Uttar Pradesh	70.6	66	69	70.7	64.3	71.6	69.8
West Bengal	71.5	73.4	73.7	78.5	74.3	76.2	78.6
Total	**82.2**	**78.3**	**78.3**	**76.1**	**77.4**	**80.1**	**78.6**

1997-98 are revised numbers and 1998-99 are from annual plans

Source: Planning Commission, 1999 Annual Report on the Working of State Electricity Boards and Electricity Departments, New Delhi, Power and Energy Division, Government of India

Table 18.9 reveals two important aspects of the structure of the pricing of electricity in India. In almost every state there is a subsidy to the agricultural and household sectors. Industrial railways and commercial sectors are cross-subsidizing these sectors to a considerable extent. This is inefficient enough. Furthermore, there are no estimates of the incidence of such cross-subsidization so that we are unaware of the final impact on the economy. Second, there is no reason to believe that the absolute level of the costs considered here are the minimum, given technology, for the output vector produced. In fact given the high level of inefficiency in SEBs these costs are likely to be much higher than minimum.

Tables 18.10, 18.11and 18.12 provide an overview of operating performance and the level of subsidies provided by some of the selected (large states) electricity boards for different consumer categories.

Another financial problem plaguing SEBs is their inability to collect dues. On an average, the SEBs customers owe them money in excess of three to four months of supply. The Boards, in turn, do not pay their suppliers (mainly public sector undertakings supplying them coal for power).

The above tables indicate an overall deterioration in the performance of the SEBs over time. If the SEBs were to break even in 1999 they would have needed budgetary support in excess of 5 per cent of states' total revenues. If the SEBs are to earn a commercial rate of return (15–16 per cent) on their assets, the subsidies have to five times more than those needed for break-even, taking the required subsidy, in 1999, to be 25 per cent of the State Government revenues or US$12 billion.

Table 18.9: Recovery of Cost of Supply of Electricity by Category of User (percentage of cost of supply)

State Electricity Board	Domestic	Commercial	Agriculture	Industrial	Railway	Outside State	Average
Andhra Pradesh	71.37	157.18	6.88	141.15	159.96	34.15	80.38
Assam	34.72	70.62	37.24	55.40	0.00	0.00	51.55
Bihar	40.68	78.67	5.21	102.68	116.48	66.09	78.45
Delhi	70.62	64.70	31.67	81.73	0.00	0.00	73.78
Gujrat	96.95	161.84	7.63	151.35	160.70	0.00	124.06
Haryana	86.46	122.34	19.73	122.34	122.34	49.51	64.76
Himachal Pradesh	39.70	130.45	34.03	110.03	0.00	107.76	97.95
Jammu & Kashmir	16.71	29.95	6.40	23.88	0.00	0.00	20.24
Karnataka	69.38	262.60	41.44	156.60	159.01	0.00	90.92
Kerala	41.38	146.60	27.34	82.31	0.00	0.00	85.93
Madya Pradesh	32.32	161.29	3.95	167.04	229.63	43.94	73.09
Maharashtra	69.01	161.29	11.21	155.06	160.36	77.62	94.53
Meghalaya	22.92	44.52	12.28	45.38	0.00	42.68	38.55
Orissa	50.22	100.80	25.04	98.84	149.94	0.00	85.49
Punjab	63.12	117.04	0.00	102.21	0.00	79.89	61.65
Rajasthan	54.42	116.39	14.36	117.86	120.93	82.59	75.01
Tamil Nadu	68.27	188.16	0.00	149.86	155.40	86.54	92.03
Uttar Pradesh	44.22	146.19	18.92	138.72	158.57	2.96	69.81
West Bengal	39.12	88.74	12.30	102.30	118.45	144.77	78.61
Average	**54.70**	**144.06**	**12.37**	**124.14**	**166.41**	**65.36**	**82.55**

Source: Planning Commission, 1999 Annual Report on the Working of State Electricity Boards and Electricity Departments, NewDelhi, Power and Energy Division, Government ofIndia

5. Oil and Gas

The Administered Price Mechanism (APM) came into existence in its present form during 1977. The Ministry of Petroleum and Natural Gas through the Oil Coordination Committee administers the scheme. OCC undertakes a cost updating study for each of the oil firms every three years to determine whether they are earning the desired revenue. APM's stated objectives are:

- Optimisation of utilisation of refining and marketing infrastructure by treating it to be the common industry infrastructure.
- Make available products at uniform price ex-refineries (all).
- Ensure that the oil firms earn a reasonable rate of return.
- Ensure stable prices by insulating domestic market from volatility of international prices.

- Achieve socio-economic objective by ensuring availability of certain products at subsidised rates for weaker sections of society and priority sectors in the Industry through cross-subsidisation of products.

Table 18.10: Electricity Transmission and Distribution Losses (percentage of plant availability)

State	1990/91	1991/92	1992/93	1993/94	1994/95	1995/96	1996/97	1997/98	1998/99
Andhra Pradesh	22.9	20.3	19.2	19.1	18.9	18.9	30.5	25.0	23.0
Arunachal Pradesh	20.0	28.2	34.9	31.6	31.0	36.0	32.0	30.0	32.0
Assam	24.1	22.7	21.0	20.8	24.9	26.2	24.9	24.0	23.0
Bihar	16.5	18.3	20.5	19.0	24.0	25.9	25.3	23.0	23.0
Daman and Diu	16.9	15.9	0.0	0.0	0.0	0.0	0.0	0.0	0.0
Goa	25.0	23.8	20.8	21.8	26.2	28.5	26.7	26.0	25.0
Gujrat	23.4	23.6	21.1	21.3	20.0	18.3	18.2	18.0	17.0
Haryana	27.5	26.8	25.4	25.5	28.5	31.4	31.7	32.2	31.1
Himachal Pradesh	21.0	19.2	18.5	17.3	17.4	17.5	17.9	17.4	16.7
Jammu & Kashmir	43.0	50.1	45.3	47.7	46.9	48.6	48.0	47.5	47.0
Karnataka	20.2	19.3	18.7	18.6	18.9	18.5	18.5	18.4	17.4
Kerala	22.4	22.5	21.0	20.2	20.1	20.1	20.0	19.0	18.0
Lakshadweep	18.6	17.4	0.0	0.0	0.0	0.0	0.0	0.0	0.0
Madya Pradesh	18.0	25.8	22.2	20.2	20.1	19.5	19.3	19.0	18.5
Maharashtra	18.3	18.6	16.4	15.8	15.3	15.4	15.3	15.2	15.2
Manipur	28.0	24.4	22.5	22.5	22.0	21.5	21.5	21.5	21.0
Meghalaya	11.5	11.7	12.2	10.7	18.7	17.8	19.3	16.9	16.0
Mizoram	29.6	34.9	28.1	28.0	28.0	27.0	26.0	26.0	25.0
Nagaland	26.1	23.1	32.4	31.6	30.8	30.0	29.7	29.0	28.5
Orissa	25.8	25.3	23.5	23.4	23.8	46.9	45.1	39.0	35.0
Punjab	19.3	21.8	18.7	18.5	18.3	18.2	18.0	18.0	17.8
Rajasthan	25.8	23.1	24.5	25.2	25.0	28.5	25.3	23.0	22.5
Sikkim	24.5	25.9	21.8	21.5	21.2	21.0	20.2	20.0	20.0
Tamil Nadu	18.0	18.4	17.5	17.3	16.9	17.0	17.0	17.0	17.0
Tripura	29.6	32.0	30.5	30.0	30.0	30.0	30.0	29.8	29.0
Uttar Pradesh	27.1	26.1	24.1	23.2	22.6	22.8	24.6	23.0	21.0
West Bengal	17.7	19.7	23.7	22.4	21.1	20.7	20.1	19.7	18.9
All India (Utilities)	**22.9**	**22.8**	**19.8**	**20.2**	**20.3**	**22.2**	**23.0**	**21.8**	**20.8**

1997-98 numbers are revised and 1998-99 are the estimates

Source: Planning Commission, 1999 Annual Report on the Working of State Electricity Boards and Electricity Departments, New Delhi, Power and Energy Division, Government of India

The reality is that APM has not led to any significant increases in operating efficiency of public sector plants. A study on APM (R-Group) suggested that improvement in operating efficiency could result in cost savings of over US$500 million. In addition APM has led to substantial allocative inefficiency in industry (Jha and Sahni 1993).

Recent energy sector reforms have attempted to bring prices for many of the petroleum products (naphtha, furnace oil, LSHS, LDO and bitumen) in line with international prices. In particular there has been a linking of diesel prices to international prices and a reduction in subsidy. However, LPG and kerosene, consumed mainly by private consumers continue to be heavily subsidised. Subsidies and cross-subsidies have resulted in serious distortions in prices, as they do not reflect economic costs at all in many cases. Total petroleum subsidy has been registering very high increases over the years. For the year ending March 2000 this subsidy stood at Rs.178.5 billion.

Table 18.11: Value of Subsidy for Agricultural Consumers in India (million rupees)

State Electricity Board	1992/93	1993/94	1994/95	1995/96	1996/97	1997/98	1998/99
Andhra Pradesh	7 259	9 254	13 503	17 477	16 788	18 155	21 428
Assam	62	88	11	87	60	141	163
Bihar	2 676	2 519	2 971	2 995	3 507	3 908	4 478
Delhi Vidyut Board	86	0	0	0	0	0	254
Gujrat	10 554	12 060	12 662	16 468	18 126	25 039	31 806
Haryana	4 563	5 400	4 898	6 123	7 274	7 427	8 898
Himachal Pradesh	10	15	9	7	9	14	16
Jammu & Kashmir	275	534	668	706	907	1167	1319
Karnataka	4 965	6 679	8 707	11 092	9 100	8 252	9 228
Kerala	0	164	230	357	470	517	672
Madya Pradesh	4 211	7 562	11 037	14 164	17 249	18 542	20 463
Maharashtra	10 309	11 309	16 470	22 498	25 536	28 758	33 731
Meghalaya	0	1	1	2	2	2	7
Orissa	207	392	202	303	408	483	574
Punjab	6 871	7 973	7 809	8 285	10 083	14 731	15 532
Rajasthan	3 475	4 684	6 226	8 076	10 550	10 409	11 474
Tamil Nadu	6 425	7 598	9 468	11 333	12 802	15 617	17 823
Uttar Pradesh	10 354	12 274	12 751	14 024	17 623	18 900	2 019
West Bengal	1 042	1 150	1 688	2 065	2 496	3 249	3 916
Total	73 344	89 656	109 311	136 062	152 990	175 311	183 801

1997-98 numbers are revised and 1998-99 are the estimates

Source: Planning Commission, 1999 Annual Report on the Working of State Electricity Boards and Electricity Departments, New Delhi, Power and Energy Division, Government of India

Note: The subsidy in 1998–9 works out to be nearly US$4 billion and it has doubled in less than 5 years.

6. Conclusions

The challenge facing India in the infrastructure sector is immense. On the one hand, it is clear that infrastructural development is critical to higher economic growth and poverty alleviation and, on the other, it is also clear that there are serious impediments to the reforms that will ensure rapid development of the infrastructure. The sector needs large doses of investment, an overhaul of regulatory and governance structures and rational pricing mechanisms. This chapter has examined some of the issues involved — particularly in the case of electricity. Other infrastructural sectors such as transport[10] and ports face similar difficulties. The policy establishment, including government, academics and business, is involved in a meaningful debate on the contours that reforms policy toward infrastructure should take. The annual *India Infrastructure Report* published by the 3iNetwork[11] is a good summary of such deliberations. However, fundamental improvement in the infrastructure sector hinges on the ability to effect price and regulatory reforms and thus attract large doses of investment. Such reform is likely to encounter stiff political opposition in the short run as subsidies are cut and user fees for infrastructural services rise. This would lead to political opposition, especially from the poorer areas of the country which are also characterised by inadequate infrastructure. Success in infrastructure reform thus depends upon forming enough political consensus to weather these short run problems. An important inducement, of course, is that with such reform not only will infrastructure services improve but economic growth should accelerate. Thus, the political establishment needs to have a sufficiently long horizon to contemplate such reforms.

---

[10] For an analysis of the challenges facing India's transport sector see World Bank (2002).

[11] The 3iNetwork consists of the Infrastructure Development Finance Company, the Indian Institute of Management, Ahmedabad, and the Indian Institute of Technology, Kanpur.

Table 18.12: Value of Subsidy for Domestic Electricity Consumers (million rupees)

State Electricity Board	1992/93	1993/94	1994/95	1995/96	1996/97	1997/98	1998/99
Andhra Pradesh	404	636	1 187	1 593	2 380	2 558	3 682
Assam	372	824	793	901	1 191	1 189	1 635
Bihar	400	563	892	1 189	1 583	1 779	1 929
Delhi Vidyut Board	2 974	0	0	0	0	0	4 227
Gujrat	880	949	1 218	1 361	1 122	921	228
Haryana	956	1 372	1 132	1 231	1 096	110	681
Himachal Pradesh	137	259	232	199	296	451	530
Jammu & Kashmir	495	620	700	938	1 277	1 564	1 630
Karnataka	225	92	353	1 185	2 523	2 207	2 114
Kerala	605	834	1 147	2 040	3 748	3 443	4 830
Madya Pradesh	2 527	2 584	3 154	4 015	5 104	5 929	7 149
Maharashtra	1 516	1 933	1 902	3 257	4 238	2 955	4 574
Meghalaya	14	11	28	59	67	76	296
Orissa	804	1 224	921	1 435	1 963	2 283	2 534
Punjab	543	831	1 081	1 196	1 623	2 521	3 207
Rajasthan	1 833	1 275	1 634	2 207	2 180	2 648	2 979
Tamil Nadu	1 418	1 476	1 586	1 927	2 375	3 046	3 379
Uttar Pradesh	3 318	4 685	5 635	5 575	8 071	9 877	11 354
West Bengal	929	1 140	1 773	1 926	2 588	3 293	3 854
Total	**20 350**	**21 308**	**25 368**	**32 234**	**43 425**	**46 850**	**60 812**

1997-98 numbers are revised and 1998-99 are the estimates

Source: Planning Commission, 1999 Annual Report on the Working of State Electricity Boards and Electricity Departments, New Delhi, Power and Energy Division, Government of India

References

Ahluwalia, M.S., 'Economic Performance of States in Post-Reforms Period', *Economic and Political Weekly*, 35 (2000), 780–92.

Banerjee, Abhijit 'Who is getting public goods in India: some evidence and some speculation', mimeo, Department of Economics, MIT (2002).

Barro, Robert J and X. Sala-I-Martin *Economic Growth;* (Singapore: McGraw Hill International Edition, 1995).

Binswanger, Hans P. and S.R. Khandker 'How Infrastructure and Financial Institutions Affect Agricultural Output and Investments in India', *Journal of Economic Development* 41 (1993), 337–66.

Chitkara, P., *Estimation of Performance Benchmarks, Inefficiency Measurement and Pricing of Power*, unpublished Ph.D. Dissertation (Mumbai, India: IGIDR, 1998)

Chitkara, P., 'A Data Envelopment Analysis Approach to Evaluation of Operational Inefficiencies in Power Generating Units: A case study of Indian Power Plants'. *IEEE Trans. On Power Systems* 14(2) (1999), 150–6.

Das, Keshab "Endowments and Rural Infrastructure: Issues Today" in Sebastian Moriss (ed.) India Infrastructure Report 2002, 3iNetwork, 187–95.

DFAT (Department of Foreign Affairs and Trade, Commonwealth of Australia, *India: New Economy Old Economy*, Economic Analytical Unit, Department of Foreign Affairs and Trade (Canberra: Commonwealth of Australia, 2001).

Dreze, Jean and Amartya Sen *India, Economic Development and Social Opportunity* (Delhi: Oxford University Press, (1995).

GOI, *India: National Human Development Report 2001*, Planning Commission, New Delhi: Government of India, 2002).

Jha, R., M.N. Murty and B.S. Sahni, 'Cross-Sectional and Time Series Variations in Technical Efficiency in the Public Sector: State Electricity Boards in India' *Indian Economic Review* (special number) 27 (1992), 361–72.

Jha, R. and B.S. Sahni, *Industrial Efficiency: An Indian Perspective* (New Delhi: Wiley Eastern, 1993).

Kurian, N.J., 'Widening Regional Disparities in India: Some Indicators', *Economic and Political Weekly*, 37 (2002), 559–71.

Mitra, Arup 'Productivity and Technical Efficiency in Indian States' Manufacturing: The Role of Infrastructure', *Economic Development and Cultural Change* 50(2) (2002), 395–426.

Moriss, Sebastian (ed.), *India Infrastructure Report 2002: Governance Issues for Commercialization* (New Delhi: Oxford Unviersity Press, 2002)

Moriss, Sebastian (ed.), *India Infrastructure Report 2001* (New Delhi: Oxford University Press, 2001).

NCAER, *The India Infrastructure Report*, Expert Group on the Commercialization of Infrastructure Projects (New Delhi: National Council of Applied Economic Research, 1996).

Rao, M.G., R.T. Shand and K.P. Kalirajan 'Convergence of Incomes Across Indian States — A divergent view', *Economic and Political Weekly,* 34, 27 March 1999).

Sachs, J., N. Bajpai and A. Ramiah, 'Understanding Regional Economic Growth in India', *Working Paper No. 88* (Harvard University, Centre for International Development,). 2002).

World Bank W*orld Development Report: Infrastructure for Development*, Washington D.C.: World Bank, 1994).

World Bank, *India: Country Framework Report for Private Participation in Infrastructure* World Bank/Public-Private Infrastructure Facility, 2000).
World Bank, *India's Transport Sector: The Challenges Ahead* (in two volumes), Washington D.C.: World Bank, 2002.

PART VI

INDIAN SOCIAL SECTOR

19

Income Generation Program and Empowerment of Women — A case study in India

Saswati Basu and Parikshit Basu

1. Introduction

The economic reform agenda set against the backdrop of globalization is dominating the socio-economic-cultural scenario in recent years. In India the process was started in the second half of the 1980s, although officially embraced in 1991. Since then India's socio-economic structure has been in flux. Among many others, public sector activities are being significantly affected and that, in turn, has affected the conduct of economic development programs. Traditionally development programs in India have been primarily conducted and controlled by the public sector. The effectiveness and extent of success of most of these programs have been questioned time and again. With economic reforms and the consequent falling importance of the public sector, the picture is changing rapidly. With the increasing importance of accountability a participatory approach is gaining higher importance.

The nature and operation of economic development programs targeting women in particular are also undergoing changes. Improving empowerment of women, one of the major targets of economic development programs in this area, is highly dependent on accountability and participation. As a result, the potential of the non-government sector is now increasingly being recognised. Non-government organizations (NGOs) are becoming increasingly involved in the economic development program.

Empowerment has been a catchword in the lexicon of economic development analysis for women. Women suffer from different types of powerlessness in social and economic spheres of life. The lack of power, or disempowerment, is reflected in lower attainments of education, income levels, lower control over their own income, lower bargaining power in selling their own produce and labour, lower participation in decision-making bodies, lower access to production inputs, resources and employment opportunities than men. This increased vulnerability of women characterizes many countries — particularly developing ones. Their dependence on men makes them a burden on a family and lowers their self-esteem. Development practitioners are concerned with raising women's empowerment levels and enabling them to overcome their dependency within their families.

Until the Sixth Five-Year Plan (1980–85) the approach to women's development programs was welfare based. Their role in economic development was considered secondary. The Sixth Plan adopted an approach with a thrust on employment along with education and health. In programs such as the Integrated Rural Development Program (IRDP) and Training for Rural Youth for Self-Employment (TRYSEM), women have been considered as a unit to get the resources of these programs. The Development of Women and Children in Rural Areas (DWACRA) program was established to provide loans for poor women on a group basis. The degree of success of these programs was limited (Swaminathan 1990; Mayox 1987; World Bank 1991).

The Ninth Five-Year Plan (1997–2002) has initiated certain major steps towards gender justice and empowerment of women. To create an enabling environment for women to exercise their rights, both within and outside the home as equal partners along with men, National Policy for Empowerment of Women is being adopted during this plan period (Shrivastava 2000).

This chapter attempts to review the increasingly important role of accountability and participatory approach in the empowerment of women under the umbrella of an economic reform agenda in India in recent years. The study has used a socio-economic case study in the districts of South 24 Parganas in West Bengal, India.

2. Definition and Literature Review

The definition of empowerment according to UNDP (1995) includes the expansion of choices for women and increasing their ability to exercise their choice. Thus improvement in women's access to economic opportunities through credit and employment programs could expand their choices to take over. Health and education related programs could enhance their capability to take advantage of those choices. It is perceived that when a development program increases women's choices of employment by providing credit facilities, it expands their choice set and raises their ability to exercise those choices. Schooling programs for women should both increase their voice in the family and the range of job options open to them (Mehra 1997).

However, researchers are arguing over the nature of development programs best suited to empowering women. Buvinic (1989) and Kandiyoti (1988) suggest that economic development programs could automatically improve the economic status of women and thereby their overall status in the community and the family.

Sometimes women cannot exercise their choices because of social restrictions practiced by their families. One study contends that one should not assume that generation of income or economic empowerment would automatically increase women's independence, bargaining power and overall status in the family or in the community (McCormack et al. 1986).

Some researchers find that the best way of achieving women's empowerment is to organise them under a common group or forum with an income generation program support (Carr et al. 1996; Viswanath 1995). They find that NGOs in different countries of south Asia have achieved this goal by following multiple development strategies. NGOs generally take participatory and community development approaches, which differ from traditional approaches usually taken by government institutions. Viswanath (1995) found that the overall empowerment of women in southern states of India improved when they had been organised under NGOs' economic development programs. SEWA (Self Employed Women Association), a NGO from western India, realised from their practical experience in the field of union strategy the necessity of undertaking income generation programs for bringing women under a common organisation (SEWA 1989; Carr et al. 1996). Smith (1995) pointed out that the participatory element embodied in the development strategy of NGOs might not always enhance the economic benefit of women beneficiaries of an economic development program. It requires the accountability of an organisation towards their members to increase the economic benefit. Higher member accountability of an organisation brings larger socio-economic benefit to their beneficiaries.

Thus the existing literature suggests that employment or income generation programs or economic development programs, participatory approach to development and member accountability of organisation are key elements of any development strategy that aims to empower women. We use a case study to assess whether the economic empowerment of women generated by economic development programs increases overall empowerment of women.

3. Methodology of the case study

3.1 Methodology

We examine a socio-economic case study using Rapid Rural Appraisal (RRA) method (Nichols 1991). This survey technique relies on quantitative information obtained through the use of a pre-designed schedule or questionnaire. The qualitative technique used relies on extracting information from the respondent by being with them, experimenting with them and talking to a whole range of people related to the program.

The case study interviewed seventy women beneficiaries of two economic development programs of a government organisation and a NGO, based in South 24 Parganas district of West Bengal in India. Systematic sampling method was followed for selecting the sample as the population for each organisation was small (Groebner and Patrick 1989). Every third woman beneficiary was selected until the required sample size was reached.

As the sample size is small, the present study primarily depends on interpretation of data rather than application of any econometric model. However, to justify sample consistency, analysis of variance (ANOVA) procedure has been used (Anderson et al. 1989). ANOVA is used as a method for testing hypothesis involving the difference between two population variances using F distribution. If the estimated value of the F ratio is higher than the critical F distribution value with respective degrees of freedom, the hypothesis (of different characteristics of population) is accepted. We used ANOVA procedures to determine the difference between NGO and GO (government organization) for variables relating to member accountability.

We analyse a credit programme. Economic and social indicators have been used to determine the impact of the credit program on economic empowerment of women. We use member accountability of a development organisation to judge the effectiveness of development strategy to achieve the goal of economic empowerment. The following indicators have been used

i) Income per month has been considered as the indicator of the economic empowerment. A successful economic development program should lead to higher level of income to its beneficiaries.

ii) Two indicators have been used to identify the social empowerment of women. These are:

   a. business knowledge and established market links by women beneficiaries; and

   b. participation in the intra-family decision making process.

3.2 Member Accountability Indicators

Typically accountability is interpreted as the means by which individuals and organisations report to a recognised authority or authorities, and are held responsible for their actions (Edwards and Hulme 1995). Although accountability is viewed as a desirable organisational characteristic empirical studies commonly indicate that both leaders and subordinates in public and private organisations seek to avoid accountability (Smith 1995).

Accountability in the literature on NGOs covers more than financial accountability and covers several aspects of a development organisation (Smith 1995). It operates 'downward' to partners, beneficiaries, staff and supporters and 'upward' to their trustees, donors and host governments. In the present case study 'downwards' or member/beneficiary accountability is the only criterion chosen for judging the effectiveness of NGOs and GOs performance. Some studies (Smith 1995; Edwards and Hulme 1995) argue that the higher the accountability of an organisation to its members the better is its performance.

We examine three aspects of accountability. We check whether an organization:

(a) addresses problems, complaints and suggestions made by members;

(b) offers timely support and assistance to its member; two specific indicators have been chosen to measure the extent of this response:
- Initial support with business management and associated skill;
- Role of organization in loan sanction and associated formalities; and

(c) shares power and financial information with its members.

3.3 Case Study Context

The case study was undertaken in 1999-2000 at the Jaynagar Blocks 1 and 2 in South 24 Parganas district. The two economic development programs selected were the credit program (the Jeevandeep Prokalpo) of the Youth Club (YC) — a NGO; and the Integrated Rural Development Program (IRDP) managed by the District Rural Development Agency (DRDA) — a GO. The common objective of both the programs is to help poor men and women to be self-employed in off-farm enterprise.

From the lists of the beneficiaries who received credit from the two programs within the preceding three years from the survey date, seventy beneficiaries were chosen for detailed interviews (thirty from the NGO and forty from the GO) following a systematic sampling procedure. Four YCs under a Cluster Club at Jaynagar were selected for examination. The YCs, community organisations, started development activities in 1980 under Lokasiksha Parisad (LSP), a national NGO based in the state of West Bengal. The community organizations of the village under the

LSP's operational area are known as Youth Clubs. The Club plays a catalytic role between villages and external agencies such as LSP, Government of India and foreign bodies. The local YCs identify problems of villagers through periodical meetings or by talking to them directly. The LSP formulates policies and the YCs execute and implement these policies in villages.

Jeevandeep Prokolpo (JP), a credit and savings programme of the YC, promoted habits of thrift and provide credit, particularly to women members in the local areas. It started in 1982 and has provided small credits to more than 300 members so far. Major operational strategies of the program include providing help with skill training and business knowledge, monitoring business situation of borrower through post credit follow up programs etc.

The IRDP was introduced in 1979 with the objective of providing credit as a capital subsidy to poor, small and marginal farmers (with less than two acres of land holdings) to enhance or supplement their earnings from agriculture. It is the largest credit-based development program initiated by the Government of India and provides loans through commercial banks to households that are officially identified to be below the poverty line. The purpose of this loan is to finance purchase of assets that serve as the basis for self-employment. It was initiated during the Sixth Five-Year Plan (Planning Commission, 1980).

The responsibility for the implementation of the IRDP lies with the District Rural Development Agencies (DRDA). It works under the Department of Rural Development, Ministry of Agriculture. The office of the South 24 Parganas DRDA is located at the district headquarters in Alipore, Calcutta.

4. Case study results

4.1 Economic Indicators

The primary objective of the programs studied here is to offer opportunities for employment to their members and thus, increasing their incomes. After obtaining loans, some women started business and some began wage employment. While evaluating the economic and social impacts, the study has considered only those beneficiaries who are engaged in income earning activities using credit provided by the programs. However, to evaluate the perception of the women beneficiaries about member accountability of the organizations, the entire sample has been considered.

Table 19.1 reveals that eighteen (60 per cent) female borrowers in the NGO program are engaged in income earning business activities, whereas only six (15 per cent) borrowers from the GO programme are so engaged.

Their income earnings range between Rs.150 to more than Rs.1000 per month (the then prevailing exchange rate: US$ 1 = Rs 45).

Some employed women invested their loan in family businesses such as vegetable vending, vegetable cultivation, *bidi* rolling and tea stalls. All of them work in their family businesses and substitute for hired labour. In such cases, their income level is assessed on the basis of the market wage for the relevant hired labour. Although these women earn profits (as part owner of the family business), only the wage income has been considered, as it is not possible to disentangle the amount of profit generated by the women alone.

Table 19.1: Average Per Capita Monthly Income of Female Borrowers (for employed women only)

Average monthly income (Indian Rupees)	*NGO program*		*GO program*	
	Number	*% of total*	*Number*	*% of total*
Less than 300	2	11.1	4	66.6
301 – 500	4	22.3	-	-
501 – 700	5	27.8	-	-
701 – 900	4	22.2	-	-
More than 900	3	16.6	2	33.4
All Groups	18	100.0	6	100.0

***Source*: Case study undertaken during December 1999 to January 2000.**

Female borrowers from the NGO earn a better income than those from the GO. About 39 per cent of total employed women under the NGO programme earn more than Rs.700 compared to 33 per cent under GO programme. Two-thirds of the employed women under the GO programme fall within the lowest income range (below Rs.300 per month). Only 11 per cent of the employed women under NGO program earn such a low level of income. These women are considered to be very poor. Some of them are the sole income earners in their families.

4.2 Social Indicators

4.2.1 Business knowledge and marketing links established by borrowers

Employed women borrowers from the NGO and GO were asked questions regarding their business knowledge and marketing links. The case-study results show that more employed women under the NGO credit program have knowledge about the price of raw materials and different marketing sources for selling their final products.

A possible reason behind the success of the NGO women lies in the operational strategy of the NGOs. First, for business loans NGOs assign priority to those who are already in business and have some entrepreneurial ability. Second, when an applicant for a business loan lacks any business knowledge, the NGO staff advises her about the business she intends to take up, the differences in wholesale and retail prices of raw materials, the market prices of the product, target markets, possible exploitation by the middlemen, associated risks etc. In this process, a woman under the NGO program gathers basic business knowledge from the NGO staff. Women under the GO programme have to submit a business proposal with the application for a business loan. The proposal has little real significance, and can be written by anybody or even 'bought' from the market. One local council (*Panchayat*) member reported during the interview that women applicants often don't know what a proposal means.

4.2.2 Participation in the intra-family decision-making process

Women's participation in intra-family decision-making process indicates their level of social development. The economic independence of women and their share of contribution to the family fund are considered major factors influencing the participation of women in intra-family decision-making. The case study reveals that women under the NGO program participated more than GOs women in intra-family decision making. There is only a weak relation between money contribution of women and their level of participation.

4.2.3 Member accountability indicators

Member-accountability of an organization is one of the most important indicators used to judge its performance in assisting development. The performance of an implementing organization depends on its operational strategy and implementation procedure. The accountability of an organization to its members might be considered as one part of its implementing procedure. The higher the accountability the better should be the performance. Women members and the beneficiaries of the NGO and GO programs were asked to rank their perceptions of the member accountability in a scale of 'good', 'satisfactory', 'not-satisfactory' and 'no comment'.

4.2.4 Adequately addressing problems/complaints and suggestions

Member-accountable organizations create a conducive environment for voicing their member's problems, complaints and suggestions.

Most women members of the YC (NGO) ranked their perceptions as either 'good' or 'satisfactory' (Table 19.2). Half the women who borrowed from the YCs ranked its member-accountability as 'good'. Another 26.7 per cent ranked it as 'satisfactory'. The women saw the authorities as listening to their complaints and trying to address them adequately. Moreover, such assistance was received within a reasonable time. Some women reported that they had an informal relationship with YC staff. As they are all local, members can easily voice their problems at any time. When they were unable to pay their loan instalments on time the secretary of the YC permitted extensions depending on the situation. Our findings confirm that the NGOs work closely at grassroots level (Tendler 1982; Robinson 1991; Smith 1995).

Table 19.2: Ranking of Member Accountability in Addressing the Problems, Complaints and Suggestions as Perceived by the Women Borrowers

Ranks	*NGO*		*GO*	
	Number	*% of total*	*Number*	*% of total*
Good	15	50.0	-	-
Satisfactory	8	26.7	24	60.0
Not-satisfactory	6	20.0	6	15.0
No Comment	1	3.3	10	25.0
All Groups	30	100.0	40	100.0
F Ratio : 52.73 – Significant at 1% level of confidence				

***Source*: Case study undertaken during December 1999to January 2000.**

However, about 20 per cent of the NGO members are unhappy about their suggestions/ complaints not being addressed and ranked the member accountability as 'not-satisfactory'. They reported that the authorities did not listen to their complaints.

In the case of the GO 60 per cent of the women borrowers from GO rank the members' accountability of their organisation as 'satisfactory'. Most of them were defaulters and could not repay their loans. The *Panchayat* members listened to their problems and assured them that loan repayment was not necessary. This confirms extant findings that politicians often play a negative role by assuring beneficiaries that they need not repay the loan (Mayoux 1989).

About 15 per cent of the GO borrowers perceive member accountability in addressing problems and suggestions as 'non-satisfactory'. They never met any person in their locality from the DRDA office or the banks and thus could not discuss their problems. One borrower found, after taking a loan for incense-stick business, that the loan amount was too small to start the business. Another woman reported that she had taken a loan and afterwards received a letter from the bank asking her to repay a much higher amount. They never had the opportunity to discuss their problem with local authorities.

4.3 Providing Timely Support and Assistance

Two aspects are examined:

i) Initial support with business management and associated skills;

ii) The role of organization in the loan sanction and associated formalities; and

i) Initial support in business management and other required skills

Women borrowers generally need to acquire some knowledge of business management. They also need direct encouragement to stay in the business and overcome the difficulties. A member-accountable organization should help its members to gain basic business knowledge.

The case study reveals that more women borrowers of the NGO were happy about the member accountability of their organization regarding initial support in starting a business. Most rank this aspect as 'good' or 'satisfactory'. None of the GO members did the same (Table 19.3).

Table 19.3: Ranking of Member Accountability Regarding Initial Support for Starting a Business as Perceived by Women Borrowers

Rank	NGO		GO	
	Number	% of total	Number	% of total
Good	2	6.7	-	-
Satisfactory	15	50.0	-	-
Not-satisfactory	9	30.0	6	15.0
No Comment	4	13.3	34	85.0
All Groups	30	100.0	40	100.0
F Ratio : 86.81 – Significant at 1% level of confidence				

Source: **Case study undertaken during December 1999 - January 2000.**

When a member applies for a business loan, she is asked in detail about the type of business activities she intends to undertake. The NGO arranges some business related training if needed. Women members who obtained such active support from the NGO ranked member accountability as 'good'. Most of the NGO women had a basic knowledge of their business before obtaining a loan — and updated their knowledge from the YC's staff. Thus half of the women ranked the accountability of the YCs as 'satisfactory'.

Not all the borrowers were equally satisfied. Some lost their business in spite of help due to lack of market knowledge. Some of them trained in stitching saris with 'jari', and some others trained in small-scale fish cultivation in a home reservoir. They failed in business due to insufficient demand. They did not receive much active support from the NGO staff. These women ranked NGO accountability as 'not-satisfactory'.

On the other hand, women borrowers of GO did not receive initial support. They reported during interviews that bank officers came with local council members to ask them about the type of business they intended to start but never offered any business knowledge. Each local DRDA office had a technical service department. The IRDP borrowers could use this service by attending business-related training through TRYSEM (the Government of India's training scheme for rural youth for self-employment). They could also ask to market their products through government marketing cells or showrooms. However, most women in business were unaware of such facilities and ranked accountability as 'not-satisfactory'. The borrowers of the IRDP reported that they never received any business related advice from DRDA and the staff never encouraged them to become motivated entrepreneurs.

ii) Role of the organisation regarding loan sanction and associated formalities

Women need assistance in processing loan application and other related formalities. A member-accountable organization should support its members actively in this area. Our results testing this are presented in Table 19.4.

Almost two-thirds of women borrowers from the NGO ranked its member accountability as 'good'. They obtained help in the technical formalities and received a loan within a reasonable period. These women considered the whole process of taking out a loan as being very simple. The YCs play the role of guarantor for the loan. Another 16.7 per cent of NGO women rank this aspect of member accountability as 'satisfactory'. Only 10 per cent of women ranked the NGO as 'not-satisfactory' and reported that they did not receive loans within a reasonable period of time.

Table 19.4: Ranking of Member Accountability Regarding Loan Sanction and Associated Formalities as Perceived by Women Borrowers

Rank	*NGO*		*GO*	
	Number	*% of total*	*Number*	*% of total*
Good	20	66.7	-	-
Satisfactory	5	16.7	15	37.5
Not-satisfactory	3	10.0	20	50.0
No Comment	2	6.6	5	12.5
All Groups	30	100.0	40	100.0
F Ratio : 37.89 – Significant at 1 per cent level of confidence				

Source: **Case study undertaken during December 1999 – January 2000.**

About 37.5 per cent of women borrowers from the IRDP ranked the member accountability of the organisation in sanctioning and other associated formalities as 'satisfactory'. The process is very complicated and takes a very long time to complete. Half of the GO borrowers ranked the loan sanctioning aspect as 'not-satisfactory' as they disliked the common system of charging 'commission' by the local council members for selecting them as a candidate for getting a loan and helping them in the process. They received the loan after a long wait and suspected that the local council members are partly responsible for these delays. It appears that NGOs can provide faster service than GOs (Aremo 1983; Heijden 1986).

4.4 Sharing Power with Beneficiaries

An organization's ability to share power with its members is one of the important indicators of its member accountability. This indicator reflects the extent of participation and involvement of members with the organization. Women borrowers from the credit program of the NGO and the GO were asked several questions regarding their perceptions of the way organisation shared power of management and financial information with the members. Results (Table 19.5) show that most of female borrowers from the NGO credit program rank it as 'good' while borrowers from the GO credit program rank it as 'not-satisfactory'.

Two-thirds of the NGO borrowers who ranked the member accountability as 'good', reported during interviews that they had an informal relationships with the secretary. Some NGO women members offered suggestions, for example, on poultry farming and kitchen gardening at the monthly meetings. These suggestions were subsequently incorporated by the YCs into the guidelines. Some members suggested the timing and date for monthly meetings; others criticised board members for not creating sufficient pressure on defaulters and others recommended higher ceilings on loans.

Table 19.5: Ranking of Member Accountability in Sharing Power with its Members as Perceived by Women Borrowers

Rank	*NGO*		*GO*	
	Number	*% of total*	*Number*	*% of total*
Good	20	66.7	-	-
Satisfactory	5	16.7	-	-
Not-satisfactory	2	6.6	32	80.0
No Comment	3	10.0	8	20.0
All Groups	30	100.0	40	100.0
F Ratio : 82.79 – Significant at 1% level of confidence				

***Source*: Case study undertaken during December 1999 – January 2000.**

These women attended monthly meetings regularly where their information was updated. Personal visits to the secretary helped them to gather additional information. The secretary visits them every month to collect instalments. These women reported that their ideas on the objective and profit and loss of the organization were taken seriously and were satisfied with the NGOs way of sharing power of management and financial information.

About 17 per cent of the women borrowers of the NGO ranked it as 'satisfactory' and reported that they had no time to attend regular meetings but kept themselves informed about the activities of the organization. They never offered suggestions regarding any activity of the organization and did not have clear ideas about the profit and loss of the organisation. Only 6.6 per cent of the NGO borrowers ranked its accountability as 'not-satisfactory'. On the other hand, 80 per cent of the GO borrowers ranked this accountability as 'not-satisfactory'. They knew only the local council members and never received any information from them. They responded negatively to every question.

5. Conclusion

Our analysis has shown that the NGO's development strategy involved more accountability to their members and achieved higher economic and social empowerment of women beneficiaries. NGOs' development programs have contributed more than the GOs' programs. NGOs have certain positive qualities that make them more successful in reaching the poorer sections of society. These qualities include participation, partnership and member accountability. The participation of recipients in the organization is one of the major reasons for the NGOs' achieving greater success than the GOs. This study also points to the difference in approach between NGOs and GOs in sharing power with their members. Women beneficiaries of the NGOs had greater participation in the development process than those of the GOs programs. The NGOs' members participated in the identification process of their business activities and in the policy making body. The LSP, the parent body of YCs (NGO), followed a group approach for ensuring the active participation of local people.

The loan approval procedures also made a difference. The simple procedures of the NGOs credit system with lower interest rate, fewer formalities (paper work) for loan application and quick delivery of loans helped in emergencies. NGOs follow a strategy of partnership in their development approach and seek help from other organisations such as government, commercial banks, private companies, co-operative societies and other NGOs to achieve their goals.

Another factor responsible for greater success of the NGOs was the accountability of their staff to members. Through addressing the problems and suggestions of the members, by providing timely assistance and support and through sharing power and information with members, the NGOs demonstrated strong accountability to its members.

References

Agarwal, Bina, 'Rural Women, Poverty and Natural Resources: Sustenance, Sustainability and Struggle for Change', *Economic and Political Weekly* 24(43) (1989), 46–65.

Anderson, D., D. Sweeney, and T. Williams, *Statistics for Business and Economics* (Sydney: Harper & Row Publishers, 1989).

Aremo, J.A., 'Popular Participation in Rural Development', *Cares* 16 (May–June 1983), 19–23.

Buvinic, Mayra, *Women, Poverty and Progress in the Third World* (New York: Foreign Policies Association, 1989).

Carr, M.; M. Chen and R. Jabvala, *Speaking Out, Women's Economic Empowerment in South Asia* (London: IT Publications, 1996).

Centre for Monitoring Indian Economy, *Approach Paper to Ninth Five-Year Plan* (Bombay CMIE, 1997).

Edwards, Michael and David Hulme, *NGOs Performance & Accountability, beyond the Magic Bullet* (London: Save the Children, Earthscah Publications Ltd, 1995).

Groebner, D.F. and W.S. Patrick, *Business Statistics. A Decision-Making Approach* (Toronto: Merrill Publishing Company, 1989).

Heijden, H.V., 'Development Impact and Effectiveness of Non-Governmental Organisations: The Record of Progress in Rural Development Co-operation', mimeo, 1986).

Joseph, M., *Women participation and development strategies* (New Delhi: Kaniska Publishers, 1997).

Kandiyoti, D., *Women and Rural Development Policies: The Changing Agenda* (Brighton, UK: Institute of Development Studies, 1988).

Lokasiksha Parishad, *Gram Seva — Annual Report 1997* (Narendrapur, India: Ramakrishna Mission Ashrama, 1998).

McCormack, J.; M. Walsh and C. Nelson, *Women's Group Enterprises — A Study of the Structure and Opportunity on the Kenya Coast*, Report of USAID Human Resource Division (Boston: World Education Inc., 1986).

Mehra, R. 'Women, Empowerment and Economic Development', *The Annals of the American Academy of Political and Social Science* 554 (November 1997), 136–49.

Mayoux, L.C. 'Income Generation for Women in India: Problems and Prospects', *Development Policy Review* 17(1) (1989), 5–27.

Morris, William; C. P. Chadsey and Harold Wentworth (eds), *The Grosset Webster Dictionary* (New York: Grosset and Dunlop Publishers (1966).

Nichols, P., *Social Survey Method. A Field Guide for Development Workers* (Oxford: Oxfam, 1991).

Planning Commission *Draft Sixth Five-Year Plan 1980-85* (New Delhi: Government of India, 1980).

Robinson, M., 'Evaluating the Impact of NGOs in Rural Poverty Alleviation – India Country Study' (Overseas Development Institute Working Paper No. 49, ODI, London, 1991).

Roy, K.C.; C.A. Tisdell and H. C. Blomqvist *Economic Development and Women in the World Community* (West Port, US: Praeger Publisher, 1996).

SEWA (Self Employed Women Association), *Shramshakti – A Summary of the Report of the National Commission on Self-employed Women and Women in the Informal Sector* (Ahmedabad, India: SEWA publication, 1989).

Shrivastava, C.R., 'Ensuring Gender Equity and Equality', *Social Welfare* 47(4) (2000) 33–9.

Smith, S., *Accoutability in Development Organizations. Experiences of Women organizations in India* (New Delhi: Sage Publications, 1995).
Swaminathan, M., 'Village Level Implementation of IRDP – comparison of West Bengal and Tamil Nadu', *Economic and Political Weekly* 25(13) (1990), A17–26.
Tendler, J. 'Turning Private Voluntary Agencies into Development Agencies: Questions for Evaluation' (Washington DC: Aid Program Evaluation Discussion Paper No. 12, USAID, 1982).
UNDP, *World Development Report* (New York: Oxford University Press, 1995).
Viswanath, V. *NGOs and Women's Development in Rural South India. A Comparative Analysis* (Oxford: Westview Press, 1995).

20
Are the Poor More Vulnerable to Income Shocks? An analysis of consumption insurance in rural India

Pushkar Maitra

1. Introduction

The literature on risk and insurance argues that income risks are pervasive in poor rural economies. That leads us to the question of how well (if at all) are households in rural economies able to insure consumption against such shocks to income? In the recent past this question has led to a large volume of literature that evaluates the success or otherwise of households in insuring consumption and identifies the different mechanisms that could potentially be used to enable these households to insure against different kinds of income shocks.

The literature has concluded that households take actions aimed at protecting consumption, by drawing on both private and social risk sharing arrangements. Townsend (1994) lists five potential risk-bearing mechanisms: (1) Spatial diversification of land holdings; (2) Storage of grains from one year to the next; (3) Purchases and sales of assets such as bullocks and land; (4) Credit from formal and informal sources; and (5) Gifts and Transfers within the family networks.[1] However, not all households are equally able to insure consumption against income shocks and differentiated access to markets, particularly financial markets result in differential ability of households to insure against income shocks.

If risks are idiosyncratic (household specific) in nature, then households will pool together to share all risks. Further if risks are fully pooled then

[1] See Alderman and Paxson (1992), Deaton (1997), Fafchamps (1992), Grimard (1997), Morduch (1995) and Townsend (1994, 1995a) for a review of the theories and empirical evidence using different data sets. Morduch (1995) categorises the different mechanisms into two categories: exante income smoothing and expost consumption smoothing.

there is complete risk sharing among households and changes in household consumption will track changes in the community average consumption and nothing else. In particular, changes in factors specific to the household like changes in household income will not have a statistically significant impact on changes in household consumption. In such a case consumption is said to be fully insured. As a consequence the estimated marginal propensity to consume out of changes in income should not be statistically different from zero. Consider a regression of a change in household consumption on a change in community average consumption and a change in household income. If consumption is fully insured then the coefficient estimate of the change in community average consumption should be one and the coefficient estimate of the change in household income should be zero. The actual amount of risk sharing that actually takes place can now be compared to this benchmark of complete risk sharing. Note however that the community average consumption, which is a measure of aggregate risk (common to all households in the community), will continue to fluctuate.

In addition to the general question of risk sharing by rural households, this paper also examines whether the arrangements for consumption insurance in rural economies work better for some households (belonging to specific wealth groups) compared to others. *A-priori* one cannot say whether poor households are more vulnerable or not. On the one hand poorer households are likely to be more risk averse and hence they are more likely to undertake specific measures to reduce the variability of their income and hence directly reduce the variability of consumption. On the other hand poorer households are more likely to be rationed in the availability of credit and insurance, so they are less likely to be able to insure consumption once the income shock has occurred.

Different versions of this empirical specification have been tested using household level data from both developed and developing countries. Mace (1991) in her study on risk sharing in the US economy finds that the evidence is conditional on the preference specification. Results are mostly consistent with consumption insurance for the exponential utility specification but not for the power utility specification. Townsend (1995) finds overwhelming rejection of the null hypothesis for different regions in Thailand. He finds that consumption in one *ampoe* (region or state) tracks income in that region. Deaton (1992) obtains a similar conclusion using data from Côte d'Ivoire. He finds that the marginal propensities to consume out of current income are always positive and significant. Jalan and Ravallion (1999) using data from rural China find that that while full insurance is always rejected, there is evidence of partial insurance for certain wealth groups and the rejection of full insurance is the strongest for the poorest wealth decile. Results from rural India are somewhat varied.

Townsend (1994) in his study of risk and insurance in three ICRISAT villages finds that full consumption insurance is a fairly good benchmark.[2] Maitra (1998) on the other hand using data from rural Punjab finds no evidence in favour of consumption insurance against idiosyncratic income shocks.

This chapter uses a household level panel data set from rural India to examine the extent of consumption insurance. India is characterised by considerable regional variations in income and as such is an interesting country to examine. This is the first examination of consumption insurance using data from all parts of India, without focusing on specific regions as the Semi-Arid tropics (Townsend 1994) or rural Punjab (Maitra 1998).

The issue of consumption insurance has important policy implications. In many developing countries, governments and policy makers have implemented programs (like food for work programs, credit schemes, buffer stocks and crop insurance schemes) aimed at reducing the riskiness of income and provide insurance for the poor. The basic premise is that left to themselves (and in the absence of such government programs) poor households will be unable to insure themselves against income shocks. Given that these programs are expensive it is important to examine whether this argument is correct or not because it is an important issue from the point of view of designing efficient policies.

2. Data and Descriptive Statistics

This chapter tests for insurance against income shocks in rural India. For this purpose I use a panel data set from rural India obtained from a survey conducted by the National Council of Applied Economic Research (NCAER) in three rounds for the years 1968–69, 1969–70 and 1970–71 — the Additional Rural Income Survey (ARIS). The data set will henceforth be referred to as the ARIS–NCAER data. The main purpose of the survey was to measure the changes in income levels and income distribution and the consequent changes in the patterns of consumption, investment and savings of households in rural areas. The final data set I use consists of 4118 households residing in 257 villages. Detailed information was collected on the demographic composition of the household including household size and composition, the number of earners in the household, income by source, expenditure on different accounts, savings and asset holdings by type. More details about the survey can be obtained from NCAER (1975).

---

2 Data collected by the International Crop Research Institute for the Semi Arid Tropics (ICRISAT). This data is referred to as the ICRISAT data and the villages included in this survey the ICRISAT villages.

The measure of consumption I used here includes expenditure on food, non-food items (including toiletry), fuel and lighting, clothing, education, medical items, services and entertainment. The measure of income used includes income earned from crop profits, livestock, agricultural wages, regular salaries earned and income from self-employment.

To test for systematic inter-household differences in the extent of consumption smoothing, the sample is stratified on the basis of landownership. This method of stratification is used because in rural India landholding is the primary indicator of wealth because of the collateral value associated with land. This pattern of sample stratification is also a good indicator of how credit constrained a household is likely to be. The households are grouped into 4 categories depending on the amount of land owned: the landless (907 households), the small landowners owning between 1.0 and 2.5 hectares (1699 households), the medium landowners owning between 2.6 and 6.5 hectares (980 households) and finally the large landowners owning in excess of 6.5 hectares (532 households). I examine the sensitivity of the estimates to alternative sample stratification in Section 6.

Table 20.1 presents the summary statistics (sample size, mean and standard deviation) for income and consumption for each of the three years, for the full sample and also for the sample stratified on the basis of landownership. Also presented are the Coefficient of Variation (CV) of both Total Income and Total Consumption Expenditure for each of the three years. The CV is a unit free measure of volatility. Notice that income is much more volatile compared to consumption, irrespective of the landholding of the household. Also presented are the correlation between the change in income and change in consumption expenditure. Generally consumption tracks income more closely for the poorer households (that is, the correlation between change in total income and change in total consumption expenditure is higher) but the correlation is always statistically significant.

Thus while the volatility of consumption expenditure is generally less than the volatility of income (indicating some amount of consumption smoothing), income and consumption generally co-move, irrespective of the wealth group. However to test whether there is sharing of idiosyncratic risk within a village, one needs to control for aggregate village level shock. I do that next.

3. Conditions for Risk Sharing — Theory

Let us assume that income risk is the only form of risk faced by a particular community. Complete risk sharing will result in each household in the community being protected from idiosyncratic risk. Consumption will still

Table 20.1: Selected Descriptive Statistics

	Sample Size	1968–69 Mean	1968–69	1968–69 Std. Dev.	1969–70 Mean	1969–70	1969–70 Std. Dev.	1970–71 Mean	1970–71	1970–71 Std. Dev.
All Households										
Total Income	4118	3840.516		4239.807	3975.463		3762.848	4208.211		4095.707
Total Expenditure	4118	3002.369		2576.365	3118.308		2418.402	3186.873		2458.127
CV (Total Income)			110.397			94.6518			97.3266	
CV (Total Expenditure)			85.8111			77.5549			77.1329	
Correlation*						0.3883 (0.0000)			0.5149 (0.0000)	
Landless Households										
Total Income	907	2178.840		2421.497	2116.427		1802.195	2256.591		2404.215
Total Expenditure	907	1851.308		1917.734	1922.929		1451.966	1954.802		1607.362
CV (Total Income)			111.137			85.1527			106.542	
CV (Total Expenditure)			103.588			75.508			82.2263	
Correlation*						0.6035 (0.0000)			0.5271 (0.0000)	
Small Landowners										
Total Income	1699	2895.491		2565.156	2920.519		2236.783	2990.534		2195.875
Total Expenditure	1699	2453.692		1865.769	2521.446		1697.379	2564.243		1637.806
CV (Total Income)			88.5914			76.5885			73.4275	
CV (Total Expenditure)			76.0393			67.3177			63.8709	
Correlation*						0.4765 (0.0000)			0.6711 (0.0000)	
Medium Landowners										
Total Income	980	4986.281		4244.981	5212.728		3382.835	5468.707		3507.855
Total Expenditure	980	3865.374		2719.264	3999.813		2409.040	4079.836		2347.032
CV (Total Income)			85.1332			64.8957			64.1441	
CV (Total Expenditure)			70.3493			60.2288			57.5276	
Correlation*						0.3858 (0.0000)			0.4978 (0.0000)	
Large Landowners										
Total Income	532	7580.904		7147.765	8234.820		6055.951	9102.318		6626.628
Total Expenditure	532	5127.310		3361.450	5438.615		3380.523	5630.923		3523.768
CV (Total Income)			94.2864			73.5408			72.8015	
CV (Total Expenditure)			65.5597			62.1578			62.5789	
Correlation*						0.3143 (0.0000)			0.4734 (0.0000)	

Notes: CV = (SD/Mean)*100; *Correlation between change in Total Income and change in Total Expenditure; Figures in Parenthesis indicate p-values vary but that is only because of the risk common to all households (aggregate community level risk). The test for full insurance is therefore a test of the validity of Pareto Optimality for the economy under consideration.[3] The problem for the social planner is to

$$\text{Max} \sum_{i=1}^{I}\sum_{t=0}^{T}\sum_{s=0}^{S} \mu_{is}\,\pi_s \rho^t U(c_{its};\theta_{its}) \tag{1}$$

subject to the full income constraint

$$\sum_{i=1}^{I} c_{its} = \sum_{i=1}^{I} y_{its} \,\forall(t,s) \tag{2}$$

where π_s is the probability of state $s, s=1,\ldots,S$; c_{its} is household consumption and y_{its} is household income; μ_{is} is the time invariant Pareto Weight associated with household $i, i=1,\ldots,I$ in state s and I is the number of households; ρ is the rate of time preference assumed to be the same for all households, σ_{its} incorporates factors that change tastes. The Langrangian associated with this problem is:

$$L = \sum_t \rho^t \left[\sum_i \mu_{is} \sum_s \pi_s U(c_{its};\theta_{its}) + \lambda_{ts}\left\{\sum_i (y_{its} - c_{its})\right\}\right] \tag{3}$$

Different specifications of the utility function $(U(c_{its};\theta_{its}))$ will give different empirical specifications. Consider an exponential utility function with the specific functional form given by

$$U(c_{its};\theta_{its}) = -\frac{1}{\alpha}\exp\{-\alpha(c_{its} - \theta_{its})\} \tag{4}$$

With this functional form the first order conditions (after manipulations and disregarding the notation for the state) can be written as

$$\Delta c_{it} = \Delta c_t^a + (\Delta\theta_{it} - \Delta\theta_t^a);\, c_t^a = \frac{1}{I}\sum_i c_{it},\, \theta_t^a = \frac{1}{I}\sum_i \theta_{it} \tag{5}$$

Under the assumption of full consumption insurance, change in individual consumption Δc_{it} depends only on change in aggregate consumption Δc_t^a.

For the power utility function we have

$$U(c_{its};\theta_{its}) = \frac{c_{its}^{1-\alpha}}{1-\alpha}\exp(\theta_{its}) \tag{6}$$

---

[3] The test described below closely follows Mace (1991). Cochrane (1991) and Townsend (1994) present similar tests.

the first order conditions (again after manipulations and disregarding the notation for the state) can be written as:

$$\Delta\log(c_{it}) = \Delta c_t^a + \left(\Delta\theta_{it} - \Delta\theta_t^a\right); c_t^{*a} = \frac{1}{I}\sum_i \log(c_{it}), \theta_t^a = \frac{1}{I}\sum_i \theta_{it} \tag{7}$$

Once again under the assumption of full insurance, change in household consumption depends only on change in community average consumption.

To examine how Pareto Optimal allocation is attained in a decentralised economy, I assume the existence of a complete set of Arrow Debreu securities. This allows me to decentralise the economy and examine whether full insurance can be attained through market mechanisms and enables me to test for consumption insurance for subsets of the population. In particular we test for consumption insurance for households classified by land holding. It can easily be shown that if there exists a complete set of Arrow Debreu securities, then the equilibrium consumption allocation will be identical to that obtained under a social planner's problem.

I now turn to the empirical specification.

4. Empirical Framework

Let c_{ivt}^{w} denote the per capita consumption of household *i* in village *v* in year *t* and belonging to the wealth group *w* $(i = 1,\ldots,I; v = 1,\ldots,V; t = 0,\ldots,T; w = 1,\ldots,W)$. Under the assumption of complete risk pooling (full insurance), the change in household consumption from year t to year $t+1$ depends only on the corresponding change in the aggregate village level consumption. The empirical specification follows immediately. Regress the change in the consumption of the ith household on the change in the village level average consumption and other explanatory variables like the change in household consumption. All variables with the exception of changes in average village level consumption are predicted to enter insignificantly. If the utility function is given by (4), the empirical specification can be written as

$$\Delta c_{ivt}^{w} = \beta_0^{w} + \beta_1^{w}\Delta c_{vt}^{aw} + \beta_2^{w}\Delta y_{ivt}^{w} + \beta_3^{w}\Delta n_{ivt}^{w} + \varepsilon_{ivt}^{w} \tag{8}$$

Here Δy_{ivt}^{w} is the change in household i's per capita income and Δn_{ivt}^{w} is the change in the household size. The error term ε_{ivt}^{w} includes both preference shocks (θ_{it}) and measurement error and is distributed identically and independently. The null hypothesis of full risk sharing predicts that $\beta_1^{w} = 1, \beta_2^{w} = 0$.

If on the other hand the utility function is given by (5), the empirical specification can be written as

$$\Delta\log\left(c_{ivt}^{w}\right)=\beta_0^{w}+\beta_1^{w}\Delta c_{vt}^{*aw}+\beta_2^{w}\Delta\log\left(y_{ivt}^{w}\right)+\beta_3^{w}\Delta\log\left(n_{ivt}^{w}\right)+\varepsilon_{ivt}^{w} \qquad (9)$$

Once again the null hypothesis of full risk sharing predicts that $\beta_1^w = 1, \beta_2^w = 0$.

5. Results

Table 20.2 presents the coefficient estimates for the regression of the change in the level of consumption on the change in the level of income and the change in the community average level of consumption (estimates of equation (8)). This will be referred to as the baseline specification. In this and in all subsequent regressions we control for the change in household size. The coefficient of the change in household size (β_3^w) is always negative and statistically significant. Results are presented for all households (full sample) and the sample stratified on the basis of landholding. The joint test presented in the table refers to the test for full insurance $\beta_1^w = 1, \beta_2^w = 0$. Note that β_2^w is the estimated marginal propensity to consume out of total income. Two alternative specifications are considered. In the first household income is assumed to be exogenous. The estimates are computed using OLS. I then account for the possibility that household income might actually be endogenous in that households might be using some component of income for the purposes of consumption smoothing — for example one response to crop failure might be to look for additional non-farm work. Lagged levels of income, savings and the number of earners in the household are used as instruments to compute the instrumental variable (IV/2SLS) estimates. There is a second reason to use 2SLS estimation methodology. This arises from the standard problem of errors in variables. In most developing countries data on income is measured with error, while data on consumption is relatively error free. Use of instruments will allow us to account for this problem.

The following results are worth noting. First, the estimated marginal propensities to consume are generally higher when income is assumed to be exogenous (OLS estimates) compared to the case where income is assumed to be endogenous (2SLS estimates). Second the estimated marginal propensities to consume are always significantly greater than zero and this is true for all households and separately for households belonging to the different land classes. Third, the null hypothesis of full insurance (that changes in household consumption is related to changes in community level average consumption and not to changes in household income) is always rejected. Fourth, the estimated marginal propensities to consume out of changes in income are higher for the landless households and the small landowners compared to the medium and large landowners. These results therefore imply that the poorest households are the most vulnerable to idiosyncratic income shocks as consumption generally tracks income more closely for the poorer households (landless households and small landowners).

Table 20.2: Consumption Changes Regressed on Income Changes — Levels

	OLS		2SLS	
	Δy^{w}_{ivt}	*Joint Test*[a]	Δy^{w}_{ivt}	*Joint Test*[a]
All Households	0.179*** (0.006)	477.34***	0.162*** (0.012)	50.68***
Landless Households	0.322*** (0.021)	115.53***	0.315*** (0.033)	46.84***
Small Landowners	0.311*** (0.010)	461.81***	0.167*** (0.027)	19.08***
Medium Landowners	0.119*** (0.009)	83.35***	0.104*** (0.015)	25.46***
Large Landowners	0.126*** (0.013)	51.19***	0.118*** (0.029)	8.17***

Notes: Figures in Parenthesis are Standard Errors
***: Significant at 1%
Joint Test[a]: $\beta^{w}_{1} = 1, \beta^{w}_{2} = 0 \sim F$

6. Robustness

How sensitive are the results to the estimation methodology used and the sample stratification used. I consider several tests to ensure that the results are robust to alternative estimation methodologies used and alternative sample stratification used. The results are presented in Tables 20.3 to 20.5.

Column (1) in Table 20.3 presents the estimated coefficients corresponding to equation (9) — growth rates in consumption regressed on growth rates of income and growth rates in community average consumption. Here the estimated coefficients of β^{w}_{2} may be interpreted as the elasticity of consumption with respect to change in income. Only the 2SLS estimates are presented. The null hypothesis of full insurance is always rejected. I again find that the poorest households are the most vulnerable to income shocks as consumption generally tracks income more closely for the poorer households. The results are in general comparable to the baseline results presented in Table 20.2.

The second specification test that we consider is yet another test of the sensitivity of the results to the estimation methodology used. The estimation methodology used thus far did not take into account the panel structure of the data. I re-estimate equation (8) taking into account the panel structure of the data by including household level fixed effects that corrects for the potential omitted variable bias caused by the unobserved household fixed effects. The results are presented in Column 2 in Table 20.3. The results are quite similar to the baseline results presented in Table 20.2. To re-iterate, once again the null hypothesis of full insurance $(\beta_1^w = 1, \beta_2^w = 0)$ is always rejected and I again find that consumption tracks income more closely for the poorer households. The estimated marginal propensities to consume out of idiosyncratic income changes are always significantly greater than zero.

Ravallion and Chaudhuri (1997) and Jalan and Ravallion (1999) criticise the estimation methodology used above arguing that this test gives biases estimates of the excess sensitivity parameter against the alternative of risk-market failure whenever there is a common village level component in household level income changes. They instead use the following specification:

$$\Delta c_{ivt}^{w} = \sum_{jk} \beta_{1jk}^{w} D_{ivt}^{jk} + \beta_2^{w} \Delta y_{ivt}^{w} + \beta_3^{w} \Delta n_{ivt}^{w} + \varepsilon_{ivt}^{w} \tag{10}$$

where D_{ivt}^{jk} is a village-time dummy variable such that

$$D_{ivt}^{jk} = \begin{cases} 1, \text{if } j = v \text{ and } k = t \\ 0, \text{otherwise} \end{cases}$$

The rest of the variables are the same as in equation (8). Notice that we again control for changes in household size. In this specification aggregate income risk is captured by the interacted village-time dummies and idiosyncratic income risk is captured by changes in income, which may be endogenous. If there is perfect income insurance within the village, then changes in household income will have no effect on consumption, after controlling for the village-time effects, i.e., $\beta_2^w = 0$. I also consider a restricted version of equation (10) where I do not control for the village-time effects

$$\Delta c_{ivt}^{w} = \beta_2^{*w} \Delta y_{ivt}^{w} + \beta_3^{*w} \Delta n_{ivt}^{w} + \varepsilon_{ivt}^{*w} \tag{11}$$

Once again if consumption is fully insured against both idiosyncratic and covariate shocks, then $\beta_2^{*w} = 0$.

Table 20.3: 2SLS Regressions of Consumption Changes Regressed on Income Changes — Robustness

	2SLS Regressions – Growth Rates[#] *(1)*		*Fixed Effects Regressions – Levels*[#] *(2)*		*2SLS Regressions –Including Village Level Dummies (3)*	*2SLS Regressions – Without Village Level Dummies (4)*
	$\Delta\log(y^w_{ivt})$	*Joint Test*[a]	Δy^w_{ivt}	*Joint Test*[b]		
All Households	0.188*** (0.010)	182.27***	0.139*** (0.010)	181.82***	0.235*** (0.014)	0.238*** (0.014)
Landless Households	0.276*** (0.023)	75.72***	0.267*** (0.038)	50.46***	0.364*** (0.036)	0.451*** (0.035)
Small Landowners	0.172*** (0.016)	64.27***	0.244*** (0.018)	193.03***	0.178*** (0.031)	0.228*** (0.029)
Medium Landowners	0.115*** (0.018)	20.70***	0.066*** (0.015)	18.52***	0.166*** (0.019)	0.162*** (0.017)
Large Landowners	0.184*** (0.020)	40.28***	0.137*** (0.022)	39.40***	0.237*** (0.042)	0.166*** (0.036)

Notes: Figures in Parenthesis are Standard Errors
***: Significant at 1%
*: Significant at 10%
Joint Test[a]: $\beta_1^w = 1, \beta_2^w = 0 \sim F$
Joint Test[b]: $\beta_1^w = 1, \beta_2^w = 0 \sim \chi^2$
[#]: Regressions Control for Community Average Consumption.

Table 20.4: 2SLS Regressions of Consumption Changes Regressed on Income Changes, by Region – Levels

	East		*West*		*North*		*South*	
	Δy^{w}_{ivt}	*Joint Test*[a]	Δy^{w}_{ivt}	*Joint Test*[a]	Δy^{w}_{ivt}	*Joint Test*[a]	Δy^{w}_{ivt}	*Joint Test*[a]
All Households	0.163*** (0.030)	16.04***	0.211*** (0.032)	22.24***	0.163*** (0.024)	23.63***	0.122*** (0.016)	29.91***
Landless Households	0.264*** (0.082)	5.99***	0.499*** (0.079)	19.86***	0.194*** (0.050)	7.71***	0.143*** (0.024)	19.18***
Small Landowners	0.268*** (0.046)	17.32***	0.133*** (0.046)	4.50**	0.125*** (0.039)	5.40***	0.162*** (0.079)	2.19
Medium Landowners	0.117 (0.075)	1.43	0.173*** (0.034)	13.14***	0.085** (0.037)	2.60*	0.084*** (0.084)	9.97***
Large Landowners	0.113*** (0.036)	5.00***	0.021 (0.043)	0.22	0.168*** (0.047)	6.40***	0.166* (0.084)	1.94

Notes: Figures in Parenthesis are Standard Errors
***: Significant at 1%
**: Significant at 5%
Joint Test[a]: $\beta_1^{w} = 1, \beta_2^{w} = 0 \sim F$
Regressions Control for Community Average Consumption

The estimated coefficients are presented in Column 3 in Table 20.3. The estimated marginal propensities to consume out of idiosyncratic changes in income is always rejected and consumption tracks income closely for the poorer households. It might be noted that the estimated marginal propensities are generally higher compared to those presented in Table 20.2. I also present in column 4 the 2SLS regression results corresponding to equation (11). Interestingly note that the estimated marginal propensities to consume are higher for the poor households but lower for the richer households, compared to the estimated coefficients of equation (10). In the regressions with the village level dummies note that the estimated marginal propensities to consume out of changes in income is higher for the large landowners compared to the small (and medium) landowners, though significantly lower compared to the landless households.

India is characterised by significant regional variations; therefore it is likely that institutions vary significantly across these very different regions. To examine whether there are any regional variations in the extent of consumption insurance, the households are additionally stratified on the basis of the region of residence: East (comprising of the states of Assam, Bihar, Orissa and West Bengal), West (comprising of the states of Gujarat, Maharashtra and Rajastan), North (comprising of the states of Haryana, Himachal Pradesh, Jammu and Kashmir, Haryana, Punjab and Uttar Pradesh) and South (comprising of the states of Andhra Pradesh, Karnataka, Kerala and Tamil Nadu). The results are presented in Table 20.4. The following results are worth noting. In general consumption tracks income more closely for the poorer households (the landless and the small landowners) compared to the richer households (the medium and large landowners). For example, estimates show that the estimated marginal propensity to consume out of income is as high as 0.499 for the landless households residing in the West compared to 0.021 for the large landowners in the same region. One exception appears to be the households residing in the Southern region of the country. In this case the estimated marginal propensities to consume are actually the highest for the large landowners. The null hypothesis of full insurance $\left(\beta_1^w = 1, \beta_2^w = 0\right)$ is generally rejected. They are always rejected for the poorer households and in the few cases where consumption is insured against household specific income shocks (i.e., household consumption changes in response to changes in the community average consumption and not in response to changes in household income), the households belong to the medium or large landowning category.

In the estimation thus far, I have stratified the sample on the basis of landownership, based on the argument that in rural India landownership is the primary indicator of wealth because of the collateral value associated with land. How sensitive are the estimates to this particular form of stratification used? I next consider an alternative method of stratification using the highest level of education attained by any member of the household. Households are stratified into one of the following four categories: No education (EDUC = 1), the most educated member of the household has some primary schooling or is literate without any formal education (EDUC = 2), the most educated member of the household has more than primary but less than matriculation (EDUC = 3) and the most educated member of the household has more than high school education (EDUC = 4). The descriptive statistics presented in Table 20.A1 shows that Total household income increases with the educational attainment of the most educated member of the household. The 2SLS estimates are presented in Table 20.5. The null hypothesis of full insurance $(\beta_1^w = 1, \beta_2^w = 0)$ is rejected. Further the null hypothesis that the estimated marginal propensities to consume out of income are zero $(\beta_2^w = 0)$ are also rejected. The estimated marginal propensity to consume is however the lowest for the poorest households (no member of the household has any education — EDUC = 0).

Table 20.5: 2SLS Regressions of Consumption Changes Regressed on Income Changes (Levels) — Stratified by the Highest Level of Education Attained by any Member of the Household

	Δy_{ivt}^{w}	Joint Test[a]
All Households	0.141*** (0.010)	90.92***
Illiterate	0.078*** (0.023)	5.69***
Some Primary Schooling	0.118*** (0.026)	11.09***
Middle Schooling	0.182*** (0.024)	29.35***
Post Secondary	0.145*** (0.018)	33.07***

Notes: Figures in Parenthesis are Standard Errors
***: Significant at 1%
*: Significant at 10%
Joint Test[a]: $\beta_1^w = 1, \beta_2^w = 0 \sim F$
Regressions Control for Community Average Consumption

7. Conclusions

This chapter examines the extent of consumption insurance against income risk by households in rural India. Motivated by the theory of risk sharing we estimate the effects of income changes on consumption after controlling for aggregate shocks through changes in village level consumption and household size. I also test whether there is a systematic wealth effect on the extent of consumption insurance against idiosyncratic income shocks by classifying the households on the basis of landholding, which is the primary source of wealth for rural households in India.

Consumption regressions using the ARIS–NCAER data show that the null hypothesis of full insurance is rejected both for the population as a whole and for the different land classes. The estimation results also show that consumption tracks income more closely for the poorer households — the estimated marginal propensity to consume out of idiosyncratic changes in income is significantly higher for the poorer households compared to the richer households. The results are robust to alternative estimation methodologies and alternative methods of sample stratification.

The implications of the results are quite significant. Governments and non-governmental organisations have implemented various programs designed specifically to reduce the riskiness of rural incomes and the stated aim of such programs is often to provide a safety net to the rural poor. It appears however that the programs are not being targeted adequately — the poorest continue to be the most vulnerable. The results in this chapter strengthen the case for improved public insurance programs, targeted at the most vulnerable, in underdeveloped rural economies. What specific form the program should take is left open to debate.

References

Alderman, H. and Paxson, C., 'Do the Poor Insure? A Synthesis of the Literature on Risk and Consumption in Developing Countries', in *Economics in a Changing World: Proceedings of the Tenth World Congress of the International Economic Association, Moscow, Volume 4, Development, Trade and the Environment*, E. Bacha (ed.), IEA Conference Volume, no. 110 (New York: St. Martin's Press; London: Macmillan Press in association with the International Economic Association 1994).

Cochrane, J.H., 'A Simple Test for Consumption Insurance', *Journal of Political Economy*, 99(5) (1991), 957–76.

Deaton, A., 'Saving and Income Smoothing in Côte d'Ivoire', mimeo (Princeton University, 1992).

Fafchamps, M., 'Solidarity Networks in Pre-industrial Societies: Rational Peasants With a Moral Economy', *Economic Development and Cultural Change*, 41 (1992), 147–76.

Grimard, F., 'Household Consumption Smoothing Through Ethnic Ties: Evidence from Côte d'Ivoire', *Journal of Development Economics*, 41 (1997), 391–422.

Jalan, J. and M. Ravallion, 'Are the Poor Less Well Insured? Evidence on Vulnerability to Income Risk in Rural China', *Journal of Development Economics*, 58 (1999), 61–81.

Mace, B.J., 'Full Insurance in the Presence of Aggregate Uncertainty', *Journal of Political Economy*, 99(5) (1991), 928–56.

Maitra, P., 'Consumption Smoothing in Rural Punjab in the Green Revolution Years', *Indian Economic Review*, 33(2) (1998), 185–96.

Morduch, J., 'Income Smoothing and Consumption Smoothing', *Journal of Economic Perspectives*, 9(3) (1995), 103–14.

NCAER (National Council of Applied Economic Research), *Changes in Rural Income in India: 1968–69, 1969–70, 1970–71*, Technical Report (New Delhi: NCAER, 1975).

Nelson, J.A., 'On Testing for Full Insurance in the Presence of Aggregate Uncertainty', *Journal of Political Economy*, 102(2) (1994), 384–94.

Ravallion, M. and S. Chaudhuri, 'Risk and Insurance in Village India: Comment', *Econometrica*, 65(1) (1997), 171–84.

Townsend, R.M., 'Risk and Insurance in Village India', *Econometrica*, 62(3) (1994), 539–91

Townsend, R. M., 'Consumption Insurance: An Evaluation of Risk Bearing Systems in Low-Income Countries', *Journal of Economic Perspectives*, 9(3) (1995), 83–102.

Table 20.A1: Selected Descriptive Statistics, by Highest Level of Education Attained by Any Member of the Household

		1968–69		*1969–70*		*1970–71*	
	Sample Size	*Mean*	*Std. Dev.*	*Mean*	*Std. Dev.*	*Mean*	*Std. Dev.*
Total Expenditure	4118	3002.369	2576.365	3118.308	2418.402	3186.873	2458.127
CV (Total Income)			110.397		94.652		97.327
CV (Total Expenditure)			85.811		77.555		77.133
Correlation*					0.3883		0.5149
Illiterate							
Total Income	1207	2128.398	2273.001	2303.018	2193.617	2375.377	2325.620
Total Expenditure	1207	1887.103	1501.150	1926.482	1410.737	1943.415	1548.077
CV (Total Income)			106.794		95.250		97.905
CV (Total Expenditure)			79.548		73.229		79.658
Correlation*					0.5267		0.5662
Some Primary Schooling							
Total Income	1058	2965.426	3156.603	3258.303	2753.288	3373.452	2780.150
Total Expenditure	1058	2524.117	1845.060	2620.101	1830.307	2668.278	1677.431
CV (Total Income)			106.447		84.501		82.413
CV (Total Expenditure)			73.097		69.856		62.866
Correlation*					0.3436		0.5721
Middle Schooling							
Total Income	1049	4744.193	4378.537	4824.318	4150.351	5096.947	4349.467
Total Expenditure	1049	3621.650	2724.226	3747.765	2605.418	3812.117	2555.716
CV (Total Income)			92.293		86.030		85.335
CV (Total Expenditure)			75.221		69.519		67.042
Correlation*					0.3706		0.4891
Post Secondary Schooling							
Total Income	804	6383.320	5771.572	6322.413	4644.247	6898.660	5363.884
Total Expenditure	804	4498.004	3401.262	4741.862	2847.690	4920.265	2992.373
CV (Total Income)			90.416		73.457		77.753
CV (Total Expenditure)			75.617		60.054		60.817
Correlation*					0.3838		0.4962

Notes: CV = (SD/Mean)*100
*: Correlation between change in Total Income and change in Total Expenditure
Figures in Parenthesis indicate p-values

21

Rural Poverty in India: Structure, determinants and suggestions for policy reform

Raghbendra Jha

1. Introduction

This chapter addresses the important issue of anti-poverty policy in India. The poverty measures used are all drawn from the popular Foster-Greer-Thorbecke class of functions written as:

$$Y_\alpha = \sum_{y_i<z} [(z - y_i)/z]^\alpha / n \tag{1}$$

where Y is the measure of poverty, y_i is the consumption of the ith household or the ith class of household, z is the poverty line[1], n is the population size, and α is a non-negative parameter. The headcount ratio, *HC*, given by the percentage of the population who are poor is obtained when α=0. This measure fails to capture the extent to which individual income (or expenditure) falls below the poverty line. A second measure is the poverty gap index (PG) given by setting α=1 in (1) is the aggregate income shortfall of the poor as a proportion of the poverty line and normalized by the population size. PG captures the acuteness of poverty since it measures the total short fall of the poor from the poverty line. A further indicator of severe poverty is abbreviated as SPG and is obtained by setting α=2 in (1).

2. Poverty in India

Table 21.1 reports on existing poverty trends for India. (For state level figures see Jha 2000b). The data set used is the National Sample Survey

[1] The poverty line is defined as per capita monthly expenditure of Rs. 49 (Rs. 57) at 1973–74 prices for the rural (urban) sector.

Table 21.1: India Poverty Trends (1951–1997) Corrected for CPIAL Changes (Poverty line = Rs. 49 per capita per month at Oct 73 to Jun 74 for rural sector) (For urban sector Rs. 57 per capita per month at 1973–74 prices)

NSS Round	*Survey period*	*Headcount index*			*Poverty gap index*			*Squared poverty gap index*		
		Rural	*Urban*	*National*	*Rural*	*Urban*	*National*	*Rural*	*Urban*	*National*
3	Aug 51–Nov 52	47.37	35.46	45.31	16.05	11.14	15.20	7.53	4.82	7.06
4	Apr 52–Sep 52	43.87	36.71	42.63	14.64	10.91	13.99	6.71	4.41	6.31
5	Dec 52–Mar 53	48.21	40.14	46.80	16.29	13.25	15.76	7.56	5.96	7.28
6	May 53–Sep 53	54.13	42.77	52.15	19.03	13.83	18.12	9.12	6.29	8.62
7	Oct 53–Mar 54	61.29	49.92	59.30	21.95	17.24	21.12	10.26	7.74	9.82
8	Jul 54–Mar 55	64.24	46.19	61.07	25.04	15.76	23.41	12.50	7.02	11.54
9	May 55–Nov 55	51.83	43.92	50.44	18.44	14.65	17.78	8.80	6.40	8.38
10	Dec 55–May 56	48.34	43.15	47.43	15.65	13.34	15.24	6.71	5.41	6.48
11	Aug 56–Feb 57	58.86	51.45	57.55	19.45	18.16	19.22	8.50	8.51	8.50
12	Mar 57–Aug 57	62.11	48.88	59.77	21.69	16.31	20.73	10.01	7.25	9.52
13	Sep 57–May 58	55.16	47.75	53.84	19.01	15.95	18.47	8.78	7.00	8.46
14	Jul 58–Jun 59	53.26	44.76	51.75	17.74	13.75	17.03	7.88	5.87	7.52
15	Jul 59–Jun 60	50.89	49.17	50.58	15.29	15.83	15.39	6.13	6.75	6.24
16	Jul 60–Aug 61	45.40	44.65	45.27	13.60	13.84	13.64	5.53	5.83	5.59
17	Sep 61–Jul 62	47.20	43.55	46.54	13.60	13.79	13.64	5.31	6.05	5.45
18	Feb 63–Jan 64	48.53	44.83	47.85	13.88	13.29	13.77	5.49	5.17	5.43
19	Jul 64–Jun 65	53.66	48.78	52.75	16.08	15.24	15.93	6.60	6.38	6.56
20	Jul 65–Jun 66	57.60	52.90	56.71	17.97	16.82	17.75	7.60	6.98	7.49
21	Jul 66–Jun 67	64.30	52.24	62.00	22.01	16.81	21.02	10.01	7.19	9.47
22	Jul 67–Jun 68	63.67	52.91	61.60	21.80	16.93	20.86	9.85	7.22	9.35
23	Jul 68–Jun 69	59.00	49.29	57.11	18.96	15.54	18.29	8.17	6.54	7.85
24	Jul 69–Jun 70	57.61	47.16	55.56	18.24	14.32	17.47	7.73	5.86	7.36
25	Jul 70–Jun 71	54.84	44.98	52.88	16.55	13.35	15.91	6.80	5.35	6.51
27	Oct 72–Sep 73	55.36	45.67	53.37	17.35	13.46	16.55	7.33	5.26	6.90
28	Oct 73–Jun 74	55.72	47.96	54.10	17.18	13.60	16.43	7.13	5.22	6.73
32	Jul 77–Jun 78	50.60	40.50	48.36	15.03	11.69	14.28	6.06	4.53	5.72
38	Jan 83–Dec 83	45.31	35.65	43.00	12.65	9.52	11.90	4.84	3.56	4.53
42	Jul 86–Jun 87	38.81	34.29	37.69	10.01	9.10	9.79	3.70	3.40	3.63
43	Jul 87–Jun 88	39.23	36.20	38.47	9.28	9.12	9.24	2.98	3.06	3.00
44	Jul 88–Jun 89	39.06	36.60	38.44	9.50	9.54	9.51	3.29	3.29	3.29
45	Jul 89–Jun 90	34.30	33.40	34.07	7.80	8.51	7.98	2.58	3.04	2.69
46	Jul 90–Jun 91	36.43	32.76	35.49	8.64	8.51	8.61	2.93	3.12	2.98
47	Jul 91–Dec 91	37.42	33.23	36.34	8.29	8.24	8.28	2.68	2.90	2.74
48	Jan 92–Dec 92	43.47	33.73	40.93	10.88	8.82	10.35	3.81	3.19	3.65
50	Jul 93–Jun 94	36.66	30.51	35.04	8.39	7.41	8.13	2.79	2.42	2.69
51	Jul 94–Jun 95	39.75	33.50	38.40	8.89	8.38	..	2.90	2.80	..
52	Jul 95–Jun 96	37.46	28.04	35.00	8.31	6.78	..	2.64	2.22	..
53	Jan 97–Dec 97	35.69	29.99	34.40	8.39	7.77	..	2.83	2.73	..

Note: All poverty measures are expressed as percentage.
Source: Datta (1999), Jha (2000a).

(NSS) consumption data from the 13th. to the 55th. Rounds. The 55th Round of the NSS (1999–2000) has some comparability problems. In NSS Rounds including and after the 50th. the reference period was uniform with respondents asked about their consumption (in all categories) in the past thirty days. During the 55th. Round however, the question on consumption of clothing, footwear, education and institutional health were asked with a reference period of 365 days and that on food consumption only for (alternately) thirty and seven days. Several economists welcomed this change since they felt that the 7-day recall period for food consumption would give a better indication of actual consumption. However, since the poverty estimates of the earlier rounds were done with the uniformly longer recall period, comparison of poverty estimates becomes difficult. National (state level) results for the 55th round are presented in Table 21.2 (Table 21.3).

Table 21.2: India: Poverty in the 55th Round of NSS, 1999–2000

Rural Sector	*Mean Consumption (Rs.)*	*Gini (%)*	*HCR (%)*	*PGR (%)*	*SPGR (%)*	*Preferred Distribution*
30 day recall	483.85	26.22	27.61	5.45	1.61	Beta
7 day recall	502.02	26.23	24.49	4.75	1.42	Beta
Urban Sector	*Mean Consumption (Rs.)*	*Gini (%)*	*HCU (%)*	*PGU (%)*	*SPGU(%)*	*Preferred Distribution*
30 day recall	838.57	34.40	25.09	5.75	1.86	Beta
7 day recall	860.87	34.25	23.22	5.20	1.67	Beta

Source: Author's calculations.

Table 21.3: Number and Percentage of Population Below Poverty Line by States: 1999–2000 (30-day Recall)

No	States/U.T.'s	Rural		Urban		Combined	
		No. of Persons (Lakhs)	% of Persons	No. of Persons (Lakhs)	% of Persons	No. of Persons (Lakhs)	% of Persons
	Andhra Pradesh	58.13	11.05	60.88	26.63	119.01	15.77
1.	Arunachal Pradesh	3.80	40.04	0.18	7.47	3.98	33.47
2.	Assam	92.17	40.04	2.38	7.47	94.55	36.09
3.	Bihar	376.51	44.30	49.13	32.91	425.64	42.60
4.	Goa	0.11	1.35	0.59	7.52	0.70	4.40
5.	Gujarat	39.80	13.17	28.09	15.59	67.89	14.07
6.	Haryana	11.94	8.27	5.39	9.99	17.34	8.74
7.	Himachal Pradesh	4.84	7.94	0.29	4.63	5.12	7.63
8.	Jammu & Kashmir	2.97	3.97	0.49	1.98	3.46	3.48
9.	Karnataka	59.91	17.38	44.49	25.25	104.40	20.04
10.	Kerala	20.97	9.38	20.07	20.27	41.04	12.72
11.	Madhya Pradesh	217.32	37.06	81.22	38.44	298.54	37.43
12.	Maharashtra	125.12	23.72	102.87	26.81	227.99	25.02
13.	Manipur	6.53	40.04	0.66	7.47	7.19	28.54
14.	Meghalaya	7.89	40.04	0.34	7.47	8.23	33.87
15.	Mizoram	1.40	40.04	0.45	7.47	1.85	19.47
16.	Nagaland	5.21	40.04	0.28	7.47	5.49	32.67
17.	Orissa	143.69	48.01	25.40	42.83	169.09	47.15
18.	Punjab	10.20	6.35	4.29	5.75	14.49	6.16
19.	Rajasthan	55.06	13.74	26.78	19.85	81.83	15.28
20.	Sikkim	2.00	40.04	0.04	7.47	2.05	36.55
21.	Tamil Nadu	80.51	20.55	49.97	22.11	130.48	21.12
22.	Tripura	12.53	40.04	0.49	7.47	13.02	34.44
23.	Uttar Pradesh	412.01	31.22	117.88	30.89	529.89	31.15
24.	West Bengal	180.11	31.85	33.38	14.86	213.49	27.02
25.	A & N Island	0.58	20.55	0.24	22.11	0.82	20.99
26.	Chandigarh	0.06	5.75	0.45	5.75	0.51	5.75
27.	Dadra & Nagar Haveli	0.30	17.57	0.03	13.52	0.33	17.14
28.	Daman & Diu	0.01	1.35	0.05	7.52	0.06	4.44
29.	Delhi	0.07	0.40	11.42	9.42	11.49	8.23
30.	Lakshadweep	0.03	9.38	0.08	20.27	0.11	15.60
31.	Pondicherry	0.64	20.55	1.77	22.11	2.41	21.67
32.	All India	1932.43		670.07		2602.50	

Source: Government of India (2001)

Notes: 1 Poverty Ratio of Assam is used for Sikkim, Arunachal Pradesh, Meghalaya, Mizoram, Manipur, Nagaland and Tripura.

2 Poverty Line of Maharashtra and expenditure distribution of Goa is used to estimate poverty ratio of Goa.

3 Poverty Line of Himachal Pradesh and expenditure distribution of Jammu & Kashmir is used to estimate poverty ratio of Jammu & Kashmir.

4 Poverty Ratio of Tamil Nadu is used for Pondicherry and A & N Island.

5 Urban Poverty Ratio of Punjab used for both rural and urban poverty of Chandigarh.

6 Poverty Line of Maharashtra and expenditure distribution of Dadra & Nagar Haveli is used to estimate poverty ratio of Dadra & Nagar Haveli.

7 Poverty Ratio of Goa is used for Daman & Diu.

8 Poverty Ratio of Kerala is used for Lakshadweep.

9 Urban Poverty Ratio of Rajasthan may be treated as tentative.

10 One lakh = 100,000

Table 21.4: Number and Percentage of Population Below Poverty Line by State — 1999–2000 (7-day Recall)

No.	States/U.T.'s	Rural		Urban		Combined	
		No. of Persons (Lakhs)	% of Persons	No. of Persons (Lakhs)	% of Persons	No. of Persons (Lakhs)	%of Persons
1.	Andhra Pradesh	48.14	9.15	55.96	24.48	104.10	13.79
2.	Arunachal Pradesh	3.23	34.00	0.15	6.29	3.38	28.41
3.	Assam	78.27	34.00	2.00	6.29	80.27	30.64
4.	Bihar	322.96	38.00	43.64	29.23	366.60	36.69
5.	Goa	0.23	2.80	0.40	5.03	0.62	3.90
6.	Gujarat	36.87	12.20	24.80	13.76	61.66	12.78
7.	Haryana	11.13	7.71	4.33	8.02	15.46	7.79
8.	Himachal Pradesh	4.63	7.61	0.24	3.95	4.88	7.27
9.	Jammu & Kashmir	3.10	4.14	0.42	1.70	3.52	3.53
10.	Karnataka	47.02	13.64	39.35	22.33	86.36	16.58
11.	Kerala	18.20	8.14	17.73	17.91	35.93	11.14
12.	Madhya Pradesh	202.78	34.58	74.93	35.46	277.70	34.81
13.	Maharashtra	109.25	20.71	96.81	25.23	206.05	22.61
14.	Manipur	5.54	34.00	0.56	6.29	6.10	24.21
15.	Meghalaya	6.70	34.00	0.29	6.29	6.99	28.75
16.	Mizoram	1.19	34.00	0.38	6.29	1.57	16.50
17.	Nagaland	4.42	34.00	0.24	6.29	4.66	27.73
18.	Orissa	131.63	43.98	23.92	40.33	155.55	43.38
19.	Punjab	8.53	5.31	4.03	5.40	12.56	5.34
20.	Rajasthan	48.97	12.22	25.36	18.80	74.33	13.88
21.	Sikkim	1.70	34.00	0.04	6.29	1.74	31.03
22.	Tamil Nadu	73.19	18.68	45.81	20.27	119.00	19.26
23.	Tripura	10.64	34.00	0.41	6.29	11.05	29.24
24.	Uttar Pradesh	379.41	28.75	110.82	29.04	490.23	28.82
25.	West Bengal	154.04	27.24	31.06	13.83	185.10	23.43
26.	A & N Island	0.52	18.68	0.22	20.27	0.75	19.13
27.	Chandigarh	0.06	5.40	0.42	5.40	0.48	5.40
28.	Dadra & Nagar Haveli	0.26	15.31	0.02	10.89	0.28	14.84
29.	Daman & Diu	0.02	2.80	0.04	5.03	0.05	3.92
30.	Delhi	0.12	0.63	6.52	5.38	6.64	4.75
31.	Lakshadweep	0.02	8.14	0.07	17.91	0.10	13.72
32.	Pondicherry	0.58	18.68	1.62	20.27	2.20	19.83
	All India	1713.35		612.57		2325.92	

Source: Government of India (2001)

Notes: 1. Poverty Ratio of Assam is used for Sikkim, Arunachal Pradesh, Meghalaya, Mizoram, Manipur, Nagaland and Tripura.
2. Poverty Line of Maharashtra and expenditure distribution of Goa is used to estimate poverty ratio of Goa.
3. Poverty Line of Himachal Pradesh and expenditure distribution of Jammu & Kashmir is used to estimate poverty ratio of Jammu & Kashmir.
4. Poverty Ratio of Tamil Nadu is used for Pondicherry and A & N Island.
5. Urban Poverty Ratio of Punjab used for both rural and urban poverty of Chandigarh.
6. Poverty Line of Maharashtra and expenditure distribution of Dadra & Nagar Haveli is used to estimate poverty ratio of Dadra & Nagar Haveli.
7. Poverty Ratio of Goa is used for Daman & Diu.
8. Poverty Ratio of Kerala is used for Lakshadweep.
9. Urban Poverty Ratio of Rajasthan may be treated as tentative

Poverty at the disaggregated level of NSS regions is portrayed in Table 21.5. All regions in the northeast corner should be of concern to policy makers. Southern Bihar (now Jharkhand), Coastal Orissa and Eastern Maharashtra are of greatest concern since the rise in HCR was more than 5 per cent and these regions had HCR of more than 50 per cent in 1987–88.

Table 21.5: Characteristics of Rural Poverty Change between 1987–88 and 1993–94 among NSS Regions

Low and Increasing	*High and Increasing*
Manipur Plains; Himachal Pradesh; Haryana; Himalayan UP; Mizoram	Four regions in Northern, Central and Eastern Maharashtra; South-west region of Madhya Pradesh; Assam; Arunachal Pradesh; Manipur Hills; Himalayan Region of West Bengal
Low and Decreasing	*High and Decreasing*
Inland and Southern Andhra Pradesh; Saurashtra Region of Gujarat; Coastal and Inland Eastern Karnataka; Malwa and North Madhya Pradesh; Punjab; Goa; North-Eastern Rajasthan; Coastal Maharashtra; Andaman and Nicobar; Chandigarh; Delhi; Lakshdweep; Pondicherry	Central and northern Bihar; Southern, central and Eastern UP: Inland northern Karnataka; South, southwest and central Madhya Pradesh; Orissa, Southern Rajasthan; Sikkim; Coastal and southern Tamilnadu; Eastern, western and central plains of West Bengal; Dadra and Nagar Haveli.

N.B. (i) 'High' denotes HCR of 40% and above in 1993–94.
(ii) Increase/decrease between two periods of 1987–88 and 1993–94.
Source: Dubey and Gangopadhyay (1998).

Table 21.6 reports on inequality. The rural Gini does not show any particular trend. The coefficient of variation of rural Ginis across states has fallen. Thus the Gini rose for most states during this period. The urban Gini, which is always higher than the rural Gini, has grown since 1994–95. Overall inequality in India has increased over time (Jha 2000a).

Since data from the NSS regions are available for just two time periods, no analysis of trends in spatial variation is possible using these regions. Figure 21.1 depicts the increasing variation of rural poverty over time across states. Figure 21.2 shows that since the mid 1990s the HCR has behaved in a fundamentally different manner than the PGR and SPGR. Between 1995–96 and 1997 although the HCR fell, the PGR and SPGR rose. The early 1990s rise in poverty was greater for the PGR and SPGR than for the HCR. In fact whenever there are sharpest adverse poverty shocks (defined as a 10 per cent or higher increase in SPG) the worsening of PGR and SPGR is greater[2] than HCR. Hence, the data seems to suggest that the poorest suffer disproportionately during a period of severe adverse shocks and they did not benefit as much as the other poor during rapid economic growth.

Table 21.6: Gini Coefficient: 1957–97

Rural	*Rural Gini (%)*
1957–58	33.74
1963–64	29.01
1968–69	30.70
1973–74	28.30
1977–78	31.20
1983	30.10
1986–87	30.15
1987–88	30.16
1989–90	28.23
1990–91	27.71
1992	29.88
1993–94	28.50
1994–95	29.19
1995–96	28.97
1997	30.11

Source: Jha (2000a).

Figure 21.1: Spatial Variation of rural poverty over time

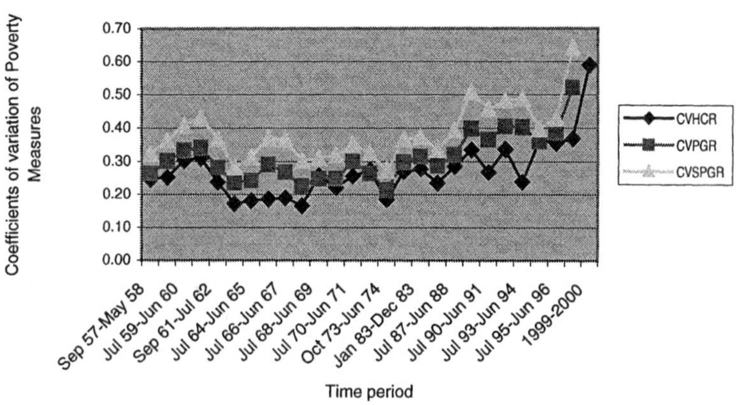

2 A further example of this is the increase in poverty following the severe drought in 1987.

Figure 21.2: Percentage Changes in Rural Poverty Indicators

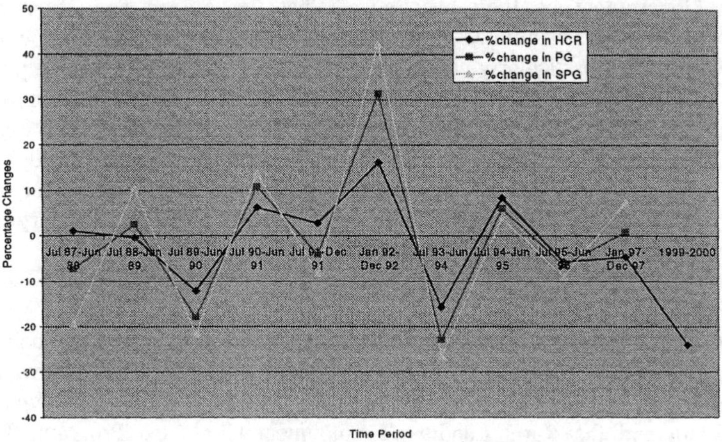

Rural Gini rose in India as a whole between 1993–94 and 1994–95, but fell in Andhra Pradesh, Madhya Pradesh, Orissa, Punjab, Tamilnadu, and West Bengal. The aggregate rural Gini fell between 1994–95 and 1995–96, but rose in Assam, Bihar, Kerala, Madhya Pradesh, Orissa, and Uttar Pradesh. Some states, e.g., Punjab and Andhra Pradesh, have reduced poverty impressively. In contrast, poverty has worsened in Assam, and its incidence remains disturbingly high in a populous state such as Bihar.

Some states that have had high rates of economic growth and enjoy high per capita consumption also show low inequality (and poverty levels) compared to states that are lagging behind. Thus, the rural Gini for Bihar was 31.65 in 1957–58 and deteriorated to 38.9 by 1995–96. Bihar has also had low rates of economic growth and is among the poorest states in India. On the other hand, in Punjab, the richest state in the country, the rural Gini coefficient dropped from 32.2 to 24.4 over the same time period, with poverty falling sharply.

Rank tests for statistical convergence reveal considerable stability in ranks across Indian states in regards to poverty and inequality. The Evans and Karras (1996) test for level convergence reveals that in respect of poverty, inequality and mean consumption each state appears to be gravitating towards its own mean rather than to the grand mean. Convergence is conditional rather than absolute. Regional inequality is becoming increasingly important (Jha 2000a).

3. Policy Responses to Poverty

The Government of India was aware that the reform and structural adjustment program initiated by it would result in a temporary fall in public expenditure — particularly consumption subsidies geared towards the poor and that economic growth did not automatically 'trickle down' to the poor.[3] A number of poverty reduction programs (PRP) were initiated. The Food for Work program begun in 1977, subsidized food supplies through a Public Distribution System[4] (PDS) and concessional loan schemes for on- and off-farm development for both small farmers (SFDP) and marginal farmers and agricultural laborers (MFALP).

Other current programs concentrate on the creation of rural self-employment through asset endowment rather than on needs-oriented programs, which were designed to ensure access to basic amenities such as drinking water to the poor. The most prominent among these is the Jawahar Rozgar Yojana (JRY), which combines the National Rural Employment Program and the Rural Landless Employment Guarantee Program. The Maharashtra Employment Guarantee Scheme (MEGS), which derives its success mainly from the strong political commitment of the state government (Hirway and Terhal 1994), is well known. The MESG employs labor to create productive assets such as small-scale irrigation schemes, maintain roads and the like and pays wages on par with prevailing agricultural wages. Since the non-poor also find these jobs attractive, the MESG does not offer the poor the opportunity to self select themselves into its schemes. Other programs include the Integrated Rural Development Program (IRDP), the Employment Assurance Scheme and the Accelerated Rural Water Supply Program. These programs assist marginal and small farmers, agricultural laborers and artisans with investments in minor irrigation, livestock purchases and the like through grants and loans at subsidized interest rates. JRY and IRDP have recently been renamed as Jawahar Gram Samridhi Yojana (JGSY) and Swaranjayanthi Gram Swarozgar Yojana (SGSY), respectively, with some restructuring. JGSY involves two changes: (i) the implementing agency is exclusively the

[3] There is disagreement about the extent of increase in poverty during the initial phase of the reform and the extent to which the reforms are responsible for this increase. See Jha (2000a) for a review.

[4] The PDS designed to reduce disruptions in food supply and interstate differences in food availability. The GOI and the Food Corporation of India procure food grain — particularly rice, wheat and sugar — from farmers and sell them to state governments at a subsidized price — the issue price. The state governments then sell this food to ration cardholders. Recently there has been a move to differentiate between ration card hordes that are above the poverty line from those that are below it and to charge the two groups different prices. For an evaluation of the PDS see Jha, Murty, Nagarajan and Seth (1999).

village Panchayats; and (ii) the main focus has been shifted to infrastructure development with employment generation being considered a secondary objective. Since efforts to improve infrastructure will have beneficial effects on poverty reduction only after a lag, the main short-run responsibility for a social safety net has been shifted to Employment Assurance Scheme (EAS). SGSY is an improvement on IRDP as it replaces individual lending with group lending, but the subsidy is retained. (Gaiha 2000b). The Ninth Five Year Plan document, GOI (1997) set ambitious targets for poverty reduction which are unlikely to be realized. Saxena (2000) enumerates serious problems in both formulation as well as implementation of PRP. The IRDP, for instance, has involved 'sub-critical investment, unviable projects, lack of technological and institutional capabilities in designing and executing projects utilizing local resources and expertise; illiterate and unskilled beneficiaries with no experience in managing an enterprise; indifferent delivery of credit by banks (high transactions cost, complex procedure, corruption, one time credit, poor recovery), overcrowding of lending in certain projects such as dairying, poor targeting and selection of non-poor, absence of linkage between different components of the IRDP, rising indebtedness, and sale of IRDP outstripping capacity of government and banks to absorb.' IRDP beneficiaries were also likely to remain indebted for long. RPW programs were also ineffective as they involved violation of material-labor (60:40) norms and fudging of muster rolls. Many of the contractors hired labor from outside the scheme. Central norms for setting aside 40 per cent of funds for watershed development and 20 per cent for minor irrigation have been disregarded. 'Today Rs.60 out of Rs.100 in wage schemes is reserved for wages, but in reality only Rs.10 to Rs.15 actually goes to the poor worker, the rest is illegal income for bureaucracy, contractors and politicians' Saxena (2000).

Other PRP include programs to counter area specific endemic poverty caused by hostile agro-climatic conditions and a degeneration of the eco-system (Gaiha 1991). A National Renewal Fund was set up in February 1992 to provide assistance to workers who would become redundant as a result of the adjustment program. This program was expected to finance the retraining, redeployment or retrenchment of redundant workers following a restructuring of industries. Despite budgetary pressures, funds have been maintained and even enhanced for these social programs[5] but their performance has been disappointing. To make programs more decentralized

5 PRP designed specifically for the urban sector provide basic physical and social amenities to urban slums. The focus is on mother and infant survival through immunization, nutritional supplements and preschool care as well as hygiene, water supply.and low-interest loans.

the Indian Parliament passed the 73rd. Amendment to the Constitution of India in 1993. The *Panchayat,* a village level organization, was made directly responsible for implementing PRP.[6]

4. Elements of a Strategy for Rural Poverty Reduction

That 'Poverty is a multi dimensional problem' is a well-known cliché. In the Indian case this problem is more important than probably anywhere else because of the vast numbers of people who are poor and the fact that poverty in India has been so well entrenched for so long. We structure our approach to such poverty reduction as answers to select questions.

4.1 Who are the poor in rural India?

The vast majority of the rural poor in India are engaged in agriculture (including fishery and livestock) either as agricultural wage laborers or marginal farmers and self-employed. Table 21.7 gives a breakdown for 1993–94.

Table 21.7: Livelihood Characteristics of the Rural Poor in 1993–94 (percentages)

		Social Groups			
	Livelihood Category	*Scheduled Tribe*	*Scheduled Caste*	*Others*	*All Households in Livelihood Category*
1	Self-Employed House holds in Non-Agriculture	0.75	2.38	7.70	10.83
2	Agricultural Labor Households	6.49	16.19	18.91	41.59
3	Other Rural Labor Households	1.45	2.40	3.98	7.83
4	Self-employed Households in Agriculture	5.62	4.76	22.49	32.87
5	Other (Residual Households)	0.73	1.46	4.69	6.88
6	All Households	15.04	27.19	57.77	100.00

Source: Sarvekshana

[6] The salient features of this amendment were ' a three tier structure comprising District, Block and Village panchayats with the Gram Sabha (Village Assembly) as the foundation; direct and periodic elections; quotas for Scheduled Castes/Scheduled Tribes (SCs/STs) backward classes and women; delineation of major areas of financial and administrative requirements; a rational basis for sharing of resources between state governments and panchayats, provision for executive and supporting staff; clear-cut procedures for dissolution/suppression of panchayats, and mandatory elections within six months of dissolution' Gaiha and Kulkarni (1998).

Almost 42 per cent of the rural poor are agricultural labourers. More than half of this group consists of scheduled castes (SC) and scheduled tribes (ST). SC and ST are about 32 per cent of the rural population but account for more than 42 per cent of the poor. Table 21.8 reports on asset ownership for select social groups for the year 1993–94.

Table 21.8: Percentage Distribution of Rural Poor Across Land Possessed Categories: All-India for 1993–94

	All Households		*Percentage non-SC and non-ST*	
Land Possessed (hectares)	*SC*	*ST*	*Ag. Lab.*	*Self Employed in Agriculture*
Less than 0.01	16.95	11.0	15.82	0.69
0.01-0.40	52.13	28.41	59.72	11.47
0.41-1.00	16.51	22.46	16.49	29.74
1.01-2.00	8.84	20.07	6.09	30.11
2.01-4.00	3.88	20.07	6.09	30.11
4.01 and above	1.69	4.97	0.16	10.51
All Categories	100.00	100.00	100.00	100.00
HCR for category	50.3	54.2	54.4	27.3
Total Estimated Rural Population in category (millions)	123.4	63.2	79.3	187.9

Source: National Sample Survey Organization: Report No. 422.

Almost 85 per cent of SC are marginal farmers with farm sizes less than 2 hectares. More ST own land, however these are mostly forests related. 19 per cent of the ST poor and 28 per cent of non-SC and non-ST self employed agricultural poor, numbering about 21 million belong to the category of large farmers. Since a third of the rural poor population consists of households that are self-employed in agriculture, their poverty is clearly related to poor productivity in agriculture.

Hence, the rural poor are primarily those with limited ownership of assets — including land. They are also getting increasingly concentrated in certain parts of this country and certain social groups SC and ST in particular, form disproportionately large sections of the poor. The ST pockets of poverty can be relatively easily identified, e.g., the eastern part of the country and pockets with preponderance of tribal population such as Bastar in Chattisgarh and Santhal Pargana in Jharkhand. SC, on the other hand, are widely dispersed.

Tables 21.9 and 21.10 reveal that among rural households there was a sharp drop in loans for productive purposes for cultivators, non-cultivators and all households between 1981 and 1991. For cultivators' loans for

Table 21.9: Cash Debt by Households Classified by Purpose of Loan, 1971–91 (%)

Purpose	*Rural Households*									*Urban Households*					
	Cultivators			*Non-Cultivators*			*All Households*			*Self Employed*		*Others*		*All Households*	
	1971	*1981*	*1991*	*1971*	*1981*	*1991*	*1971*	*1981*	*1991*	*1981*	*1991*	*1981*	*1991*	*1981*	*1991*
1. In farm Business															
Capital Expenses	34.7	45.3	14.4	5.0	8.4	2.4	31.2	42.4	12.0	7.2	5.7	4.3	0.3	5.6	2.5
Current Expenses	15.0	18.5	3.2	2.5	5.9	0.7	13.5	17.6	2.7	8.1	0.2	1.1	0.1	4.4	0.1
2. In non-farm business															
Capital expense	3.2	6.3	4.7	8.0	18.8	9.8	3.7	7.2	5.8	41.6	21.1	7.3	3.3	23.2	10.8
Current expense	1.1	1.5	1.5	5.7	4.5	3.8	1.7	1.7	2.0	15.0	8.1	2.5	1.0	8.3	4.0
3. Household Expenses															
Residential	37.8	20.0	5.1	63.3	51.0	11.8	40.9	22.4	6.5	13.1	28.7	54.3	44.6	35.0	37.9
Current expenses	N.A.	N.A.	0.5	N.A.	N.A.	0.4	N.A.	N.A.	0.5	N.A.	0.1	N.A.	2.5	N.A.	1.5
4. Productive expense (1+2)	54.0	71.6	23.8	21.2	37.8	16.7	50.1	69.2	22.5	74.9	35.1	15.2	4.7	41.6	17.4
5. Other Purposes	7.9	8.2	45.4	15.5	11.4	57.6	8.7	8.5	48.0	14.7	33.9	30.4	46.6	23.2	41.4
6. Unspecified	0.3	0.2	25.2	0.4	-	13.5	0.3	0.2	22.8	0.3	2.2	0.2	1.4	0.2	1.8
7. All Purposes	100.0	100.0	100.0		100.0	100.0	100.0	100.0	100.0	100.0	100.0	100.0	100.0	100.0	100.0

Notes: (i) 'Other purposes' relate to repayment of debt, expenditure on litigation, financial investment and other expenditures of households for 1971 and 1981, and also include 'other purposes' of farm and non-farm business for 1991.
(ii) The use of the term 'productive purposes' is consistent with the definition used by NSS.
(iii) N.A. = not available.

Source: All India Debt and Investment Survey (1991-92) reported in *RBI Bulletin* February 2000.

Table 21.10: Proportion of Households Reporting Debt and Share in Total Amount Outstanding According to Credit Agency and Asset Group, 1991

Asset Group (Rs. 000)	*Rural*						*Urban*					
	Institutional Agencies		*Non-Institutional Agencies*		*Total*		*Institutional Agencies*		*Non-Institutional Agencies*		*Total*	
	P	*S*	*P*	*S*	*P*	*S*	*P*	*S*	*P*	*S*	*P*	*S*
Less than 5	5.3	37.1	14.2	62.0	18.9	100.0	2.9	31.7	14.2	65.7	16.1	100.0
5–10	9.8	38.4	22.2	56.8	30.7	100.0	4.9	23.0	19.5	72.4	23.1	100.0
10–20	10.7	35.2	21.3	52.0	30.2	100.0	8.8	37.3	20.3	58.8	27.1	100.0
20–30	15.5	55.7	19.4	38.0	32.2	100.0	8.1	36.9	17.4	52.5	24.8	100.0
30–50	15.3	46.9	20.3	50.4	32.6	100.0	11.2	42.0	19.4	53.2	27.3	100.0
50–70	15.8	47.6	19.7	49.2	31.9	100.0	12.0	51.5	18.4	47.3	27.6	100.0
70–100	16.8	49.8	20.7	46.3	33.1	100.0	12.4	47.3	23.3	48.0	32.7	100.0
100–150	19.4	52.2	21.5	41.3	35.3	100.0	19.0	82.4	18.8	16.4	31.8	100.0
150–250	20.2	58.8	19.6	27.8	38.2	100.0	21.2	72.0	14.2	24.4	31.1	100.0
250 and above	25.5	56.6	20.0	39.6	32.0	100.0	11.8	64.3	18.0	32.0	26.9	100.0
Total	15.6	56.6	20.0	39.6	32.0	100.0	11.8	64.3	18.0	32.0	26.9	100.0

Notes: (i) Debt comprises cash loans and current liabilities.
(ii) Total includes unspecified; P = proportion of households reporting (percent), S = Percentage share in total.

Source: All India Debt and Investment Survey (1991-92) reported in *RBI Bulletin* February 2000.

Table 21.11: Literacy Status of Persons belonging to Bottom 40 per cent of Rural Population (1986-87) (%)

S. No.	State	Literacy Codes									
		0	1	2	3	4	5	6	7	8	9
1	Andhra Pradesh										
	Male	53.20	17.54	9.56	4.80	-	1.20	0.29	0.12	0.09	-
	Female	67.64	9.67	3.70	1.08	0.01	0.23	0.14	0.42	0.04	-
2	Assam										
	Male	49.17	10.48	20.64	13.42	-	4.28	1.38	0.30	0.10	-
	Female	61.50	10.16	16.83	7.67	-	1.53	0.36	-	-	-
3	Bihar										
	Male	62.47	10.82	8.12	7.76	0.05	2.68	0.76	0.10	0.30	0.89
	Female	80.52	4.62	2.43	1.46	0.04	0.24	0.05	0.04	0.01	-
4	Gujarat										
	Male	47.19	15.85	16.15	21.13	0.09	3.78	0.42	0.24	0.33	0.10
	Female	71.60	11.30	9.65	4.45	0.12	1.07	0.45	0.03	0.01	-
5	Haryana										
	Male	77.19	19.39	14.76	6.27	-	3.72	0.98	0.06	0.53	0.04
	Female	54.77	11.99	8.28	1.30	-	0.16	0.04	-	-	-
6	Jammu & Kashmir										
	Male	49.43	16.16	11.85	8.94	0.03	2.85	0.50	0.14	0.39	0.11
	Female	70.71	9.15	5.13	1.65	0.13	0.55	0.07	-	-	-
7	Karnataka										
	Male	42.05	15.36	14.45	8.24	-	2.36	0.60	0.14	0.33	0.01
	Female	56.92	7.99	6.99	3.69	-	0.43	0.17	-	0.05	0.02
8	Kerala										
	Male	20.66	21.46	30.40	16.67	0.04	4.36	0.49	0.35	0.11	0.08
	Female	23.51	20.46	28.47	14.58	-	4.88	0.60	0.35	0.25	0.19
9	Madhya Pradesh										
	Male	64.78	19.35	9.71	2.66	0.010	0.61	0.75	0.03	0.09	0.02
	Female	89.25	5.17	2.98	1.08	-	0.36	0.10	0.01	0.02	-
10	Maharashtra										

	Male	39.51	15.48	19.01	11.18	0.03	2.83	0.53	0.15	0.44	0.05
	Female	56.03	11.48	10.60	4.20	-	0.77	0.11	0.06	0.03	-
11	Orissa										
	Male	66.16	15.91	9.35	6.12	-	0.77	0.46	0.08	0.11	-
	Female	84.89	7.96	3.32	2.23	-	0.27	0.03	0.03	-	-
12	Punjab										
	Male	47.14	15.25	15.15	6.70	0.21	4.01	0.61	0.25	0.21	0.22
	Female	68.44	14.84	12.88	2.58	0.09	0.25	0.23	0.25	0.06	-
13	Rajasthan										
	Male	64.14	17.10	8.37	5.52	-	1.05	0.70	0.04	0.31	0.05
	Female	91.08	4.14	1.88	0.42	-	0.04	0.01	-	-	-
14	Tamil Nadu										
	Male	41.51	26.32	7.97	8.75	-	1.80	0.26	0.26	0.19	0.05
	Female	64.87	17.67	10.42	2.90	0.01	0.51	0.10	0.02	0.05	-
15	Uttar Pradesh										
	Male	62.93	14.89	9.73	7.21	0.02	2.45	1.24	0.13	0.38	0.15
	Female	89.25	5.17	2.98	1.08	-	0.36	0.10	0.02	0.05	-
16	West Bengal										
	Male	62.71	15.42	14.29	3.48	-	0.97	0.40	0.08	0.23	0.01
	Female	76.69	8.87	7.45	1.28	-	0.21	0.03	0.01	-	-

0: Not Literate
1: Literate but below primary/Not undergone any formal education
2: Primary/Junior basic
3: Middle/Senior basic
4: Technical/Vocational school course
5: Matric/Secondary
6: Higher secondary/Per-university/ Intermediate
7: Under graduate, diploma/Certificate not equivalent to degree
8: Degree/Diploma equivalent to degree (at Graduation level)
9: Post graduate/Diploma certificate

Source: Sarvekshana, 55th Issue, Vol. XVI, No.4, and April–June 1993.

capital expenditures related to farm business fell sharply from 45.3 per cent to 14.4 per cent. There was a smaller drop for non-farm business capital expenditure for cultivators. Debts for current expenditures related to non-farm business for cultivators remained stagnant whereas there was a sharp drop in loans for current expenditures for farm business.

For non-cultivators there was a drop in share of loans for capital and current (productive) purposes. Debts for 'other purposes' increased from 8.2 per cent in 1981 to 45.4 per cent in 1991 for cultivators and from 11.4 to 57.6 per cent for non-cultivators. Hence the rural credit situation in India is shifting toward more and more loans for non-productive purposes. Thus along with stagnating public sector investment we should also expect stagnating private sector investment.

Table 21.10 shows that for the smallest asset group the share of non-institutional credit is the highest. This share falls as the asset size increases. The poor still have to rely largely on non-institutional credit — particularly from moneylenders and relatives. Since the relatives of poor people are likely to also be poor, the share of moneylenders is likely to be high.

There are important inequalities within the typical rural family. Women and children are less well looked after than men. Table 21.11 presents evidence on the education status of the bottom 40 per cent of the rural population. Illiteracy among the poor is uniformly higher among females than males (Table 21.12). In no state, including Kerala, are females less illiterate than men.

Table 21.12: Female Literacy in India — 1961 to 2001 (%)

Year	*Rural*	*Urban*	*Overall*
1961*	10.13	40.46	15.33
1971*	15.52	48.84	21.97
1981*	20.66	54.40	28.47
1991**	30.62	64.05	39.29
2001+	54.16	NA	NA

* = Relates to population 5 years and above
** = Relates to population 7 years and above
NA = Not Available.
Source: Statistical Database for Literacy - Vol.2, 1993, National Institute of Adult Education
+ Source of data for 2001 is Census of India, 2001.

Children are also quite vulnerable. A majority under 5 (irrespective of the poverty status of their families) is underweight and the percentage of children that are wasting is among the highest in India.

Table 21.13: Select Social Indicators: India in Comparison to Asia

Country	Adult Illiteracy Rate (age 15 and older) (%), 1997	Female Illiteracy Rate (Age 15-24) (%), 1997	Children under five who are underweight (%) 1990-98	Children under five who are Wasting (%) 1990-98	People not expected to survive to age 15, (%) 1997	People not expected to survive to age 40 (%), 1997
Bangladesh	61	63	56	18	13	21
Cambodia	.	43	52	13	17	28
China	17	4	16	.	5	8
India	47	44	53	18	11	16
Indonesia	15	4	34	13	7	13
Iran	27	10	16	7	6	10
South Korea	3	0	.	.	2	5
Lao	41	.	40	11	19	29
Malaysia .	14	3	19	.	2	5
Mongolia	16	11	39	.	13	18
Myanmar	16	11	39	.	13	18
Nepal	62	62	47	11	14	23
Pakistan	59	61	38	.	12	15
Philippines	5	2	28	6	5	9
Singapore	9	0	.	.	1	2
Sri Lanka	9	4	34	14	2	5
Thailand	5	2	19	6	4	11
Vietnam	8	3	41	14	7	12

Source: UNDP, Poverty Report 2000.

Table 21.14: Percentage Distribution of Child Workers in India by Industry of Occupation

Location of Child Workers	*Urban*	*Rural*	*Total*
Cultivation	5.32	38.87	35.93
Agricultural Labor	14.73	45.42	42.74
Livestock, Forestry, Fishing Plantation	3.07	6.61	6.30
Mining and Quarrying	0.20	0.25	0.24
Manufacturing, Processing, Servicing and Repairs	39.16	5.72	8.65
Construction	3.27	0.47	0.72
Trade and Commerce	15.03	0.96	2.19
Transport, Storage and Communication	2.45	0.10	0.30
Other Services	16.77	1.60	2.93

Source: Census of India, 1981.

Nearly 85 per cent of child workers in India are employed in cultivation, agricultural laborers and livestock maintenance. Since these involve low productivity of labor, one would not expect the economic conditions of these children to improve when they become adults.[7] Table 21.15 gives information on the educational status of the children of the poor and Table 21.16 on dropout rates for girls.

Table 21.15: Distribution of Rural Children (6–14 years) Over Levels of Education (1986–87) (%)

S. No.	*State*	*Level of Education*							
		1	1	2	2	3	3	4	4
		Male	Female	Male	Female	Male	Female	Male	Female
1	Andhra Pradesh	26.53	41.73	30.70	18.64	15.11	9.62	0.45	0.53
2	Assam	27.73	33.40	13.65	14.63	35.03	29.33	5.75	4.24
3	Bihar	46.44	65.04	20.50	16.83	14.50	6.51	1.92	0.51
4	Gujarat	20.76	32.54	17.95	18.77	24.11	23.03	3.22	3.35
5	Haryana	13.34	32.23	33.77	27.82	12.67	11.10	0.21	14.27
6	Jammu & Kashmir	24.66	46.57	32.84	25.27	7.60	4.25	13.99	6.56
7	Karnataka	21.97	32.36	17.98	18.22	22.28	16.85	13.66	1.55
8	Kerala	0.93	1.53	1.16	8.73	36.52	40.38	0.45	0.77
9	Madhya Pradesh	36.43	32.99	38.46	23.47	8.64	4.20	0.08	0.25
10	Maharashtra	13.33	24.05	19.86	20.92	31.28	24.44	1.75	1.29
11	Orissa	39.30	55.53	26.92	26.02	19.05	12.41	1.09	1.01
12	Punjab	23.74	28.67	23.32	30.19	13.16	11.46	0.63	0.51
13	Rajasthan	32.72	75.53	35.81	12.09	7.70	4.42	0.43	0.27
14	Tamil Nadu	15.39	28.00	28.32	37.38	22.53	19.09	0.43	0.73
15	Uttar Pradesh	34.00	66.87	29.07	17.45	12.56	4.78	0.55	0.53
16	West Bengal	38.50	51.46	25.40	24.20	13.03	10.48	0.24	0.22

Codes: 1: Not Literate.
2: Literate but below primary/not undergone any formal education.
3: Primary/Junior basic.
4: Middle/Senior basic.

Source: Sarvekshana, 55th Issue, Vol. XVI, No: 4, April-June 1993.

Table 21.16: School Drop-out Rates (%) for Girls (Rural + Urban)

Stage/year	*1993–94*	*1995–96**	*1996–97**
I-V	35.05	41.31	38.35
I-VIII	49.95	61.70	52.77
I-X	68.41	74.01	73.04

* Provisional
Source: Annual Report 1997-98, Ministry of Human Resource Development

7 On a more general note, Grootaert and Kanbur (1995) note that 'children's earnings are consistently lower than those of adults, even where these two groups are engaged in the same tasks'.

4.2 Do the identified poor lend themselves for easy targeting in Poverty Reduction Programs (PRP)?

At first glance, an important strategy for a PRP would be to target the most vulnerable of the social/economic groups. Most PRP — no matter how poorly targeted — are effective initially but their impact wears off over time. A new program is under considerable scrutiny and, hence, is under pressure to perform. As time goes by, programs often develop leaks. Targeting becomes weak as entrenched social interests (the rich among the rural population) take over these programs. Most PRP err on both sides – by including those who are not to be included (the non-poor) and by excluding those that are to be included (the poor) (Lipton 2001).

Even the best-designed PRP can fail if its clientele (the poor) fail to assert themselves and participate fully in the program[8]. Targeting of women can influence the pattern of household expenditure and lead to some savings from the program. Children will be sent to school rather than being asked to look after/work on assets such as land or cattle.[9] Targeting is straightforward in geographical areas where there is a large concentration of the poor — say ST dominated regions. But targeting by SC may create divisions within the poor. Thus there is a tradeoff.

One can thus make a distinction between **statistical targeting** (targeting of easily identifiable groups) and **strategic targeting** — which recognizes the need to form coalitions of the poor when the poor are not overwhelmingly from a small number of identifiable groups.

Table 21.17 illustrates this point. Punjab- a state with low poverty — has the highest proportion of SC. Bihar and Orissa have high poverty but low proportions of SC population. A poor district such as Koch Bihar in West Bengal shows high SC concentration. The union territory with the highest SC population is Delhi — but Delhi has low poverty. The highest concentration of ST is in Mizoram, where poverty is low. At the district level the highest concentration of ST is in West Khasi Hills in Meghalaya, which is not particularly poor However, some very poor areas of Bihar and

---

[8] The need for the empowerment of the poor is noted by official documents as well. The Ninth Five Year Plan document writes 'Poverty (can be eradicated) through a process of social mobilization, encouraging participatory approaches and institutions and empowerment of the poor' Ninth Five Year document, volume 2, chapter 2.

[9] UNDP (2000) notes the benefits of targeting and empowering women in its mandal samakyas in Andhra Pradesh. Through this program, women and young girls benefited by gaining new self-confidence and became much more involved in community affairs. Credit and technical assistance targeted to these women have enabled them to augment their family incomes and earn respect within and outside their families. Women have been able to make decisions of critical importance to their families such as avoiding early marriages, the promotion of family planning, sending children to school rather than to work and saving and investment.

Uttar Pradesh have low proportion of ST. Some areas with the dual characteristics of high ST population and high poverty can be identified, e.g., Chattishgarh and Jharkhand.

Table 21.17: SC and ST Population (Excluding Jammu and Kashmir)

SC	138 223 277	16.48% of population
Scheduled Tribes	67 758 380	8.08% of population
State with the highest proportion of SC		Punjab (28.3%)
State with the lowest proportion of SC		Mizoram (0.1%)
UT with the highest proportion of SC		Delhi (19.1%)
UT with the lowest proportion of SC		D and N Haveli (2.0%)
District with the highest proportion of SC		Koch Bihar (51.8%) W.B.
Districts with lowest proportion of SC		Tamenglong (0%) Manipur, West Khasi Hills (0%) Meghalaya
State with the highest proportion of ST		Mizoram (94.8%)
State with the lowest proportion of ST		Uttar Pradesh (0.2%)
UT with the highest proportion of ST		Lashwadeep (93.1%)
UT with the lowest proportion of ST		A&N Islands (9.5%)
District with the highest proportion of ST		West Khasi Hills (98.1%) Meghalaya
District with lowest proportion of ST		46 Districts in UP (0%) 11 Districts in Bihar (0%) 1 District in HP (0%)

Source: Census of India, 1991

4.3 Why has poverty alleviation slowed down in the 1990s?

Traditionally economists have emphasized economic growth as a tool for poverty reduction (Dollar and Kraay 2000). In India growth in the 1980s was accompanied by a sharp reduction in poverty. Over the 1990s the trend rate of growth of agriculture was 3.3 per cent — comparable to that in the 1980s. The growth rate of food production was 2.6 per cent per annum, which is in excess of population growth (1.6 per cent per annum) (World Bank 2000). However, the impact of growth on rural poverty reduction in the 1990s fell. Agricultural growth in the 1980s was concentrated in the North and Eastern parts of the country where poverty is high. During the 1990s agricultural growth in these areas was lower, mainly because of slower productivity growth in agriculture as a result of falling public investment. Investment is biased towards irrigated areas although irrigation opportunities are limited. About two-thirds of agriculture takes place in rain-fed areas and this can at best be brought down to a half. Rising population led to greater pressure on land. Thus rapid development of non-farm activities in the rural sector would be crucial for poverty alleviation. Official credit machinery has not been able to impact the poor very much. Also, the post-reforms rate of economic growth in India, although impressive by her own standards, has never been high as per the standards of East Asian countries. There are real constraints to economic growth discussed in Chapter 2.

4.4 What should be the broad contours of a strategy of Rural Poverty Reduction?

The broad thrust of anti poverty measures must combine sectoral policies with intervention at the microeconomic level of decision making within the family.

Interventions at the Sectoral Level

<u>Demand Side of the Labor Market</u>

Labour demand can be increased through (i) augmentation of skills to enhance labour skills; and b) the development of a vibrant non-farm sector. There may be activities such as rural industries and infrastructure development, which are complementary to agriculture and which could raise the demand for labour as well as agricultural wages. By opening up and linking hitherto isolated rural areas, roads and improved transport and increasing electricity and telephone connections can raise labour demand and facilitate the growth of poverty-reducing non-farm activities. Further, labor-intensive technology can be used in a number of key areas, without compromising on quality or cost-effectiveness. ILO's experience with rural public works (RPW) programs in several countries shows that it is possible to involve the private sector and communities in executing infrastructure schemes. Core labour standards (e.g., those relating to force and child labor, non-discrimination, safety requirements, etc.) can be introduced. Although many experiences with RPW have been rather disappointing, that need not be an argument against this approach. Indeed, evaluations show that with good program design, especially based on decentralized planning and community involvement, and effective implementation, labor based approaches in infrastructure can help reduce poverty. [Lipton (2001)]. To be effective, RPW should be self targeting in that they should pay less than the going market agricultural wage in order to attract the real poor and repel the non-poor. The RPW should be monitored to ensure that fictitious payments are not being made to the non-poor by showing them as workers even when they are not working on it. Further, the RPW by their very nature, have typically focussed on giving current gains to the poor and downplayed rural capital formation. To be sustainable, the RPW programs should concentrate on creating skills among the target workforce. This would create assets to work on in the future. Further, a RPW program during the lean season is surely more appropriate than during the busy harvest season. The RPW program must allow for flexibility and fungibility of time spent. To improve women's participation allowance must be made for time to be spent for the family and child support systems should be set up in conjunction with the program. Payment should permit combining of piece and time rates since workers may have set targets for income and piece rates give them the flexibility to pursue these targets. Self-targeting rather than direct targeting by group seems to be important in this case. The emergence of pressure groups to help detect leakage and identify obvious mistargeting should be encouraged.

Labor Supply

Policy should aim to organize workers in order to increase their negotiation powers. Greater representation of the poor — particularly SC and ST — in major decision making bodies (e.g. Panchayati Raj Institutions (PRI) and the Gram Sabha (GS)) should be encouraged, Whether the minimum wage is a useful anti-poverty measure depends on how widely it can be applied and the labor market conditions. If payment of the minimum wage entails that the poor are denied work in RPW, for example, this policy would be counterproductive.

Institutional Reform

These include: a) reform of non-institutional credit particularly in economically depressed areas; where employers are an important source of credit to workers, labor and credit contracts can be interlinked. In such cases a policy concentrating only on one market or one that is isolated may not serve much purpose. b) Investment in education and training in the rural economy would raise labor productivity directly and encourage easier adaptation to modern farming practices, better medical and sanitary practices, better response to non-farm opportunities, and greater awareness of rights and obligations. There is an important role for the community both in motivating the poor to get literate/acquire education and providing them support — in terms of sharing family chores and other activities -during this process. (Dreze and Sen 1997).

PRI have been the basic conduit for funds for rural development and rural poverty alleviation since they are presumed to have better knowledge of the needs of the people. However, PRI are accountable to higher levels of government such as those in the Blocks, which are often interested only in achieving budgetary targets. The GS, on the other hand, is concerned with social development but, without administrative or financial power, it is moribund. If the PRI were answerable to GS and if such accountability was an input into budgetary decisions by higher-level governments in respect of

PRI, it is likely that the anti-poverty performance of PRI would improve. Further the PRI and GS should not get overtaken by the rich and powerful of village society.

To address the higher incidence of risk among the poor insurance funds are needed. Some of the poor may be transients in poverty and appropriate risk management would attend to their problems more than anything else. However since the poorest may be the most vulnerable to risk they may be compelled to shift some of the burden of adjustment to the weakest members in the family leading to the emergence of child labour. Given the almost continual nature of the risk that the rural poor are exposed to, social insurance should be considered a mainstream rather than a residual activity or a 'social safety net.' Such funds should also create physical assets that the poor may fall back upon in the event of a future crisis. This capital may take physical as well as social form, for example, transfers between households who run out of food, communal labor for households with sick members, management of common property resources for the dry season, and sharing of knowledge between farmers about how to protect against bad harvests.

Clearly defining property rights is important. There are vast tracks of wastelands in central India with ill-defined property rights. As a consequence local powerful interests have taken over these lands. If these lands were given to communal ownership of the poor, these could probably be developed for their benefit.

Family Level Interventions

The design of a PRP must be sensitive to decision-making within the family. A micro-finance program can influence savings decisions by making interest charged on loans contingent upon the profile of saving of the household. Households that send children to work may be penalized when selecting workers for a RPW. Household able to produce report cards and school attendance records of their children could be preferred for selection for work or credit. Such decisions could be discussed and rationalized within the community to create public awareness.

5. Concluding Comments

This chapter has presented an overview of the evolution of rural poverty in India. It has characterized the poor and discussed how economic reforms have impacted upon poverty. It has also made a number of suggestions relating both to economic policy reform as well as the design of PRP that might accelerate the reduction of poverty in India. The future of poverty alleviation - indeed of economic reforms — in India depends upon whether official agencies at various levels, village organizations, NGOs and international organizations can coordinate a systematic response to these challenges.

References

Datt, G., 'Has Poverty in India Declined since the Reforms?' *Economic and Political Weekly,* 34 (1999), 1371–90.

Datt, G. & Ravallion, M., 'Macroeconomic crises and poverty monitoring: a case study of India', *Review of Development Economics*, 1(2) (1997), 135–52.

Dollar, D. and A. Kraay, 'Growth is Good for the Poor' (World Bank, Washington D.C. USA, 2000).

Dreze. J. and A. Sen, *India :Economic Development and Social Opportunity* (New Delhi: Oxford University Press, (1997)

Dubey, A. and S. Gangopadhyay (1998) *Where Are the Poor in India,* CSO, New Delhi.

Evans, P. & Karras, G., 'Convergence revisited', *Journal of Monetary Economics*, 37(2) (1996), 249–65.

Fan, S. and P. Hazell, 'Should Developing Countries Invest more in Less-Favoured Areas? — An Empirical Analysis of Rural India' *Economic and Political Weekly,* 35 (2000), 1455–64.

Foster, J., Greer, J. & Thorbecke, E., 'A class of decomposable poverty measures', *Econometrica*, 52(3) (1984), 761–5.

Gaiha, R., Poverty alleviation programs in rural India: an assessment, *Development and Change*, 22(1) (1991), 117–54.

Gaiha, R. & Kulkarni, V., Is growth central to poverty alleviation in India?, *Journal of International Affairs*, 52 (1) (1998), 145–80.

Gaiha, R., 'On the Targeting of the Employment Guarantee Scheme in the Indian State of Maharashtra' *Economics of Planning*, .3(2) (2000A), 203–19.

Gaiha, R., '*The Exclusion of the Poorest: Emerging Lessons from the Maharashtra Rural Credit Projects*' (Rome: PI, IFAD, (2000b).

Government of India *Ninth Five year Plan (1997–2002)* (Planning Commission., 1997).

Government of India, 'Poverty Estimates for 1999-2000' (New Delhi: Press Information Bureau, (2001)

Grootaert, C. and R. Kanbur, 'Child Labor: An Economic Perspective' *International Labor Review*, 134 (1995), 187–201.

Gupta, S. (1995) 'Economic reform and its impact on the poor', *Economic and Political Weekly*, 30 (1995), 1295–313.

Hirway, I. & Terhal, P., *Towards Employment Guarantee in India* (New Delhi, Sage Publication, 1994).

International Labor Office, *Indonesia Strategies for Employment-Led Recovery and Reconstruction,* Report of an ILO Mission (Geneva and Jakarta, 1996), *World Employment Report 1996/9* (Geneva, 1999).

International Labor Organisation, *World Labor Report* (Geneva, 1995)

Jha, R., Murthy, K. V., Nagarajan, H., & Seth, A.,'Real consumption levels and the public distribution system in India', *Economic and Political Weekly,* 34 (15) (1999), 919–27.

Jha, R., 'Reducing Poverty and Inequality in India: Has Liberalization Helped' *Discussion Paper 204* (Helsinki :WIDER,.2000a)

Jha, R., 'Growth, Inequality and Poverty in India: Spatial and Temporal Characteristics' *Economic and Political Weekly,* 35 (2000b), 921–8.

Jha, R., *Country Strategic Opportunities Paper: India* (Rome: IFAD, 2001).

Lipton, M., 'Successes in Anti-Poverty', *Discussion Paper 8* (Geneva: ILO,.2001)

Ravallion, M. and G. Datt, 'How Important to India's poor is the sectoral Composition of Economic Growth' *The World Bank Economic Review,* 10(1) (1996), 1–25.

Ravallion, M. Does aggregation hide the harmful effects of inequality on growth?, *Economics Letters*, 61(1) (1998), 73–7.
Ravallion, M. & Datt, G. (1999) When is growth pro-poor?: evidence from the diverse experiences of Indian states, mimeo (Washington, DC: World Bank, 1999).
Ravallion, M. and G. Datt, 'Farm Productivity and Rural Poverty in India' *Journal of Development Studies*, 34(4) (1998),.62–85.
Saxena, N., 'How have the Poor Done? — Mid-term review of Ninth Plan', *Economic and Political Weekly*, 35 (2000), 846–55.
UNDP, *Overcoming Human Poverty*, UNDP Poverty Report 2000 (2000).
World Bank, *India — Poverty Reduction: Progress and Challenges*, Washington, D.C. (2000).

Index